THE
POLITICAL WRITINGS
OF
THOMAS PAINE

THE
POLITICAL WRITINGS
OF
THOMAS PAINE

VOLUME II

Athens ‡ Manchester

The Political Writings of Thomas Paine

Old Book Publishing Ltd

Book Cover Design: Old Book Publishing Ltd

Title of original: The Political Writings of Thomas Paine, secretary to the committee of Foreign Affairs in the American Revolution. To which is prefixed a brief sketch of the author's life. In two volumes.

Volume II

Originally published in 1824 George Davidson

Cover image: In *Fashion before Ease; —or,— A good Constitution sacrificed for a Fantastic Form* (1793), James Gillray caricatured Paine tightening the corset of Britannia; protruding from his coat pocket is a measuring tape inscribed "Rights of Man".

ISBN–10: 1-78107-064-4 volume I
ISBN–10: 1-78107-065-2 **volume II**
ISBN–10: 1-78107-066-0 set

ISBN–13: 978-1-78107-064-2 volume I
ISBN–13: 978-1-78107-065-9 **volume II**
ISBN–13: 978-1-78107-066-6 set

EDITOR'S NOTE

THE

Political Writings

OF

THOMAS PAINE,

SECRETARY TO THE COMMITTEE OF FOREIGN AFFAIRS IN THE AMERICAN
REVOLUTION.

TO WHICH IS PREFIXED

A BRIEF SKETCH OF THE AUTHOR'S LIFE.

IN TWO VOLUMES.

VOL II.

CHARLESTOWN (Ms.)

PRINTED AND PUBLISHED BY GEORGE DAVIDSON.

1824.

CONTENTS

OF THE SECOND VOLUME.

———◆———

PROSPECTS ON THE RUBICON:

OR, AN INVESTIGATION INTO THE
CAUSES AND CONSEQUENCES OF THE POLITICS TO BE AGITATED AT
THE NEXT MEETING OF PARLIAMENT.

PREFACE.

AN expression in the British parliament respecting the American war, alluding to Julius Cæsar having passed the Rubicon, has on several occasions introduced that river as the figurative river of war.

Fortunately for England, she is yet on the peaceable side of the Rubicon; but as the flames once kindled are not always easily extinguished, the hopes of peace are not so clear as before the late mysterious dispute began.

But while the calm lasts, it may answer a very good purpose to take a view of the prospects, consistent with the maxim, that he that goeth to war should first sit down and count the cost.

The nation has a young and ambitious minister at its head, fond of himself, and deficient in experience: and instances have often shown that judgment is a different thing from genius, and that the affairs of a nation are but unsafely trusted where the benefit of experience is wanting.

Illustrations have been drawn from the circumstances of the war before last, to decorate the character of the present minister, and, perhaps, they may have been greatly over-drawn; for the management must have been bad to have done less than what was then done, when we impartially consider the means, the force, and the quantity of money employed.

It was then Great Britain and America against France singly, for Spain did not join till near the close of the war. The great number of troops which the American colonies then raised, and paid themselves, were sufficient to turn the scale, if all other parts had been equal. France had not at that time attended to naval affairs so much as she has done since; and the capture of French sailors before any declaration of war was made; which, however it may be justified upon policy, will always be ranked among the clandestine arts of war, assured a certain, but unfair advantage against her, because it was like a man administering a disabling dose over night to the person whom he intends to challenge in the morning.

THE AUTHOR.

PROSPECTS ON THE RUBICON.

RIGHT by chance and wrong by system, are things so frequently seen in the political world, that it becomes a proof of prudence neither to censure nor applaud too soon.

" The Rubicon is passed," was once given as a reason for prosecuting the most expensive war that England ever knew. Sore with the event, and groaning beneath a galling yoke of taxes, she has again been led ministerially on to the shore of the same delusive and fatal river, without being permitted to know the object or reason why.

Expensive preparations have been gone into ; fears, alarms, dangers and apprehensions, have been mystically held forth, as if the existence of the nation was at stake, and at last the mountain has brought forth a Dutch mouse.

Whoever will candidly review the present national characters of England and France, cannot but be struck with surprise at the change that is taking place. The people of France are beginning to think for themselves, and the people of England are resigning up the privilege of thinking.

The affairs of Holland have been the bubble of the day ; and a tax is to be laid on shoes and boots (so say the newspapers) for the service of the statdholder of Holland. This will undoubtedly do honor to the nation, by verifying the old English proverb, " over shoes over boots."

But though Democritus could scarcely have forborne laughing at the folly, yet as serious argument and sound reasoning are preferable to ridicule, it will be best to quit the vein of unprofitable humor, and give the cause a fair investigation. But before we do this, it may not be improper to take a general review of sundry political matters that will naturally lead to a better understanding of the subject.

What has been the event of all the wars of England, but an amazing accumulation of debt, and an unparalleled burden of taxes? Sometimes the pretence has been to support one outlandish cause and sometimes another. At one time Austria, and another time Prussia, another to oppose Russia, and so on; but the consequence has always been *taxes*. A few men have enriched themselves by jobs and contracts, and the groaning multitude borne the burden. What has England gained by war since the year 1738, only fifty years ago, to recompense her for *two hundred millions* sterling, incurred as a debt within that time, and under the annual interest of which, besides what was incurred before, she is now groaning? Nothing at all.

The glare of fancied glory has often been held up, and the shadowy recompense imposed itself upon the senses. Wars that might have been prevented have been madly gone into, and the end has been debt and discontent. A sort of something which man cannot account for is mixed in his composition, and renders him the subject of deception by the very means he takes not to be deceived.

That jealousy which individuals of every nation feel at the supposed designs of foreign powers, fits them to be the prey of ministers, and of those among themselves, whose trade is war, or whose livelihood is jobs and contracts. "Confusion to the politics of Europe, and may every nation be at war in six months," was a toast given in my hearing not long since.—The man was in court to the ministry for a job.—Ye gentle graces, if any such there be who preside over human actions how must ye weep at the viciousness of man!

When we consider, for the feelings of nature cannot be dismissed, the calamities of war and the miseries it inflicts upon the human species, the thousands and tens of thousands of every age and sex who are rendered wretched by the event, surely there is something in the heart of man that calls upon him to think! Surely there is some tender chord tuned by the hand of its creator, that struggles to emit in the hearing of the soul a note of sorrowing sympathy. Let it then be heard, and let men learn to feel, that the true greatness of a nation is founded on the principles of humanity ; and that to avoid a war when her own existence is not endangered, and wherein the happiness of man must be wantonly sacrificed, is a higher principle of true honor than madly to engage in it.

But independent of all civil and moral considerations, there is no possible event that a war could produce benefits to England or France, on the present occasion, that could in the most distant proportion recompense to either the expense she must be at. War involves in its progress such a train of unforeseen and unsupposed circumstances, such a combination of foreign matters, that no human wisdom can calculate the end. It has but one thing certain, and that is increase of *taxes.* The policy of European courts is now so cast, and their interest so interwoven with each other, that however easy it may be to begin a war, the weight and influence of interfering nations compel even the conqueror to unprofitable conditions of peace.

Commerce and maritime strength are now becoming the fashion, or rather the rage of Europe, and this naturally excites in them a combined wish to prevent either England or France increasing its comparative strength by destroying, or even relatively weakening the other, and therefore, whatever views each may have at the commencement of a war, new enemies will arise as either gains the advantage, and continual obstacles ensue to embarrass success.

The greatness of Louis the fourteenth, made Europe his enemy, and the same cause will produce the same consequence to any other European power. That nation, therefore, is only truly wise, who, contenting herself with the means of defence, creates to herself no unnecessary enemies by seeking to be greater than the system of Europe admits. The monarch or the minister who exceeds this line, knows but little of his business. It is what the poet, on another occasion, calls,

" The point where sense and nonsense join."

Perhaps there is not a greater instance of the folly of calculating upon events, than is to be found in the treaties of alliance. As soon as they have answered the immediate purpose of either of the parties, they are but little regarded. Pretences, afterwards, are never wanting to explain them away, nor reasons to render them abortive. And if half the money which nations lavish on speculative alliances were reserved for their own immediate purposes, whenever the occasion shall arrive, it would be more productively and advantageously employed.

Monarchs and ministers, from ambition or resentment, often contemplate to themselves schemes of future greatness, and set out with what appears to them the fairest prospect; in the mean while, the great wheel of time and fate revolves unobserved, and something, never dreamed of, turns up and blasts the whole. A few fancied or unprofitable laurels supply the absence of success, and the exhausted nation is *huzza'd into new taxes.*

The politics and interests of European courts are so frequently varying with regard to each other, that there is no fixing even the probability of their future conduct. But the great principle of alliancing seems to be but little understood, or little cultivated in courts, perhaps the least of all, in that of England.—No alliance can be operative, that does not embrace within itself, not only the attachment of the sovereigns, but the real interest of the nations.

The alliance between France and Spain, however it may be spoken of as a mere family compact, derives its greatest strength from national interest. The mines of Peru and Mexico, are the soul of this alliance. Were those mines extinct, the family compact would most probably dissolve.

There exists not a doubt in the mind of Spain, what part England would act, respecting those mines, could she demolish the maritime power of France; and therefore the interest of Spain feels itself continually united with France. Spain has high ideas of honor, but has not the same ideas of English honor. They consider England as wholly governed by principles of interest, and that whatever she thinks it her interest to do, and supposes she has the power of doing, she makes very little ceremony of attempting. But this is not all—There is not a nation in Europe but what is more satisfied that those mines should be in the possession of Spain, than in that of any other European nation; because the wealth of those mines, sufficient to ruin Europe in the hands of some of its powers, is innocently employed with respect to Europe, and better and more peaceably distributed among them all, though the medium of

Spain, than it would be through that of any other nation. This is one of the secret causes that combine so large a part of Europe in the interest of France, because they cannot but consider her as a standing barrier to secure to them the free and equal distribution of this wealth throughout all the dominions of Europe.

This alliance of interest is likewise one of the unseen cements that prevents Spain and Portugal, two nations not very friendly to each other, proceeding to hostilities. They are both in the same situation, and whatever their dislikes may be they cannot fail to consider, that by giving way to resentment that would weaken and exhaust themselves, each would be exposed a prey to some stronger power.

In short, this alliance of national interest is the only one that can be trusted, and the only one that can be operative. All other alliances formed on the mere will and caprice of sovereigns, of family connexions, uncombined with national interest, are but the quagmire of politics, and never fail to become a loss to that nation who wastes its present substance on the expectancy of distant returns.

With regard to Holland, a man must know very little of the matter, not to know that there exists a stronger principle of rivalship between Holland and England in point of commerce, than prevails between England and France in point of power: and, therefore, whenever a stadtholder of Holland shall see it his interest to unite with the principle of his country, and act in concert with the sentiments of the very people who pay him for his services, the means now taken by England to render him formidable, will operate contrary to the political expectations of the present day.

Circumstances will produce their own natural effects, and no other, let the hopes or expectations of man be what they may. It is not our doing a thing with a design that it shall answer such or such an end, that will cause it to produce that end; the means taken must have a natural ability and tendency within themselves to produce no other, for it is this, and not our wishes or policy, that governs the event.

The English navigation act was levelled against the interest of the Dutch as a whole nation, and therefore it is not to be supposed that the catching at the accidental circumstances of one man, as in the case of the present stadtholder, can combine the interest of that country with this.

A few years, perhaps a less time, may remove him to the place where all things are forgotten, and his successor, contemplating his father's troubles, will be naturally led to reprobate the means that produced them, and to repose himself on the interests of his country, in preference to the accidental and tumultuous assistance of exterior power.

England herself exhibits at this day, a species of this kind of policy. The present reign, by embracing the Scotch, has tranquillized and conciliated the spirit that disturbed the two former reigns. Accusations were not wanting at that time to reprobate the policy as tinctured with ingratitude towards those who were the immediate means of the Hanover succession. The brilliant pen of Junius was drawn forth, but in vain. It enraptured without convincing; and though in the plenitude of its rage it might be said to give elegance to bitterness, yet the policy survived the blast.

What then will be the natural consequence of this expense, on account of the stadtholder, or of a war entered into from that cause? Search the various windings and caverns of the human heart, and draw from thence the most probable conclusion, for this is more to be depended upon than the projects or declarations of ministers.

It may do very well for a paragraph in a newspaper, or the wild effusions of romantic politicians, or the mercenary views of those who wish for war on any occasion, merely for the sake of jobs and contracts, to talk of French finesse or French intrigue; but the Dutch are not a people to be impressed by the finesse or intrigue of France or England, or any other nation. If there has been any finesse in the case, it has been between the electorate of Hanover, the king of Prussia, and the stadtholder, in which it is most probable the people of England will be finessed out of a sum of money.

The Dutch, as is already observed, are not a people open to the impression of finesse. It is lost upon them. They are impressed by their commercial interest. It is the political soul of their country, the spring of their actions, and when this principle coincides with their ideas of freedom, it has all the impulse a Dutchman is capable of feeling.

The opposition in Holland were the enemies of the stadtholder, upon a conviction that he was not the friend of their national interests. They wanted no other impulse but this.

Whether this defect in him proceeded from foreign attachment, from bribery or corruption, or from the well known defect of his understanding, is not the point of inquiry. It was the effect rather than the cause that irritated the Hollanders.

If the stadtholder made use of the power he held in the government to expose and endanger the interest and property of the very people who supported him, what other incentive does any man in any country require? If the Hollanders conceived the conduct of the stadtholder injurious to their national interest, they had the same right to expel him which England had to expel the Stuarts; and the interference of England to re-establish him, serves only to confirm in the Hollanders the same hatred against England which the attempt of Louis XIV. to re-establish the Stuarts caused in England against France; therefore, if the present policy is intended to attach Holland to England, it goes on a principle exceedingly erroneous.

Let us now consider the situation of the stadtholder, as making another part of the question.

He must place the cause of his troubles to some secret influence which governed his conduct during the late war, or in other words, that he was suspected of being the tool of the then British administration. Therefore, as every part of an argument ought to have its weight, instead of charging the French of intriguing with the Hollanders, the charge more consistently lies against the British ministry, for intriguing with the stadtholder, and endangering the nation in a war without a sufficient object. That which the ministry are now doing confirms the suspicion, and explains to the Hollanders that collusion of the stadtholder, against their national interests, which he must wish to have concealed, and the explanation does him more hurt than the unnecessary parade of service has done him good.

Nothing but necessity should have operated with England to appear openly in a case that must put the stadtholder on still worse terms with his countrymen. Had France made any disposition for war, had she armed, had she made any one hostile preparation, there might then have been some pretence for England taking a step, that cannot fail to expose to the world that the suspicions of the Hollanders against the stadtholder were well founded, and that their cause was just, however unsuccessful has been the event.

As to the consequence of Holland in the scale of Europe
(the great stake, says some of the newspapers, for which
England is contending) that is naturally pointed out by
her condition: as merchants for other nations her interest
dictates to her to be a neutral power, and this she always
will be unless she is made war upon, as was the case in the
last war; and any expectation beyond what is the line of
her interest, that is, beyond neutrality, either in England
or France, will prove abortive. It therefore cannot be
policy to go to war to effect that at a great expense, which
will naturally happen of itself, and beyond which there is
nothing to expect.

Let Holland be allied with England or with France, or
with neither, or with both; her national conduct, consequently arising out of her circumstances, will be nearly the
same, that is, she will be neutral. Alliances have such a
natural tendency to sink into harmless unoperative things,
that to make them a cause for going to war, either to prevent their being formed, or to break any already formed,
is the silliest speculation that war can be made upon, or
wealth wasted to accomplish. It would scarcely be worth
the attempt, if war could be carried on without expense,
because almost the whole that can be hoped at the risk and
expense of a war, is effected by their natural tendency to
inactivity.

However pompous the declarations of an alliance may
be, the object of many of them is no other than good-will,
and reciprocally securing, as far as such security can go,
that neither shall join the enemies of the other in any war
that may happen. But the national circumstances of Holland, operate to insure this tranquillity on her part as effectually to the power she is not allied with, as the engagement
itself does to the power with whom she is allied; therefore
the security from circumstances is as good as the security
from engagement.

As to a cordial union of interest between Holland and
England, it is as unlikely to happen as between two individual rivals in the same trade: and if there is any step
that England could take, to put it at a still greater distance,
it is the part she is now acting. She has increased the animosity of Holland on the speculative politics of interesting
the stadtholder, whose future repose depends upon uniting
with the opposition in Holland, as the present reign did
with the Scotch. How foolish then has been the policy,

how needless the expense of engaging in a war on account
of the affairs of Holland?

A cordiality between England and France is less improbable than between England and Holland. It is not how
an Englishman feels, but how a Dutchman feels, that decides this question. Between England and France there is
no real rivalship of interest; it is more the effect of temper,
disposition, and the jealousy of confiding in each other, than
any substantial cause, that keeps up the animosity. But
on the part of Holland towards England, there is over and
above the spirit of animosity, the more powerful motives of
interested commercial rivalship, and the galling remem-
brance of past injuries. The making war upon them under
lord North's administration, when they were taking no part
in the hostilities, but merely acting the business of merchants, is a circumstance that will not be easily forgotten
by them. On these reasons, therefore, which are naturally deduced from the operative feelings of mankind, any
expectation of attaching Holland to England as a friendly
power, is vague and futile. Nature has her own way of
working in the heart, and all plans of politics not founded
thereon will disappoint themselves.

Any one who will review the history of English politics for
several years past, must perceive that they have been
directed without system. To establish this, it is only necessary to examine one circumstance, fresh in the mind of
every man.

The American war was prosecuted at a very great expense, on the publicly declared opinion, that the retaining
America was necessary to the existence of England; but
America being now separated from England, the present
politics are, that she is better without her than with her.
Both these cannot be true, and their contradiction to each
other shows want of system. If the latter is true, it amounts
to an impeachment of the political judgment of government
because the discovery ought to have been made before the
expense was incurred. This single circumstance, yet fresh
in every man's mind, is sufficient to create a suspicion,
whether the present measures are more wisely founded
than the former ones; and whether experience may not
prove, that going to war for the sake of the stadtholder, or
for the hope of retaining a partial interest in Holland, which,
under any connexion, can, from circumstances, be no more

than a neutral power, is not as weak policy as going to
war to retain America.

If England is powerful enough to maintain her own
ground and consequence in the world as an independent
nation, she needs no foreign connexion. If she is not, the
fact contradicts the popular opinion that she is. Therefore, either her politics are wrong, or her true condition is
not what she supposes it to be. Either she must give up
her opinion to justify her politics, or renounce her politics
to vindicate her opinion.

If some kind of connexion with Holland is supposed to be
an object worthy some expense to obtain, it may be asked
why was that connexion broken by making war upon her
in the last war? If it was not then worth preserving without expense, is it now worth re-obtaining at a vast expense? If the Hollanders do not like the English, can
they be made to like them against their wills? If it shall
be said that under the former connexion they were unfriendly, will they be more friendly under any other?—
They were then in as free a situation to choose as any future
circumstances can make them, and, therefore, the national
governing sentiment of the country can be easily discov-
ed; for it signifies not what or who a stadtholder may be,
that which governs Holland is, and always must be, a
commercial principle, and it will follow this line in spite
of politics. Interest is as predominant and as silent in its
operations as love; it resists all the attempts of force, and
countermines all the stratagem of control.

The most able English statesmen and politicians have
always held it as a principle, that foreign connexions served only to embarrass and exhaust England. That surrounded by the ocean she could not be invaded as countries are on the continent of Europe, and that her insular
situation dictated to her a different system of politics to
what those countries required, and that to be leagued
with them was sacrificing the advantages of situation to a
capricious system of politics. That though she might
serve them, they could not much serve her, and that as
the service must at all times be paid for, it could always
be procured when it was wanted; and that it would be
better to take it up in this line than to embarrass herself
with speculative alliances that served rather to draw her
into a continental war on their account, than extricate her
from a war undertaken on her own account.

From this discussion of the affairs of Holland, and of the inadequacy of Holland as an object of war, we will proceed to show that neither England nor France are in a condition to go to war ; and that there is no present object to the one or the other to recompense the expense that each must be at, or atone to the subjects of either for the additional burdens that must be brought upon them.   I defend the cause of the poor, of the manufacturers, of the tradesmen, of the farmer, and of all those on whom the real burden of taxes fall—but above all, I defend the cause of humanity.

It will always happen, that any rumor of war will be popular among a great number of people in London.— There are thousands who live by it : it is their harvest ; and the clamor which those people keep up in newspapers and conversations passes unsuspiciously for the voice of the people, and it is not till after the mischief is done, that the deception is discovered.

Such people are continually holding up in very magnified terms the wealth of the nation, and the depressed condition of France, as reasons for commencing a war, without knowing any thing of either of these subjects.

But admitting them to be as true, as they are false, as will be hereafter shown, it certainly indicates a vileness in the national disposition of any country, that will make the accidental internal difficulties to which all nations are subject, and sometimes encumbered with, a reason for making war upon them.   The amazing increase and magnitude of the paper currency now floating in all parts of England, exposes her to a shock as much more tremendous than the shock occasioned by the bankruptcy of the South Sea funds, as the quantity of credit and paper currency is now greater than they were at that time.   Whenever such a circumstance shall happen, and the wisest men in the nation are, and cannot avoid being, impressed with the danger, it would be looked upon as baseness in France to make the distress and misfortune of England a cause and opportunity for making war upon her, yet this hideous infidelity is publicly avowed in England.   The bankruptcy of 1719, was precipitated by the great credit which the funds then had, and the confidence which people placed in them.   Is not credit making infinitely greater strides now than it made then ?   Is not confidence equally as blind now as at that day ?   The people then supposed themselves as wise

as they do now, yet they were miserably deceived, and
the deception that has once happened will happen again
from the same causes.

Credit is not money, and therefore it is not pay, neither
can it be put in the place of money in the end. It is only
the means of getting into debt, not the means of getting
out, otherwise the national debt could not accumulate ;
and the delusion which nations are under respecting the
extension of credit is exactly like that which every man
feels respecting life, the end is always nearer than was expected ; and we become bankrupts in time by the same delusion that nations become bankrupts in property.

The little which nations know, or are sometimes willing
to know, of each other, serves to precipitate them into
wars which neither would have undertaken, had they fully
known the extent of the power and circumstances of each
other ; it may therefore be of some use to place the circumstances of England and France in a comparative point
of view.

In order to do this the accidental circumstances of a nation must be thrown out of the account. By accidental
circumstances is meant, those temporary disjointings and
derangements of its internal system which every nation in
the world is subject to, and which, like accidental fits of
sickness in the human body, prevents in the interim the
full exertion and exercise of its natural powers.

The substantial basis of the power of a nation arises out
of its population, its wealth and its revenues. To these
may be added the disposition of the people. Each of
these will be spoken of as we proceed.

Instances are not wanting to show that a nation confiding too much on its natural strength, is less inclined to be
active in its operations than one of less natural powers
who is obliged to supply that deficiency by increasing its
exertions. This has often been the case between England
and France. The activity of England, arising from its
fears, has sometimes exceeded the exertions of France re-
posing on its confidence.

But as this depends on the accidental disposition of a
people, it will not always be the same. It is a matter well
known to every man who has lately been in France, that
a very extraordinary change is working itself in the minds
of the people of that nation. A spirit that will render
France exceedingly formidable whenever its government

shall embrace the fortunate opportunity of doubling its strength by allying, if it may be so expressed (for it is difficult to express a new idea by old terms) the majesty of the sovereign with the majesty of the nation; for of all alliances that is infinitely the strongest and the safest to be trusted to, because the interest so formed, and operating against external enemies can never be divided.

It may be taken as a certain rule, that a subject of any country attached to the government on the principles abovementioned is of twice the value he was before. Freedom in the subject is not a diminution, as was formerly believed, of the power of government, but an increase of it. Yet the progress by which changes of this kind are effected, requires to be nicely attended to.

Were governments to offer freedom to the people, or to show an anxiety for that purpose, the offer most probably would be rejected. The purpose for which it was offered, might be mistrusted. Therefore the desire must originate with, and proceed from the mass of the people, and when the impression becomes universal, and not before, is the important moment for the most effectual consolidation of national strength and greatness that can take place.

While this change is working, there will appear a kind of chaos in the nation; but the creation we enjoy arose out of chaos, and our greatest blessings appear to have a confused beginning.

Therefore we may take it for granted, that what has at this moment the appearance of disorder in France, is no more than one of the links in that great chain of circumstances by which nations acquire the summit of their greatness. The provincial assemblies already begun in France, are as full, or rather a fuller representation of the people than the parliaments of England are.

The French, or, as they were formerly called, the Franks (from whence came the English word frank and free) were once the freest people in Europe; and as nations appear to have their periodical revolutions, it is very probable they will be so again. The change is already begun. The people of France, as it was before observed, are beginning to think for themselves, and the people of England resigning up the prerogative of thinking.

We shall now proceed to compare the present condition of England and France as to population, revenues and wealth, and show that neither is in a condition of going to war, and that war can end in nothing but loss, and most probably, a temporary ruin to both nations.

To establish this point so necessary for both nations to be impressed with, a free investigation of all the matters connected with it is indispensable : if, therefore, any thing herein advanced shall be disagreeable, it can be justified on the ground that it is better to be known in order to prevent ruin, than to be concealed, when such concealment serves only to hasten the ruin.

Of POPULATION.—The population of France being upwards of twenty-four millions, is more than double that of Great Britain and Ireland ; besides which France recruits more soldiers in Switzerland than England does in Scotland and Ireland. To this may likewise be added, that England and Ireland are not on the best terms. The suspicion that England governs Ireland for the purpose of keeping her low to prevent her becoming a rival in trade and manufactures, will always operate to hold Ireland in a state of sentimental hostilities with England.

REVENUES.—The revenues of France are twenty-four millions sterling. The revenues of England fifteen millions and an half. The taxes per head in France are twenty shillings sterling ; the taxes per head in England are two pounds four shillings and two pence. The national debt of France including the life annuities (which are two-fifths of the whole debt, and are annually expiring) at eleven years purchase, is one hundred and forty-two millions sterling. The national debt of England, the whole of which is on perpetual interest, is two hundred and forty-five millions. The national debt of France contains a power of annihilating itself without any new taxes for that purpose ; because it needs no more than to apply the life annuities as they expire to the purchase of the other two-fifths, which are on perpetual interest : but the national debt of England has not this advantage, and therefore the million a year that is to be applied towards reducing it is so much additional tax upon the people, over and above the current service.

WEALTH.—This is an important investigation : it ought therefore to be heard with patience, and judged of without prejudice.

Nothing is more common than for people to mistake one thing for another. Do not those who are crying up the wealth of the nation mistake a paper currency for riches?

To ascertain this point may be one of the means of preventing that ruin which cannot fail to follow by persisting in the mistake.

The highest estimation that is made of the quantity of gold and silver in Britain at this present day is twenty millions : and those who are most conversant with money transactions, believe it to be considerably below that sum. Yet this is no more money than what the nation possessed twenty years ago, and therefore, whatever her trade may be, it has produced to her no profit. Certainly no man can be so unwise as to suppose that increasing the quantity of bank notes, which is done with as little trouble as printing of newspapers, is national wealth.

The quantity of money in the nation was very well ascertained in the years 1773, '74, and '76, by calling in the light gold coin.

There were upwards of fifteen millions and a half of gold coin then called in, which with upwards of two millions of heavy guineas that remained out, and the silver coin, made about twenty millions, which is more than there is at this day. There is an amazing increase in the circulation of bank paper, which is no more national wealth than newspapers are ; because an increase of promissory notes, the capital remaining unincreasing in the same proportion, is no increase of wealth. It serves to raise false ideas which the judicious soon discover, and the ignorant experience to their cost.

Out of twenty millions sterling, the present quantity of real money in the nation, it would be too great an allowance to say that one-fourth of that sum, which is five millions, was in London. But even admitting this to be the case, it would require no very superior powers to ascertain pretty nearly what proportion of that sum of five millions could be in the bank. It would be ridiculous to suppose it could be less than half a million, and extravagant to suppose it could be two millions.

It likewise requires no very extraordinary discernment to ascertain how immense the quantity of bank notes, compared to its capital in the bank must be, when it is considered, that the national taxes are paid in bank notes; that all great transactions are done in bank notes; and that were a loan for twenty millions to be opened at the meeting of parliament, it would most probably be subscribed in a few days: yet all men must know the loan could not be paid in money, because it is at least four times greater than all the money in London, including the bankers and the bank amount too. In short, every thing shows, that the rage that overrun America, for paper money, or paper currency, has reached to England under another name. There it was called continental money, and here it is called bank notes. But it signifies not what name it bears, if the capital is not equal to the redemption.

There is likewise another circumstance that cannot fail to strike with some force when it is mentioned, because every man that has any thing to do with money transactions, will feel the truth of it, though he may not before have reflected upon it. It is the embarrassed condition into which the gold coin is thrown by the necessity of weighing it, and by refusing guineas that are even standing weight, and there appear to be but few heavy ones. Whether this is intended to force the paper currency into circulation, is not here attempted to be asserted, but it certainly has that effect to a very great degree, because people, rather than submit to the trouble and hazard of weighing, will take paper in preference to money. This was once the case in America.

The natural effect of increasing and continuing to increase paper currencies is that of banishing the real money. The shadow takes place of the substance till the country is left with only shadows in its hands.

A trade that does not increase the quantity of real money in a country, cannot be styled a profitable trade; yet this is certainly the case with England : and as to credit, of which so much has been said, it may be founded on ignorance or a false belief, as well as on real ability.

In Amsterdam, the money deposited in the bank is never taken out again. The depositors, when they have debts to pay, transfer their right to the persons to whom they are indebted, and those again proceed by the same practice, and the transfer of the right goes for payment; now could all the money deposited in the bank of Amsterdam be privately removed away, and the matter be kept a secret, the ignorance or the belief that the money was still there, would give the same credit as if it had not been removed. In short, credit is often no more than opinion, and the difference between credit and money, is, that money requires no opinion to support it.

All the countries in Europe annually increase in their quantity of gold and silver except England. By the registers kept at Lisbon and Cadiz, the two ports into which the gold and silver from South-America are imported, it appears that above eighty millions sterling have been imported within twenty years.* This has spread itself over Europe, and increased the quantity in all the countries on the continent; yet twenty years ago there was as much gold and silver in England as there is at this time.

The value of the silver imported into Europe exceeds that of the gold, yet every one can see there is no increase of silver coin in England; very little silver coin appearing except what are called Birmingham shillings, which have a faint impression of king William on one side, and are smooth on the other.

In what is the profits of trade to show itself but by increasing the quantity of that which is the object of trade, money? An increase of paper is not an increase of national money, and the confounding paper and money together, or not attending to the distinction, is a rock that the nation will one day split upon.

Whether the payment of interest to foreigners, or the trade to the East-Indies, or the nation embroiling itself in foreign wars, or whether the amount of trade which England carries on with different parts of the world, collectively taken, balances itself without profit; whether one or all of these is the cause, why the quantity of money does not increase in England is not, in this place, the object of inquiry. It is the fact and not the cause that is the matter here treated of.

Men immersed in trade and the concerns of a comptinghouse, are not the most speculative in national affairs, nor always the best judges of them. Accustomed to run risks in trade, they are habitually prepared to run risks with government, and though they are the first to suffer, they are often the last to foresee an evil.

Let us now cast a look towards the manufactures. A great deal has been said of their flourishing condition, and perhaps a great deal too much, for it may again be asked, where is the profit if there is no increase of money in the nation?

* From 1763 to 1777, a period of fifteen years of peace, the registered importations of gold and silver into Lisbon and Cadiz, was seventy millions sterling, besides what was privately landed.

The woollen manufacture is the staple manufacture of England, and this is evidently on the decline, in some, if not in all its branches. The city of Norwich, one of the most populous cities in England, and wholly dependant on the woollen manufacture, is, at this day, in a very impoverished condition, owing to the decline of its trade.

But not to rest the matter on a general assertion, or embarrass it with numerous statements, we will produce a circumstance by which the whole progress of the trade may be ascertained.

So long as thirty years ago, the price paid to the spinners of wool was one shilling for twenty-four skeins, each skein containing five hundred and sixty yards. This, according to the term of the trade, was giving a shilling for a shilling. A good hand would spin twelve skeins, which was six pence a day.

According to the increase of taxes, and the increased price of all the articles of life, they certainly ought now to get at least fifteen pence, for what thirty years ago they got one shilling. But such is the decline of the trade, that the case is directly the contrary. They now get but nine pence for the shilling, that is, they get but nine pence for what thirty years ago they got one shilling. Can these people cry out for war, when they are already half ruined by the decline of trade, and half devoured by the increase of taxes ?

But this is not the whole of the misfortunes which that part of the country suffers, and which will extend to others. The Norfolk farmers were the first who went into the practice of manuring their land with marl : but time has shown, that though it gave a vigor to the land for some years, it operated in the end to exhaust its stamina ; that the lands in many parts are worse than before they began to marl, and that it will not answer to marl a second time.

The manufactures of Manchester, Birmingham and Sheffield have had of late a considerable spring, but this appears to be rather on speculation than certainty. The speculations on the American market have failed, and that on Russia is becoming very precarious. Experience likewise was wanting to ascertain the quantity which the treaty of commerce with France would give sale to, and it is most probable the estimations have been too high, more especially as English goods will now become upopular in

France, which was not the case before the present injudicious rupture.

But in the best state which manufactures can be in, they are very unstable sources of national wealth. The reasons are, that they seldom continue long in one state. The market for them depends upon the caprice of fashions, and sometimes of politics in foreign countries, and they are at all times exposed to rivalship as well as to change. The Americans have already several manufactures among them, which they prefer to the English, such as axes, scythes, sickles, hoes, planes, nails, &c. Window glass, which was once a considerable article of exportation from England to America, the Americans now procure from other countries, nearly as good as the English crown glass, and but little dearer than the common green window glass.

It is somewhat remarkable that so many pens have been displayed to show what is called the increase of the commerce of England, and yet all of them have stepped short of the grand point, that is, they have gone no further than to show that a larger proportion of shipping, and a greater quantity of tonnage have been employed of late years than formerly: but this is no more than what is happening in other parts of Europe. The present fashion of the world is commerce, and the quantity increases in France as well as in England.

But the object of all trade is profit, and profit shows itself, not by an increase of paper currency, for that may be nationally had without the trouble of trade, but by an increase of real money: therefore the estimation should have ended, not in the comparative quantity of shipping and tonnage, but in the comparative quantity of gold and silver.

Had the quantity of gold and silver increased in England, the ministerial writers would not have stopped short at shipping and tonnage; but if they know any thing of the matter, they must know that it does not increase, and that the deception is occasioned by the increase of paper money, and that as paper continues to increase, gold and silver will diminish. Poorer in wealth and richer in delusion.

Something is radically wrong, and time will discover it to be putting paper in the room of money.

Out of one hundred millions sterling of gold and silver, which must have been imported into Europe from South-

America since the commencement of the peace before last, it does not appear that England has derived or retains any portion of it.

M. Neckar states the annual increase of gold and silver in France, that is, the proportion which France draws of the annual importation into Europe, to be upwards of one million sterling. But England, in the space of twenty years, does not appear to have increased in any thing but paper currency.

Credulity is wealth while credulity lasts, and credit is, in a thousand instances, the child of credulity. It requires no more faith to believe paper to be money, than to believe a man could go into a quart bottle; and the nation whose credulity can be imposed upon by bottle conjuring, can, for a time, be imposed upon by paper conjuring.

From these matters we pass on to make some observations on the national debt, which is another species of paper currency.

In short, to whatever point the eye is directed, whether to the money, the paper, the manufactures, the taxes, or the debt, the inability of supporting a war is evident, unless it is intended to carry it on by fleecing the skin over people's ears by taxes; and therefore the endangering the nation in a war for the sake of the stadtholder of Holland, or the king of Prussia, or any other foreign affairs, from which England can derive no possible advantage, is an absurd and ruinous system of politics.

France perhaps is not in a better situation, and therefore, a war where both must lose, and wherein they could only act the part of seconds, must historically have been denominated a boyish, foolish, unnecessary quarrel.

But before we enter on the subject of the national debt, it will be proper to make a general review of the different manner of carrying on war since the revolution to what was the practice before.

Before the revolution the intervals of peace and war always found means to pay off the expense, and leave the nation clear of incumbrance at the commencement of any succeeding war; and even for some years after the revolution this practice was continued.

From the year 1688, (the era of the revolution) to the year 1702, a period of fourteen years, the sums borrowed by government at different times, amounted to forty-four millions; yet this sum was paid off almost as fast as it was borrowed; thirty-four millions was paid off, at the commencement of the year 1702. This was a greater exertion than the nation has ever made since, for exertion is not in borrowing but in paying.

From that time wars have been carried on by borrowing and funding the capital on a perpetual interest, instead of paying it off, and thereby continually carrying forward and accumulating the weight and expense of every war into the next. By this means that which was light at first becomes immensely heavy at last. The nation has now on its shoulders the weight of all the wars from the time of queen Anne. This practice is exactly like that of loading a horse with a feather at a time till you break his back.

The national debt exhibits at this day a striking novelty. It has travelled on in a circular progression till the amount of the annual interest has exactly overtaken, or become equal to, the first capital of the national debt, *nine millions*. Here begins the evidence of the predictions so long foretold by the ablest calculators in the nation. The interest will in succession overtake all the succeeding capitals, and that with the proportioned rapidity with which those capitals accumulated; because by continuing the practice, not only higher and higher premiums must be given for loans, but the money, or rather the paper, will not go so far as it formerly did, and therefore the debt will increase with a continual increasing velocity.

The expense of every war, since the national debt began, has, upon an average, been double the expense of the war preceding it; the expense of the next war will be at least two hundred millions, which will increase the annual interest to at least seventeen millions, and consequently the taxes in the same proportion; the following war will increase the interest to thirty-three millions, and a third war will mount up the interest to sixty-five millions. This is not going on in the spirit of prediction, but taking what has already been as a rule for what will again be, and therefore the nation has but a miserable prospect to look at. The weight of accumulating interest is not much felt till after many years have passed over; but when it begins to be heavy, as it does now, the burden increases like that of purchasing a horse with a farthing for the first nail of the shoe and doubling it.

As to Mr. Pitt's scheme of reducing the national debt by a million a year, applied to the purchase of stock, it will turn out, to say the least of it, a ridiculous and frivolous project: for if a minister has not experience enough to distinguish a feather floating in the air, from the god of war, nor the clamors and interest of those who are seeking for jobs and contracts, from the voice and interest of the people, he will soon precipitate the nation into some unnecessary war; and therefore any scheme of redemption of the debt, founded on the supposed continuance of peace, will, with such conduct, be no more than a balloon.

That the funding system contains within itself the seeds of its own destruction, is as certain as that the human body contains within itself the seeds of death. The event is as fixed as fate, unless it can be taken as a proof that because we are not dead we are not to die.

The consequence of the funding scheme, even if no other event takes place, will be to create two violent parties in the nation. The one, goaded by the continual increase of taxes to pay the interest; the other reaping a benefit from the taxes by receiving the interest. This is very strongly shadowed forth, like the hand writing on the wall, by the ingenious author of the Commercial Atlas, in his observations on the national debt.

The slumber that for several years has overshadowed the nation, in all matters of public finance, cannot be supposed to last for ever. The people have not yet awakened to the subject, and it is taken for granted that they never will. But, if a supposed unnecessary expenditure of between five and six millions sterling, in the finances of France (for the writer undertakes not to judge of the fact) has awakened that whole nation, a people supposed to be perfectly docile in all national matters, surely the people of England will not be less attentive to their rights and properties. If this should not be the case, the inference will be fairly drawn, that England is losing the spirit that France is taking up, and that it is an ingenious device in the ministry to compose the nation to unpopular and unnecessary taxes, by shamming a victory when there was no enemy at hand.

In short, every war serves to increase every kind of paper currency in the nation, and to diminish the quantity of gold and silver, by sending it to Prussia and other foreign countries.

It will not be denied that credulity is a strong trait in the English character; and this has in no instance shown itself more than in mistaking paper for money, except it be in the unaccountable ignorance of mistaking the debt of the nation for riches. But the suspicion is beginning to awaken.

We will close this article with observing, that a new kind of paper currency has arisen within a few years, which is that of country bank notes; almost every town now has its bank, its paper mint, and the coinage of paper has become universal. In the mean time the melting down the light guineas, and recoining them, passes with those who know no better, for an increase of money; because every new guinea they see, and which is but seldom, they naturally suppose to be a guinea more, when it is really nothing else than an old guinea new cast.

From this account of the money, paper, and national debt of England, we proceed to compare it with the money, paper, and national debt of France.

It is very well known that paper has not the same credit in France which it has in England, and that, consequently, there is much less of it. This has naturally operated to increase the quantity of gold and silver in France, and prevent the increase of paper.

The highest estimation of the quantity of gold and silver in England, as already stated, is twenty millions sterling, and the quantity of paper grafted thereon, immense.

The quantity of gold and silver in France is ninety millions sterling, and the quantity of paper grafted thereon, trifling. France, therefore, has a long run of credit in reserve, which England has already expended; and it will naturally follow, that when the government of France and the nation shall adjust their differences by an amicable embrace of each other, that this reserved credit will be brought forth, and the power of France will be doubly increased. The adjustment of these differences is but the business of a day, whenever its government shall see the proper moment for doing it, and nothing would precipitate this event more than a war. The cry of war, from the injudicious provocations given by the British ministry, and the disadvantageous effect of the commercial treaty, is becoming popular in France.

The near situation of France to Spain and Portugal, the two countries which import gold and silver, and her

manufactures being better adapted to the warm climate
of those countries, than the manufactures of England, give
her superior opportunities of drawing money into the nation, and as she has but little trade to the East-Indies, the
money so drawn in is not drawn out again as in England.
Another advantage is, that from the greatness of her dominions she has no occasion to waste her wealth in hiring
foreign troops, as is the practice with England; and a
third advantage is, that the money which England squan-
ders in Prussia and other countries on the continent serves
to increase the wealth of France, because a considerable
part of it centres there through the medium of her commerce.

Admitting Great Britain and Ireland to contain ten millions of inhabitants, the quantity of money per head is forty shillings: the money per head in France is three
pounds fifteen shillings, which is nearly double.

The national debt of England, compared to the whole
amount of money in the nation, is as twelve to one, that is,
the debt is twelve times greater than all the money
amounts to.

The national debt of France, compared to the whole
amount of her money, is considerably less than as two are
to one, that is, her debt is not so much as twice the amount
of her money. France, therefore, as already stated, has
an immense credit in reserve whenever the settlement of
her present internal differences shall furnish her with the
means of employing it, and that period, so much to be
dreaded by England, is hastening on.

The annual interest of the national debt of England and
France are nearly equal, being *nine millions* sterling ; but
with this difference, that above three millions and a half of
the annual interest of France are only life annuities. The
interest, therefore, of her debt lessens every year, and she
will have a surplus up to the amount of three millions and
an half, to apply to the purchase of that part of the debt
which is on perpetual interest ; therefore, without any new
taxes for that purpose, she can discharge her whole debt
in less than a third of the time on which it can be done in
England, according to Mr. Pitt's plan, with his additional
tax of a million a year.

But let the event of Mr. Pitt's plan be what it may, as
to reducing the debt, there is one circumstance that cannot
fail to accompany it, which is, that of making it the interest

of government, in executing this plan, to undermine the interest of its creditors, or the value of the funds, for the purpose of purchasing at a cheaper rate.

The plan is founded on the presumption of a long uninterrupted peace, and that future loans would not be wanted, which cannot now be expected, for France in her turn is getting into a temper for war. The plan naturally strikes at the credit of government, in contracting further debts, for were a loan to be opened to-morrow, the subscribers naturally perceiving that it was the interest of government to undermine them as soon as they became creditors, would consequently seek to secure themselves, by demanding higher premiums at first. It is a question, whether a premium of thirty per cent. is now as good as ten was before, and therefore the plan, in case of a war, instead of lessening the debt, serves to push it more rapidly on.

The minister certainly never understood the natural operation of his plan, or he would not have acted as he has done. The plan has two edges, while he has supposed it to have only one. It strikes at the debt in peace, and at the credit in war.

The gentleman who originally furnished the minister with this plan, now gives it totally up. He knew its operation both in peace and war, but the minister appears not to have comprehended it: but if he has made a mistake, his youth and inexperience must be his apology.

The plan, unless it should be altered, that is given out for providing for the expense of the late armaments, is in reality no other than the American plan of paper money, and it is very probable that the minister has received it from some American refugee.

The plan given out is, that the minister is to borrow the *money* of the bank. Here is the delusion. The name of *money* covers the deception. For the case is, that the bank does not lend the real money, but it issues out an emission of bank paper, and the presumption is, that there will be no run upon the bank in consequence of such an extraordinary emission, but if there should, no man can be at a loss in foreseeing the issue.

There are those who remember that on a former run the bank was obliged to prolong the time by paying shillings and sixpences, and it is universally credited that a quantity of silver is now preserved in the bank for the same purpose; but the device, to every person of reflection, shows that the capital is not equal to the demands, and that the chapter of accidents is part of the bible of the bank.

It may be asked why does not the government issue the paper instead of the bank? The answer is, that it is exactly the same thing in the end, only with this difference in the mode, that were the government to do it, it would be too visible a system of paper currency, and that a disguise is necessary.

Having recourse to the bank, is a kind of playing the bank off against the funds. Fighting one kind of paper against another, and in the combat both of them will be sufferers.

In short, the delusion of paper riches is working as rapidly in England as it did in America. A young and inexperienced minister, like a young and inexperienced congress, may suppose that he sees mines of wealth in a printing press, and that a nation cannot be exhausted while there is paper and ink enough to print paper money.— Every new emission, until the delusion bursts, will appear to the nation an increase of wealth. Every merchant's coffers will appear a treasury, and he will swell with paper riches until he becomes a bankrupt.

When a bank makes too free with its paper, it exposes itself in much the same manner which a government does that makes too free with its power; too much credit is as bad as too little; and there is such a thing as governing too much, as well in a bank, as in government. But nothing exposes a bank more than being under the influence, instead of the protection of government, and whenever either the property or the credit of a bank, can be commanded or influenced by a government, or a minister, its destruction is not far off.

We have now stated the comparative condition of England and France as to money matters. But there yet remain some things necessary to be touched upon.

It is an error very frequently committed in the world to mistake disposition for condition.

France with a much better permanent condition for war than England, is in a less disposition to enter into one, and this disposition in her is mistaken in England for want of condition; and on the other hand, the apparent disposition in England for war is mistaken by her for a condition to undertake and carry one on.

There appears a uniformity in all the works of nature, from individual animals up to nations. The smaller animals are always the most fretful, passionate, and insulting. They mistake temper for strength, and often fall a sacrifice to vexatious impetuosity; while larger ones go calmly on, and require repeated provocations to incense them. France may yet be aggravated into a war, and very probably will. Where the condition exists the disposition may at any time take place. We may create temper, but we cannot create strength.

While the literature of England preserves an honorable rank among the nations of Europe, her national character is most miserably suffering in the world through her newspapers. The most barefaced perfidiousness, the most abandoned principles are daily propagated. A total disregard to all the obligations of national faith and honor are publicly professed. Instead of that true greatness of heart, that generous disdain of vulgar littleness that ought always to accompany the disputes of nations, scarcely any thing is to be seen but mean abuse and low scurrility. This is not the case in any other country in the world but England.

We will now proceed to conclude with a few additional observations on the state of politics.

For several weeks the nation was amused with the daily rumors of some great cabinet secret, and admiring how profoundly the secret was kept, when the only secret was, that there was no secret to divulge.

But this opinion of a secret very well shows that the opinion of the nation was opposed to the opinion of the minister, or the supposition of some great secret would not have taken place, as the affairs of the stadtholder were then publicly known. It shows that the nation did not think the stadtholder of Holland a sufficient reason for laying new taxes on England, and running into the risk and expense of a war, and great was the surprise when the declaration and counter declaration, like twin mice, peeped from the cabinet.

But there is one secret that requires to be investigated, which is, whether the minister did not know that France would not engage in a war, and whether the preparations were not an idle parade, founded on that knowledge.

Whether it was not meanly putting England under the banners of Prussia, and taking thereby a dishonorable advantage of the internal perplexity which France was then in, and which in its turn may happen to England, to assume the air of a challenge, which it must be known would not be accepted, because there was nothing to make the acceptance necessary.

Whether this conduct in the minister does not mischievously operate to destroy the harmony that appeared to be growing up between the two nations; to lessen, if not totally destroy, the advantages of the commercial treaty, and to lay the seeds of future wars, when there was a prospect of a long and uninterrupted peace.

When there are two ways of accomplishing the same object, it almost always happens that the one is better than the other; and whether the minister has not chosen the worst, a few observations will elucidate.

It signifies not what airy schemes, projects, or even treaties may be formed, especially if done under the point of the bayonet, for all that can be expected of Holland is neutrality. Her trade is with all nations, and it is from her neutrality that this trade has arisen. Destroy this neutrality and Holland is destroyed. Therefore it matters not what sentiments party men may be of in Holland as to the stadtholdership, because there is still a superior banner under which all will unite.

Holland will not expose her trade to the devastations of England by joining France in a war, neither will she expose it to France by joining England. It may very well be asked, what is England or France to Holland, that she should join with either in a war, unless she is compelled to it by one or the other making war upon her, as was the case in the last war?

Events may soon happen in Europe to make all the force that Prussia can raise necessary to her own defence, and Holland must be wise enough to see, that by joining England she not only exposes her trade to France but likewise her dominions, because France can invade her in a quarter in which England cannot defend her, for Holland lies open to France by land. It is, therefore, more immediately the interest of Holland to keep on good terms with France;

neither can England give her any equivalent to balance this circumstance. How foolish then are the politics which are directed to unnatural and impossible objects! Surely the experience of a century past is sufficient to show to any man, except one of yesterday, what the conduct of Holland in all cases must be.

But there is another circumstance that does not fail to impress foreigners, and especially Holland, which is, that the immensity of the national debt of England, the prospect of its still increasing, and the exorbitancy of her paper currencies, render her too insecure in herself to be much confided in by foreign nations for any length of time. Because that which must happen may very soon happen.

Concerning the rescript delivered by the French minister, there is one certain explanation to be put upon it, which is, that if France had been disposed for war, she would not have made that communication. The very making it goes to a full explanation of the parts ; and as soon as Mr. Pitt obtained this knowledge, it appeared to him a safe moment to gird on his sword, and when he found that France was as well weaponed as himself, to propose to take it off again. This is in a few words the whole history of the campaign. A war minister in peace, and a peace minister in war. Brave where there is no danger, and prudent when there is any.

The rescript could be nothing else than an explanation, on the part of France, of the situation she conceived herself to be subject to, and the probable consequences that might follow from it. This she was not obliged to make, and therefore her making it was a matter of civil communication towards a power she was at peace with, and which in return entitled her to a similar communication on the part of the British cabinet. All this might have been done without either the expense, the tumult, the provocations, or the ill blood that has been created between the two nations.

The alliance between France and Holland, was formed while the stadtholder was a part of the government, therefore, France could not from that alliance take a part either for or against him. She could only act when the whole interest of the republic was exposed to a foreign enemy, and it was not certain that this might not be the case.

The rescript, therefore, instead of being taken as a ground for war, was in itself a ground for peace, because it tended to bring on a discussion of all the circumstances of France and England relative to Holland, which would not have failed to place Holland in a state of neutrality, and that only will be the final event now; because, independent of all parties, no other is consistent with the whole national interest of that republic.

But this not being done, it is now left to the Dutch to do it for themselves.

An alliance with England, at the same time there is one existing with France, will secure this neutrality, so necessary to the Dutch republic. By this stroke of politics she will be free from all obligations, to join with either in a war, and be guaranteed to both. Her alliance with England will debar England from molesting her trade by sea, and that with France will debar France from the same thing, and likewise from invading her by land in all future cases. There are so many probable circumstances to arise on the continent of Europe, that the situation of Holland requires this safeguard, more especially from France, on account of her land connexion.

The rising greatness of the Russian empire, the probable union of this empire with that of Germany and France, and consequently with Spain, whose interests cannot be separated, and the probability of a rupture between the emperor and the king of Prussia, are matters that cannot fail to impress the Dutch with the necessity of securing themselves by land as well as by sea, and to prevent their being drawn into the quarrels either of England or France.

Upon the whole, as there was a civil as well as an uncivil line of politics to be pursued, every man of humane and generous sentiments must lament it was not chosen.

A disposition for peace was growing up in every part of France, and there appeared at the same time a mutual one rising in England. A silent wish on both sides, was universally expanding itself, that wars, so fatal to the true interest and burdensome by taxes to the subjects of both countries, might exist no more, and that a long and lasting peace might take place.

But instead of cultivating this happy opportunity, the pettish vanity of a young and inexperienced minister, who balanced himself between peace and war to take his choice of circumstances, instead of principles, and who went into an expensive armament when there was none to contend with, and not till after the affairs of Holland might be said to be terminated, has destroyed those seeds of harmony that might have been considered of more value to both nations than their fleets and armies.

He has permitted the nation to run mad under the universal influence of a groundless belief of vast hostile armaments in the East and West-Indies, and the supposition of a secret that never existed. By this means the sparks of ill-will are afresh kindled up between the nations, the fair prospect of lasting peace is vanished, and a train of future evils fills up the scene, and that at a time when the internal affairs of France, however confused they at present appear, are naturally approaching to a great and harmonious increase of its power.

THOMAS PAINE.

London, Aug. 1787.

RIGHTS OF MAN.

BEING

AN ANSWER

TO MR. BURKE'S ATTACK ON THE FRENCH REVOLUTION.

———

PART I.

TO

GEORGE WASHINGTON,

PRESIDENT OF THE UNITED STATES OF AMERICA.

SIR,

I PRESENT you a small treatise in defence of those principles of freedom which your exemplary virtue hath so
eminently contributed to establish. That the rights of
man may become as universal as your benevolence can
wish, and that you may enjoy the happiness of seeing the
new world regenerate the old, is the prayer of

Sir,

Your much obliged, and

Obedient humble servant,

THOMAS PAINE.

RIGHTS OF MAN.

Among the incivilities by which nations or individuals provoke and irritate each other, Mr. Burke's pamphlet on the French revolution is an extraordinary instance. Neither the people of France, nor the national assembly, were troubling themselves about the affairs of England, or the English parliament; and why Mr. Burke should commence an unprovoked attack upon them, both in parliament and in public, is a conduct that cannot be pardoned on the score of manners, nor justified on that of policy.

There is scarcely an epithet of abuse to be found in the English language, with which Mr. Burke has not loaded the French nation and the national assembly. Every thing which rancor, prejudice, ignorance or knowledge could suggest, are poured forth in the copious fury of near four hundred pages. In the strain and on the plan Mr. Burke was writing, he might have wrote on to as many thousand. When the tongue or the pen is let loose in a phrenzy of passion, it is the man, and not the subject that becomes exhausted.

Hitherto Mr. Burke has been mistaken and disappointed in the opinions he had formed on the affairs of France; but such is the ingenuity of his hope, or the malignancy of his despair, that it furnishes him with new pretences to go on. There was a time when it was impossible to make Mr. Burke believe there would be any revolution in

France. His opinion then was, that the French had neither spirit to undertake it, nor fortitude to support it; and
now that there is one, he seeks an escape by condemning it.

Not sufficiently content with abusing the national assembly, a great part of his work is taken up with abusing Dr.
Price (one of the best hearted men that exists) and the two
societies in England, known by the name of the Revolution
and the Constitutional societies.

Dr. Price had preached a sermon on the 4th of Novem-
ber, 1789, being the anniversary of what is called in England the revolution, which took place in 1688. Mr. Burke,
speaking of this sermon, says, " the political divine proceeds dogmatically to assert, that, by the principles of the
revolution, the people of England have acquired three fundamental rights :

1st, To choose our own governors.

2d, To cashier them for misconduct.

3d. To frame a government for ourselves."

Dr. Price does not say that the right to do these things
exists in this or in that person, or in this or in that description of persons, but that it exists in the *whole*—that it is a
right resident in the nation.   Mr. Burke, on the contrary,
denies that such a right exists in the nation, either in whole
or in part, or that it exists any where; and what is still
more strange and marvellous, he says, that "the people
of England utterly disclaim such right, and that they will
resist the practical assertion of it with their lives and fortunes."   That men will take up arms, and spend their lives
and fortunes *not* to maintain their rights, but to maintain
that they have *not* rights, is an entire new species of discovery, and suited to the paradoxical genius of Mr. Burke.

The method which Mr. Burke takes to prove that the
people of England have no such rights, and that such rights
do not exist in the nation, either in whole or in part, or any
where at all, is of the same marvellous and monstrous kind
with what he has already said; for his arguments are, that
the persons, or the generation of persons in whom they did
exist, are dead, and with them the right is dead also.   To
prove this, he quotes a declaration made by parliament
about an hundred years ago, to William and Mary, in these
words: " The lords spiritual and temporal, and commons,
do, in the name of the people aforesaid—(meaning the
people of England then living) most humbly and faithfully

submit themselves, their *heirs* and *posterity*, for ever."—
He also quotes a clause of another act of parliament made
in the same reign, the terms of which, he says, "bind us—
(meaning the people of that day)—our *heirs* and our *posterity*, to *them*, their *heirs* and *posterity*, to the end of time."

Mr. Burke considers his point sufficiently established by
producing those clauses, which he enforces by saying that
they exclude the right of the nation *for ever:* and not yet
content with making such declarations, repeated over and
over again, he further says, "that if the people of England
possessed such a right before the revolution" (which he
acknowledges to have been the case, not only in England,
but throughout Europe, at an early period) " yet that the
English nation did, at the time of the revolution, most solemnly renounce and abdicate it, for themselves, and *for all
their posterity for ever."*

As Mr. Burke occasionally applies the poison drawn
from his horrid principles (if it is not a profanation to call
them by the name of principles) not only to the English nation, but to the French revolution and the national assembly, and charges that august, illuminated and illuminating
body of men with the epithet of *usurpers,* I shall, *sans cere-
monie,* place another system of principles in opposition to
his.

The English parliament of 1688, did a certain thing,
which for themselves and their constituents, they had a right
to do, and which appeared right should be done; but, in
addition to this right, which they possessed by delegation,
they set up another right by assumption, that of binding and
controlling posterity to the end of time. The case, therefore, divides itself into two parts; the right which they
possessed by delegation, and the right which they set up
by assumption. The first is admitted; but with respect to
the second, I reply :—

There never did, nor never can exist a parliament, or
any description of men, or any generation of men, in any
country, possessed of the right or the power of binding or
controlling posterity to the " end of time," or of commanding for ever how the world shall be governed, or who shall
govern it; and therefore all such clauses, acts, or declarations, by which the makers of them attempt to do what
they have neither the right nor the power to do, nor the
power to execute, are in themselves null and void. Every
age and generation must be as free to act for itself, *in all*

cases, as the ages and generations which preceded it. The vanity and presumption of governing beyond the grave, is the most ridiculous and insolent of all tyrannies. Man has no property in man; neither has any generation a property in the generations which are to follow. The parliament or the people of 1688, or of any other period, had no more right to dispose of the people of the present day, or to bind or to control them *in any shape whatever*, than the parliament or the people of the present day have to dispose of, bind or control those who are to live an hundred or a thousand years hence. Every generation is and must be competent to all the purposes which its occasions require. It is the living and not the dead, that are to be accommodated. When man ceases to be, his power and his wants cease with him; and having no longer any participation in the concerns of this world, he has no longer any authority in directing who shall be its governors, or how its government shall be organized, or how administered.

I am not contending for, nor against, any form of government, nor for nor against any party, here or elsewhere. That which a whole nation chooses to do, it has a right to do. Mr. Burke denies it. Where then does the right exist? I am contending for the right of the *living*, and against their being willed away, and controlled and contracted for, by the manuscript-assumed authority of the dead; and Mr. Burke is contending for the authority of the dead over the rights and freedom of the living. There was a time when kings disposed of their crowns by will upon their deathbeds, and consigned the people, like beasts of the field, to whatever successor they appointed. This is now so exploded as scarcely to be remembered, and so monstrous as hardly to be believed: but the parliamentary clauses upon which Mr. Burke builds his political church, are of the same nature.

The laws of every country must be analogous to some common principle. In England, no parent or master, nor all the authority of parliament, omnipotent as it has called itself, can bind or control the personal freedom even of an individual beyond the age of twenty-one years: on what ground of right then could the parliament of 1688, or any other parliament bind all posterity for ever?

Those who have quitted the world, and those who are not arrived yet in it, are as remote from each other as the utmost stretch of mortal imagination can conceive: what possible obligation then can exist between them, what rule or principle can be laid down, that two nonentities, the one out of existence, and the other not in, and who never can meet in this world, that the one should control the other to the end of time?

In England, it is said that money cannot be taken out of the pockets of the people without their consent: but who authorized, and who could authorize the parliament of 1688 to control and take away the freedom of posterity, and limit and confine their rights of acting in certain cases for ever, who were not in existence to give or withhold their consent?

A greater absurdity cannot present itself to the understanding of man, than what Mr. Burke offers to his readers. He tells them, and he tells the world to come, that a certain body of men who existed an hundred years ago, made a law, and that there does not now exist in the nation, nor never will, nor never can, a power to alter it.— Under how many subtleties, or absurdities, has the divine right to govern been imposed on the credulity of mankind : Mr. Burke has discovered a new one, and he has shortened his journey to Rome, by appealing to the power of this infallible parliament of former days; and he produces what it has done, as of divine authority : for that power must be certainly more than human, which no human power to the end of time can alter.

But Mr. Burke has done some service, not to his cause, but to his country, by bringing those clauses into public view. They serve to demonstrate how necessary it is at all times to watch against the attempted encroachment of power, and to prevent its running to excess. It is somewhat extraordinary, that the offence for which James II. was expelled, that of setting up power by *assumption*, should be re-acted under another shape and form, by the parliament that expelled him. It shows, that the rights of man were but imperfectly understood at the revolution ; for certain it is that the right which that parliament set up by *assumption* (for by delegation it had not, and could not have it, because none could give it) over the persons and freedom of posterity for ever, was of the same tyrannical, unfounded kind which James attempted to set up over the parliament and the nation, and for which he was expelled. The only difference is, (for in principle they differ not) that the one was an usurper over the living, and the other over the unborn; and as the one has no better authority to stand upon than the other, both of them must be equally null and void, and of no effect.

From what or whence, does Mr. Burke prove the right of any human power to bind posterity for ever? He has produced his clauses; but he must produce also his proofs that such a right existed, and show how it existed. If it ever existed, it must now exist; for whatever appertains to the nature of man, cannot be annihilated by man. It is the nature of man to die, and he will continue to die as long as he continues to be born. But Mr. Burke has set up a sort of political Adam, in whom all posterity are bound for ever; he must therefore prove that his Adam possessed such a power or such a right.

The weaker any cord is, the less it will bear to be stretched, and the worse is the policy to stretch it, unless it is intended to break it. Had a person contemplated the overthrow of Mr. Burke's positions, he would have proceeded as Mr. Burke has done. He would have magnified the authorities, on purpose to have called the *right* of them into question; and the instant the question of right was started, the authorities must have been given up.

It requires but a very small glance of thought to perceive, that although laws made in one generation often continue in force through succeeding generations, yet they continue to derive their force from the consent of the living. A law not repealed continues in force, not because it *cannot* be repealed, but because it *is not* repealed; and the non-repealing passes for consent.

But Mr. Burke's clauses have not even this qualification in their favor. They become null, by attempting to become immortal. The nature of them precludes consent. They destroy the right which they *might* have, by grounding it on a right which they *cannot* have. Immortal power is not a human right, and therefore cannot be a right of parliament. The parliament of 1688 might as well have passed an act to have authorized itself to live for ever, as to make their authority live for ever. All, therefore, that can be said of them is, that they are a formality of words, of as much import, as if those who used them had addressed a congratulation to themselves, and, in the oriental style of antiquity, had said, O! parliament, live for ever!

The circumstances of the world are continually changing, and the opinions of men change also; and as government is for the living, and not for the dead, it is the living only that has any right in it. That which may be thought right and found convenient in one age, may be thought wrong and found inconvenient in another. In such cases, who is to decide, the living, or the dead?

As almost one hundred pages of Mr. Burke's book are employed upon these clauses, it will consequently follow, that if the clauses themselves, so far as they set up an *assumed, usurped* dominion over posterity for ever, are unauthoritative, and in their nature, null and void, that all his voluminous inferences and declamation drawn therefrom, or founded thereon, are null and void also: and on this ground I rest the matter.

We now come more particularly to the affairs of France. Mr. Burke's book has the appearance of being written as instruction to the French nation; but if I may permit myself the use of an extravagant metaphor, suited to the extravagance of the case, it is darkness attempting to illuminate light.

While I am writing this, there is accidentally before me some proposals for a declaration of rights by the marquis de la Fayette (I ask his pardon for using his former address, and do it only for distinction's sake) to the national assembly on the 11th of July 1789, three days before the taking of the Bastile; and I cannot but be struck how opposite the sources are from which that gentleman and Mr. Burke draw their principles. Instead of referring to musty records and mouldy parchments, to prove that the rights of the living are lost, "renounced and abdicated for ever" by those who are now no more, as Mr. Burke has done, M. de la Fayette applies to the living world, and emphatically says, "Call to mind the sentiments which nature has engraved in the heart of every citizen, and which take a new force when they are solemnly recognized by all:— for a nation to love liberty, it is sufficient that she knows it; and to be free, it is sufficient that she wills it." How dry, barren and obscure, is the source from which Mr. Burke labors; and how ineffectual, though embellished with flowers, is all his declamation and his argument, compared with these clear, concise and soul-animating sentiments: few and short as they are, they lead on to a vast field of generous and manly thinking, and do not finish, like Mr. Burke's periods, with music in the ear, and nothing in the heart.

As I have introduced the mention of M. de la Fayette, I
will take the liberty of adding an anecdote respecting his
farewell address to the congress of America in 1783, and
which occurred fresh to my mind when I saw Mr. Burke's
thundering attack on the French revolution.—M. de la
Fayette went to America at an early period of the war,
and continued a volunteer in her service to the end.   His
conduct through the whole of that enterprise is one of the
most extraordinary that is to be found in the history of a
young man, scarcely then twenty years of age. Situated in
a country that was like the lap of sensual pleasure, and with
the means of enjoying it, how few are there to be found who
would exchange such a scene for the woods and wilderness
of America, and pass the flowery years of youth in unprofitable danger and hardship ! But such is the fact. When
the war ended, and he was on the point of taking his final
departure, he presented himself to congress, and contemplating, in his affectionate farewell, the revolution he had
seen, expressed himself in these words : *" May this great
monument raised to Liberty, serve as a lesson to the oppressor,
and an example to the oppressed !"* When this address came
to the hands of Dr. Franklin, who was then in France, he
applied to count Vergennes to have it inserted in the
French gazette, but never could obtain his consent. The
fact was, that count Vergennes was an aristocratical despot, at home, and dreaded the example of the American
revolution in France, as certain other persons now dread
the example of the French revolution in England ; and Mr.
Burke's tribute of fear (for in this light his book must be
considered) runs parallel with count Vergennes' refusal.
But to return more particularly to his work.

"We have seen (says Mr. Burke) the French rebel
against a mild and lawful monarch, with more fury, outrage
and insult, than any people has been known to rise against
the most illegal usurper, or the most sanguinary tyrant."—
This is one among a thousand other instances, in which Mr.
Burke shows that he is ignorant of the springs and principles of the French revolution.

It was not against Louis XVI. but against the despotic
principle of the government, that the nation revolted.
These principles had not their origin in him, but in the
original establishment, many centuries back ; and they
were become too deeply rooted to be removed, and the
Augean stable of parasites and plunderers too abominably

filthy to be cleansed, by any thing short of a complete and universal revolution.

When it becomes necessary to do a thing, the whole heart should join in the measure, or it should not be attempted. That crisis was then arrived, and there remained no choice but to act with determined vigor, or not to act at all. The king was known to be the friend of the nation, and this circumstance was favorable to the enterprise. Perhaps no man bred up in the style of an absolute king, ever possessed a heart so little disposed to the exercise of that species of power as the present king of France. But the principles of the government itself still remained the same. The monarch and monarchy were distinct and separate things; and it was against the established despotism of the latter, and not against the person or principles of the former, that the revolt commenced, and the revolution has been carried on.

Mr. Burke does not attend to this distinction between men and principles, and therefore he does not see that a revolt may take place against the despotism of the latter, while there lies no charge of despotism against the former.

The natural moderation of Louis XVI. contributed nothing to alter the hereditary despotism of the monarchy. All the tyrannies of former reigns, acted under that hereditary despotism, were still liable to be revived in the hands of a successor. It was not the respite of a reign that would satisfy France, enlightened as she was then become. A casual discontinuance of the *practice* of despotism, is not a discontinuance of its *principles*; the former depends on the virtue of the individual who is in immediate possession of the power; the latter, on the virtue and fortitude of the nation. In the case of Charles I. and James II. of England, the revolt was against the personal despotism of the men; whereas in France, it was against the hereditary despotism of the established government. But men who can consign over the the rights of posterity for ever on the authority of a mouldy parchment, like Mr. Burke, are not qualified to judge of this revolution. It takes in a field too vast for their views to explore, and proceeds with a mightiness of reason they cannot keep pace with.

But there are many points of view in which this revolution may be considered. When despotism has established itself for ages in a country, as in France, it is not in the person of the king only that it resides. It has the

appearance of being so in show, and in nominal authority;
but it is not so in practice, and in fact. It has its standard every where. Every office and department has its
despotism, founded upon custom and usage. Every place
has its Bastile, and every Bastile its despot. The original
hereditary despotism resident in the person of the king,
divides and sub-divides itself into a thousand shapes and
forms, till at last the whole of it is acted by deputation.—
This was the case in France; and against this species of
despotism, proceeding on through an endless labyrinth of
office till the source of it is scarcely perceptible, there is
no mode of redress. It strengthens itself by assuming the
appearance of duty, and tyrannizes under the pretence of
obeying.

When a man reflects on the condition which France was
in from the nature of her government, he will see other
causes for revolt than those which immediately connect
themselves with the person or character of Louis XVI.—
There were, if I may so express it, a thousand despotisms
to be reformed in France, which had grown up under the
hereditary despotism of the monarchy, and become so
rooted as to be in a great measure independent of it. Between the monarchy, the parliament, and the church, there
was a *rivalship* of despotism : besides the feudal despotism
operating locally, and the ministerial despotism operating
every where. But Mr. Burke, by considering the king as
the only possible object of a revolt, speaks as if France
was a village, in which every thing that passed must be
known to its commanding officer, and no oppression could
be acted but what he could immediately control. Mr.
Burke might have been in the Bastile his whole life, as
well under Louis XVI. as Louis XIV. and neither the one
nor the other known that such a man as Mr. Burke existed. The despotic principles of the government were the
same in both reigns, though the dispositions of the men
were as remote as tyranny and benevolence.

What Mr. Burke considers as a reproach to the French
revolution, that of bringing it forward under a reign more
mild than the preceding ones, is one of its highest honors.
The revolutions that have taken place in other European
countries, have been excited by personal hatred. The
rage was against the man, and he became the victim.—
But, in the instance of France, we see a revolution generated in the rational contemplation of the rights of man, and

distinguishing from the beginning between persons and principles.

But Mr. Burke appears to have no idea of principles, when he is contemplating governments. "Ten years ago," says he, "I could have felicitated France on her having a government, without inquiring what the nature of that government was, or how it was administered." Is this the language of a rational man? Is it the language of a heart feeling as it ought to feel for the rights and happiness of the human race? On this ground, Mr. Burke must compliment every government in the world, while the victims who suffer under them, whether sold into slavery or tortured out of existence, are wholly forgotten. It is power, and not principles that Mr. Burke venerates; and under this abominable depravity, he is disqualified to judge between them. Thus much for his opinion as to the occasion of the French revolution. I now proceed to other considerations.

I know a place in America called Point-no-Point; because as you proceed along the shore, gay and flowery as Mr. Burke's language, it continually recedes and presents itself at a distance a-head; and when you have got as far as you can go, there is no point at all. Just thus is it with Mr. Burke's three hundred and fifty-six pages. It is therefore difficult to reply to him. But as the points that he wishes to establish may be inferred from what he abuses, it is in his paradoxes that we must look for his arguments.

As to the tragic paintings by which Mr. Burke has outraged his own imagination, and seeks to work upon that of his readers, they are very well calculated for theatrical representation, where facts are manufactured for the sake of show, and accommodated to produce, through the weakness of sympathy, a weeping effect. But Mr. Burke should recollect that he is writing history, and not *plays ;* and that his readers will expect truth, and not the spouting rant of high-toned exclamation.

When we see a man dramatically lamenting in a publication intended to be believed, that " *The age of chivalry is gone ;*" that " *the glory of Europe is extinguished forever !*" that " *the unbought grace of life* (if any one knows what it is,) *the cheap defence of nations, the nurse of manly sentiment and heroic enterprise is gone !*" And all this because the Quixote age of chivalric nonsense is gone, what opinion can we form of his judgment, or what regard can we pay to his facts? In the rhapsody of his imagination, he has discovered a world of windmills, and his sorrows are, that there are no Quixotes to attack them. But if the age of aristocracy, like that of chivalry, should fall, and they had originally some connexion, Mr. Burke, the trumpeter of the order, may continue his parody to the end, and finish with exclaiming—" *Othello's occupation's gone !*"

Notwithstanding Mr. Burke's horrid paintings, when the French revolution is compared with that of other countries, the astonishment will be, that it is marked with so few sacrifices; but this astonishment will cease when we reflect that it was *principles*, and not *persons*, that were the meditated objects of destruction. The mind of the nation was acted upon by a higher stimulus than what the consideration of persons could inspire, and sought a higher conquest than could be produced by the downfal of an enemy.—Among the few who fell, there do not appear to be any that were intentionally singled out. They all of them had their fate in the circumstances of the moment, and were not pursued with that long, cold-blooded, unabated revenge which pursued the unfortunate Scotch in the affair of 1745.

Through the whole of Mr. Burke's book I do not observe that the Bastile is mentioned more than once, and that with a kind of implication as if he was sorry it is pulled down, and wished it was built up again. "We have rebuilt Newgate (says he) and tenanted the mansion; and we have prisons almost as strong as the Bastile for those who dare to libel the queen of France."* As to what a madman, like the person called lord George Gordon, might say, and to whom Newgate is rather a bedlam than a prison, it is unworthy a rational consideration. It was a madman that libelled—and that is sufficient apology and it afforded an opportunity for confining him, which was the thing that was wished for: but certain it is that Mr. Burke, who does not call himself a madman, whatever other people may do, has libelled, in the most unprovoked manner,

---

* Since writing the above, two other places occur in Mr. Burke's pamphlet, in which the name of Bastile is mentioned but in the same manner.—In the one, he introduces it in a sort of obscure question, and asks—" Will any ministers who now serve such a king with but a decent appearance of respect, cordially obey the orders of those whom but the other day, in his name, they had committed to the Bastile ?" In the other the taking it is mentioned as implying criminality in the French guards who assisted in demolishing it. "They have not" says he "forgot the taking the king's castles at Paris." This is Mr. Burke, who pretends to write on constitutional freedom.

and in the grossest style of the most vulgar abuse, the whole representative authority of France; and yet Mr. Burke takes his seat in the British house of commons!— From his violence and his grief, his silence on some points and his excess on others, it is difficult not to believe that Mr. Burke is sorry, extremely sorry, that arbitrary power, the power of the pope and the Bastile, are pulled down.

Not one glance of compassion, not one commiserating reflection, that I can find throughout his book, has he bestowed on those that lingered out the most wretched of lives, a life without hope, in the most miserable of prisons. It is painful to behold a man employing his talents to corrupt himself. Nature has been kinder to Mr. Burke than he has to her. He is not affected by the reality of distress touching upon his heart, but by the showy resemblance of it striking his imagination. He pities the plumage, but forgets the dying bird. Accustomed to kiss the aristocratical hand that hath purloined him from himself, he degenerates into a composition of art, and the genuine soul of nature forsakes him. His hero or his heroine must be a tragedy-victim, expiring in show, and not the real prisoner of misery, sliding into death in the silence of a dungeon.

As Mr. Burke has passed over the whole transaction of the Bastile (and his silence is nothing in his favor) and has entertained his readers with reflections on supposed facts, distorted into real falsehoods, I will give, since he has not, some account of the circumstances which preceded that transaction. They will serve to show, that less mischief could scarce have accompanied such an event, when considered with the treacherous and hostile aggravations of the enemies of the revolution.

The mind can hardly picture to itself a more tremendous scene than what the city of Paris exhibited at the time of taking the Bastile, and for two days before and after, nor conceive the possibility of its quieting so soon. At a distance, this transaction has appeared only as an act of heroism, standing on itself: and the close political connexion it had with the revolution is lost in the brilliancy of the achievement. But we are to consider it as the strength of the parties, brought man to man, and contending for the issue. The Bastile was to be either the prize or the prison of the assailants. The downfal of it included the idea of

the downfal of despotism; and this compounded image
was become as figuratively united as Bunyan's Doubting
Castle and giant Despair.

The national assembly, before and at the time of taking
the Bastile, was sitting at Versailles, twelve miles distant
from Paris. About a week before the rising of the Parisians and their taking the Bastile, it was discovered that a
plot was forming, at the head of which was the count
d'Artois, the king's youngest brother, for demolishing the
national assembly, seizing its members, and thereby crush-
ing, by a *coup de main*, all hopes and prospects of forming
a free government. For the sake of humanity, as well as
of freedom, it is well this plan did not succeed. Examples
are not wanting to show how dreadfully vindictive and
cruel are all old governments, when they are successful
against what they call a revolt.

This plan must have been some time in contemplation;
because in order to carry it into execution, it was necessary to collect a large military force round Paris, and to cut
off the communication between that city and the national
assembly at Versailles. The troops destined for this service were chiefly the foreign troops in the pay of France,
and who, for this particular purpose, were drawn from the
distant provinces where they were then stationed. When
they were collected, to the amount of between twenty-five
and thirty thousand, it was judged time to put the plan in
execution. The ministry who were then in office, and who
were friendly to the revolution, were instantly dismissed,
and a new ministry formed of those who had concerted
the project:—among whom was count de Broglio, and to
his share was given the command of those troops. The
character of this man, as described to me in a letter which
I communicated to Mr. Burke before he began to write his
book, and from an authority which Mr. Burke well knows
was good, was that of "an high-flying aristocrat, cool, and
capable of every mischief."

While these matters were agitating, the national assembly stood in the most perilous and critical situation that a
body of men can be supposed to act in. They were the
devoted victims, and they knew it. They had the hearts
and wishes of their country on their side, but military authority they had none. The guards of Broglio surrounded the hall where the assembly sat, ready, at the word of
command, to seize their persons, as had been done the

year before to the parliament in Paris. Had the national assembly deserted their trust, or had they exhibited signs of weakness or fear, their enemies had been encouraged, and the country depressed. When the situation they stood in, the cause they were engaged in, and the crisis then ready to burst which should determine their personal and political fate, and that of their country, and probably of Europe, are taken into one view, none but a heart callous with prejudice, or corrupted by dependance, can avoid interesting itself in their success.

The archbishop of Vienne was at this time president of the national assembly; a person too old to undergo the scene that a few days, or a few hours, might bring forth. A man of more activity, and bolder fortitude, was necessary; and the national assembly chose (under the form of vice-president, for the presidency still rested in the archbishop) M. de la Fayette; and this is the only instance of a vice-president being chosen. It was at the moment this storm was pending, July 11, that a declaration of rights was brought forward by M. de la Fayette, and is the same which is alluded to in page 51. It was hastily drawn up, and makes only a part of a more extensive declaration of rights, agreed upon and adopted afterwards by the national assembly. The particular reason for bringing it forward at this moment (M. de la Fayette has since informed me) was, that if the national assembly should fall in the threatened destruction that then surrounded it, some traces of its principles might have the chance of surviving the wreck.

Every thing now was drawing to a crisis. The event was freedom or slavery. On one side an army of nearly thirty thousand men; on the other an unarmed body of citizens, for the citizens of Paris on whom the national assembly must then immediately depend, were as unarmed and as undisciplined as the citizens of London are now.— The French guards had given strong symptoms of their being attached to the national cause; but their numbers were small, not a tenth part of the force that Broglio commanded, and their officers were in the interest of Broglio.

Matters being now ripe for execution, the new ministry made their appearance in office. The reader will carry in his mind, that the Bastile was taken the 14th of July: the point of time I am now speaking to, is the 12th. As soon as the news of the change of the ministry reached

Paris in the afternoon, all the play-houses and places of entertainment, shops and houses, were shut up. The change of ministry was considered as the prelude of hostilities, and the opinion was rightly founded.

The foreign troops began to advance towards the city. The prince de Lambesc, who commanded a body of German cavalry, approached by the palace of Louis XV. which connects itself with some of the streets. In his march he insulted and struck an old man with his sword. The French are remarkable for their respect to old age, and the insolence with which it appeared to be done, uniting with the general fermentation they were in, produced a powerful effect, and a cry of *to arms! to arms!* spread itself in a moment over the whole city.

Arms they had none, nor scarcely any who knew the use of them; but desperate resolution, when every hope is at stake, supplies, for a while, the want of arms. Near where the prince de Lambesc was drawn up, were large piles of stones collected for building the new bridge, and with these the people attacked the cavalry. A party of the French guards, upon hearing the firing, rushed from their quarters and joined the people; and night coming on the cavalry retreated.

The streets of Paris, being narrow, are favorable for defence; and the loftiness of the houses, consisting of many stories, from which great annoyance might be given, secured them against nocturnal enterprises; and the night was spent in providing themselves with every sort of weapon they could make or procure : guns, swords, blacksmiths' hammers, carpenters' axes, iron crows, pikes, halberds, pitchforks, spits, clubs, &c.

The incredible numbers with which they assembled the next morning, and the still more incredible resolution they exhibited, embarrassed and astonished their enemies.— Little did the new ministry expect such a salute. Accustomed to slavery themselves, they had no idea that liberty was capable of such inspiration, or that a body of unarmed citizens would dare to face the military force of thirty thousand men. Every moment of this day was employed in collecting arms, concerting plans, and arranging themselves in the best order which such an instantaneous movement could afford. Broglio continued lying round the city, but made no further advances this day, and the

succeeding night passed with as much tranquillity as such
a scene could possibly produce.

But the defence only was not the object of the citizens.
They had a cause at stake, on which depended their freedom or their slavery. They every moment expected an
attack, or to hear of one made on the national assembly;
and in such a situation, the most prompt measures are
sometimes the best. The object that now presented itself,
was the Bastile; and the *eclat* of carrying such a fortress
in the face of such an army, could not fail to strike terror
into the new ministry, who had scarcely yet had time to
meet. By some intercepted correspondence this morning,
it was discovered, that the mayor of Paris, M. de Flesseles
who appeared to be in their interest, was betraying them;
and from this discovery, there remained no doubt that
Broglio would reinforce the Bastile the ensuing evening.
It was therefore necessary to attack it that day; but before this could be done, it was first necessary to procure a
better supply of arms than they were then possessed of.

There was, adjoining to the city, a large magazine of
arms deposited at the hospital of the invalids, which the
citizens summoned to surrender; and as the place was not
defensible, nor attempted much defence, they soon succeeded. Thus supplied, they marched to attack the Bastile; a vast mixed multitude of all ages, and of all degrees,
and armed with all sorts of weapons. Imagination would
fail of describing to itself the appearance of such a procession, and of the anxiety for the events which a few hours
or a few minutes might produce. What plans the ministry
was forming, were as unknown to the people within the city
as what the citizens were doing was unknown to them; and
what movements Broglio might make for the support or relief of the place, were to the citizens equally unknown.
All was mystery and hazard.

That the Bastile was attacked with an enthusiasm of
heroism, such only as the highest animation of liberty
could inspire, and carried in the space of a few hours, is
an event which the world is fully possessed of. I am not
undertaking a detail of the attack, but bringing into view,
the conspiracy against the nation which provoked it, and
which fell with the Bastile. The prison to which the new
ministry were dooming the national assembly, in addition
to its being the high altar and castle of despotism, became
the proper object to begin with. This enterprise broke up

the new ministry, who began now to fly from the ruin they had prepared for others. The troops of Broglio dispersed and himself fled also.

Mr. Burke has spoken a great deal about plots, but he has never once spoken of this plot against the national assembly, and the liberties of the nation; and that he might not, he has passed over all the circumstances that might throw it in his way. The exiles who have fled from France, whose cause he so much interests himself in, and from whom he has had his lesson, fled in consequence of the miscarriage of this plot. No plot was formed against them : it was they who were plotting against others; and those who fell, met, not unjustly, the punishment they were preparing to execute. But will Mr. Burke say, that if this plot, contrived with the subtlety of an ambuscade, had succeeded, the successful party would have restrained their wrath so soon? Let the history of all old governments answer the question.

Whom has the national assembly brought to the scaffold? None. They were themselves the devoted victims of this plot, and they have not retaliated; why then are they charged with revenge they have not acted? In the tremendous breaking forth of a whole people, in which all degrees, tempers and characters are confounded, and delivering themselves by a miracle of exertion, from the destruction meditated against them, is it to be expected that nothing will happen? When men are sore with the sense of oppressions, and menaced with the prospect of new ones, is the calmness of philosophy, or the palsy of insensibility to be looked for? Mr. Burke exclaims against outrage; yet the greatest is that which he has committed. His book is a volume of outrage, not apologized for by the impulse of a moment, but cherished through a space of ten months; yet Mr. Burke had no provocation, no life, no interest at stake.

More citizens fell in this struggle than of their opponents: but four or five persons were seized by the populace, and instantly put to death; the governor of the Bastile, and the mayor of Paris, who was detected in the act of betraying them; and afterwards Foulon, one of the new ministry, and Berthier, his son-in-law, who had accepted the office of intendant of Paris. Their heads were stuck upon pikes, and carried about the city; and it is upon this mode of punishment that Mr. Burke builds a great part of his tragic scenes. Let us therefore examine how men came by the idea of punishing in this manner.

They learn it from the governments they live under; and retaliate the punishments they have been accustomed to behold. The heads stuck upon pikes, which remained for years upon Temple-bar, differed nothing in the horror of the scene from those carried about on pikes at Paris : yet this was done by the English government. It may perhaps be said, that it signifies nothing to a man what is done to him after he is dead; but it signifies much to the living : it either tortures their feelings, or hardens their hearts; and in either case, it instructs them how to punish when power falls into their hands.

Lay then the axe to the root and teach governments humanity. It is their sanguinary punishments which corrupt mankind. In England, the punishment in certain cases, is by *hanging, drawing* and *quartering;* the heart of the sufferer is cut out, and held up to the view of the populace. In France under the former government, the punishments were not less barbarous. Who does not remember the execution of Damien, torn to pieces by horses ? The effect of these cruel spectacles exhibited to the populace, is to destroy tenderness, or excite revenge; and by the base and false idea of governing men by terror instead of reason, they become precedents. It is over the lowest class of mankind that government by terror is intended to operate, and it is on them that it operates to the worst effect. They have sense enough to feel that they are the objects aimed at ; and they inflict in their turn the examples of terror they have been instructed to practise.

There are in all European countries, a large class of people of that description which in England are called the " *mob.*" Of this class were those who committed the burnings and devastations in London in 1780, and of this class were those who carried the heads upon pikes in Paris. Foulon and Berthier were taken up in the country, and sent to Paris, to undergo their examination at the hôtel de Ville; for the national assembly immediately on the new ministry coming into office, passed a decree, which they communicated to the king and cabinet, that they (the national assembly) would hold the ministry, of which Foulon was one, responsible for the measures they were advising and pursuing ; but the mob incensed at the appearance of Foulon and Berthier, tore them from their conductors

before they were carried to the hotel de Ville, and executed them on the spot. Why then does Mr. Burke charge
outrages of this kind on a whole people? As well may he
charge the riots and outrages of 1780 on all the people of
London, or those in Ireland on all his country.

But every thing we see or hear offensive to our feelings,
and derogatory to the human character, should lead to
other reflections than those of reproach. Even the beings
who commit them have some claim to our consideration.
How then is it that such vast classes of mankind as are
distinguished by the appellation of the vulgar, or the ignorant mob, are so numerous in all old countries? The instant we ask ourselves this question, reflection finds an answer. They arise, as an unavoidable consequence, out of
the ill construction of all the old governments in Europe,
England included with the rest. It is by distortedly exalting some men, that others are distortedly debased, till
the whole is out of nature. A vast mass of mankind are
degradedly thrown into the back ground of the human
picture, to bring forward, with greater glare, the puppet-
show of state and aristocracy. In the commencement of a
revolution, those men are rather the followers of the *camp*
than of the *standard* of liberty, and have yet to be instructed how to reverence it.

I give to Mr. Burke all his theatrical exaggerations for
facts, and I then ask him, if they do not establish the certainty of what I here lay down? Admitting them to be true,
they show the necessity of the French revolution, as much
as any one thing he could have asserted. These outrages
were not the effect of the principles of the revolution, but
of the degraded mind that existed before the revolution,
and which the revolution is calculated to reform. Place
them then to their proper cause, and take the reproach of
them to your own side.

It is to the honor of the national assembly, and the city
of Paris, that during such a tremendous scene of arms and
confusion, beyond the control of all authority, that they
have been able, by the influence of example and exhortation, to restrain so much. Never was more pains taken
to instruct and enlighten mankind, and to make them see
that their interest consisted in their virtue, and not in their
revenge, than what have been displayed in the revolution
of France.—I now proceed to make some remarks on Mr.

Burke's account of the expedition to Versailles, on the 5th and 6th of October.

I can consider Mr. Burke's book in scarcely any other light than a dramatic performance; and he must, I think, have considered it in the same light himself, by the poetical liberties he has taken of omitting some facts, distorting others, and making the machinery bend to produce a stage effect. Of this kind is his account of the expedition to Versailles. He begins this account by omitting the only facts which as causes are known to be true; every thing beyond these is conjecture even in Paris: and he then works up a tale accommodated to his own passions and prejudices.

It is to be observed throughout Mr. Burke's book, that he never speaks of plots *against* the revolution; and it is from those plots that all the mischiefs have arisen. It suits his purpose to exhibit consequences without their causes. It is one of the arts of the drama to do so. If the crimes of men were exhibited with their suffering, the stage effect would sometimes be lost, and the audience would be inclined to approve where it was intended they should commiserate.

After all the investigations that have been made into this intricate affair (the expedition to Versailles,) it still remains enveloped in all that kind of mystery which ever accompanies events produced more from a concurrence of awkward circumstances, than from fixed design. While the characters of men are forming, as is always the case in revolutions, there is a reciprocal suspicion, and a disposition to misinterpret each other; and even parties directly opposite in principle, will sometimes concur in pushing forward the same movement with very different views, and with the hopes of its producing very different consequences. A great deal of this may be discovered in this embarrassed affair, and yet the issue of the whole was what nobody had in view.

The only things certainly known are, that considerable uneasiness was at this time excited in Paris, by the delay of the king in not sanctioning and forwarding the decrees of the national assembly, particularly that of the *declaration of the rights of man*, and the decrees of the *fourth of August*, which contained the foundation principles on which the constitution was to be erected. The kindest, and perhaps the fairest, conjecture upon this matter is, that some of the

ministers intended to make observations upon certain parts
of them, before they were finally sanctioned and sent to
the provinces; but be this as it may, the enemies of the revolution derived hopes from the delay, and the friends of
the revolution, uneasiness.

During this state of suspense, the *gardes du corps*, which
was composed, as such regiments generally are, of persons
much connected with the court, gave an entertainment at
Versailles (Oct. 1,) to some foreign regiments then arrived; and when the entertainment was at its height, on a
signal given, the *gardes du corps* tore the national cockade
from their hats, trampled it under foot, and replaced it with
a counter cockade prepared for the purpose. An indigni-
ty of this kind amounted to defiance. It was like declaring
war; and if men will give challenges, they must expect
consequences. But all this Mr. Burke has carefully kept
out of sight. He begins his account by saying, " History
will record, that on the morning of the 6th of October, 1789,
the king and queen of France, after a day of confusion,
alarm, dismay and slaughter, lay down under the pledged
security of public faith, to indulge nature in a few hours of
respite, and troubled melancholy repose." This is neither
the sober style of history, nor the intention of it. It leaves
every thing to be guessed at, and mistaken. One would
at least think there had been a battle; and a battle there
probably would have been, had it not been for the moder-
ating prudence of those whom Mr. Burke involves in his
censures. By his keeping the *gardes du corps* out of sight
Mr. Burke has afforded himself the dramatic licence of putting the king and queen in their places, as if the object of
the expedition was against them.—But, to return to my account—

This conduct of the *gardes du corps*, as might well be expected, alarmed and enraged the Parisians: the colors of
the cause, and the cause itself, were become too united to
mistake the intention of the insult and the Parisians were
determined to call the *gardes du corps* to an account. There
was certainly nothing of the cowardice of assassination in
marching in the face of day to demand satisfaction, if such
a phrase may be used, of a body of armed men who had
voluntarily given defiance. But the circumstance which
serves to throw this affair into embarrassment is, that the
enemies of the revolution appear to have encouraged it, as
well as its friends. The one hoped to prevent a civil war,

by checking it in time, and the other to make one. The hopes of those opposed to the revolution, rested in making the king of their party, and getting him from Versailles to Metz, where they expected to collect a force, and set up a standard. We have therefore two different objects presenting themselves at the same time, and to be accomplished by the same means; the one, to chastise the *gardes du corps* which was the object of the Parisians; the other, to render the confusion of such a scene an inducement to the king to set off for Metz.

On the 5th of October, a very numerous body of women, and men in the disguise of women, collected round the hotel de Ville or town hall at Paris, and set off for Versailles. Their professed object was the *gardes du corps;* but prudent men readily recollected that mischief is easier begun than ended; and this impressed itself with the more force, from the suspicions already stated, and the irregularity of such a cavalcade. As soon therefore as a sufficient force could be collected, M. de la Fayette, by orders from the civil authority of Paris, set off after them at the head of twenty thousand of the Paris militia. The revolution could derive no benefit from confusion, and its opposers might. By an amiable and spirited manner of address, he had hitherto been fortunate in calming disquietudes, and in this he was extraordinarily successful; to frustrate, therefore, the hopes of those who might seek to improve this scene into a sort of justifiable necessity for the king's quitting Versailles and withdrawing to Metz, and to prevent at the same time, the consequences that might ensue between the *gardes du corps* and this phalanx of men and women, he forwarded expresses to the king, that he was on his march to Versailles, by the orders of the civil authority of Paris, for the purpose of peace and protection, expressing at the same time the necessity of restraining the *gardes du corps* from firing on the people.*

He arrived at Versailles between ten and eleven o'clock at night. The *gardes du corps* were drawn up, and the people had arrived some time before, but every thing had remained suspended. Wisdom and policy now consisted in changing a scene of danger into a happy event. M. de la Fayette became the mediator between the enraged parties;

* I am warranted in asserting this, as I had it from M. de la Fayette, with whom I have lived in habits of friendship for fourteen years.

and the king, to remove the uneasiness which had arisen from the delay already stated, sent for the president of the national assembly, and signed the *declaration of the rights of man*, and such other parts of the constitution as were in readiness.

It was now about one in the morning. Every thing appeared to be composed, and a general congratulation took place. At the beat of drum a proclamation was made, that the citizens of Versailles would give the hospitality of their houses to their fellow-citizens of Paris. Those who could not be accommodated in this manner, remained in the streets, or took up their quarters in the churches; and at two o'clock the king and queen retired.

In this state matters passed until the break of day, when a fresh disturbance arose from the censurable conduct of some of both parties; for such characters there will be in all such scenes. One of the *gardes du corps* appeared at one of the windows of the palace, and the people who had remained during the night in the streets accosted him with reviling and provocative language. Instead of retiring, as in such a case prudence would have dictated, he presented his musket, fired, and killed one of the Paris militia. The peace being thus broken, the people rushed into the palace in quest of the offender. They attacked the quarters of the *gardes du corps* within the palace, and pursued them through the avenues of it, and to the apartments of the king. On this tumult, not the queen only, as Mr. Burke has represented it, but every person in the palace, was awakened and alarmed; and M. de la Fayette had a second time to interpose between the parties, the event of which was, that the *gardes du corps* put on the national cockade, and the matter ended, as by oblivion, after the loss of two or three lives.

During the latter part of the time in which this confusion was acting, the king and queen were in public at the balcony, and neither of them concealed for safety's sake, as Mr. Burke insinuates. Matters being thus appeased, and tranquillity restored, a general acclamation broke forth, of *le roi a Paris—le roi a Paris*—the king to Paris. It was the shout of peace, and immediately accepted on the part of the king. By this measure, all future projects of trepanning the king to Metz, and setting up the standard of opposition to the constitution, were prevented, and the suspicions extinguished. The king and his family reached

Paris in the evening, and were congratulated on their arrival by M. Bailley, the mayor of Paris, in the name of the citizens. Mr. Burke, who throughout his book confounds things, persons, and principles, has, in his remarks on M. Bailley's address, confounded time also. He censures M. Bailley for calling it, "*un bon jour*," a good day. Mr. Burke should have informed himself, that this scene took up the space of two days, the day on which it began with every appearance of danger and mischief, and the day on which it terminated without the mischiefs that threatened; and that it is to this peaceful termination that M. Bailley alludes, and to the arrival of the king at Paris. Not less than three hundred thousand persons arranged themselves in the procession from Versailles to Paris, and not an act of molestation was committed during the whole march.

Mr. Burke, on the authority of M. Lally Tollendal, a deserter from the national assembly, says, that on entering Paris, the people shouted, "*tous les eviques a la lanterne.*" All bishops to be hanged at the lantern or lamp-posts. It is surprising that nobody should hear this but Lally Tollendal, and that nobody should believe it but Mr. Burke. It has not the least connexion with any part of the transaction, and is totally foreign to every circumstance of it. The bishops have never been introduced before into any scene of Mr. Burke's drama: why then are they, all at once, and together. *tout a coup et tous ensemble*, introduced now? Mr. Burke brings forward his bishops and his lantern, like figures in a magic lantern, and raises his scenes by contrast instead of connexion. But it serves to show, with the rest of his book, what little credit ought to be given, where even probability is set at defiance, for the purpose of defaming; and with this reflection, instead of a soliloquy in praise of chivalry, as Mr. Burke has done, I close the account of the expedition to Versailles.*

I have now to follow Mr. Burke through a pathless wilderness of rhapsodies, and a sort of descant upon governments, in which he asserts whatever he pleases, on the presumption of its being believed, without offering either evidence or reasons for so doing.

* An account of the expedition to Versailles may be seen in No. 13, of the 'Revolution de Paris,' containing the events from the 5d to the 10th of October, 1789.

Before any thing can be reasoned upon to a conclusion, certain facts, principles, or data, to reason from, must be established, admitted, or denied. Mr. Burke, with his usual outrage, abuses the *declaration of the rights of man*, published by the national assembly of France, as the basis on which the constitution of France is built. This he calls " paltry and blurred sheets of paper about the rights of man." Does Mr. Burke mean to deny that *man* has any rights? If he does, then he must mean that there are no such things as rights any where, and that he has none himself; for who is there in the world but man? But if Mr. Burke means to admit that man has rights, the question then will be, what are those rights, and how came man by them originally?

The error of those who reason by precedents drawn from antiquity, respecting the rights of man, is, that they do not go far enough into antiquity. They do not go the whole way. They stop in some of the intermediate stages of an hundred or a thousand years, and produce what was then done as a rule for the present day. This is no authority at all. If we travel still further into antiquity, we shall find a directly contrary opinion and practice prevailing; and if antiquity is to be authority, a thousand such authorities may be produced, successively contradicting each other: but if we proceed on, we shall at last come out right: we shall come to the time when man came from the hand of his maker. What was he then? Man. Man was his high and only title, and a higher cannot be given him. But of titles I shall speak hereafter.

We have now arrived at the origin of man, and at the origin of his rights. As to the manner in which the world has been governed from that day to this, it is no further any concern of ours than to make a proper use of the errors or the improvements which the history of it presents. Those who lived an hundred or a thousand years ago, were then moderns as we are now. They had *their* ancients and those ancients had others, and we also shall be ancients in our turn. If the mere name of antiquity is to govern in the affairs of life, the people who are to live an hundred or a thousand years hence, may as well take us for a precedent, as we make a precedent of those who lived an hundred or a thousand years ago. The fact is, that portions of antiquity, by proving every thing, establish nothing. It is authority against authority all the way, till we come to the divine origin of the rights of man, at the creation. Here our inquiries find a resting-place, and our reason finds a home. If a dispute about the rights of man had arisen at the distance of an hundred years from the creation, it is to this source of authority they must have referred, and it is to the same source of authority that we must now refer.

Though I mean not to touch upon any sectarian principle of religion, yet it may be worth observing, that the genealogy of Christ is traced to Adam. Why then not trace the rights of man to the creation of man? I will answer the question. Because there have been an upstart of governments, thrusting themselves between, and presumptuously working to *un-make* man.

If any generation of men ever possessed the right of dictating the mode by which the world should be governed for ever, it was the first generation that existed; and if that generation did not do it, no succeeding generation can show any authority for doing it, nor set any up. The illuminating and divine principles of the equal rights of man (for it has its origin from the maker of man,) relates, not only to the living individuals, but to generations of men succeeding each other. Every generation is equal in rights to the generations which preceded it, by the same rule that every individual is born equal in rights with his contemporary.

Every history of the creation, and every traditionary account, whether from the lettered or unlettered world, however they may vary in their opinion or belief of certain particulars, all agree in establishing one point, *the unity of man*; by which I mean that man is all of *one degree*, and consequently that all men are born equal, and with equal natural rights, in the same manner as if posterity had been continued by *creation* instead of *generation*, the latter being only the mode by which the former is carried forward; and consequently, every child born into the world must be considered as deriving its existence from God. The world is as new to him as it was to the first man that existed, and his natural right in it is of the same kind.

The Mosaic account of the creation, whether taken as divine authority, or merely historical, is fully up to this point, *the unity or equality of man*. The expressions admit, of no controversy. " And God said, let us make man in our own image. In the image of God created he him;

male and female created he them." The distinction of sexes is pointed out, but no other distinction is even implied. If this be not divine authority, it is at least historical authority, and shows that the equality of man, so far from being a modern doctrine, is the oldest upon record.

It is also to be observed, that all the religions known in the world are founded, so far as they relate to man, on the *unity of man*, as being all of one degree. Whether in heaven or in hell, or in whatever state man may be supposed to exist hereafter, the good and the bad are the only distinctions. Nay, even the laws of governments are obliged to slide into this principle, by making degrees to consist in crimes, and not in persons.

It is one of the greatest of all truths, and of the highest advantage to cultivate. By considering man in this light, and by instructing him to consider himself in this light, it places him in a close connexion with all his duties, whether to his creator, or to the creation, of which he is a part; and it is only when he forgets his origin, or, to use a more fashionable phrase, his *birth and family*, that he becomes dissolute. It is not among the least of the evils of the present existing governments in all parts of Europe, that man, considered as man, is thrown back to a vast distance from his maker, and the artificial chasm filled up by a succession of barriers, or a sort of turnpike gates, through which he has to pass. I will quote Mr. Burke's catalogue of barriers that he has set up between man and his maker. Putting himself in the character of a herald, he says—"We fear God—we look with *awe* to kings—with affection to parliaments—with duty to magistrates—with reverence to priests, and with respect to nobility." Mr. Burke has forgot to put in "chivalry." He has also forgot to put in Peter.

The duty of man is not a wilderness of turnpike gates, through which he is to pass by tickets from one to the other. It is plain and simple, and consists but of two points. His duty to God, which every man must feel; and with respect to his neighbor, to do as he would be done by. If those to whom power is delegated do well, they will be respected; if not they will be despised; and with regard to those to whom no power is delegated, but who assume it, the rational world can know nothing of them.

Hitherto we have spoken only (and that but in part) of the natural rights of man. We have now to consider the

civil rights of man, and to show how the one originates out
of the other. Man did not enter into society to become
worse than he was before, nor to have less rights than he
had before, but to have those rights better secured. His
natural rights are the foundation of all his civil rights. But
in order to pursue this distinction with more precision, it is
necessary to mark the different qualities of natural and
civil rights.

A few words will explain this. Natural rights are those
which always appertain to man in right of his existence.
Of this kind are all the intellectual rights, or rights of the
mind, and also all those rights of acting as an individual
for his own comfort and happiness, which are not injurious
to the rights of others.—Civil rights are those which appertain to man in right of his being a member of society.
Every civil right has for its foundation some natural right
pre-existing in the individual, but to which his individual
power is not, in all cases, sufficiently competent. Of this
kind are all those which relate to security and protection.

From this short review, it will be easy to distinguish between that class of natural rights which man retains after
entering into society, and those which he throws into common stock as a member of society.

The natural rights which he retains, are all those in
which the power to execute is as perfect in the individual
as the right itself. Among this class, as is before mentioned, are all the intellectual rights, or rights of the mind :
consequently, religion is one of those rights. The natural
rights which are not retained, are all those in which, though
the right is perfect in the individual, the power to execute
them is defective. They answer not his purpose. A man,
by natural right, has a right to judge in his own cause ;
and so far as the right of the mind is concerned, he never
surrenders it : but what availeth it him to judge, if he has
not power to redress ? He therefore deposites this right in
the common stock of society, and takes the arm of society,
of which he is a part, in preference and in addition to his
own. Society *grants* him nothing. Every man is a proprietor in society, and draws on the capital as a matter of
right.

From these premises, two or three certain conclusions
will follow.

1st, That every civil right grows out of a natural right :
or, in other words, is a natural right exchanged.

2d, That civil power properly considered as such, is
made up of the aggregate of that class of the natural rights
of man, which becomes defective in the individual in point
of power, and answers not his purpose, but when collected to a focus, becomes competent to the purpose of every
one.

3d. That the power produced by the aggregate of natural
rights, imperfect in power in the individual, cannot be applied to invade the natural rights which are retained in the
individual, and in which the power to execute is as perfect
as the right itself.

We have now, in a few words, traced man from a natural
individual to a member of society, and shown, or endeavored to show, the quality of the natural rights retained, and of
those which are exchanged for civil rights. Let us now
apply those principles to government.

In casting our eyes over the world, it is extremely easy
to distinguish the governments which have arisen out of
society, or out of the social compact, from those which
have not : but to place this in a clearer light than what a
single glance may afford, it will be proper to take a review of the several sources from which governments have
arisen, and on which they have been founded.

They may be all comprehended under three heads—1st,
superstition : 2d, power : 3d. the common interests of society, and the common rights of man.

The first was a government of priest-craft, the second of
conquerors, and the third of reason.

When a set of artful men pretended, through the medium of oracles, to hold intercourse with the deity, as famil-
iarly as they now march up the back stairs in European
courts, the world was completely under the government of
superstition. The oracles were consulted, and whatever
they were made to say, became the law ; and this sort of
government lasted just as long as this sort of superstition
lasted.

After these a race of conquerors arose, whose government, like that of William the conqueror, was founded in
power, and the sword assumed the name of a sceptre.
Governments thus established, last as long as the power to
support them lasts ; but that they might avail themselves
of every engine in their favor, they united fraud to force,
and set up an idol which they called *divine right*, and which
in imitation of the pope, who affects to be spiritual and

temporal; and in contradiction to the founder of the Christian religion, twisted itself afterwards into an idol of another shape, called *church and state*. The key of St. Peter, and the key of the treasury, became quartered on one another, and the wondering, cheated multitude, worshipped the invention.

When I contemplate the natural dignity of man; when I feel (for nature has not been kind enough to me to blunt my feelings) for the honor and happiness of its character, I become irritated at the attempt to govern mankind by force and fraud, as if they were all knaves and fools, and can scarcely avoid feeling disgust for those who are thus imposed upon.

We have now to review the governments which arise out of society, in contradistinction to those which arose out of superstition and conquest.

It has been thought a considerable advance towards establishing the principles of freedom, to say, that government is a compact between those who govern and those who are governed: but this cannot be true, because it is putting the effect before the cause; for as man must have existed before governments existed, there necessarily was a time when governments did not exist, and consequently there could originally exist no governors to form such a compact with. The fact therefore must be, that the *individuals themselves*, each in his own personal and sovereign right, *entered into a compact with each other* to produce a government: and this is the only mode in which governments have a right to be established; and the only principle on which they have a right to exist.

To possess ourselves of a clear idea of what government is or ought to be, we must trace it to its origin. In doing this, we shall easily discover that governments must have arisen, either *out* of the people, or *over* the people. Mr. Burke has made no distinction. He investigates nothing to its source, and therefore he confounds every thing: but he has signified his intention of undertaking at some future opportunity, a comparison between the constitutions of England and France. As he thus renders it a subject of controversy by throwing the gauntlet, I take him up on his own ground. It is in high challenges that high truths have the right of appearing; and I accept it with the more readiness, because it affords me, at the same time, an opportunity of pursuing the subject with respect to governments arising out of society.

But it will be first necessary to define what is meant by a *constitution*. It is not sufficient that we adopt the word; we must fix also a standard signification to it.

A constitution is not a thing in name only, but in fact. It has not an ideal, but a real existence; and wherever it cannot be produced in a visible form there is none. A constitution is a thing antecedent to a government, and a government is only the creature of a constitution. The constitution of a country is not the act of its government, but of the people constituting a government. It is the body of elements, to which you can refer, and quote article by article; and contains the principles on which the government shall be established, the form in which it shall be organized, the powers it shall have, the mode of elections, the duration of parliaments, or by what other name such bodies may be called; the powers which the executive part of the government shall have; and, in fine, every thing that relates to the complete organization of a civil government, and the principle on which it shall act, and by which it shall be bound. A constitution, therefore is to a government, what the laws made afterwards by that government are to a court of judicature. The court of judicature does not make laws, neither can it alter them; it only acts in conformity to the laws made; and the government is in like manner governed by the constitution.

Can then Mr. Burke produce the English constitution? If he cannot we may fairly conclude, that though it has been so much talked about, no such thing as a constitution exists, or ever did exist, and consequently the people have yet a constitution to form.

Mr. Burke will not, I presume, deny the position I have already advanced; namely, that governments arise either *out* of the people, or *over* the people. The English government is one of those which arose out of a conquest, and not out of society, and consequently it arose over the people; and though it has been much modified from the opportunity of circumstances, since the time of William the conqueror, the country has never yet regenerated itself, and it is therefore without a constitution.

I readily perceive the reason why Mr. Burke declined going into the comparison between the English and French constitutions, because he could not but perceive, when he sat down to the task, that no constitution was in existence on his side of the question. His book is certainly bulky enough to have contained all he could say on this subject, and it would have been the best manner in which people could have judged of their separate merits. Why then has he declined the only thing that was worth while to write upon? It was the strongest ground he could take, if the advantages were on his side; but the weakest if they were not; and his declining to take it, is either a sign that he could not possess it, or could not maintain it.

Mr. Burke has said, in a speech last winter in parliament, that when the national assembly of France first met in three orders, (the *tiers etats*, the clergy, and the *noblesse*) that France had then a good constitution. This shows, among numerous other instances, that Mr. Burke does not understand what a constitution is. The persons so met, were not a *constitution*, but a *convention* to make a constitution.

The present national assembly of France is, strictly speaking, the personal social compact. The members of it are the delegates of the nation in its *original* character; future assemblies will be the delegates of the nation in its *organized* character. The authority of the present assembly is different to what the authority of future assemblies will be. The authority of the present one is to form a constitution: the authority of future assemblies will be to legislate according to the principles and forms prescribed in that constitution; and if experience should hereafter show that alterations, amendments, or additions are necessary, the constitution will point out the mode by which such things shall be done, and not leave it to the discretionary power of the future government.

A government on the principles on which constitutional governments, arising out of society, are established, cannot have the right of altering itself. If it had, it would be arbitrary. It might make itself what it pleased; and wherever such a right is set up, it shows that there is no constitution. The act by which the English parliament empowered itself to sit for seven years, shows there is no constitution in England. It might, by the same self-authority, have sat any greater number of years or for life. The bill which the present Mr. Pitt brought into parliament some years ago, to reform parliament, was on the same erroneous principle. The right of reform is in the

nation in its original character, and the constitutional method would be by a general convention elected for the purpose. There is moreover a paradox in the idea of vitiat-
ed bodies reforming themselves.

From these preliminaries I proceed to draw some comparisons. I have already spoken of the declaration of
rights; and as I mean to be as concise as possible, I shall
proceed to other parts of the French constitution.

The constitution of France says, that every man who
pays a tax of sixty sous per annum (2s. and 6d. English)
is an elector. What article will Mr. Burke place against
this? Can any thing be more limited, and at the same
time more capricious, than what the qualifications of electors are in England? Limited—because not one man in
an hundred (I speak much within compass) is admitted to
vote: capricious—because the lowest character that can
be supposed to exist, and who has not so much as the visible means of an honest livelihood, is an elector in some
places; while, in other places, the man who pays very
large taxes, and with a fair, known character, and the
farmer who rents to the amount of three or four hundred
pounds a year, and with a property on that farm to three
or four times that amount, is not admitted to be an elector.
Every thing is out of nature, as Mr. Burke says on another occasion, in this strange chaos, and all sorts of follies
are blended with all sorts of crimes. William the conqueror and his descendants parcelled out the country in
this manner, and bribed one part of it by what they called charters, to hold the other parts of it the better subjected to their will. This is the reason why so many charters
abound in Cornwall. The people were averse to the government established at the conquest, and the towns were
garrisoned and bribed to enslave the country. All the old
charters are the badges of this conquest, and it is from this
source that the capriciousness of election arises.

The French constitution says, that the number of representatives for any place shall be in a ratio to the number of taxable inhabitants or electors. What article will
Mr. Burke place against this? The county of Yorkshire,
which contains near a million of souls, sends two county
members; and so does the county of Rutland, which contains not an hundredth part of that number. The town of
old Sarum, which contains not three houses, sends two
members; and the town of Manchester, which contains

upwards of sixty thousand souls, is not admitted to send any. Is there any principle in these things? Is there any thing by which you can trace the marks of freedom, or discover those of wisdom? No wonder then Mr. Burke has declined the comparison, and endeavored to lead his readers from the point by a wild, unsystematical display of paradoxical rhapsodies.

The French constitution says, that the national assembly shall be elected every two years. What article will Mr. Burke place against this? Why, that the nation has no right at all in the case: that the government is perfectly arbitrary with respect to this point; and he can quote for his authority, the precedent of a former parliament.

The French constitution says, there shall be no game laws; that the farmer on whose lands wild game shall be found (for it is by the produce of those lands they are fed) shall have a right to what he can take. That there shall be no monopolies of any kind, that all trades shall be free, and every man free to follow any occupation by which he can procure an honest livelihood, and in any place, town or city throughout the nation. What will Mr. Burke say to this? In England, game is made the property of those at whose expense it is not fed; and with respect to monopolies, the country is cut up into monopolies. Every chartered town is an aristocratic monopoly in itself, and the qualification of electors proceeds out of those chartered monopolies, Is this freedom? Is this what Mr. Burke means by a constitution?

In these chartered monopolies a man coming from another part of the country, is hunted from them as if he were a foreign enemy. An Englishman is not free in his own country: every one of those places presents a barrier in his way, and tells him he is not a freeman—that he has no rights. Within these monopolies, are other monopolies. In a city, such for instance as Bath, which contains between twenty and thirty thousand inhabitants, the right of electing representatives to parliament is monopolized into about thirty-one persons. And within these monopolies are still others. A man even of the same town, whose parents were not in circumstances to give him an occupation is debarred, in many cases, from the natural right of acquiring one, be his genius or industry what it may.

Are these things examples to hold out to a country regenerating itself from slavery, like France? Certainly they

are not; and certain am I, that when the people of England come to reflect upon them, they will, like France, an-
nihilate those badges of ancient oppression, those traces of
a conquered nation. Had Mr. Burke possessed talents
similar to the author "On the Wealth of Nations," he
would have comprehended all the parts which enter into,
and, by assemblage, form a constitution. He would have
reasoned from minutiæ to magnitude. It is not from his
prejudices only, but from the disorderly cast of his genius,
that he is unfitted for the subject he writes upon. Even
his genius is without a constitution. It is a genius at ran-
dom, and not a genius constituted. But he must say something—He has therefore mounted in the air like a balloon,
to draw the eyes of the multitude from the ground they
stand upon.

Much is to be learned from the French constitution.
Conquest and tyranny transplanted themselves with William the conqueror, from Normandy into England, and the
country is yet disfigured with the marks. May then the
example of all France contribute to regenerate the freedom
which a province of it destroyed!

The French constitution says, that to preserve the national representation from being corrupt, no member of
the national assembly shall be an officer of government,
a placeman or a pensioner. What will Mr. Burke place
against this? I will whisper his answer: *loaves* and *fishes*.
Ah! this government of loaves and fishes has more mischief in it than people have yet reflected on. The national
assembly has made the discovery, and it holds out the example to the world. Had governments agreed to quarrel
on purpose to fleece their countries by taxes, they could
not have succeeded better than they have done.

Every thing in the English government appears to me
the reverse of what it ought to be, and of what it is said to
be. The parliament, imperfectly and capriciously elected
as it is, is nevertheless *supposed* to hold the national purse
in *trust* for the nation: but in the manner in which an English parliament is constructed, it is like a man being both
mortgager and mortgagee: and in the case of misapplica-
tion of trust, it is the criminal sitting in judgment on himself. If those persons who vote the supplies are the same
persons who receive the supplies when voted, and are to
account for the expenditure of those supplies to those who
voted them, it is *themselves accountable to themselves*, and the

Comedy of Errors concludes with the pantomime of *Hush.* Neither the ministerial party, nor the opposition will touch upon this case. The national purse is the common hack which each mounts upon. It is like what the country people call, " Ride and tie—You ride a little way and then I." They order these things better in France.

The French constitution says, that the right of war and peace is in the nation. Where else should it reside, but in those who are to pay the expense?

In England, this right is said to reside in a *metaphor,* shown at the tower for sixpence or a shilling a-piece; so are the lions; and it would be a step nearer to reason to say it resided in them, for any inanimate metaphor is no more than a hat or a cap. We can all see the absurdity of worshipping Aaron's molten calf, or Nebuchadnezzar's golden image; but why do men continue to practise in themselves, the absurdities they despise in others?

It may with reason be said, that in the manner the English nation is represented it matters not where this right resides, whether in the crown or in the parliament. War is the common harvest of all those who participate in the division and expenditure of public money, in all countries. It is the art of *conquering at home :* the object of it is an increase of revenue; and as revenue cannot be increased without taxes, a pretence must be made for expenditures. In reviewing the history of the English government, its wars, and taxes, an observer, not blinded by prejudice, nor warped by interest would declare, that taxes were not raised to carry on wars, but that wars were raised to carry on taxes.

Mr. Burke, as a member of the house of commons, is a part of the English government; and though he professes himself an enemy to war, he abuses the French constitution, which seeks to explode it. He holds up the English government as a model in all its parts, to France ; but he should first know the remarks which the French make upon it. They contend, in favor of their own, that the portion of liberty enjoyed in England, is just enough to enslave a country by, more productively than by despotism; and that as the real object of a despotism is revenue, a government so formed obtains more than it could either by direct despotism, or in a full state of freedom, and is, therefore, on the ground of interest, opposed to both. They account also for the readiness which always appears in such governments for engaging in wars, by remarking on the different motives which produce them.   In despotic governments, wars are the effects of pride; but in those governments in which they become the means of taxation, they acquire thereby a more permanent promptitude.

The French constitution, therefore, to provide against both those evils, has taken away from kings and ministers the power of declaring war, and placed the right where the expense must fall.

When the question on the right of war and peace was agitating in the national assembly, the people of England appeared to be much interested in the event, and highly to applaud the decision.   As a principle, it applies as much to one country as to another.   William the conqueror, *as a conqueror*, held this power of war and peace in himself, and his descendants have ever since claimed it as a right.

Although Mr. Burke has asserted the right of the parliament at the revolution to bind and control the nation and posterity *for ever*, he denies, at the same time, that the parliament or the nation had any right to alter, what he calls, the succession of the crown, in any thing but in part, or by a sort of modification.   By his taking this ground, he throws the case back to the *Norman conquest;* and by thus running a line of succession, springing from William the conqueror to the present day, he makes it necessary to inquire who and what William the conqueror was, and where he came from: and into the origin, history and nature of what are called prerogatives.   Every thing must have had a beginning, and the fog of time and antiquity should be penetrated to discover it.   Let then Mr. Burke bring forward his William of Normandy, for it is to this origin that his argument goes.   It also unfortunately happens, in running this line of succession, that another line, parallel thereto, presents itself, which is, that if the succession runs in the line of the conquest, the nation runs in the line of being conquered, and it ought to rescue itself from this reproach.

But it will perhaps be said, that though the power of declaring war descends into the heritage of the conquest, it is held in check by the right of the parliament to withhold the supplies.   It will always happen, when a thing is originally wrong, that amendments do not make it right, and it often happens that they do as much mischief one way as good the other: and such is the case here, for if the one rashly declares war as a matter of right, and the other peremptorily withholds the supplies as a matter of right, the remedy becomes as bad or worse than the disease. The one forces the nation to a combat, and the other ties its hands : but the more probable issue is, that the contrast will end in a collusion between the parties, and be made a screen to both.

On this question of war, three things are to be considered : 1st, the right of declaring it : 2d, the expense of supporting it : 3d, the mode of conducting it after it is declared. The French constitution places the *right* where the *expense* must fall, and this union can be only in the nation. The mode of conducting it after it is declared, it consigns to the executive department. Were this the case in all countries, we should hear but little more of wars.

Before I proceed to consider other parts of the French constitution, and by way of relieving the fatigue of argument, I will introduce an anecdote which I had from Dr. Franklin.

While the doctor resided in France, as minister from America, during the war, he had numerous proposals made to him by projectors of every country and of every kind, who wished to go to the land that floweth with milk and honey. America; and among the rest, there was one who offered himself to be king. He introduced his proposal to the doctor by letter, which is now in the hands of M. Beaumarchais, of Paris—stating, first, that as the Americans had dismissed or sent away their king, they would want another. Secondly, that himself was a Norman. Thirdly, that he was of a more ancient family than the dukes of Normandy, and of a more honorable descent, his line having never been bastardized. Fourthly, that there was already a precedent in England, of kings coming out of Normandy : and on these grounds he rested his offer, *enjoining* that the doctor would forward it to America. But as the doctor did not do this, nor yet send him an answer, the projector wrote a second letter ; in which he did not, it is true, threaten to go over and conquer America, but only, with great dignity, proposed, that if his offer was not accepted, that an acknowledgment of about 30,000*l.* might be made to him for his generosity! Now, as all arguments respecting succession must necessarily connect that succession with some beginning, Mr. Burke's arguments on this subject go to show, that there is no English origin of kings, and that they are descendants of the Norman line in right of the conquest. It may therefore be of service to his doctrine to make the story known, and to inform him, that in case of that natural extinction to which all mortality is subject, kings may again be had from Normandy, on more reasonable terms than William the conqueror; and consequently, that the good people of England, at the revolution of 1688, might have done much better, had such a generous Norman as *this* known *their* wants, and they *his*. The chivalric character which Mr. Burke so much admires, is certainly much easier to make a bargain with than a hard-dealing Dutchman. But, to return to the matters of the constitution—

The French constitution says, *there shall be no titles :* and of consequence, all that class of equivocal generation, which in some countries is called "*aristocracy*," and in others "*nobility*," is done away, and the *peer* is exalted into the *man*.

Titles are but nicknames, and every nickname is a title. The thing is perfectly harmless in itself, but it marks a sort of foppery in the human character which degrades it. It renders man diminutive in things which are great, and the counterfeit of woman in things which are little. It talks about its fine *riband* like a girl, and shows its *garter* like a child. A certain writer, of some antiquity, says, "When I was a child, I thought as a child; but when I became a man, I put away childish things."

It is, properly, from the elevated mind of France, that the folly of titles has been abolished. It has outgrown the baby-clothes of *count* and *duke*, and breeched itself in manhood. France has not levelled, it has exalted. It has put down the dwarf to set up the man. The insignificance of a senseless word like *duke, count,* or *earl,* has ceased to please. Even those who possessed them have disowned the gibberish, and, as they outgrew the rickets, have despised the rattle. The genuine mind of man, thirsting for its native home, society, contemns the gewgaws that separate him from it. Titles are like circles drawn by the magician's wand, to contract the sphere of man's felicity. He lives immured within the Bastile of a word, and surveys at a distance the envied life of man.

Is it then any wonder that titles should fall in France? Is it not a greater wonder they should be kept up any where? What are they? What is their worth and "what is their amount?" When we think or speak of a *judge* or a *general*, we associate with it the ideas of office and character; we think of gravity in the one and bravery in the other: but when we use a word merely as a title, no ideas associate with it. Through all the vocabulary of Adam, there is not such an animal as a duke or a count; neither can we connect any certain idea to the words. Whether they mean strength or weakness, wisdom or folly, a child or a man, or a rider or a horse, is all equivocal. What respect then can be paid to that which describes nothing, and which means nothing? Imagination has given figure and character to centaurs, satyrs, and down to all the fairy tribe; but titles baffle even the powers of fancy, and are a chimerical nondescript.

But this is not all—If a whole country is disposed to hold them in contempt, all their value is gone, and none will own them. It is common opinion only that makes them any thing or nothing, or worse than nothing. There is no occasion to take titles away, for they take themselves away when society concurs to ridicule them. This species of imaginary consequence has visibly declined in every part of Europe, and it hastens to its exit as the world of reason continues to rise. There was a time when the lowest class, of what are called nobility, was more thought of than the highest is now, and when a man in armor riding through Christendom in search of adventures was more stared at than a modern duke. The world has seen this folly fall, and it has fallen by being laughed at, and the farce of titles will follow its fate. The patriots of France have discovered in good time, that rank and dignity in society must take a new ground. The old one has fallen through. It must now take the substantial ground of character, instead of the chimerical ground of titles; and they have brought their titles to the altar, and made of them a burnt-offering to reason.

If no mischief had annexed itself to the folly of titles, they would not have been worth a serious and formal destruction, such as the national assembly have decreed them; and this makes it necessary to inquire further into the nature and character of aristocracy.

That, then, which is called aristocracy in some countries, and nobility in others, arose out of the governments founded upon conquest. It was originally a military order for the purpose of supporting military government; (for such

were all governments founded in conquests) and to keep
up a succession of this order for the purpose for which it
was established, all the younger branches of those families
were disinherited, and the law of *primogenitureship* set up.

The nature and character of aristocracy shows itself to
us in this law. It is a law against every law of nature,
and nature herself calls for its destruction. Establish family justice and aristocracy falls. By the aristocratical
law of primogenitureship, in a family of six children, five
are exposed.—Aristocracy has never but *one* child. The
rest are begotten to be devoured. They are thrown to the
cannibal for prey, and the natural parent prepares the unnatural repast.

As every thing which is out of nature in man, affects
more or less, the interest of society, so does this. All the
children which the aristocracy disowns (which are all, except the eldest) are, in general, cast like orphans on a parish, to be provided for by the public, but at a greater
charge. Unnecessary offices and places in governments and
courts are created at the expense of the public to maintain
them.

With what kind of parental reflections can the father or
mother contemplate their younger offspring. By nature
they are children, and by marriage they are heirs; but by
aristocracy they are bastards and orphans. They are the
flesh and blood of their parents in one line, and nothing
akin to them in the other. To restore, therefore, parents
to their children, and children to their parents—relations
to each other, and man to society—and to exterminate the
monster aristocracy, root and branch—the French constitution has destroyed the law of *primogenitureship*. Here,
then lies the monster, and Mr. Burke, if he pleases, may
write its epitaph.

Hitherto we have considered aristocracy chiefly in one
point of view. We have now to consider it in another.
But whether we view it before or behind, or side ways,
or any way else, domestically or publicly, it is still a monster.

In France, aristocracy had one feature less in its countenance than what it has in some other countries. It did
not compose a body of hereditary legislators. It was not
"*a corporation of aristocracy*," for such I have heard M. de
la Fayette describe an English house of peers. Let us

then examine the grounds upon which the French constitution has resolved against having such an house in France.

Because, in the first place, as is already mentioned, aristocracy is kept up by family tyranny and injustice.

2d, Because there is an unnatural unfitness in an aristocracy to be legislators for a nation. Their ideas of *distributive justice* are corrupted at the very source. They begin life trampling on all their younger brothers and sisters, and relations of every kind, and are taught and educated so to do. With what ideas of justice or honor can that man enter an house of legislation, who absorbs in his own person the inheritance of a whole family of children, or metes out some pitiful portion with the insolence of a gift?

3d, Because the idea of hereditary legislators is as inconsistent as that of hereditary judges, or hereditary juries ; and as absurd as an hereditary mathematician, or an hereditary wise man ; and as ridiculous as an hereditary poet-laureat.

4th, Because a body of men, holding themselves accountable to nobody, ought not to be trusted by any body.

5th, Because it is continuing the uncivilized principle of governments founded in conquest, and the base idea of man having property in man, and governing him by personal right.

6th, Because aristocracy has a tendency to degenerate the human species. By the universal economy of nature it is known, and by the instance of the Jews is proved, that the human species has a tendency to degenerate, in any small number of persons, when separated from the general stock of society, and intermarrying constantly with each other. It defeats even its pretended end, and becomes in time the opposite of what is noble in man. Mr. Burke talks of nobility ; let him show what it is. The greatest characters the world has known, have rose on the democratic floor. Aristocracy has not been able to keep a proportionate pace with democracy. The artificial *noble* shrinks into a dwarf before the *noble* of nature ; and in the few instances (for there are some in all countries) in whom nature, as by a miracle, has survived in aristocracy, *those men despise it.* But it is time to proceed to a new subject.

The French constitution has reformed the condition of the clergy. It has raised the income of the lower and middle classes, and taken from the higher. None are now less than twelve hundred livres (fifty pounds sterling) nor any higher than two or three thousand pounds. What will Mr. Burke place against this? Hear what he says.

He says, that "the people of England can see, without pain or grudging, an archbishop precede a duke; they can see a bishop of Durham, or a bishop of Winchester, in possession of 10,000*l*. a-year; and cannot see why it is in worse hands than estates to the like amount in the hands of this earl or that 'squire." And Mr. Burke offers this as an example to France.

As to the first part, whether the archbishop precedes the duke, or the duke the bishop, it is, I believe, to the people in general, somewhat like *Sternhold* and *Hopkins*, or *Hopkins* and *Sternhold ;* you may put which you please first : and as I confess that I do not understand the merits of this case I will not contend it with Mr. Burke.

But with respect to the latter, I have something to say. Mr. Burke has not put the case right. The comparison is out of order by being put between the bishop and the earl or the 'squire. It ought to be put between the bishop and the curate, and then it will stand thus : *the people of England can see, without grudging or pain, a bishop of Durham, or a bishop of Winchester, in possession of ten thousand pounds a-year, and a curate on thirty or forty pounds a-year, or less.* No, sir, they certainly do not see these things without great pain and grudging. It is a case that applies itself to every man's sense of justice, and is one among many that calls aloud for a constitution.

In France, the cry of "*the church! the church!*" was repeated as often as in Mr. Burke's book, and as loudly as when the dissenters' bill was before parliament ; but the generality of the French clergy were not to be deceived by this cry any longer. They knew, that whatever the pretence might be, it was themselves who were one of the principal objects of it. It was the cry of the high beneficed clergy, to prevent any regulation of income taking place between those of ten thousand pounds a-year and the parish priest. They, therefore, joined their case to those of every other oppressed class of men, and by this union obtained redress.

The French constitution has abolished tithes, that source of perpetual discontent between the tithe-holder and the parishioner. When land is held on tithe, it is in the condition of an estate held between two parties; one receiving one tenth, and the other nine-tenths of the produce: and, consequently, on principles of equity, if the estate can be improved, and made to produce by that improvement double or treble what it did before, or in any other ratio, the expense of such improvement ought to be borne in like proportion between the parties who are to share the produce. But this is not the case in tithes; the farmer bears the whole expense, and the tithe-holder takes a tenth of the improvement, in addition to the original tenth, and by this means gets the value of two tenths instead of one. This is another case that calls for a constitution.

The French constitution hath abolished or renounced *toleration*, and *intoleration* also, and hath established *universal right of conscience*.

Toleration is not the *opposite* of intoleration, but is the *counterfeit* of it. Both are despotisms. The one assumes to itself the right of withholding liberty of conscience, and the other of granting it. The one is the pope, armed with fire and faggot, and the other is the pope selling or granting indulgences. The former is church and state, and the latter is church and traffic.

But toleration may be viewed in a much stronger light. Man worships not himself, but his maker; and the liberty of conscience which he claims, is not for the service of himself, but of his God. In this case, therefore, we must necessarily have the associated idea of two beings; the *mortal* who renders the worship, and the *immortal being* who is worshipped. Toleration, therefore, places itself, not between man and man, nor between church and church, nor between one denomination of religion and another, but between God and man; between the being who worships, and the *being* who is worshipped; and by the same act of assumed authority by which it tolerates man to pay his worship, it presumptuously and blasphemously sets up itself to tolerate the almighty to receive it.

Were a bill brought into parliament, entitled, "An *act* to tolerate or grant liberty to the almighty to receive the worship of a Jew or a Turk," or "to prohibit the almighty from receiving it," all men would startle, and call it blasphemy. There would be an uproar. The presumption of toleration in religious matters would then present itself unmasked: but the presumption is not the less because the name of "man" only appears to those laws, for the associated idea of the *worshipper* and the *worshipped* cannot be separated. Who, then, art thou, vain dust and ashes! by whatever name thou art called, whether a king, a bishop, a church or a state, a parliament or any thing else, that obtrudest thine insignificance between the soul of man and his maker? Mind thine own concerns. If he believes not as thou believest, it is a proof that thou believest not as he believeth, and there is no earthly power can determine between you.

With respect to what are called denominations of religion, if every one is left to judge of his own religion, there is no such thing as a religion that is wrong; but if they are to judge of each other's religion, there is no such thing as a religion that is right; and therefore, all the world is right, or all the world is wrong. But with respect to religion itself, without regard to names, and as directing itself from the universal family of mankind to the divine object of all adoration, *it is man bringing to his maker the fruits of his heart;* and though these fruits may differ from each other, like the fruits of the earth, the grateful tribute of every one is accepted.

A bishop of Durham, or a bishop of Winchester, or the archbishop who heads the dukes, will not refuse a tithe-sheaf of wheat, because it is not a cock of hay; nor a cock of hay, because it is not a sheaf of wheat; nor a pig, because it is neither the one nor the other: but these same persons, under the figure of an established church, will not permit their maker to receive the varied tithes of man's devotion.

One of the continual choruses of Mr. Burke's book is, "church and state;" he does not mean some one particular church, or some one particular state, but any church and state; and he uses the term as a general figure to hold forth the political doctrine of always uniting the church with the state in every country, and he censures the national assembly for not having done this in France. Let us bestow a few thoughts on this subject.

All religions are in their nature mild and benign, and united with principles of morality. They could not have made proselytes at first, by professing any thing that was vicious, cruel, persecuting, or immoral. Like every thing else, they had their beginning; and they proceeded by persuasion, exhortation, and example. How then is it that they lose their native mildness, and become morose and intolerant?

It proceeds from the connexion which Mr. Burke recommends. By engendering the church with the state, a sort of mule animal, capable only of destroying, and not of breeding up, is produced, called, *the church established by law.* It is a stranger, even from its birth, to any parent mother on which it is begotten, and whom in time it kicks out and destroys.

The inquisition in Spain does not proceed from the religion originally professed, but from this mule animal, engendered between the church and the state. The burnings in Smithfield proceeded from the same heterogenous production; and it was the regeneration of this strange animal in England afterwards, that renewed rancor and irreligion among the inhabitants, and that drove the people called Quakers and Dissenters to America. Persecution is not an original feature in *any* religion ; but it is always the strongly-marked feature of all law-religions, or religions established by law. Take away the law-establishment, and every religion re-assumes its original benignity. In America, a catholic priest is a good citizen, a good character, and a good neighbor; an episcopalian minister is of the same description: and this proceeds, independent of men, from there being no law-establishment in America.

If also we view this matter in a temporal sense, we shall see the ill effects it has had on the prosperity of nations. The union of church and state has impoverished Spain. The revoking the edict of Nantz drove the silk manufacture from that country into England; and church and state are now driving the cotton manufacture from England to America and France. Let then Mr. Burke continue to preach his anti-political doctrine of church and state. It will do some good. The national assembly will not follow his advice, but will benefit by his folly. It was by observing the ill effects of it in England, that America has been warned against it; and it is by experiencing them in France, that the national assembly have abolished it, and, like America, has established *universal right of conscience, and universal right of citizenship.**

* When in any country we see extraordinary circumstances taking place, they naturally lead any man who has a talent for observation and investigation, to inquire into the causes. The manufacturers of Manchester, Birmingham, and Sheffield, are the principal manufacturers in England. From whence did this arise ? A little observation will explain the case. The principal, and the generality of the inhabitants of those places, are not of what is

I will here cease the comparison with respect to the principles of the French constitution, and conclude this part of the subject with a few observations on the organization of the formal parts of the French and English governments.

The executive power in each country is in the hands of a person styled, the king; but the French constitution distinguishes between the king and the sovereign: it considers the station of king as official, and places sovereignty in the nation.

The representatives of the nation, which compose the national assembly, and who are the legislative power, originate in and from the people by election, as an inherent right in the people. In England it is otherwise; and this arises from the original establishment of what is called its monarchy; for, as by the conquest all the rights of the people or the nation were absorbed into the hands of the conqueror, and who added the title of king to that of conqueror, those same matters which in France are now held as rights in the people, or in the nation, are held in England as grants from what is called the crown. The parliament in England, in both its branches, was erected by patents from the descendants of the conqueror. The house of commons did not originate as a matter of right in the people, to delegate or elect, but as a grant or boon.

called in England, the church established by law: and they, or their fathers (for it is within but a few years) withdrew from the persecution of the chartered towns, where test-laws more particularly operate, and established a sort of asylum for themselves in those places. It was the only asylum then offered, for the rest of Europe was worse. But the case is now changing.— France and America bid all comers welcome, and initiate them into all the rights of citizenship. Policy and interest, therefore, will, but perhaps too late, dictate in England, what reason and justice could not. Those manufacturers are withdrawing to other places. There is now erecting at Passey, three miles from Paris, a large cotton manufactory, and several are already erected in America. Soon after the rejecting the bill for repealing the test-law, one of the richest manufacturers in England said in my hearing, " England, sir, is not a country for a Dissenter to live in—we must go to France." These are truths, and it is doing justice to both parties to tell them. It is chiefly the Dissenters that have carried English manufactures to the height they are now at, and the same men have it in their power to carry them away; and though those manufactures would afterwards continue in those places, the foreign market will be lost. There frequently appears in the London Gazette, extracts from certain acts to prevent machines, and as far as it can extend to persons, from going out of the country. It appears from these, that the ill effects of the test-laws and church-establishment begin to be much suspected; but the remedy of force can never supply the remedy of reason. In the progress of less than a century, all the unrepresented part of England, of all denominations which is at least an hundred times the most numerous, may begin to feel the necessity of a constitution, and then all those matters will come regularly before them.

By the French constitution, the nation is always named before the king. The third article of the declaration of rights says, " *The nation is essentially the source* (or fountain) *of all sovereignty.*" Mr. Burke argues, that, in England, a king is the fountain—that he is the fountain of all honor. But as this idea is evidently descended from the conquest, I shall make no other remark upon it than that it is the nature of conquest to turn every thing upside down; and as Mr. Burke will not be refused the privilege of speaking twice, and as there are but two parts in the figure, the *fountain* and the *spout*, he will be right the second time.

The French constitution puts the legislative before the executive ; the law before the king ; *la loi, le roi*. This also is in the natural order of things ; because laws must have existence, before they can have execution.

A king in France does not, in addressing himself to the national assembly, say, " my assembly," similar to the phrase used in England of "*my* parliament ;" neither can he use it consistent with the constitution, nor could it be admitted. There may be propriety in the use of it in England, because, as is before mentioned, both houses of parliament originated out of what is called the crown, by patent or boon—and not out of the inherent rights of the people, as the national assembly does in France, and whose name designates its origin.

The president of the national assembly does not ask the king *to grant to the assembly the liberty of speech*, as is the case with the English house of commons. The constitutional dignity of the national assembly cannot debase itself. Speech is, in the first place, one of the natural rights of man, always retained ; and with respect to the national assembly, the use of it is their *duty*, and the nation is their *authority*. They were elected by the greatest body of men exercising the right of election the European world ever saw. They sprung not from the filth of rotten boroughs, nor are they vassal representatives of aristocratical ones. Feeling the proper dignity of their character, they support it. Their parliamentary language, whether for or against a question, is free, bold, and manly, and extends to all the parts and circumstances of the case. If any matter or subject respecting the executive department, or the person who presides in it (the king,) comes before them, it is debated on with the spirit of men, and the language of gentlemen ; and their answer, or their address, is returned

in the same style. They stand not aloof with the gaping
vacuity of vulgar ignorance, nor bend with the cringe of
sycophantic insignificance. The graceful pride of truth
knows no extremes, and preserves, in every latitude of life
the right-angled character of man.

Let us now look to the other side of the question. In
the addresses of the English parliaments to their kings, we
see neither the intrepid spirit of the old parliaments of
France, nor the serene dignity of the present national assembly; neither do we see in them any thing of the style
of English manners, which borders somewhat on bluntness.
Since then they are neither of foreign extraction, nor naturally of English production, their origin must be sought for
elsewhere, and that origin is the Norman conquest. They
are evidently of the vassalage class of manners, and emphatically mark the prostrate distance that exists in no
other condition of men than between the conqueror and
the conquered. That this vassalage idea and style of
speaking was not got rid of, even at the revolution of 1688,
is evident from the declaration of parliament to William
and Mary, in these words : "we do most humbly and
faithfully *submit* ourselves, our heirs and posterity for ever."
Submission is wholly a vassalage term, repugnant to the
dignity of freedom, and an echo of the language used at the
conquest.

As the estimation of all things is by comparison, the revolution of 1688, however from circumstances it may have
been exalted above its value, will find its level. It is already on the wane, eclipsed by the enlarging orb of reason, and the revolutions of America and France. In less
than another century, it will go, as well as Mr. Burke's labors, "to the family vault of all the Capulets." Mankind
will then scarcely believe that a country calling itself free,
would send to Holland for a man, and clothe him with power, on purpose to put themselves in fear of him, and give
him almost a million sterling a-year for leave to *submit* themselves and their posterity, like bondmen and bondwomen
for ever.

But there is a truth that ought to be made known ; I
have had the opportunity of seeing it : which is, *that, notwithstanding appearances, there is not any description of men that
despise monarchy so much as courtiers.* But they well know,
that if it were seen by others, as it is seen by them, the jug-
gle could not be kept up. They are in the condition of

men who get their living by a show, and to whom the folly
of that show is so familiar that they ridicule it ; but were
the audience to be made as wise, in this respect, as themselves, there would be an end to the show and the profits
with it. The difference between a republican and a courtier with respect to monarchy is, that the one opposes monarchy believing it to be something, and the other laughs at
it knowing it to be nothing.

As I used sometimes to correspond with Mr. Burke, believing him then to be a man of sounder principles than his
book shows him to be, I wrote to him last winter from Paris,
and gave him an account how prosperously matters were
going on. Among other subjects in that letter, I referred
to the happy situation the national assembly were placed
in ; that they had taken a ground on which their moral
duty and their political interest were united. They have
not to hold out a language which they do not believe, for
the fraudulent purpose of making others believe it. Their
station requires no artifice to support it, and can only be
maintained by enlightening mankind. It is not their interest to cherish ignorance, but to dispel it. They are not in
the case of a ministerial or an opposition party in England,
who, though they are opposed, are still united to keep up
the common mystery. The national assembly must throw
open a magazine of light. It must show man the proper
character of man ; and the nearer it can bring him to that
standard, the stronger the national assembly becomes.

In contemplating the French constitution, we see in it a
rational order of things. The principles harmonize with
the forms, and both with their origin. It may perhaps be
said as an excuse for bad forms, that they are nothing
more than forms ; but this is a mistake. Forms grow out
of principles, and operate to continue the principles they
grow from. It is impossible to practice a bad form on any
thing but a bad principle. It cannot be ingrafted on a
good one ; and wherever the forms in any government are
bad, it is a certain indication that the principles are bad
also.

I will here finally close this subject. I began it by remarking that Mr. Burke had *voluntarily* declined going into
a comparison of the English and French constitutions. He
apologizes (p. 241) for not doing it, by saying that he had
not time. Mr. Burke's book was upwards of eight months
in hand, and it extended to a volume of three hundred

and fifty-six pages. As his omission does injury to his cause, his apology makes it worse; and men on the English side of the water will begin to consider, whether there is not some radical defect in what is called the English constitution, that made it necessary in Mr. Burke to suppress the comparison, to avoid bringing it into view.

As Mr. Burke has not written on constitutions, so neither has he written on the French revolution. He gives no account of its commencement or its progress. He only expresses his wonder. " It looks," says he, " to me as if I were in a great crisis, not of the affairs of France alone, but of all Europe, perhaps of more than Europe. All circumstances taken together, the French revolution is the most astonishing that has hitherto happened in the world."

As wise men are astonished at foolish things, and other people at wise ones, I know not on which ground to account for Mr. Burke's astonishment; but certain it is that he does not understand the French revolution. It has apparently burst forth like a creation from a chaos, but it is no more than the consequence of mental revolution previously existing in France. The mind of the nation had changed beforehand, and the new order of things has naturally followed a new order of thoughts.—I will here, as concisely as I can, trace out the growth of the French revolution, and mark the circumstances that have contributed to produce it.

The despotism of Louis XIV. united with the gaiety of his court, and the gaudy ostentation of his character, had so humbled, and at the same time so fascinated the mind of France, that the people appear to have lost all sense of their own dignity, in contemplating that of their grand monarch: and the whole reign of Louis XV. remarkable only for weakness and effeminacy, made no other alteration than that of spreading a sort of lethargy over the nation, from which it showed no disposition to rise.

The only signs which appeared of the spirit of liberty during those periods, are to be found in the writings of the French philosophers. Montesquieu, president of the parliament of Bourdeaux, went as far as a writer under a despotic government could well proceed; and being obliged to divide himself between principle and prudence, his mind often appears under a veil, and we ought to give him credit for more than he has expressed.

Voltaire, who was both the flatterer and satirist of despotism, took another line. His forte lay in exposing and ridiculing the superstitions which priest-craft, united with state-craft, had interwoven with governments. It was not from the purity of his principles, or his love of mankind, (for satire and philanthropy are not naturally concordant) but from his strong capacity of seeing folly in its true shape, and his irresistible propensity to expose it that he made those attacks. They were however as formidable as if the motives had been virtuous; and he merits the thanks rather than the esteem of mankind.

On the contrary, we find in the writings of Rousseau and abbe Raynal, a loveliness of sentiment in favor of liberty, that excites respect, and elevates the human faculties; yet having raised this animation, they do not direct its operations, but leave the mind in love with an object, without describing the means of possessing it.

The writings of Quisne, Turgot, and the friends of those authors, are of a serious kind; but they labored under the same disadvantage with Montesquieu; their writings abound with moral maxims of government, but are rather directed to economise and reform the administration of the government, than the government itself.

But all those writings and many others had their weight; and by the different manner in which they treated the subject of government, Montesquieu by his judgment and knowledge of laws; Voltaire by his wit; Rousseau and Raynal by their animation, and Quisne and Turgot by their moral maxims and systems of economy, readers of every class met with something to their taste, and a spirit of political inquiry began to diffuse itself through the nation at the time the dispute between England and the then colonies of America broke out.

In the war which France afterwards engaged in, it is very well known that the nation appeared to be beforehand with the French ministry. Each of them had its views: but those views were directed to different objects; the one sought liberty and the other retaliation on England. The French officers and soldiers who after this went to America, were eventually placed in the school of freedom, and learned the practice as well as the principles of it by heart.

As it was impossible to separate the military events which took place in America from the principles of the American revolution, the publication of those events in

France necessarily connected themselves with the principles that produced them.   Many of the facts were in
themselves principles: such as the declaration of American independence, and the treaty of alliance between
France and America, which recognized the natural rights
of man, and justified resistance to oppression.

The then minister of France, count Vergennes, was not
the friend of America: and it is both justice and gratitude
to say, that it was the queen of France who gave the cause
of America a fashion at the French court.   Count Vergennes was the personal and social friend of Dr. Franklin ;
and the doctor had obtained by his sensible gracefulness,
a sort of influence over him ; but with respect to principles,
count Vergennes was a despot.

The situation of Dr. Franklin as minister from America
to France should be taken into the chain of circumstances.
A diplomatic character is the narrowest sphere of society
that man can act in.   It forbids intercourse by a reciprocity of suspicion ; and a diplomatist is a sort of unconnected
atom, continually repelling and repelled.   But this was
not the case with Dr. Franklin : he was not the diplomatist
of a court, but of *man*.   His character as a philosopher
had been long established, and his circle of society in
France was universal.

Count Vergennes resisted for a considerable time the
publication of the American constitutions in France, translated into the French language ; but even in this he was
obliged to give way to public opinion, and a sort of propriety in admitting to appear what he had undertaken to
defend.   The American constitutions were to liberty what
a grammar is to language : they define its parts of speech,
and practically construct them into syntax.

The peculiar situation of the then marquis de la Fayette
is another link in the great chain.   He served in America
as an American officer, under a commission of congress,
and by the universality of his acquaintance, was in close
friendship with the civil government of America, as well
as with the military line.   He spoke the language of the
country, entered into the discussions on the principles of
government, and was always a welcome friend at any
election.

When the war closed, a vast reinforcement to the cause
of liberty spread itself over France, by the return of the
French officers and soldiers.   A knowledge of the practice

was then joined to the theory ; and all that was wanting to give it real existence, was opportunity. Man, cannot, properly speaking, make circumstances for his purpose, but he always has it in his power to improve them when they occur : and this was the case in France.

M. Neckar was displaced in May 1781 ; and by the ill-management of the finances afterwards, and particularly during the extravagant administration of M. Calonne, the revenue of France which was nearly twenty-four millions sterling per year, was become unequal to the expenditures not because the revenue had decreased, but because the expenses had increased, and this was the circumstance which the nation laid hold of to bring forward a revolution. The English minister, Mr. Pitt, has frequently alluded to the state of the French finances in his budgets, without understanding the subject. Had the French parliaments been as ready to register edicts for new taxes, as an English parliament is to grant them, there had been no derangement in the finances, nor yet any revolution ; but this will better explain itself as I proceed.

It will be necessary here to show how taxes were formerly raised in France. The king, or rather the court or ministry, acting under the use of that name, framed the edicts for taxes at their own discretion, and sent them to the parliaments to be registered ; for until they were registered by the parliaments, they were not operative. Disputes had long existed between the court and the parliament with respect to the extent of the parliament's authority on this head. The court insisted that the authority of parliament went no further than to remonstrate or show reasons against the tax, reserving to itself the right of determining whether the reasons are well or ill-founded ; and in consequence thereof, either to withdraw the edict as a matter of choice, or to *order* it to be enregistered as a matter of authority. The parliaments on their part insisted, that they had not only a right to remonstrate, but to reject ; and on this ground they were always supported by the nation.

But, to return to the order of my narrative—M. Calonne wanted money ; and as he knew the sturdy disposition of the parliaments with respect to new taxes, he ingeniously sought either to approach them by a more gentle means than that of direct authority, or to get over their heads by a manœuvre : and, for this purpose, he revived the project of assembling a body of men from the several provinces.

under the style of an "assembly of the notables," or men
of note, who met in 1787, and who were either to recommend taxes to the parliaments, or to act as a parliament
themselves.   An assembly under this name had been called in 1687.

As we are to view this as the first practical step towards
the revolution, it will be proper to enter into some particulars respecting it.   The assembly of the notables has in
some places been mistaken for the states-general, but was
wholly a different body ; the states-general being always
by election.   The persons who composed the assembly of
the notables were all nominated by the king, and consisted of one hundred and forty-members.   But as M. Calonne
could not depend upon a majority of this assembly in his
favor, he very ingeniously arranged them in such a manner as to make forty-four a majority of one hundred and
forty : to effect this, he disposed of them into seven separate committees, of twenty members each.   Every general
question was to be decided, not by a majority of persons,
but by a majority of committees ; and as eleven votes
would make a majority in a committee, and four committees a majority of seven, M. Calonne had good reason to
conclude, that as forty-four would determine any general
question, he could not be out-voted.   But all his plans deceived him, and in the event became his overthrow.

The then marquis de la Fayette was placed in the second committee, of which count d'Artois was president ;
and as money matters was the object, it naturally brought
into view every circumstance connected with it.   M. de la
Fayette made a verbal charge against Calonne, for selling
crown land to the amount of two millions of livres, in a
manner that appeared to be unknown to the king.   The
count d'Artois (as if to intimidate, for the Bastile was then
in being) asked the marquis, if he would render the charge
in writing ? He replied that he would.   The count d'Artois
did not demand it, but brought a message from the king to
that purport.   M. de la Fayette then delivered in his charge
in writing, to be given to the king, undertaking to support
it.   No further proceedings were had upon this affair ; but
M. Calonne was soon after dismissed by the king, and went
to England.

As M. de la Fayette, from the experience he had had
in America, was better acquainted with the science of civil
government than the generality of the members who com-

posed the assembly of the notables could then be, the brunt of the business fell considerably to his share. The plan of those who had a constitution in view, was to contend with the court on the ground of taxes, and some of them openly professed their object. Disputes frequently arose between count d' Artois and M. de la Fayette upon various subjects. With respect to the arrears already incurred, the latter proposed to remedy them, by accommodating the expenses to the revenue, instead of the revenue to the expenses; and as objects of reform, he proposed to abolish the Bastile, and all the state-prisons throughout the nation (the keeping of which was attended with great expense) and to suppress *lettres de cachet:* but those matters were not then much attended to; and with respect to *lettres de cachet, a majority of the nobles appeared to be in favor of them.*

On the subject of supplying the treasury by new taxes, the assembly declined taking the matter on themselves, concurring in the opinion that they had not authority. In a debate on this subject, M. de la Fayette said, that raising money by taxes could only be done by a national assembly, freely elected by the people and acting as their representatives. Do you mean, said the count d'Artois, the states-general? M. de la Fayette replied, that he did. Will you, said the count d'Artois, sign what you say, to be given to the king? The other replied, that he not only would do this, but that he would go further, and say, that the effectual mode would be, for the king to agree to the establishment of a constitution.

As one of the plans had thus failed, that of getting the assembly to act as a parliament, the other came into view, that of recommending. On this subject, the assembly agreed to recommend two new taxes to be enregistered by the parliament, the one a stamp-act, and the other a territorial tax, or sort of land-tax. The two have been estimated at about five millions sterling, per annum. We have now to turn our attention to the parliaments, on whom the business was again devolving.

The archbishop of Thoulouse (since archbishop of Sens, and now a cardinal) was appointed to the administration of the finances, soon after the dismission of Calonne. He was also made prime minister, an office that did not always exist in France. When this office did not exist, the chief of each of the principal departments transacted business immediately with the king; but when a prime minister was appointed, they did business only with him. The archbishop arrived to more state-authority than any minister since the duke de Choiseuil, and the nation was strongly disposed in his favor; but by a line of conduct scarcely to be accounted for, he perverted every opportunity, turned out a despot, and sunk into disgrace, and a cardinal.

The assembly of the notables having broke up, the new minister sent the edicts for the two new taxes recommended by the assembly to the parliaments, to be enregistered. They of course came first before the parliament of Paris, who returned for answer, *That with such a revenue as the nation then supported, the name of taxes ought not to be mentioned, but for the purpose of reducing them;* and threw both the edicts out.*

On this refusal, the parliament was ordered to Versailles, where, in the usual form, the king held, what under the old government was called a bed of justice: and the two edicts were enregistered in presence of the parliament, by an order of state, in the manner mentioned, p. 99. On this, the parliament immediately returned to Paris, renewed their session in form, and ordered the enregistering to be struck out, declaring that every thing done at Versailles was illegal. All the members of parliament were then served with *lettres de cachet,* and exiled to Trois; but as they continued as inflexible in exile as before, and as vengeance did not supply the place of taxes, they were after a short time recalled to Paris.

The edicts were again tendered to them, and the count d'Artois undertook to act as representative for the king.— For this purpose, he came from Versailles to Paris, in a train of procession; and the parliament was assembled to receive him. But show and parade had lost their influence in France; and whatever ideas of importance he might set off with, he had to return with those of mortification and disappointment. On alighting from his carriage to ascend the steps of the parliament house, the crowd (which was numerously collected) threw out trite expressions, saying, " this is monsieur d'Artois, who wants more of our money to spend." The marked disapprobation which he

---

* When the English minister, Mr. Pitt, mentions the French finances again in the English parliament, it would be well that he noticed this as an example.

saw, impressed him with apprehensions; and the word *aux arms*, (*to arms*) was given out by the officer of the guard who attended him. It was so loudly vociferated, that it echoed through the avenues of the house, and produced a temporary confusion: I was then standing in one of the apartments through which he had to pass, and could not avoid reflecting how wretched is the condition of a disrespected man.

He endeavored to impress the parliament by great words, and opened his authority by saying, " The king, our lord and master." The parliament received him very coolly, and with their usual determination not to register the taxes: and in this manner the interview ended.

After this a new subject took place: in the various debates and contests that arose between the court and the parliaments on the subject of taxes, the parliament of Paris at last declared, that although it had been customary for parliaments to enregister edicts for taxes as a matter of convenience, the right belonged only to the states-general; and that therefore, the parliaments could no longer with propriety continue to debate on what it had not authority to act. The king after this, came to Paris, and held a meeting with the parliament, in which he continued from ten in the morning till about six in the evening; and, in a manner that appeared to proceed from him, as if unconsulted upon with the cabinet or the ministry, gave his word to the parliament, that the states-general should be convened.

But after this another scene arose, on a ground different from all the former. The minister and the cabinet were averse to calling the states-general: they well knew, that if the states-general were assembled, that themselves must fall; and as the king had not mentioned *any time*, they hit on a project calculated to elude, without appearing to oppose.

For this purpose, the court set about making a sort of constitution itself: it was principally the work of M. Lamoignon, keeper of the seals, who afterwards shot himself. The arrangement consisted in establishing a body under the name of a *cour pleniere*, or full court, in which were invested all the power that the government might have occasion to make use of. The persons composing this court to be nominated by the king; the contended right of taxation was given up on the part of the king, and a new criminal code of laws, and law proceedings, was substituted in the room of the former. The thing, in many points, contained better principles than those upon which the government had hitherto been administered: but with respect to the *cour pleniere*, it was no other than a medium through which despotism was to pass, without appearing to act directly from itself.

The cabinet had high expectations from their new contrivance. The persons who were to compose the *cour pleniere*, were already nominated; and as it was necessary to carry a fair appearance, many of the best characters in the nation were appointed among the number. It was to commence on the 8th of May, 1788: but an opposition arose to it, on two grounds—the one as to principle, the other as to form.

On the ground of principle it was contended, that government had not a right to alter itself; and that if the practice was once admitted, it would grow into a principle, and be made a precedent for any future alterations the government might wish to establish: that the right of altering the government was a national right, and not a right of government. And on the ground of form, it was contended, that the *cour pleniere* was nothing more than a large cabinet.

The then dukes de la Rochefoucault, Luxembourg, de Noailles, and many others, refused to accept the nomination, and strenuously opposed the whole plan. When the edict for establishing this new court was sent to the parliaments to be enregistered, and put into execution, they resisted also. The parliament of Paris not only refused, but denied the authority; and the contest renewed itself between the parliament and the cabinet more strongly than ever. While the parliament was sitting in debate on this subject, the ministry ordered a regiment of soldiers to surround the house, and form a blockade. The members sent out for beds and provision, and lived as in a besieged citadel; and as this had no effect, the commanding officer was ordered to enter the parliament house and seize them, which he did, and some the principal members were shut up in different prisons. About the same time a deputation of persons arrived from the province of Britanny, to remonstrate against the establishment of the *cour pleniere*; and those the archbishop sent to the Bastile. But the spirit of the nation was not to be overcome; and it was so fully sensible of the strong ground it had taken, that of withholding taxes, that it contented itself with keeping up a sort of quiet resistance, which effectually overthrew all the plans at that time formed against it. The project of the *cour pleniere* was at last obliged to be given up, and the prime minister not long afterwards followed its fate ; and M. Neckar was recalled into office.

The attempt to establish the *cour pleniere* had an effect upon the nation, which was not anticipated. It was a sort of new form of government, that insensibly served to put the old one out of sight, and to unhinge it from the superstitious authority of antiquity. It was government dethroning government ; and the old one, by attempting to make a new one, made a chasm.

The failure of this scheme renewed the subject of convening the states-general ; and this gave rise to a new series of politics. There was no settled form for convening the states-general : all that it positively meant, was a deputation from what was then called the clergy, the nobility, and the commons; but their numbers, or their proportions, had not been always the same. They had been convened only on extraordinary occasions, the last of which was in 1614; their numbers were then in equal proportions, and they voted by orders.

It could not well escape the sagacity of M. Neckar, that the mode of 1614 would answer neither the purpose of the then government, nor of the nation. As matters were at that time circumstanced, it would have been too contentious to argue upon any thing. The debates would have been endless upon privileges and exemptions, in which neither the wants of the government, nor the wishes of the nation for a constitution, would have been attended to. But as he did not choose to take the decision upon himself, he summoned again the assembly of the *notables*, and referred it to them. This body was in general interested in the decision, being chiefly of the aristocracy and the high-paid clergy ; and they decided in favor of the mode of 1614. This decision was against the sense of the nation, and also against the wishes of the court ; for the aristocracy opposed itself to both, and contended for privileges independent of either. The subject was then taken up by the parliament, who recommended that the number of the commons should be equal to the other two ; and that they should all sit in one house, and vote in one body. The number finally determined on was twelve hundred : six hundred to be chosen by the commons (and this was less than their

proportion ought to have been when their worth and consequence is considered on a national scale) three hundred by
the clergy, and three hundred by the aristocracy ; but with
respect to the mode of assembling themselves, whether together or apart, or the manner in which they should vote,
those matters were referred.*

The election that followed, was not a contested election,
but an animated one. The candidates were not men, but
principles. Societies were formed in Paris, and committees
of correspondence and communication established throughout the nation, for the purpose of enlightening the people,
and explaining to them the principles of civil government;
and so orderly was the election conducted, that it did not
give rise even to the rumor of tumult.

The states-general were to meet at Versailles in April,
1789, but did not assemble till May. They located themselves in three separate chambers, or rather the clergy and
the aristocracy withdrew each into a separate chamber.
The majority of the aristocracy claimed what they called
the privilege of voting as a separate body, and of giving
their consent or their negative in that manner ; and many
of the bishops and the high-beneficed clergy claimed the
same privilege on the part of their order.

The *tiers etat* (as they were called) disowned all knowledge of artificial orders and privileges ; and they were not
only resolute on this point but somewhat disdainful. They

---

* Mr. Burke, (and I must take the liberty of telling him that he is unacquainted with French affairs,) speaking upon this subject, says, " The first
thing that struck me in calling the states-general, was a great departure from
the ancient course;" and he soon after says. "From the moment I read the
list, I saw distinctly, and very nearly as it has happened, all that was to follow "
Mr. Burke certainly did not see all that was to follow I have endeavored to
impress him, as well before as after the states general met, that there would
be a *revolution ;* but was not able to make him see it, neither would he believe it. How then he could distinctly see all the parts, when the whole was
out of sight, is beyond my comprehension. And with respect to the " departure from the ancient course," besides the natural weakness of the remark, it shows that he is unacquainted with circumstances. The departure
was necessary. from the experience had upon it, that the ancient course was
a bad one. The states-general of 1614 were called at the commencement of
the civil war in the minority of Louis XIII. : but by the clash of arranging
them by orders, they increased the confusion they were called to compose.
The author of *l'Intrigue du Cabinet* (Intrigue of the Cabinet,) who wrote before any revolution was thought of in France, speaking of the states-general
of 1614, says, " They held the public in suspense five months : and by the
questions agitated therein, and the heat with which they were put, it appears that the great (*les grands*) thought more to satisfy their particular
passions, than to procure the good of the nation ; and the whole time passed
away in alterations, ceremonies and parade." l'Intrigue du Cabinet, vol. i.
p. 329.

began to consider aristocracy as a kind of fungus growing out of the corruption of society, that could not be admitted even as a branch of it; and from the disposition the aristocracy had shown, by upholding *lettres de cachet*, and in sundry other instances, it was manifest that no constitution could be formed by admitting men in any other character than as national men.

After various altercations on this head, the *tiers etat*, or commons, (as they were then called) declared themselves (on a motion made for that purpose by the abbe Sieyes,) " THE REPRESENTATIVES OF THE NATION ; *and that the two orders could be considered but as deputies of corporations, and could only have a deliberative voice but when they assembled in a national character, with the national representatives.*" This proceeding extinguished the style of *etas generaux* or states-general, and erected it into the style it now bears, that of *l'assemble nationale* or national assembly.

This motion was not made in a precipitate manner : it was the result of cool deliberation, and concerted between the national representatives and the patriotic members of the two chambers, who saw into the folly, mischief, and injustice of artificial privileged distinctions. It was become evident, that no constitution, worthy of being called by that name, could be established on any thing less than a national ground. The aristocracy had hitherto opposed the despotism of the court, and affected the language of patriotism ; but it opposed it as its rival ; (as the English barons opposed king John) and it now opposed the nation from the same motives.

On carrying this motion the national representatives, as had been concerted, sent an invitation to the two chambers, to unite with them in a national character, and proceed to business. A majority of the clergy, chiefly of the parish priests, withdrew from the clerical chamber, and joined the nation; and forty-five from the other chamber joined in like manner. There is a sort of secret history belonging to this last circumstance, which is necessary to its explanation : it was not judged prudent that all the patriotic members of the chamber, styling itself the nobles, should quit it at once ; and in consequence of this arrangement, they drew off by degrees, always leaving some, as well to reason the case, as to watch the suspected. In a little time, the numbers increased from forty-five to eighty, and soon after to a greater number : which with a majority of the

clergy, and the whole of the national representatives, put
the malcontents in a very diminutive condition.

The king, who, very different to the general class called
by that name, is a man of a good heart, showed himself
disposed to recommend a union of the three chambers, on
the ground the national assembly had taken; but the malcontents exerted themselves to prevent it, and began now
to have another project in view. Their numbers consisted
of a majority of the aristocratical chamber, and a minority
of the clerical chamber, chiefly of bishops and high-beneficed clergy; and these men were determined to put
every thing at issue, as well by strength as by stratagem.
They had no objection to a constitution; but it must be
such an one as themselves should dictate, and suited to
their own views and particular situations. On the other
hand, the nation disowned knowing any thing of them but
as citizens, and was determined to shut out all such upstart pretensions. The more aristocracy appeared, the
more it was despised; there was a visible imbecility and
want of intellects in the majority, a sort of *je ne scais quoi*,
that while it affected to be more than citizen, was less than
man. It lost ground more from contempt than from
hatred; and was rather jeered at as an ass, than dreaded
as a lion. This is the general character of aristocracy, or
what are called nobles or nobility, or rather no-ability, in
all countries.

The plan of the malcontents consisted now of two things;
either to deliberate and vote by chambers (or orders,) more
especially on all questions respecting a constitution (by
which the aristocratical chamber would have had a negative on any article of the constitution) or, in case they could
not accomplish this object, to overthrow the national assembly entirely.

To effect one or the other of these objects, they began
now to cultivate a friendship with the despotism they had
hitherto attempted to rival, and the count d'Artois became
their chief. The king (who has since declared himself deceived into their measures) held, according to the old form,
a bed of justice, in which he accorded to the deliberation
and vote *par tete* (by head) upon several objects; but reserved the deliberation and vote upon all questions respecting a constitution to the three chambers separately.
This declaration of the king was made against the advice
of M. Neckar, who now began to perceive that he was

growing out of fashion at court, and that another minister was in contemplation.

As the form of sitting in separate chambers was yet apparently kept up, though essentially destroyed, the national representatives, immediately after this declaration of the king, resorted to their chambers, to consult on a protest against it; and the minority of the chamber (calling itself the nobles) who had joined the national cause, retired to a private house, to consult in like manner. The malcontents had by this time concerted their measures with the court, which count d'Artois undertook to conduct: and as they saw, from the discontent which the declaration excited, and the opposition making against it, that they could not obtain a control over the intended constitution by a separate vote, they prepared themselves for their final object— that of conspiring against the national assembly, and overthrowing it.

The next morning, the door of the chamber of the national assembly was shut against them, and guarded by troops; and the members were refused admittance. On this, they withdrew to a tennis-ground in the neighborhood of Versailles, as the most convenient place they could find, and, after renewing their session, took an oath never to separate from each other, under any circumstances whatever, death excepted, until they had established a constitution. As the experiment of shutting up the house had no other effect than that of producing a closer connexion in the members, it was opened again the next day, and the public business re-commenced in the usual place.

We now are to have in view the forming the new ministry, which was to accomplish the overthrow of the national assembly. But as force would be necessary, orders were issued to assemble thirty thousand troops, the command of which was given to Broglio, one of the new-intended ministry, who was recalled from the country for this purpose. But as some management was necessary to keep this plan concealed till the moment it should be ready for execution, it is to this policy that a declaration made by the count d'Artois must be attributed, and which is here proper to be introduced.

It could not but occur, that while the malcontents continued to resort to their chambers separate from the national assembly, that more jealousy would be excited than if they were mixed with it, and that the plot might be

suspected. But as they had taken their ground, and now
wanted a pretence for quitting it, it was necessary that one
should be devised. This was effectually accomplished by
a declaration made by count d'Artois, that *"if they took
not a part in the national assembly, the life of the king would be
endangered,"* on which they quitted their chambers, and
mixed with the assembly in one body.

At the time this declaration was made, it was generally
treated as a piece of absurdity in the count d'Artois, and
calculated merely to relieve the outstanding members of
the two chambers from the diminutive situation they were
put in ; and if nothing more had followed, this conclusion
would have been good. But as things best explain themselves by events, this apparent union was only a cover to
the machinations that were secretly going on ; and the declaration accommodated itself to answer that purpose. In a
little time the national assembly found itself surrounded
by troops, and thousands daily arriving. On this a very
strong declaration was made by the national assembly to
the king, remonstrating on the impropriety of the measure,
and demanding the reason. The king, who was not in the
secret of this business, as himself afterwards declared, gave
substantially for answer, that he had no other object in view
than to preserve public tranquillity, which appeared to be
much disturbed.

But in a few days from this time the plot unravelled itself. M. Neckar and the ministry were displaced, and a
new one formed, of the enemies of the revolution ; and
Broglio, with between twenty-five and thirty thousand foreign troops, was arrived to support them. The mask was
now thrown off, and matters were come to a crisis. The
event was, that in the space of three days, the new ministry and all their abettors, found it prudent to fly the nation ; the Bastile was taken, and Broglio and his foreign
troops dispersed ; as is already related in a former part of
this work.

There are some curious circumstances in the history of
this short-lived ministry, and this brief attempt at a counter-revolution. The palace of Versailles, where the court
was sitting, was not more than four hundred yards distant
from the hall where the national assembly was sitting.
The two places were at this moment like the separate
head-quarters of two combatant enemies ; yet the court
was as perfectly ignorant of the information which had

arrived from Paris to the national assembly, as if it had resided at an hundred miles distance. The then marquis de la Fayette, who (as has been already mentioned) was chosen to preside in the national assembly on this particular occasion, named, by order of the assembly, three successive deputations to the king, on the day, and up to the evening on which the Bastile was taken, to inform and confer with him on the state of affairs: but the ministry, who knew not so much as that it was attacked, precluded all communication, and were solacing themselves how dexterously they had succeeded: but in a few hours the accounts arrived so thick and fast, that they had to start from their desks and run: some set off in one disguise, and some in another, and none in their own character. Their anxiety now was to outride the news, lest they should be stopped, which, though it flew fast, flew not so fast as themselves.

It is worth remarking, that the national assembly neither pursued those fugitive conspirators, nor took any notice of them, nor sought to retaliate in any shape whatever. Occupied with establishing a constitution, founded on the rights of man and the authority of the people, the only authority on which government has a right to exist in any country, the national assembly felt none of those mean passions which mark the character of impertinent governments, founding themselves on their own authority, or on the absurdity of hereditary succession. It is the faculty of the human mind to become what it contemplates, and to act in unison with its object.

The conspiracy being thus dispersed, one of the first works of the national assembly, instead of vindictive proclamations, as has been the case with other governments, published a declaration of the rights of man, as the basis on which the new constitution was to be built, and which is here subjoined.

Declaration of the rights of man and of citizens: by the national assembly of France.

"The representatives of the people of France, formed into a national assembly, considering that ignorance, neglect, or contempt of human rights, are the sole causes of public misfortunes, and corruptions of government, have resolved to set forth, in a solemn declaration, these natural, imprescriptible, and unalienable rights: that this declara-

tion being constantly present to the minds of the body social, they may be ever kept attentive to their rights and
their duties : that the acts of the legislative and executive
powers of government, being capable of being every moment compared with the end of political institutions, may
be more respected : and also, that the future claims of the
citizens, being directed by simple and incontestible principles, may always tend to the maintenance of the constitution and the general happiness.

" For these reasons the national assembly doth recog-
nize and declare, in the presence of the supreme being,
and with a hope of his blessing and favor, the following *sacred* rights of men and of citizens :

" I. Men are born and always continue free and equal
in respect of their rights. Civil distinctions, therefore, can
only be founded on public utility.

" II. The end of all political associations is the preservation of the natural and imprescriptible rights of man ;
and these rights are liberty, property, security, and resistance of oppression.

" III. The nation is essentially the source of all sovereignty : nor can any *individual* or *any body of men,* be entitled to any authority which is not expressly derived
from it.

" IV. Political liberty consists in the power of doing
whatever does not injure another. The exercise of the
natural rights of every man has no other limits than those
which are necessary to secure to every *other* man the free
exercise of the same rights ; and these limits are determinable only by the law.

" V. The law ought to prohibit only actions hurtful to
society. What is not prohibited by the law, should not
be hindered ; nor should any one be compelled to that
which the law does not require.

" VI. The law is an expression of the will of the community. All citizens have a right to concur, either personally, or by their representatives, in its formation. It
should be the same to all, whether it protects or punishes ;
and all being equal in its sight, are equally eligible to all
honors, places, and employments, according to their different abilities, without any other distinction than that created by their virtues and talents.

" VII. No man should be accused, arrested, or held in
confinement, except in cases determined by the law, and

according to the forms which it has prescribed. All who promote, solicit, execute, or cause to be executed, arbitrary orders, ought to be punished; and every citizen called upon or apprehended by virtue of the law, ought immediately to obey, and not render himself culpable by resistance.

" VIII. The law ought to impose no other penalties than such as are absolutely and evidently necessary : and no one ought to be punished, but in virtue of a law promulgated before the offence, and legally applied.

" IX. Every man being presumed innocent till he has been convicted, whenever his detention becomes indispensable, all rigor to him, more than is necessary to secure his person, ought to be provided against by the law.

" X. No man ought to be molested on account of his opinions, not even on account of his religious opinions, provided his avowal of them does not disturb the public order established by law.

" XI. The unrestrained communication of thoughts and opinions being one of the most precious rights of man, every citizen may speak, write, and publish freely, provided he is responsible for the abuse of this liberty in cases determined by the law.

" XII. A public force being necessary to give security to the rights of men and of citizens, that force is instituted for the benefit of the community, and not for the particular benefit of the persons with whom it is intrusted.

" XIII. A common contribution being necessary for the support of the public force, and for defraying the other expenses of government, it ought to be divided equally among the members of the community, according to their abilities.

" XIV. Every citizen has a right, either by himself or his representative, to a free voice in determining the necessity of public contributions, the appropriation of them, and their amount, mode of assessment, and duration.

" XV. Every community has a right to demand of all its agents, an account of their conduct.

" XVI. Every community in which a separation of powers and a security of rights is not provided for, wants a constitution.

" XVII. The right to property being inviolable and sacred, no one ought to be deprived of it, except in cases of

evident public necessity legally ascertained, and on condition of a previous just indemnity."

Observations on the declaration of rights.

The three first articles comprehend in general terms the
whole of a declaration of rights: all the succeeding articles either originate out of them, or follow as elucidations.
The 4th, 5th, and 6th, define more particularly what is
only generally expressed in the 1st, 2d, and 3d.

The 7th, 8th, 9th, 10th, and 11th articles are declaratory of *principles* upon which laws shall be construed conformable to *rights* already declared. But it is questioned
by some very good people in France, as well as in other
countries, whether the 10th article sufficiently guarantees
the right it is intended to accord with: besides which, it
takes off from the divine dignity of religion, and weakens
its operative force upon the mind to make it a subject of
human laws. It then presents itself to man, like light intercepted by a cloudy medium, in which the source of it is
obscured from his sight, and he sees nothing to reverence
in the dusky rays.*

The remaining articles, beginning with the twelfth, are
substantially contained in the principles of the preceding
articles; but, in the particular situation which France then
was, having to undo what was wrong, as well as to set up
what was right, it was proper to be more particular than
what in another condition of things would be necessary.

While the declaration of rights was before the national
assembly, some of its members remarked, that if a declaration of rights was published, it should be accompanied

* There is a single idea, which, if it strikes rightly upon the mind, either
in a legal or a religious sense, will prevent any man, or any body of men, or
any government, from going wrong on the subject of religion: which is, that
before any human institutions of government were known in the world, there
existed, if I may so express it, a compact between God and man, from the
beginning of time; and that as the relation and condition which man in his
individual person stands in towards his maker cannot be changed, by any human laws or human authority, that religious devotion, which is a part of this
compact, cannot so much as be made a subject of human laws; and that all
laws must conform themselves to this prior existing compact, and not assume
to make the compact conform to the laws, which, besides being human, are
subsequent thereto. The first act of man, when he looked around and saw
himself a creature which he did not make, and a world furnished for his re-
ception, must have been devotion; and devotion must ever continue sacred
to every individual man, as it appears right to him; and governments do mischief by interfering.

by a declaration of duties. The observation discovered a mind that reflected, and it only erred by not reflecting far enough. A declaration of rights is, by reciprocity, a declaration of duties also. Whatever is my right as a man, is also the right of another; and it becomes my duty to guarantee, as well as to possess.

The three first articles are the basis of liberty as well individual as national; nor can any country be called free, whose government does not take its beginning from the principles they contain, and continue to preserve them pure; and the whole of the declaration of rights is of more value to the world, and will do more good, than all the laws and statutes that have yet been promulgated.

In the declaratory exordium which prefaces the declaration of rights, we see the solemn and majestic spectacle of a nation opening its commission, under the auspices of its creator, to establish a government; a scene so new, and so transcendantly unequalled by any thing in the European world, that the name of a revolution is inexpressive of its character, and it rises into a regeneration of man. What are the present governments of Europe, but a scene of iniquity and oppression? What is that of England? Does not its own inhabitants say, it is a market where every man has his price, and where corruption is common traffic, at the expense of a deluded people? No wonder, then, that the French revolution is traduced. Had it confined itself merely to the destruction of flagrant despotism, perhaps Mr. Burke and some others had been silent. Their cry now is, " It has gone too far:" that is, gone to far for them. It stares corruption in the face, and the venal tribe are all alarmed. Their fear discovers itself in their outrage, and they are but publishing the groans of a wounded vice. But from such opposition, the French revolution, instead of suffering, receives homage. The more it is struck, the more sparks it will emit; and the fear is, it will not be struck enough. It has nothing to dread from attacks. Truth has given it an establishment; and time will record it with a name as lasting as its own.

Having now traced the progress of the French revolution through most of its principal stages, from its commencement to the taking of the Bastile, and its establishment by the declaration of rights, I will close the subject with the energetic apostrophe of M. de la Fayette—*May this great monument raised to liberty, serve as a lesson to the oppressor, and an example to the oppressed!*

MISCELLANEOUS CHAPTER.

To prevent interrupting the argument in the preceding part of this work, or the narrative that follows it, I reserved some observations to be thrown together into a miscellaneous chapter; by which variety might not be censured for confusion. Mr. Burke's book is *all* miscellany. His intention was to make an attack on the French revolution: but instead of proceeding with an orderly arrangement, he has stormed it with a mob of ideas, tumbling over and destroying one another.

But this confusion and contradiction in Mr. Burke's book, is easily accounted for. When a man in any cause attempts to steer his course by any thing else than some popular truth or principle, he is sure to be lost. It is beyond the compass of his capacity, to keep all the parts of an argument together, and make them unite in one issue, by any other means than having this guide always in view. Neither memory nor invention will supply the want of it. The former fails him, and the latter betrays him.

Notwithstanding the nonsense, for it deserves no better name, that Mr. Burke has asserted about hereditary rights, and hereditary succession, and that a nation has not a right to form a government for itself, it happened to fall in his way to give some account of what government is. " Government," says he, " is a contrivance of human wisdom."

Admitting that government is a contrivance of human wisdom, it must necessarily follow, that hereditary succession, and hereditary rights (as they are called) can make no part of it, because it is impossible to make wisdom hereditary; and on the other hand, *that* cannot be a wise contrivance, which in its operation may commit the government of a nation to the wisdom of an ideot. The

---

* See p. 52. of this work.—N. B. Since the taking the Bastile, the occurrences have been published: but the matters recorded in this narrative are prior to that period, and some of them, as may easily be seen, can be but very little known.

ground which Mr. Burke now takes is fatal to every part
of his cause. The argument changes from hereditary
rights to hereditary wisdom; and the question is, who is
the wisest man? He must now show that every one in
the line of hereditary succession was a Solomon, or his
title is not good to be a king. What a stroke has Mr.
Burke now made! to use a sailor's phrase he has *swabbed
the deck*, and scarcely left a name legible in the list of
kings; and he has mowed down and thinned the house of
peers, with a scythe as formidable as death and time.

But, Mr. Burke appears to have been aware of this re-
tort, and he has taken care to guard against it, by making
government to be not only a *contrivance* of human wisdom,
but a *monopoly* of wisdom. He puts the nation as fools on
one side, and places his government of wisdom, all wise
men of Gotham, on the other side; and he then proclaims,
and says, that " *men have a* RIGHT *that their* WANTS *should be
provided for by this wisdom*." Having thus made proclamation, he next proceeds to explain to them what their *wants*
are, and also what their *rights* are. In this he has succeeded dexterously, for he makes their wants to be a *want*
of wisdom; but as this is but cold comfort, he then informs
them, that they have a *right* (not to any of the wisdom) but
to be governed by it: and in order to impress them with
a solemn reverence for this monopoly-government of wisdom, and of its vast capacity for all purposes, possible or
impossible, right or wrong, he proceeds with astrological,
mysterious importance, to tell them its powers in these
words—"The rights of men in government are their advantages; and these are often in balances between differences of good; and in compromises sometimes between
good and *evil*, and sometimes between *evil* and *evil*. Political reason is a *computing principle;* adding, subtracting,
multiplying, and dividing, morally and not metaphysically
or mathematically, true moral demonstrations."

As the wondering audience whom Mr. Burke supposes
himself talking to, may not understand all this jargon, I
will undertake to be its interpreter. The meaning then,
good people, of all this is, *that government is governed by no
principle whatever : that it can make evil good, or good evil, just
as it pleases. In short, that government is arbitrary power.*

But there are some things which Mr. Burke has forgotten: 1st, he has not shown where the wisdom originally
came from : and, 2d, he has not shown by what authority

it first began to act. In the manner he introduced the matters, it is either government stealing wisdom, or wisdom
stealing government. It is without an origin, and its powers without authority. In short, it is usurpation.

Whether it be from a sense of shame, or from a consciousness of some radical defect in government necessary
to be kept out of sight, or from both, or from some other
cause, I undertake not to determine ; but so it is, that a monarchical reasoner never traces government to its source,
or from its source. It is one of the *shibboleths* by which he
may be known. A thousand years hence, those who shall
live in America or in France will look back with contem-
plative pride on the origin of their governments, and say,
this was the work of our glorious ancestors! But what can a
monarchical talker say ? What has he to exult in ? Alas !
he has nothing. A certain something forbids him to look
back to a beginning, lest some robber or some Robin
Hood should rise from the long obscurity of time, and say,
I am the origin. Hard as Mr. Burke labored under the regency bill and hereditary succession two years ago, and
much as he dived for precedents, he still had not boldness
enough to bring up William of Normandy, and say, *there is
the head of the list, there is the fountain of honor,* the son of a
prostitute, and the plunderer of the English nation.

The opinions of men, with respect to government, are
changing fast in all countries. The revolutions of America and France have thrown a beam of light over the world,
which reaches into man. The enormous expense of governments have provoked people to think by making them
feel : and when once the veil begins to rend, it admits not
of repair. Ignorance is of a peculiar nature : once dispel-
led, it is impossible to re-establish it. It is not originally
a thing of itself, but is only the absence of knowledge ; and
though man may be *kept* ignorant, he cannot be *made* ignorant. The mind, in discovering truths, acts in the same
manner as it acts through the eye in discovering an object ;
when once any object has been seen, it is impossible to put
the mind back to the same condition it was in before it saw
it. Those who talk of a counter-revolution in France, show
how little they understand of man. There does not exist
in the compass of language, an arrangement of words to
express so much as the means of effecting a counter-revolution. The means must be an obliteration of knowledge :

and it has never yet been discovered how to make a man *unknow* his knowledge, or *unthink* his thoughts.

Mr. Burke is laboring in vain to stop the progress of knowledge ; and it comes with the worse grace from him, as there is a certain transaction known in the city, which renders him suspected of being a pensioner in a fictitious name. This may account for some strange doctrine he has advanced in his book, which, though he points it at the Revolution society, is effectually directed against the whole nation.

" The king of England," says he, " holds *his* crown (for it does not belong to the nation, according to Mr. Burke) in *contempt* of the choice of the Revolution society, who have not a single vote for a king among them either *individually* or *collectively ;* and his majesty's heirs, each in their time and order, will come to the crown *with the same contempt* of their choice, with which his majesty has succeeded to that which he now wears."

As to who is king in England or elsewhere, or whether there is any at all, or whether the people choose a Cherokee chief, or a Hessian hussar for a king, is not a matter that I trouble myself about, be that to themselves ; but with respect to the doctrine, so far as it relates to the rights of men and nations, it is as abominable as any thing ever uttered in the most enslaved country under heaven. Whether it sounds worse to my ear, by not being accustomed to hear such despotism, than it does to the ear of another person, I am not so well a judge of : but of its abominable principle, I am at no loss to judge.

It is not the Revolution society that Mr. Burke means ; it is the nation, as well in its *original,* as in its *representative* character ; and he has taken care to make himself understood, by saying that they have not a vote either *collectively* or *individually.* The Revolution society is composed of citizens of all denominations, and of members of both houses of parliament. and consequently. if there is not a right to vote in any of the characters, there can be no right to any, either in the nation or in its parliament. This ought to be a caution to every country, how it imports foreign families to be kings. It is somewhat curious to observe that although the people of England have been in the habit of talking about kings. it is always a foreign house of kings : hating foreigners yet governed by them. It is now the house of Brunswick, one of the petty tribes of Germany.

It has hitherto been the practice of the English parliaments, to regulate what was called the succession, (taking it for granted, that the nation then continued to accord to the form of annexing a monarchical branch to its government; for without this, the parliament could not have had authority to have sent either to Holland or to Hanover, or to impose a king upon the nation against its will.) And this must be the utmost limit to which parliament can go upon the case; but the right of the nation goes to the *whole* case, because it has the right of changing its *whole* form of government. The right of a parliament is only a right in trust, a right by delegation, and that but from a very small part of the nation; and one of its houses has not even this. But the right of the nation is an original right, as universal as taxation. The nation is the paymaster of every thing, and every thing must conform to its general will.

I remember taking notice of a speech in what is called the English house of peers, by the then earl of Shelburne, and I think it was at the time he was minister, which is applicable to this case. I do not directly charge my memory with every particular; but the words and the purport as nearly as I remember, were these: *that the form of government was a matter wholly at the will of a nation at all times: that if it chose a monarchical form, it had a right to have it so, and if it afterwards chose to be a republic, it had a right to be a republic, and to say to a king, we have no longer any occasion for you.*

When Mr. Burke says that " his majesty's heirs and successors, each in their time and order, will come to the crown with the same contempt of their choice with which his majesty has succeeded to that he wears," it is saying too much even to the humblest individual in the country; part of whose daily labor goes towards making up the million sterling a-year, which the country give a person it styles a king. Government with insolence, is despotism; but when contempt is added, it becomes worse; and to pay for contempt is the excess of slavery. This species of government comes from Germany; and reminds me of what one of the Brunswick soldiers told me, who was taken prisoner by the Americans in the late war; " Ah !" said he, "America is a fine free country, it is worth people's fighting for; I know the difference by knowing my own; in my country, "if the prince say, eat straw, we eat straw."—God help that country, thought I, be it England or elsewhere, whose liberties are to be protected by German principles of government and princes of Brunswick.

As Mr. Burke sometimes speaks of England, sometimes of France, and sometimes of the world, and of government in general, it is difficult to answer his book without apparently meeting him on the same ground. Although principles of government are general subjects, it is next to impossible in many cases to separate them from the idea of place and circumstance; and the more so when circumstances are put for arguments, which is frequently the case with Mr. Burke.

In the former part of his book, addressing himself to the people of France, he says, "no experience has taught us, (meaning the English) that in any other course or method than that of an *hereditary crown*, can our liberties be regularly perpetuated and preserved sacred as our *hereditary right*." I ask Mr. Burke who is to take them away? M. de la Fayette, in speaking of France, says, "*For a nation to be free, it is sufficient that she wills it.*" But Mr. Burke represents England as wanting capacity to take care of itself; and that its liberties must be taken care of by a king, holding it in "contempt." If England is sunk to this, it is preparing itself to eat straw, as in Hanover or in Brunswick. But besides the folly of the declaration, it happens that the facts are all against Mr. Burke. It was by the government *being hereditary*, that the liberties of the people were endangered. Charles I. and James II. are instances of this truth; yet neither of them went so far as to hold the nation in contempt.

As it is sometimes of advantage to the people of one country, to hear what those of other countries have to say respecting it, it is possible that the people of France may learn something from Mr. Burke's book, and that the people of England may also learn something from the answers it will occasion. When nations fall out about freedom, a wide field of debate is opened. The argument commences with the rights of war, without its evils; and as knowledge is the object contended for, the party that sustains the defeat obtains the prize.

Mr. Burke talks about what he calls an hereditary crown, as if it were some production of nature; or as if like time, it had power to operate not only independently, but in spite of man; or as if it were a thing or a subject universally consented to. Alas! it has none of those properties, but is the reverse of them all. It is a thing of imagination, the propriety of which is more than doubted, and the legality of which in a few years will be denied.

But, to arrange this matter in a clearer view than what general expressions can convey, it will be necessary to state the distinct heads under which (what is called) an hereditary crown, or, more properly speaking, an hereditary succession to the government of a nation, can be considered, which are,

1st, The right of a particular family to establish itself.

2d. The right of a nation to establish a particular family.

With respect to the *first* of these heads, that of a family establishing itself with hereditary powers on its own authority, and independent of the consent of a nation, all men will concur in calling it despotism; and it would be trespassing on their understanding to attempt to prove it.

But the *second* head, that of a nation establishing a particular family with *hereditary powers*, does not present itself as despotism on the first reflection; but if men will permit a second reflection to take place, and carry that reflection forward but one remove out of their own persons to that of their offspring, they will then see that hereditary succession becomes in its consequences the same despotism to others, which they reprobated for themselves. It operates to preclude the consent of the succeeding generation, and the preclusion of consent is despotism. When the person who at any time shall be in possession of a government, or those who stand in succession to him, shall say to a nation, I hold this power in " contempt " of you, it signifies not on what authority he pretends to say it. It is no relief, but an aggravation to a person in slavery, to reflect that he was sold by his parent; and as that which heightens the criminality of an act cannot be produced to prove the legality of it, hereditary succession cannot be established as a legal thing.

In order to arrive at a more perfect decision on this head it will be proper to consider the generation which undertakes to establish a family with *hereditary powers*, separately from the generations which are to follow; and also to consider the character in which the *first* generation acts with respect to succeeding generations.

The generation which first selects a person, and puts him at the head of its government, either with the title of king, or any other distinction, acts its *own choice*, be it wise or foolish, as a free agent for itself. The person so set up is not hereditary, but selected and appointed; and the generation who sets him up, does not live under an hereditary government, but under a government of its own choice and establishment. Were the generation who sets him up, and the person so set up, to live for ever, it never could become hereditary succession: hereditary succession can only follow on death of the first parties.

As therefore hereditary succession is out of the question with respect to the *first* generation, we have now to consider the character in which *that* generation acts with respect to the commencing generation, and to all succeeding ones.

It assumes a character, to which it has neither right nor title. It changes itself from a *legislator* to a *testator*, and affects to make its will, which is to have operation after the demise of the makers, to bequeath the government; and it not only attempts to bequeath, but to establish on the succeeding generation, a new and different form of government under which itself lived. Itself, as is before observed, lived not under an hereditary government, but under a government of its own choice and establishment; and it now attempts, by virtue of a will and testament (and which it has not authority to make) to take from the commencing generation, and all future ones, the rights and free agency by which itself acted.

But, exclusive of the right which any generation has to act collectively as a testator, the objects to which it applies itself in this case, are not within the compass of any law, or of any will or testament.

The rights of men in society, are neither devisable, nor transferrable, nor annihilable but are descendable only; and it is not in the power of any generation to intercept finally, and cut off the descent. If the present generation, or any other, are disposed to be slaves, it does not lessen the right of the succeeding generation to be free: wrongs cannot have a legal descent. When Mr. Burke attempts to maintain, that the *English nation did, at the revolution of* 1688, *most solemnly renounce and abdicate their rights for themselves, and for all their posterity for ever*, he speaks a language that merits not reply, and which can only excite contempt for his prostitute principles, or pity for his ignorance.

In whatever light hereditary succession, as growing out of the will and testament of some former generation, presents itself, it is an absurdity. A cannot make a will to take from B his property, and give it to C; yet this is the manner in which (what is called) hereditary succession by law, operates. A certain former generation made a will to take away the rights of the commencing generation and all future ones, and convey those rights to a third person, who afterwards comes forward, and tells them, in Mr. Burke's language, that they have *no rights*, that their rights are already bequeathed to him, and that he will govern in *contempt* of them. From such principles, and such ignorance, good Lord deliver the world !

But, after all, what is this metaphor, called a crown, or rather, what is monarchy? Is it a thing, or is it a name, or is it a fraud? Is it a "contrivance of human wisdom," or human craft, to obtain money from a nation under specious pretences? Is it a thing necessary to a nation? If it is, in what does that necessity consist, what service does it perform, what is its business, and what are its merits? Doth the virtue consist in the metaphor, or in the man? Doth the goldsmith that makes the crown, make the virtue also? Doth it operate like Fortunatus's wishing cap, or Harlequin's wooden sword? Doth it make a man a conjuror? In fine, what is it? It appears to be a something going much out of fashion, falling into ridicule, and rejected in some countries both as unnecessary and expensive. In America it is considered as an absurdity, and in France it has so far declined, that the goodness of the man, and the respect for his personal character, are the only things that preserve the appearance of its existence.

If government be what Mr. Burke describes it, "a contrivance of human wisdom," I might ask him, if wisdom was at such a low ebb in England, that it was become necessary to import it from Holland and from Hanover? But I will do the country the justice to say, that that was not the case ; and even if it was, it mistook the cargo. The wisdom of every country, when properly exerted, is sufficient for all its purposes : and there could exist no more real occasion in England to have sent for a Dutch stadtholder, or a German elector, than there was in America to have done a similar thing. If a country does not understand its own affairs, how is a foreigner to understand them, who knows neither its laws, its manners, nor its language? If there existed a man so transcendantly wise above all others, that his wisdom was necessary to instruct a nation, some reason might be offered for monarchy; but when we cast our eyes about a country, and observe how every part understands its own affairs; and when we look around the world, and see that of all men in it, the race of kings are the most insignificant in capacity, our reason cannot fail to ask us—What are those men kept for?

If there is any thing in monarchy which we people of America do not understand, I wish Mr. Burke would be so kind as to inform us. I see in America, a government extending over a country ten times as large as England, and conducted with regularity for a fortieth part of the expense which government costs in England. If I ask a man in America, if he wants a king, he retorts, and asks me if I take him for an ideot. How is it that this difference happens; are we more or less wise than others? I see in America, the generality of people living in a style of plenty unknown in monarchical countries; and I see that the principle of its government, which is that of the *equal rights of man*, is making a rapid progress in the world.

If monarchy is a useless thing, why is it kept up any where? And if a necessary thing, how can it be dispensed with? That *civil government* is necessary, all civilized nations will agree in; but civil government is republican government. All that part of the government of England which begins with the office of constable, and proceeds through the department of magistrate, quarter-session, and general assize, including the trial by jury, is republican government. Nothing of monarchy appears in any part of it, except the name which William the conqueror imposed upon the English, that of obliging them to call him " their sovereign lord the king."

It is easy to conceive, that a band of interested men, such as placemen, pensioners, lords of the bed-chamber, lords of the kitchen, lords of the necessary-house, and the Lord knows what besides, can find as many reasons for monarchy as their salaries, paid at the expense of the country, amount to; but if I ask the farmer, the manufacturer, the merchant, the tradesman, and down through all the occupations of life to the common laborer, what service monarchy is to him, he can give me no answer. If I ask him what monarchy is, he believes it is something like a sinecure.

Notwithstanding the taxes of England amount to almost seventeen millions a-year, said to be for the expenses of government, it is still evident that the sense of the nation is left to govern itself, and does govern itself by magistrates and juries, almost at its own charge, on republican principles, exclusive of the expense of taxes. The salaries of the judges are almost the only charge that is paid out of the revenue. Considering that all the internal government is executed by the people, the taxes of England ought to be the lightest of any nation in Europe; instead of which, they are the contrary. As this cannot be accounted for on the score of civil government, the subject necessarily extends itself to the monarchical part.

When the people of England sent for George I. (and it would puzzle a wiser man than Mr. Burke to discover for what he could be wanted, or what service he could render) they ought at least to have conditioned for the abandonment of Hanover. Besides the endless German intrigues that must follow from a German elector's being king of England, there is a natural impossibility of uniting in the same person the principles of freedom and the principles of despotism, or, as it is called in England, arbitrary power. A German elector is, in his electorate, a despot: how then could it be expected that he should be attached to principles of liberty in one country, while his interest in another was to be supported by despotism? The union cannot exist: and it might easily have been foreseen, that German electors would make German kings, or in Mr. Burke's words, would assume government with "contempt." The English have been in the habit of considering a king of England only in the character in which he appears to them: whereas the same person, while the connexion lasts, has a home-seat in another country, the interest of which is at variance with their own, and the principles of the government in opposition to each other. To such a person England will appear as a town-residence, and the electorate as the estate. The English may wish, as I believe they do, success to the principles of liberty in France, or in Germany; but a German elector trembles for the fate of despotism in his electorate; and the duchy of Mecklenburg, where the present queen's family governs, is under the same wretched state of arbitrary power, and the people in slavish vassalage.

There never was a time when it became the English to watch continental intrigues more circumspectly than at the present moment, and to distinguish the politics of the electorate from the politics of the nation. The revolution of France has entirely changed the ground with respect to England and France, as nations : but the German despots, with Prussia at their head, are combining against liberty ; and the fondness of Mr. Pitt for office, and the interest which all his family connexions have obtained, do not give sufficient security against this intrigue.

As every thing which passes in the world becomes matter for history, I will now quit this subject, and take a concise review of the state of parties and politics in England, as Mr. Burke has done in France.

Whether the present reign commenced with contempt, I leave to Mr. Burke : certain however it is, that it had strongly that appearance. The animosity of the English nation, it is very well remembered, ran high ; and, had the true principles of liberty been as well understood then as they now promise to be, it is probable the nation would not have patiently submitted to so much. George I. and II. were sensible of a rival in the remains of the Stuarts : and as they could not but consider themselves as standing on their good behaviour, they had prudence to keep their German principles of government to themselves ; but as the Stuart family wore away, the prudence became less necessary.

The contest between rights, and what were called prerogatives, continued to heat the nation till some time after the conclusion of the American revolution, when all at once it fell a calm ; execration exchanged itself for applause, and court popularity sprung up like a mushroom in the night.

To account for this sudden transition, it is proper to observe, that there are two distinct species of popularity ; the one excited by merit, the other by resentment. As the nation had formed itself into two parties, and each was extolling the merits of its parliamentary champions for and against the prerogative, nothing could operate to give a more general shock than an immediate coalition of the champions themselves. The partisans of each being thus suddenly left in the lurch, and mutually heated with disgust at the measure, felt no other relief than uniting in a common execration against both. A higher stimulus of resentment

being thus excited, than what the contest on prerogatives
had occasioned, the nation quitted all former objects of
rights and wrongs, and sought only that of gratification.—
The indignation at the coalition, so effectually superseded
the indignation against the court, as to extinguish it; and
without any change of principles on the part of the court.
the same people who had reprobated its despotism, united
with it, to revenge themselves on the coalition parliament.
The case was not, which they liked best—but, which they
hated most; and the least hated passed for love. The
dissolution of the coalition parliament, as it afforded the
means of gratifying the resentment of the nation, could not
fail to be popular; and from hence arose the popularity
of the court.

Transitions of this kind exhibit to us a nation under the
government of temper, instead of a fixed and steady principle: and having once committed itself, however rashly,
it feels itself urged along to justify by continuance its first
proceeding. Measures which at other times it would censure, it now approves, and acts persuasion upon itself to
suffocate its judgment.

On the return of a new parliament, the new minister,
Mr. Pitt, found himself in a secure majority: and the nation gave him credit, not out of regard to himself, but because it had resolved to do it out of resentment to another.
He introduced himself to public notice by a proposed reform of parliament, which in its operation would have
amounted to a public justification of corruption. The nation was to be at the expense of buying up the rotten boroughs, whereas it ought to punish the persons who deal in
the traffic.

Passing over the two bubbles, of the Dutch business, and
the million a-year to sink the national debt, the matter
which is most prominent, is the affair of the regency.
Never in the course of my observation, was delusion more
successfully acted, nor a nation more completely deceived.
But, to make this appear, it will be necessary to go over
the circumstances.

Mr. Fox had stated in the house of commons, that the
prince of Wales, as heir in succession, had a right in himself to assume the government. This was opposed by Mr.
Pitt; and, so far as the opposition was confined to the doctrine, it was just. But the principles which Mr. Pitt maintained on the contrary side, were as bad, or worse in their

extent, than those of Mr. Fox; because they went to establish an aristocracy over the nation, and over the small representation it has in the house of commons.

Whether the English form of government be good or bad, is not in this case the question; but, taking it as it stands, without regard to its merits or demerits, Mr. Pitt was further from the point than Mr. Fox.

It is supposed to consist of three parts; while, therefore, the nation is disposed to continue this form, the parts have a *national standing*, independent of each other, and are not the creatures of each other. Had Mr. Fox passed through parliament, and said, that the person alluded to claimed on the ground of the nation, Mr. Pitt must then have contended for (what he called) the right of the parliament, against the right of the nation.

By the appearance which the contest made, Mr. Fox took the hereditary ground; and Mr. Pitt the parliamentary ground, but the fact is, they both took hereditary ground, and Mr. Pitt took the worst of the two.

What is called the parliament, is made up of two houses; one of which is more hereditary, and more beyond the control of the nation, than what the crown (as it is called) is supposed to be. It is an hereditary aristocracy, assuming and asserting indefeasible, irrevocable rights and authority, wholly independent of the nation. Where then was the merited popularity of exalting this hereditary power over another hereditary power less independent of the nation than what itself assumed to be, and of absorbing the rights of the nation into a house over which it has neither election nor control?

The general impulse of the nation was right; but it acted without reflection. It approved the opposition made to the right set up by Mr. Fox, without perceiving that Mr. Pitt was supporting another indefeasible right more remote from the nation, in opposition to it.

With respect to the house of commons, it is elected but by a small part of the nation; but were the election as universal as taxation, which it ought to be, it would still be only the organ of the nation, and cannot possess inherent rights. When the national assembly of France resolves a matter, the resolve is made in right of the nation; but Mr. Pitt, on all national questions, so far as they refer to the house of commons, absorbs the rights of the nation into the organ, and makes the organ into a nation, and the nation itself into a cypher.

In a few words, the question on the regency was a question on a million a-year, which is appropriated to the executive department: and Mr. Pitt could not possess himself of any management of this sum, without setting up the supremacy of parliament; and when this was accomplished, it was indifferent who should be regent, as he must be regent at his own cost. Among the curiosities which this contentious debate afforded, was that of making the great seal into a king; the affixing of which to an act, was to be royal authority. If, therefore, royal authority is a great seal, it consequently is in itself nothing; and a good constitution would be of infinitely more value to the nation, than what the three nominal powers, as they now stand are worth.

The continual use of the word *constitution* in the English parliament, shows there is none; and that the whole is merely a form of government without a constitution, and constituting itself with what powers it pleases. If there was a constitution, it certainly would be referred to; and the debate on any constitutional point, would terminate by producing the constitution. One member says, this is constitutional? another says, that is constitutional—To-day it is one thing; and to-morrow, it is something else—while the maintaining the debate proves there is none. Constitution is now the cant word of parliament, turning itself to the ear of the nation. Formerly it was the *universal supremacy and the omnipotence of parliament*. But, since the progress of liberty in France, those phrases have a despotic harshness in their note; and the English parliament has caught the fashion from the national assembly, but without the substance, of speaking of *a constitution*.

As the present generation of people in England did not make the government, they are not accountable for any of its defects; but that sooner or later it must come into their hands to undergo a constitutional reformation, is as certain as that the same thing has happened in France. If France, with a revenue of nearly twenty-four millions sterling, with an extent of rich and fertile country above four times larger than England, with a population of twenty-four millions of inhabitants to support taxation, with upwards of ninety millions sterling of gold and silver circulating in the nation, and with a debt less than the present debt of England—still found it necessary, from whatever cause, to come to a settlement of its affairs, it solves the problem of funding for both countries.

It is out of the question to say how long, what is called the English constitution, has lasted, and to argue from thence how long it is to last; the question is, how long can the funding system last? It is a thing but of modern invention, and has not yet continued beyond the life of a man; yet in that short space it has so far accumulated, that, together with the current expenses, it requires an amount of taxes at least equal to the whole landed rental of the nation in acres, to defray the annual expenditures. That a government could not always have gone on by the same system which has been followed for the last seventy years, must be evident to every man; and for the same reason it cannot always go on.

The funding system is not money; neither is it, properly speaking, credit. It in effect, creates upon paper the sum which it appears to borrow, and lays on a tax to keep the imaginary capital alive by the payment of interest, and sends the annuity to market, to be sold for paper already in circulation. If any credit is given, it is to the disposition of the people to pay the tax, and not to the government which lays it on. When this disposition expires, what is supposed to be the credit of government expires with it. The instance of France under the former government shows that it is impossible to compel the payment of taxes by force, when a whole nation is determined to take its stand upon that ground.

Mr. Burke, in his review of the finances of France, states the quantity of gold and silver in France, at about eighty-eight millions sterling. In doing this he has, I presume, divided by the difference of exchange, instead of the standard of twenty-four livres to a pound sterling; for M. Neckar's statement, from which Mr. Burke's is taken, is *two thousand two hundred millions of livres*, which is upwards of ninety-one millions and an half sterling.

M. Neckar in France, and Mr. George Chalmers of the office of trade and plantation in England, of which lord Hawkesbury is president, published nearly about the same time (1786) an account of the quantity of money in each nation, from the returns of the mint of each nation. Mr. Chalmers from the returns of the English mint at the Tower of London, states the quantity of money in England, including Scotland and Ireland, to be twenty millions sterling.*

M. Neckar† says, that the amount of money in France, recoined from the old coin which was called in, was two thousand five hundred millions of livres (upwards of one hundred and four millions sterling,) and, after deducting for waste, and what may be in the West-Indies, and other possible circumstances, states the circulating quantity at home, to be ninety-one millions and an half sterling; but, taking it as Mr. Burke has put it, it is sixty-eight millions more than the national quantity in England.

That the quantity of money in France cannot be under this sum, may at once be seen from the state of the French revenue, without referring to the records of the French mint for proofs. The revenue of France prior to the revolution, was nearly twenty-four millions sterling; and as paper had then no existence in France, the whole revenue was collected upon gold and silver; and it would have been impossible to have collected such a quantity of revenue upon a less national quantity than M. Neckar has stated. Before the establishment of paper in England, the revenue was about a fourth part of the national amount of gold and silver, as may be known by referring to the revenue prior to king William, and the quantity of money stated to be in the nation at that time, which was nearly as much as it is now.

It can be of no real service to a nation, to impose upon itself, or to permit itself to be imposed upon ; but the prejudices of some, and the imposition of others, have always represented France as a nation possessing but little money, whereas the quantity is not only more than four times what the quantity is in England, but is considerably greater on a proportion of numbers. To account for this deficiency on the part of England, some reference should be had to the English system of funding. It operates to multiply paper, and to substitute it in the room of money, in various shapes ; and the more paper is multiplied, the more opportunities are afforded to export the specie ; and it admits of a possibility (by extending it to small notes) of increasing paper, till there is no money left.

* See Estimate of the Comparative Strength of Great Britain, by Geo. Chalmers.

† See Administration of the Finances of France, vol. iii. by M. Neckar.

I know this is not a pleasant subject to English readers; but the matters I am going to mention, are so important in themselves, as to require the attention of men interested in money transactions of a public nature. There is a circumstance stated by M. Neckar, in his treatise on the administration of the finances, which has never been attended to in England, but which forms the only basis whereon to estimate the quantity of money (gold and silver) which ought to be in every nation in Europe, to preserve a relative proportion with other nations.

Lisbon and Cadiz are the two ports into which (money) gold and silver from South America are imported, and which afterwards divides and spreads itself over Europe by means of commerce, and increases the quantity of money in all parts of Europe. If, therefore, the amount of the annual importation into Europe can be known, and the relative proportion of the foreign commerce of the several nations by which it is distributed can be ascertained, they give a rule, sufficiently true, to ascertain the quantity of money which ought to be found in any nation at any given time.

M. Neckar shows from the registers of Lisbon and Cadiz, that the importation of gold and silver into Europe, is five millions sterling annually. He has not taken it on a single year, but on an average of fifteen succeeding years, from 1763, to 1777, both inclusive; in which time, the amount was one thousand eight hundred million livres, which is seventy-five millions sterling.*

From the commencement of the Hanover succession in 1714, to the time Mr. Chalmers published, is seventy-two years; and the quantity imported into Europe, in that time, would be three hundred and sixty millions sterling.

If the foreign commerce of Great Britain be stated at a sixth part of what the whole foreign commerce of Europe amounts to (which is probably an inferior estimation to what the gentlemen at the exchange would allow) the proportion which Britain should draw by commerce, of this sum, to keep herself on a proportion with the rest of Europe, would be also a sixth part, which is sixty millions sterling; and if the same allowance for waste and accident be made for England, which M. Neckar makes for France, the quantity remaining after these deductions, would be

* Administration of the Finances of France, vol. iii.

fifty-two millions, and this sum ought to have been in the nation (at the time Mr. Chalmers published) in addition to the sum which was in the nation at the commencement of the Hanover succession, and to have made in the whole at least sixty-six millions sterling; instead of which there were but twenty millions, which is forty-six millions below its proportionate quantity.

As the quantity of gold and silver, imported into Lisbon and Cadiz is more easily ascertained than that of any commodity imported into England; and as the quantity of money coined at the Tower of London, is still more positively known, the leading facts do not admit of a controversy. Either, therefore, the commerce of England is unproductive of profit, or the gold and silver which it brings in, leak continually away by unseen means, at the average rate of about three quarters of a million a-year, which in the course of seventy-two years, accounts for the deficiency; and its absence is supplied by paper.*

* Whether the English commerce does not bring in money, or whether the government sends it out after it is brought in, is a matter which the parties concerned can best explain: but that the deficiency exists, is not in the power of either to disprove. While Dr. Price, Mr. Eden, (now Auckland) Mr. Chalmers, and others, were debating whether the quantity of money was greater or less than at the revolution, the circumstance was not adverted to, that since the revolution, there cannot have been less than four hundred millions sterling imported into Europe: and therefore the quantity in England ought at least to have been four times greater than it was at the revolution, to be on a proportion with Europe. What England is now doing by paper, is what she should have been able to do by solid money, if gold and silver had come into the nation in the proportion it ought, or had not been sent out; and she is endeavoring to restore by paper, the balance she has lost by money. It is certain, that the gold and silver which arrive annually in the register-ships to Spain and Portugal, do not remain in those countries. Taking the value half in gold and half in silver, it is about four hundred tons annually: and from the number of ships and galleons employed in the trade of bringing those metals from South-America to Portugal and Spain, the quantity sufficiently proves itself, without referring to the registers.

In the situation England now is, it is impossible she can increase in money. High taxes not only lessen the property of the individuals but they lessen also the money capital of the nation, by inducing smuggling, which can only be carried on by gold and silver. By the politics which the British government have carried on with the inland powers of Germany and the continent, it has made an enemy of all the maritime powers, and is therefore obliged to keep up a large navy: but though the navy is built in England, the naval stores must be purchased from abroad, and that from countries where the greatest part must be paid for in gold and silver. Some fallacious rumors have been set afloat in England to induce a belief of money, and, among others, that of the French refugees bringing great quantities. The idea is ridiculous. The general part of the money in France is silver; and it would take upwards of twenty of the largest broad wheel wagons, with ten horses each, to remove one million sterling of silver. Is it then to be supposed, that a few people fleeing on horseback or in post-chaises, in a secret manner, and having the French custom-house to pass, and the sea to cross, could bring even a sufficiency for their own expenses?

The revolution of France is attended with many novel circumstances, not only in the political sphere, but in the circle of money transactions. Among others, it shows that a government may be in a state of insolvency, and a nation rich. So far as the fact is confined to the late government of France, it was insolvent; because the nation would no longer support its extravagance, and therefore it could no longer support itself—but with respect to the nation all the means existed. A government may be said to be insolvent every time it applies to a nation to discharge its arrears. The insolvency of the late government of France, and the present government of England, differed in no other respect than as the disposition of the people differ. The people of France refused their aid to the old government, and the people of England submit to taxation without inquiry. What is called the crown in England has been insolvent several times; the last of which, publicly known, was in May 1777, when it applied to the nation to discharge upwards of 600,000l. private debts, which otherwise it could not pay.

It was the error of Mr. Pitt, Mr. Burke, and all those who were unacquainted with the affairs of France, to confound the French nation with the French government. The French nation in effect, endeavored to render the late government insolvent, for the purpose of taking government into its own hands; and it reserved its means for the support of the new government. In a country of such vast extent and population as France, the natural means cannot be wanting; and the political means appear the instant the nation is disposed to permit them. When Mr. Burke, in a speech last winter in the British parliament, *cast his eyes over the map of Europe, and saw a chasm that once was France,* he talked like a dreamer of dreams. The same natural France existed as before, and all the natural means existed with it. The only chasm was that which the extinction of despotism had left, and which was to be filled

---

When millions of money are spoken of, it should be recollected, that such sums can only accumulate in a country by slow degrees, and a long procession of time. The most frugal system that England could now adopt, would not recover in a century the balance she has lost in money since the commencement of the Hanover succession. She is seventy millions behind France, and she must be in some considerable proportion behind every country in Europe, because the returns of the English mint do not show an increase of money, while the registers of Lisbon and Cadiz show an European increase of between three and four hundred millions sterling.

up with a constitution more formidable in resources than the power which had expired.

Although the French nation rendered the late government insolvent, it did not permit the insolvency to act towards the creditors; and the creditors considering the nation as the real paymaster, and the government only as the agent, rested themselves on the nation, in preference to the government. This appears greatly to disturb Mr. Burke, as the precedent is fatal to the policy by which governments have supposed themselves secure. They have contracted debts, with a view of attaching what is called the monied interest of a nation to their support; but the example in France shows, that the permanent security of the creditor is in the nation, and not in the government; and that in all possible revolutions that may happen in governments, the means are always with the nation, and the nation always in existence. Mr. Burke argues, that the creditors ought to have abided the fate of the government which they trusted; but the national assembly considered them as the creditors of the nation, and not of the government— of the master, and not of the steward.

Notwithstanding the late government could not discharge the current expenses, the present government has paid off a great part of the capital. This has been accomplished by two means; the one by lessening the expenses of government, and the other by the sale of the monastic and ecclesiastical landed estates. The devotees and penitent debauchees, extortioners and misers of former days, to ensure themselves a better world than that they were about to leave, had bequeathed immense property in trust to the priesthood for *pious uses;* and the priesthood kept it for themselves. The national assembly has ordered it to be sold for the good of the whole nation, and the priesthood to be decently provided for.

In consequence of the revolution, the annual interest of the debt of France will be reduced at least six millions sterling, by paying off upwards of one hundred millions of the capital; which, with lessening the former expenses of government at least three millions, will place France in a situation worthy the imitation of Europe.

Upon a whole review of the subject, how vast is the contrast! While Mr. Burke has been talking of a general bankruptcy in France, the national assembly have been paying off the capital of the national debt; and while taxes have increased near a million a-year in England, they have lowered several millions a-year in France. Not a word has either Mr. Burke or Mr. Pitt said about French affairs, or the state of the French finances, in the present session of parliament. The subject begins to be too well understood, and imposition serves no longer.

There is a general enigma running through the whole of Mr. Burke's book. He writes in a rage against the national assembly; but what is he enraged about? If his assertions were as true as they are groundless, and if France by her revolution had annihilated her power, and become what he calls a *chasm*, it might excite the grief of a Frenchman (considering himself as a national man) and provoke his rage against the national assembly; but why should it excite the rage of Mr. Burke? Alas! it is not the nation of France that Mr. Burke means, but the *court;* and every court in Europe, dreading the same fate, is in mourning. He writes neither in the character of a Frenchman nor an Englishman, but in the fawning character of that creature, known in all countries, as a friend to none, a *courtier*. Whether it be the court of Versailles, or the court of St. James or of Carlton-house, or the court in expectation, signifies not; for the caterpillar principles of all courts and courtiers are alike. They form a common policy throughout Europe, detached and separate from the interest of the nations, and while they appear to quarrel, they agree to plunder. Nothing can be more terrible to a court or a courtier, than the revolution of France. That which is a blessing to nations, is bitterness to them; and as their existence depends on the duplicity of a country, they tremble at the approach of principles, and dread the precedent that threatens their overthrow.

CONCLUSION.

Reason and ignorance, the opposites of each other, influence the great bulk of mankind. If either of these can be rendered sufficiently extensive in a country, the machinery of government goes easily on. Reason shows itself, and ignorance submits to whatever is dictated to it.

The two modes of government which prevail in the world, are, 1st, government by election and representation : 2d, government by hereditary succession. The former is generally known by the name of republic; the latter by that of monarchy and aristocracy.

Those two distinct and opposite forms, erect themselves on the two distinct and opposite bases of reason and ignorance. As the exercise of government requires talents and abilities, and as talents and abilities cannot have hereditary descent, it is evident that hereditary succession requires a belief from man, to which his reason cannot subscribe, and which can only be established upon his ignorance ; and the more ignorant any country is, the better it is fitted for this species of government.

On the contrary, government in a well constituted republic, requires no belief from man beyond what his reason authorizes. He sees the *rationale* of the whole system, its origin and its operation; and as it is best supported when best understood, the human faculties act with boldness, and acquire, under this form of government, a gigantic manliness.

As, therefore, each of those forms acts on a different basis, the one moving freely by the aid of reason, the other by ignorance; we have next to consider, what it is that gives motion to that species of government which is called mixed government, or, as it is sometimes ludicrously styled, a government of *this, that, and t'other.*

The moving power in this species of government is, of necessity, corruption. However imperfect election and representation may be in mixed governments, they still give exertion to a greater portion of reason than is convenient to the hereditary part ; and therefore it becomes necessary to buy the reason up. A mixed government is an imperfect every-thing, cementing and soldering the discordant parts together by corruption, to act as a whole. Mr. Burke appears highly disgusted, that France, since she had resolved on a revolution, did not adopt what he calls " a British constitution;" and the regret which he expresses on this occasion, implies a suspicion, that the British constitution needed something to keep its defects in countenance.

In mixed governments there is no responsibility ; the parts cover each other till responsibility is lost ; and the corruption which moves the machine, contrives at the same

time its own escape. When it is laid down as a maxim,
that *a king can do no wrong*, it places him in a state of similar security with that of idiots and persons insane, and responsibility is out of the question with respect to himself.
It then descends upon the minister, who shelters himself
under a majority in parliament, which, by places, pensions,
and corruption, he can always command; and that majority justifies itself by the same authority with which it protects the minister. In this rotatory motion, responsibility
is thrown off from the parts, and from the whole.

When there is a part in a government which can do no
wrong, it implies that it does nothing; and is only the machine of another power, by whose advice and direction it
acts. What is supposed to be the king, in mixed governments, is the cabinet; and as the cabinet is always a part
of the parliament, and the members justifying in one character what they act in another, a mixed government becomes a continual enigma; entailing upon a country, by
the quantity of corruption necessary to solder the parts,
the expense of supporting all the forms of government at
once, and finally resolving itself into a government by committee; in which the advisers, the actors, the approvers,
the justifiers, the persons responsible, and the persons not
responsible, are the same persons.

By this pantomimical contrivance, and change of scene
and character, the parts help each other out in matters,
which, neither of them singly, would presume to act.
When money is to be obtained, the mass of variety apparently dissolves, and a profusion of parliamentary praises
passes between the parts. Each admires, with astonishment, the wisdom, the liberality and disinterestedness of
the other; and all of them breathe a pitying sigh at the
burdens of the nation.

But in a well-conditioned republic, nothing of this soldering, praising, and pitying, can take place; the representation being equal throughout the country, and complete in itself, however it may be arranged into legislative
and executive, they have all one and the same natural
source. The parts are not foreigners to each other, like
democracy, aristocracy and monarchy. As there are no
discordant distinctions, there is nothing to corrupt by compromise, nor confound by contrivance. Public measures
appeal of themselves to the understanding of the nation,
and, resting on their own merits, disown any flattering

application to vanity. The continual whine of lamenting
the burden of taxes, however successfully it may be practised in mixed governments, is inconsistent with the sense
and spirit of a republic. If taxes are necessary, they are
of course advantageous; but if they require an apology,
the apology itself implies an impeachment. Why then is
man thus imposed upon, or why does he impose upon himself ?

When men are spoken of as kings and subjects, or when
government is mentioned under distinct or combined heads
of monarchy, aristocracy, and democracy, what is it that
reasoning man is to understand by the terms? If there really
existed in the world two more distinct and separate *elements*
of human power, we should then see the several origins to
which those terms would descriptively apply : but as there
is but one species of man, there can be but one element of
human power, and that element is man himself. Monarchy, aristocracy and democracy are but creatures of imagination; and a thousand such may be contrived as well
as three.

. . . .

From the revolutions of America and France, and the
symptoms that have appeared in other countries, it is evident that the opinion of the world is changing with respect
to systems of government, and that revolutions are not
within the compass of political calculations. The progress
of time and circumstances, which men assign to the accom-
plishment of great changes, is too mechanical to measure
the force of the mind, and the rapidity of reflection, by
which revolutions are generated : all the old governments
have received a shock from those that already appear, and
which were once more improbable, and are a greater subject of wonder, than a general revolution in Europe would
be now.

When we survey the wretched condition of man under
the monarchical and hereditary systems of government,
dragged from his home by one power, or driven by another, and impoverished by taxes more than by enemies,
it becomes evident that those systems are bad, and that a
general revolution in the principle and construction of governments is necessary.

What is government more than the management of the affairs of a nation? It is not, and from its nature cannot be, the property of any particular man or family, but of the whole community, at whose expense it is supported; and though by force or contrivance it has been usurped into an inheritance, the usurpation cannot alter the right of things. Sovereignty, as a matter of right, appertains to the nation only, and not to any individual; and a nation has at all times an inherent, indefeasible right to abolish any form of government it finds inconvenient, and establish such as accords with its interest, disposition and happiness. The romantic and barbarous distinctions of men into kings and subjects, though it may suit the condition of courtiers cannot that of citizens; and is exploded by the principle upon which governments are now founded. Every citizen is a member of the sovereignty, and as such, can acknowledge no personal subjection; and his obedience can be only to the laws.

When men think of what government is, they must necessarily suppose it to possess a knowledge of all the objects and matters upon which its authority is to be exercised. In this view of government, the republican system, as established by America and France, operates to embrace the whole of a nation; and the knowledge necessary to the interest of all the parts, is to be found in the centre, which the parts by representation form: but the old governments are on a construction that excludes knowledge as well as happiness; government by monks, who know nothing of the world beyond the walls of a convent, is as consistent as government by kings.

What were formerly called revolutions, were little more than a change of persons, or an alteration of local circumstances. They rose and fell like things of course, and had nothing in their existence or their fate that could influence beyond the spot that produced them. But what we now see in the world, from the revolutions of America and France, are a renovation of the natural order of things, a system of principles as universal as truth and the existence of man, and combining moral with political happiness and national prosperity.

"I. Men are born and always continue free and equal in respect to their rights. Civil distinctions, therefore, can be founded only on public utility.

"II. The end of all political associations is the preservation of the natural and imprescriptible rights of man, and these rights are liberty, property, security and resistance of oppression.

"III. The nation is essentially the source of all sovereignty; nor can any individual, or any body of men, be entitled to any authority which is not expressly derived from it."

In these principles there is nothing to throw a nation into confusion, by inflaming ambition. They are calculated to call forth wisdom and abilities, and to exercise them for the public good, and not for the emolument or aggrandizement of particular descriptions of men or families. Monarchical sovereignty, the enemy of mankind and the source of misery, is abolished; and sovereignty itself is restored to its natural and original place, the nation.— Were this the case throughout Europe, the cause of wars would be taken away.

It is attributed to Henry IV. of France, a man of an enlarged and benevolent heart, that he proposed, about the year 1620, a plan for abolishing war in Europe. The plan consisted in constituting an European congress, or, as the French authors style it, a pacific republic; by appointing delegates from the several nations, who were to act, as a court of arbitration, in any disputes that might arise between nation and nation.

Had such a plan been adopted at the time it was proposed, the taxes of England and France, as two of the parties, would have been at least ten millions sterling annually, to each nation, less than they were at the commencement of the French revolution.

To conceive a cause why such a plan has not been adopted (and that instead of a congress for the purpose of preventing war, it has been called only to *terminate* a war, after a fruitless expense of several years) it will be necessary to consider the interest of governments as a distinct interest to that of nations.

Whatever is the cause of taxes to a nation, becomes also the means of revenue to a government. Every war terminates with an addition of taxes, and consequently with an addition of revenue; and in any event of war, in the manner they are now commenced and concluded, the power and interest of governments are increased. War, therefore, from its productiveness, as it easily furnishes the pretence of necessity for taxes and appointments to places and offices, becomes the principal part of the system of old governments; and to establish any mode to abolish war, however advantageous it might be to nations, would be to take from such government the most lucrative of its branches. The frivolous matters upon which war is made, show the disposition and avidity of governments to uphold the system of war, and betray the motives upon which they act.

Why are not republics plunged into war, but because the nature of their government does not admit of an interest distinct from that of the nation? Even Holland, though an ill-constructed republic, and with a commerce extending over the world, existed nearly a century without war: and the instant the form of government was changed in France, the republican principles of peace, and domestic prosperity and economy, arose with the new government; and the same consequences would follow the same causes in other nations.

As war is the system of government on the old construction, the animosity which nations reciprocally entertain, is nothing more than what the policy of their governments excite, to keep up the spirit of the system. Each government accuses the other of perfidy, intrigue and ambition, as a means of heating the imagination of their respective nations, and incensing them to hostilities. Man is not the enemy of man, but through the medium of a false system of government. Instead therefore of exclaiming against the ambition of kings, the exclamation should be directed against the principle of such governments; and instead of seeking to reform the individual, the wisdom of a nation should apply itself to reform the system.

Whether the forms and maxims of governments which are still in practice, were adapted to the condition of the world at the period they were established, is not in this case the question. The older they are the less correspondence can they have with the present state of things. Time, and change of circumstances and opinions have the same progressive effect in rendering modes of government obsolete, as they have upon customs and manners. Agriculture, commerce, manufactures and the tranquil arts, by which the prosperity of nations is best promoted, require a different system of government, and a different species of knowledge to direct its operations, to what might have been the former condition of the world.

As it is not difficult to perceive, from the enlightened state of mankind, that hereditary governments are verging to their decline, and that revolutions on the broad basis of national sovereignty, and government by representation, are making their way in Europe, it would be an act of wisdom to anticipate their approach, and produce revolutions by reason and accommodation, rather than commit them to the issue of convulsions.

From what we now see, nothing of reform in the political world ought to be held improbable. It is an age of revolutions, in which every thing may be looked for. The intrigue of courts, by which the system of war is kept up, may provoke a confederation of nations to abolish it : and an European congress to patronize the progress of free government, and promote the civilization of nations with each other is an event nearer in probability, than once were the revolutions and alliance of France and America.

RIGHTS OF MAN.

PART II.

COMBINING PRINCIPLES AND PRACTICE.

TO M. DE LA FAYETTE.

AFTER an acquaintance of nearly fifteen years, in difficult situations in America, and various consultations in Europe, I feel a pleasure in presenting you this small treatise, in gratitude for your services to my beloved America, and as a testimony of my esteem for the virtues, public and private, which I know you to possess.

The only point upon which I could ever discover that we differed, was not as to principles of government, but as to time. For my own part, I think it equally as injurious to good principles to permit them to linger, as to push them on too fast. That which you suppose accomplishable in fourteen or fifteen years, I may believe practicable in a much shorter period. Mankind, as it appears to me, are always ripe enough to understand their true interest, provided it be presented clearly to their understanding, and that in a manner not to create suspicion by any thing like self-design, nor to offend by assuming too much. Where we would wish to reform we must not reproach.

When the American revolution was established, I felt a disposition to sit serenely down and enjoy the calm. It did not appear to me that any object could afterwards arise great enough to make me quit tranquillity, and feel as I had felt before. But when principle, and not place, is the energetic cause of action, a man, I find, is every where the same.

I am now once more in the public world; and as I have
not a right to contemplate on so many years of remaining
life as you have, I am resolved to labor as fast as I can;
and as I am anxious for your aid and your company, I
wish you to hasten your principles and overtake me.

If you make a campaign the ensuing spring, which it is
most probable there will be no occasion for, I will come
and join you. Should the campaign commence, I hope it
will terminate in the extinction of German despotism, and
in establishing the freedom of all Germany. When France
shall be surrounded with revolutions, she will be in peace
and safety, and her taxes, as well as those of Germany,
will consequently become less.

Your sincere,

Affectionate friend,

THOMAS PAINE.

London, Feb. 9, 1792.

PREFACE.

WHEN I began the chapter entitled the *Conclusion*, in the former part of the Rights of Man, published last year, it was my intention to have extended it to a greater length; but in casting the whole matter in my mind which I wished to add, I found that I must either make the work too bulky, or contract my plan too much. I therefore brought it to a close as soon as the subject would admit, and reserved what I had further to say to another opportunity.

Several other reasons contributed to produce this determination. I wished to know the manner in which a work, written in a style of thinking and expression at variance with what had been customary in England, would be received before I proceeded further. A great field was opening to the view of mankind by means of the French revolution. Mr. Burke's outrageous opposition thereto brought the controversy into England. He attacked principles which he knew (from information) I would contest with him, because they are principles I believe to be good and which I have contributed to establish, and conceive myself bound to defend. Had he not urged the controversy, I had most probably been a silent man.

Another reason for deferring the remainder of the work was, that Mr. Burke promised in his first publication to renew the subject at another opportunity, and to make a comparison of what he called the English and French constitutions. I therefore held myself in reserve for him. He has published two works since, without doing this;

which he certainly would not have omitted, had the comparison been in his favor.

In his last work, his " Appeal from the New to the Old Whigs," he has quoted about ten pages from the Rights of Man, and having given himself the trouble of doing this, says, " he shall not attempt in the smallest degree to refute them," meaning the principles therein contained. I am enough acquainted with Mr. Burke, to know, that he would if he could. But instead of contesting them, he immediately after consoles himself with saying that " he has done his part."—He has not done his part. He has not performed his promise of a comparison of constitutions. He started a controversy, he gave the challenge, and has fled from it ; and he is now a *case in point* with his own opinion that " *the age of chivalry is gone !*"

The title, as well as the substance of his last work, his Appeal, is his condemnation. Principles must rest on their own merits, and if they are good they certainly will. To put them under the shelter of other men's authority, as Mr. Burke has done, serves to bring them into suspicion. Mr. Burke is not very fond of dividing his honors, but in this case he is artfully dividing the disgrace.

But who are those to whom Mr. Burke has appealed ? A set of childish thinkers and half-way politicians born in the last century ; men who went no further with any principle than as it suited their purpose as a party ; the nation sees nothing in such works, or such politics worthy its attention. A little matter will move a party, but it must be something great that moves a nation.

Though I see nothing in Mr. Burke's Appeal worth taking notice of, there is, however, one expression upon which I shall offer a few remarks.—After quoting largely from the Rights of Man, and declining to contest the principles contained in that work, he says, " This will most probably be done (*if such writings shall be thought to deserve any other refutation than that of criminal justice*) by others, who may think with Mr. Burke and with the same zeal."

In the first place, it has not been done by any body. Not less, I believe, than eight or ten pamphlets, intended as answers to the former part of the Rights of Man have been published by different persons, and not one of them, to my knowledge, has extended to a second edition, nor are even the titles of them so much as generally remembered. As I am averse to unnecessarily multiplying publications, I have answered none of them. And as I believe that a man may write himself out of reputation when nobody else can do it, I am careful to avoid that rock.

But as I decline unnecessary publications on the one hand, so would I avoid any thing that looked like sullen pride on the other. If Mr. Burke, or any person on his side the question, will produce an answer to the Rights of Man, that shall extend to an half, or even a fourth part of the number of copies to which the Rights of Man extended, I will reply to his work. But until this be done, I shall so far take the sense of the public for my guide (and the world knows I am not a flatterer) that what they do not think worth while to read, is not worth mine to answer. I suppose the number of copies to which the first part of the Rights of Man extended, taking England, Scotland, and Ireland, is not less than between forty and fifty thousand.

I now come to remark on the remaining part of the quotation I have made from Mr. Burke.

" If," says he, " such writings shall be thought to deserve any other refutation than that of *criminal* justice."

Pardoning the pun, it must be *criminal* justice indeed that should condemn a work as a substitute for not being able to refute it. The greatest condemnation that could be passed upon it would be a refutation. But in proceeding by the method Mr. Burke alludes to, the condemnation would in the final event, pass upon the criminality of the process and not upon the work, and in this case, I had rather be the author, than be either the judge or the jury that should condemn it.

But to come at once to the point. I have differed from some professional gentlemen on the subject of prosecutions, and I since find they are falling into my opinion, which I shall here state as fully, but as concisely as I can.

I will first put a case with respect to any law, and then compare it with a government, or with what in England is, or has been, called a constitution.

It would be an act of despotism, or what in England is called arbitrary power, to make a law to prohibit investigating the principles, good or bad, on which such a law, or any other is founded.

If a law be bad, it is one thing to oppose the practice of it, but it is quite a different thing to expose its errors, to reason on its defects, and to show cause why it should be repealed, or why another ought to be substituted in its place. I have always held it an opinion (making it also my practice) that it is better to obey a bad law, making use at the same time of every argument to show its errors, and procure its repeal, than forcibly to violate it; because the precedent of breaking a bad law might weaken the force, and lead to a discretionary violation, of those which are good.

The case is the same with respect to principles and forms of government, or to what are called constitutions, and the parts of which they are composed.

It is for the good of nations, and not for the emolument or aggrandizement of particular individuals, that government ought to be established, and that mankind are at the expense of supporting it. The defects of every government and constitution both as to principle and form, must, on a parity of reasoning, be as open to discussion as the defects of a law, and it is a duty which every man owes to society to point them out. When those defects and the means of remedying them, are generally seen by a nation that nation will reform its government or its constitution in the one case, as the government repealed or reformed the law in the other. The operation of government is

restricted to the making and the administering of laws ;
but it is to a nation that the right of forming or reforming,
generating or regenerating constitutions and governments
belong ; and consequently those subjects, as subjects of investigation, are always before a country *as a matter of right*,
and cannot, without invading the general rights of that country, be made subjects for prosecution. On this ground I
will meet Mr. Burke whenever he pleases. It is better that
the whole argument should come out, than to seek to stifle
it. It was himself that opened the controversy, and he
ought not to desert it.

I do not believe that monarchy and aristocracy will continue seven years longer in any of the enlightened countries of Europe. If better reasons can be shown for them
than against them, they will stand ; if the contrary, they
will not. Mankind are not now to be told they shall not
think, or they shall not read : and publications that go no
further than to investigate principles of government, to invite men to reason and to reflect, and to show the errors
and excellencies of different systems, have a right to appear. If they do not excite attention, they are not worth
the trouble of a prosecution ; and if they do the prosecution will amount to nothing, since it cannot amount to a
prohibition of reading. This would be a sentence on the
public, instead of the author, and would also be the most
effectual mode of making or hastening revolutions.

On all cases that apply universally to a nation, with respect to systems of government, a jury of *twelve* men is not
competent to decide. Where there are no witnesses to be
examined, no facts to be proved, and where the whole matter is before the whole public, and the merits or demerits
of it resting on their opinion ; and where there is nothing
to be known in a court, but what every body knows out of
it, every twelve men are equally as good a jury as the other
and would most probably reverse each other's verdict ; or
from the variety of their opinions, not be able to form one.

It is one case whether a nation approve a work, or a plan; but it is quite another case whether it will commit to any such jury the power of determining whether that nation has a right to, or shall reform its government, or not. I mention these cases, that Mr. Burke may see I have not written on government without reflecting on what is law, as well as on what are rights.—The only effectual jury in such cases would be a convention of the whole nation fairly elected; for in all such cases the whole nation is the vicinage.

As to the prejudices which men have from education and habit, in favor of any particular form or system of government, those prejudices have yet to stand the test of reason and reflection. In fact such prejudices are nothing. No man is prejudiced in favor of a thing knowing it to be wrong. He is attached to it on the belief of its being right; and when he sees it is not so, the prejudice will be gone. We have but a defective idea of what prejudice is. It might be said that until men think for themselves the whole is prejudice and *not opinion;* for that only is opinion which is the result of reason and reflection. I offer this remark, that Mr. Burke may not confide too much in what has been the customary prejudices of the country.

But admitting governments to be changed all over Europe, it certainly may be done without convulsion or revenge. It is not worth making changes or revolutions, unless it be for some great national benefit, and when this shall appear to a nation, the danger will be, as in America and France, to those who oppose; and with this reflection I close my preface.

THOMAS PAINE.

London, Feb. 9, 1792.

RIGHTS OF MAN.

PART II.

—

INTRODUCTION.

What Archimedes said of the mechanical powers, may be applied to reason and liberty: " *Had we,*" said he, "*a place to stand upon, we might raise the world.*"

The revolution in America presented in politics what was only theory in mechanics. So deeply rooted were all the governments of the old world, and so effectually had the tyranny and the antiquity of habit established itself over the mind, that no beginning could be made in Asia, Africa, or Europe, to reform the political condition of man. Freedom had been hunted round the globe; reason was considered as rebellion; and the slavery of fear had made men afraid to think.

But such is the irresistible nature of truth, that all it asks, and all it wants, is the liberty of appearing. The sun needs no inscription to distinguish him from darkness, and no sooner did the American governments display themselves to the world, than despotism felt a shock, and man began to contemplate redress.

The independence of America, considered merely as a separation from England, would have been a matter but of little importance, had it not been accompanied by a revolution in the principles and practice of government. She made a stand, not for herself only, but for the world, and looked beyond the advantages which *she* could receive. Even the Hessian, though hired to fight against her, may live to bless his defeat; and England, condemning the viciousness of its government, rejoice in its miscarriage.

As America was the only spot in the political world where the principles of universal reformation could begin, so also was it the best in the natural world. An assemblage of circumstances conspired, not only to give birth, but to add gigantic maturity to its principles. The scene which that country presents to the eye of the spectator, has something in it which generates and enlarges great ideas. Nature appears to him in magnitude. The mighty objects he beholds, act upon his mind by enlarging it, and he partakes of the greatness he contemplates. Its first settlers were emigrants from different European nations, and of diversified professions of religion, retiring from the governmental persecutions of the old world, and meeting in the new, not as enemies, but as brothers. The wants which necessarily accompany the cultivation of a wilderness, produced among them a state of society, which countries long harassed by the quarrels and intrigues of governments, had neglected to cherish. In such a situation man becomes what he ought to be. He sees his species, not with the inhuman idea of a natural enemy, but as kindred; and the example shows to the artificial world, that man must go back to nature for information.

From the rapid progress which America makes in every species of improvement, it is rational to conclude, that if the governments of Asia, Africa and Europe, had begun on a principle similar to that of America, or had they not been very early corrupted therefrom, those countries must, by this time, have been in a far superior condition to what they are. Age after age has passed away, for no other purpose than to behold their wretchedness. Could we suppose a spectator who knew nothing of the world, and who was put into it merely to make his observations, he would take a great part of the old world to be new, just struggling with the difficulties and hardships of an infant settlement. He could not suppose that the hordes of miserable poor, with which old countries abound, could be any other than those who had not yet been able to provide for themselves. Little would he think they were the consequence of what in such countries is called government.

If, from the more wretched parts of the old world, we look at those which are in an advanced state of improvement, we still find the greedy hand of government thrusting itself into every corner and crevice of industry, and grasping the spoil of the multitude. Invention is continually exercised, to furnish new pretences for revenue and taxation. It watches prosperity as its prey, and permits none to escape without a tribute.

As revolutions have begun, (and as the probability is always greater against a thing beginning, than of proceeding after it has begun) it is natural to expect that other revolutions will follow. The amazing and still increasing expenses with which old governments are conducted, the numerous wars they engage in or provoke, the embarrassments they throw in the way of universal civilization and commerce, and the oppression and usurpation acted at home, have wearied out the patience, and exhausted the property of the world. In such a situation, and with such examples already existing, revolutions are to be looked for. They are become subjects of universal conversation, and may be considered as the *order of the day*.

If systems of government can be introduced less expensive, and more productive of general happiness, than those which have existed, all attempts to oppose their progress will in the end prove fruitless. Reason, like time, will make its own way, and prejudice will fall in the combat with interest. If universal peace, harmony, civilization and commerce are ever to be the happy lot of man, it cannot be accomplished but by a revolution in the present system of governments. All the monarchical governments are military. War is their trade, plunder and revenue their objects. While such governments continue, peace has not the absolute security of a day. What is the history of all monarchical governments but a disgustful picture of human wretchedness, and the accidental respite of a few years repose? Wearied with war, and tired with human butchery, they sat down to rest and called it peace. This certainly is not the condition that heaven intended for man; and if *this be monarchy*, well might monarchy be reckoned among the sins of the Jews.

The revolutions which formerly took place in the world, had nothing in them that interested the bulk of mankind. They extended only to a change of persons and measures, but not of principles, and rose or fell among the common transactions of the moment. What we now behold, may not improperly be called a "*counter revolution*." Conquest and tyranny, at some early period, dispossessed man of his rights, and he is now recovering them. And as the tide of human affairs has its ebb and flow in directions contrary to each other, so also is it in this. Government founded on a *moral theory, on a system of universal peace, on the indefeasible, hereditary rights of man*, is now revolving from west to east by a stronger impulse than the government of the sword revolved from east to west. It interests not particular individuals but nations in its progress, and promises a new era to the human race.

The danger to which the success of revolutions is most exposed, is that of attempting them before the principles on which they proceed, and the advantages to result from them, are sufficiently understood. Almost every thing appertaining to the circumstances of a nation has been absorbed and confounded under the general and mysterious word *government*. Though it avoids taking to its account the errors it commits, and the mischiefs it occasions, it fails not to arrogate to itself whatever has the appearance of prosperity. It robs industry of its honors, by pedantically making itself the cause of its effects; and purloins from the general character of man, the merits that appertain to him as a social being.

It may therefore be of use, in this day of revolutions, to discriminate between those things which are the effect of government, and those which are not. This will best be done by taking a review of society and civilization, and the consequences resulting therefrom, as things distinct from what are called governments. By beginning with this investigation, we shall be able to assign effects to their proper causes, and analyze the mass of common errors.

CHAPTER 1.

OF SOCIETY AND CIVILIZATION.

A GREAT part of that order which reigns among mankind is not the effect of government. It had its origin in the principles of society, and the natural constitution of man. It existed prior to government, and would exist if the formality of government was abolished. The mutual dependance and reciprocal interest which man has in man, and all the parts of a civilized community upon each other, create that great chain of connexion which holds it together. The landholder, the farmer, the manufacturer, the merchant, the tradesman, and every occupation prospers by the aid which each receives from the other, and from the whole. Common interest regulates their concerns, and forms their laws; and the laws which common usage ordains, have a greater influence than the laws of government. In fine, society performs for itself almost every thing which is ascribed to government.

To understand the nature and quantity of government proper for man, it is necessary to attend to his character. As nature created him for social life, she fitted him for the station she intended. In all cases she made his natural wants greater than his individual powers. No one man is capable, without the aid of society, of supplying his own wants; and those wants acting upon every individual, impel the whole of them into society, as naturally as gravitation acts to a centre.

But she has gone further. She has not only forced man into society by a diversity of wants, which the reciprocal aid of each other can supply, but she has implanted in him a system of social affections, which though not necessary to his existence, are essential to his happiness. There is no period in life when this love for society ceases to act. It begins and ends with our being.

If we examine, with attention, into the composition and constitution of man, the diversity of his wants, and the diversity of talents in different men for reciprocally accommodating the wants of each other, his propensity to society, and consequently to preserve the advantages resulting from it, we shall easily discover, that a great part of what is called government is mere imposition.

Government is no further necessary than to supply the few cases to which society and civilization are not conveniently competent; and instances are not wanting to show that every thing which government can usefully add thereto, has been performed by the common consent of society, without government.

For upwards of two years from the commencement of the American war, and a longer period, in several of the American states, there were no established forms of gov-

ernment. The old governments had been abolished, and
the country was too much occupied in defence, to employ
its attention in establishing new governments; yet during
this interval, order and harmony were preserved as inviolate as in any country in Europe. There is a natural apt-
ness in man, and more so in society, because it embraces
a greater variety of abilities and resources, to accommodate
itself to whatever situation it is in. The instant formal
government is abolished, society begins to act. A general
association takes place, and common interest produces
common security.

So far is it from being true, as has been pretended, that
the abolition of any formal government is the dissolution
of society, it acts by a contrary impulse, and brings
the latter the closer together. All that part of its organization which it had committed to its government, devolves
again upon itself, and acts through its medium. When
men, as well from natural instinct, as from reciprocal benefits, have habituated themselves to social and civilized
life, there is always enough of its principles in practice to
carry them through any changes they may find necessary
or convenient to make in their government. In short, man
is so naturally a creature of society, that it is almost impossible to put him out of it.

Formal government makes but a small part of civilized
life; and when even the best that human wisdom can devise is established, it is a thing more in name and idea,
than in fact. It is to the great and fundamental principles
of society and civilization—to the common usage universally consented to, and mutually and reciprocally maintained—to the unceasing circulation of interest, which,
passing through its innumerable channels, invigorates the
whole mass of civilized man—it is to these things, infinitely more than to any thing which even the best instituted
government can perform, that the safety and prosperity
of the individual and of the whole depends.

The more perfect civilization is, the less occasion has it
for government, because the more does it regulate its own
affairs, and govern itself; but so contrary is the practice
of old governments to the reason of the case, that the expenses of them increase in the proportion they ought to
diminish. It is but few general laws that civilized life requires, and those of such common usefulness, that whether
they are enforced by the forms of government or not, the

effect will be nearly the same. If we consider what the principles are that first condense men into society, and what the motives that regulate their mutual intercourse afterwards, we shall find, by the time we arrive at what is called government, that nearly the whole of the business is performed by the natural operation of the parts upon each other.

Man, with respect to all those matters, is more a creature of consistency than he is aware of, or than governments would wish him to believe. All the great laws of society are laws of nature. Those of trade and commerce, whether with respect to the intercourse of individuals, or of nations, are laws of mutual and reciprocal interest. They are followed and obeyed, because it is the interest of the parties so to do, and not on account of any formal laws their governments may impose or interpose.

But how often is the natural propensity to society disturbed or destroyed by the operations of government! When the latter, instead of being ingrafted on the principles of the former, assumes to exist for itself, and acts by partialities of favor and oppression, it becomes the cause of the mischiefs it ought to prevent.

If we look back to the riots and tumults, which at various times have happened in England, we shall find, that they did not proceed from the want of a government, but that government was itself the generating cause; instead of consolidating society, it divided it; it deprived it of its natural cohesion, and engendered discontents and disorders, which otherwise would not have existed. In those associations which men promiscuously form for the purpose of trade, or of any concern, in which government is totally out of the question, and in which they act merely on the principles of society, we see how naturally the various parties unite; and this shows, by comparison, that governments, so far from being always the cause or means of order, are often the destruction of it. The riots of 1780 had no other source than the remains of those prejudices, which the government itself had encouraged. But with respect to England there are also other causes.

Excess and inequality of taxation, however disguised in the means, never fail to appear in their effect. As a great mass of the community are thrown thereby into poverty and discontent, they are constantly on the brink of commotion; and, deprived, as they unfortunately are, of the means of information, are easily heated to outrage. Whatever the apparent cause of any riots may be, the real one is always want of happiness. It shows that something is wrong in the system of government, that injures the felicity by which society is to be preserved.

But as fact is superior to reasoning, the instance of America presents itself to confirm these observations.— If there is a country in the world, where concord, according to common calculation, would be least expected, it is America. Made up, as it is, of people from different nations,* accustomed to different forms and habits of government, speaking different languages, and more different in their modes of worship, it would appear that the union of such a people was impracticable ; but by the simple operation of constructing government on the principles of society and the rights of man, every difficulty retires, and all the parts are brought into cordial unison. There, the poor are not oppressed, the rich are not privileged. Industry is not mortified by the splendid extravagance of a court rioting at its expense. Their taxes are few, because their government is just ; and as there is nothing to render them wretched, there is nothing to engender riots and tumults.

A metaphysical man, like Mr. Burke, would have tortured his invention to discover how such a people could be governed. He would have supposed that some must be managed by fraud, others by force, and all by some contrivance ; that genius must be hired to impose upon ignorance, and show and parade to fascinate the vulgar. Lost in the abundance of his researches, he would have resolved and re-resolved, and finally overlooked the plain and easy road that lay directly before him.

One of the great advantages of the American revolution has been, that it led to a discovery of the principles, and laid open the imposition of governments. All the revolutions till then had been worked within the atmosphere of

* That part of America which is generally called New-England, including New-Hampshire, Massachusetts, Rhode-Island, and Connecticut, is peopled chiefly by English descendants. In the state of New-York, about half are Dutch, the rest English, Scotch, and Irish. In New-Jersey, a mixture of English and Dutch, with some Scotch and Irish. In Pennsylvania, about one third are English, another Germans, and the remainder Scotch and Irish, with some Swedes. The states to the southward have a greater proportion of English than the middle states, but in all of them there is a mixture ; and besides those enumerated, there are a considerable number of French, and some few of all the European nations, lying on the coast. The most numerous religious denomination are the Presbyterians ; but no one sect is established above another, and all men are equally citizens.

a court, and never on the great floor of a nation. The parties were always of the class of courtiers; and whatever was their rage for reformation, they carefully preserved the fraud of the profession.

In all cases they took care to represent government as a thing made up of mysteries, which only themselves understood : and they hid from the understanding of the nation, the only thing that was beneficial to know, namely, *that government is nothing more than a national association acting on the principles of society.*

Having thus endeavored to show, that the social and civilized state of man is capable of performing within itself, almost every thing necessary to its protection and government, it will be proper, on the other hand, to take a review of the present old governments, and examine whether their principles and practice are correspondent thereto.

CHAPTER II.

OF THE ORIGIN OF THE PRESENT OLD GOVERNMENTS.

It is impossible that such governments as have hitherto existed in the world, could have commenced by any other means than a total violation of every principle, sacred and moral. The obscurity in which the origin of all the present old governments is buried, implies the iniquity and disgrace with which they began. The origin of the present governments of America and France will ever be remembered, because it is honorable to record it; but with respect to the rest, even flattery has consigned them to the tomb of time, without an inscription.

It could have been no difficult thing in the early and solitary ages of the world, while the chief employment of men was that of attending flocks and herds, for a banditti of ruffians to overrun a country, and lay it under contribution. Their power being thus established, the chief of the band contrived to lose the name of robber in that of monarch; and hence the origin of monarchy and kings.

The origin of the government of England, so far as relates to what is called its line of monarchy, being one of the latest, is perhaps the best recorded. The hatred which the Norman invasion and tyranny begat, must have been deeply rooted in the nation, to have outlived the contrivance to obliterate it. Though not a courtier will talk of the curfew-bell, not a village in England has forgotten it.

Those bands of robbers having parcelled out the world, and divided it into dominions, began, as is naturally the case, to quarrel with each other. What at first was obtained by violence, was considered by others as lawful to be taken, and a second plunderer succeeded the first. They alternately invaded the dominions which each had assigned to himself, and the brutality with which they treated each other explains the original character of monarchy.— It was ruffian torturing ruffian. The conqueror considered the conquered not as his prisoner, but his property.— He led him in triumph rattling in chains, and doomed him, at pleasure, to slavery or death. As time obliterated the history of their beginning, their successors assumed new appearances, to cut off the entail of their disgrace, but their principles and objects remained the same. What at first was plunder assumed the softer name of revenue ; and the power originally usurped, they affected to inherit.

From such beginning of governments, what could be expected, but a continual system of war and extortion? It has established itself into a trade. The vice is not peculiar to one more than to another, but is the common principle of all. There does not exist within such governments a stamina whereon to ingraft reformation ; and the shortest and most effectual remedy is to begin anew.

What scenes of horror, what perfection of iniquity, present themselves in contemplating the character, and reviewing the history of such governments! If we would delineate human nature with a baseness of heart, and hypocrisy of countenance, that reflection would shudder at and humanity disown, it is kings, courts, and cabinets, that must sit for the portrait. Man, as he is naturally, with all his faults about him, is not up to the character.

Can we possibly suppose that if government had originated in a right principle, and had not an interest in pursuing a wrong one, that the world could have been in the wretched and quarrelsome condition we have seen it?— What inducement has the farmer, while following the plough, to lay aside his peaceful pursuits, and go to war with the farmer of another country ? Or what inducement has the manufacturer ? What is dominion to them, or to any class of men in a nation ? Does it add an acre to any man's estate, or raise its value? Are not conquest and defeat each of the same price, and taxes the never-failing consequence ? Though this reasoning may be good to a nation, it is not so to a government. War is the faro-table of governments, and nations the dupes of the game.

If there is any thing to wonder at in this miserable scene of governments, more than might be expected, it is the progress which the peaceful arts of agriculture, manufacture, and commerce have made, beneath such a long accumulating load of discouragement and oppression. It serves to show, that instinct in animals does not act with stronger impulse than the principles of society and civilization operate in man. Under all discouragements, he pursues his object, and yields to nothing but impossibilities.

CHAPTER III.

OF THE OLD AND NEW SYSTEMS OF GOVERNMENT.

NOTHING can appear more contradictory than the principles on which the old governments began, and the condition to which society, civilization, and commerce, are capable of carrying mankind. Government on the old system, is an assumption of power, for the aggrandizement of itself; on the new, a delegation of power, for the common benefit of society. The former supports itself by keeping up a system of war; the latter promotes a system of peace, as the true means of enriching a nation. The one encourages national prejudices; the other promotes universal society, as the means of universal commerce.— The one measures its prosperity by the quantity of revenue it extorts; the other proves its excellence, by the small quantity of taxes it requires.

Mr. Burke has talked of old and new whigs. If he can amuse himself with childish names and distinctions, I shall not interrupt his pleasure. It is not to him, but to the Abbe Sieyes, that I address this chapter. I am already engaged to the latter gentleman, to discuss the subject of monarchical government; and as it naturally occurs in comparing the old and new systems, I make this the opportunity of presenting to him my observations. I shall occasionally take Mr. Burke in my way.

Though it might be proved that the system of government now called the *new*, is the most ancient in principle of all that have existed, being founded on the original inherent rights of man : yet, as tyranny and the sword have suspended the exercise of those rights for many centuries past, it serves better the purpose of distinction to call it the *new*, than to claim the right of calling it the old.

The first general distinction between those two systems, is, that the one now called the old is *hereditary*, either in whole or in part; and the new is entirely *representative*. It rejects all hereditary government :

1st, As being an imposition on mankind.

2d, As inadequate to the purposes for which government is necessary.

With respect to the first of these heads—It cannot be proved by what right hereditary government could begin : neither does there exist within the compass of mortal power, a right to establish it. Man has no authority over posterity in matters of personal right ; and therefore, no man, or body of men, had, or can have, a right to set up hereditary government. Were even ourselves to come again into existence, instead of being succeeded by posterity, we have not now the right of taking from ourselves the rights which would then be ours. On what ground, then, do we pretend to take them from others?

All hereditary government is in its nature tyranny. An heritable crown, or an heritable throne, or by what other fanciful name such things may be called, have no other significant explanation than that mankind are heritable property. To inherit a government, is to inherit the people, as if they were flocks and herds.

With respect to the second head, that of being inadequate to the purposes for which government is necessary, we have only to consider what government essentially is, and compare it with the circumstances to which hereditary succession is subject.

Government ought to be a thing always in full maturity. It ought to be so constructed as to be superior to all the accidents to which individual man is subject : and therefore, hereditary succesion, by being *subject to them all*, is the most irregular and imperfect of all the systems of government.

We have heard the *rights of man* called a *levelling* system ; but the only system to which the word *levelling* is truly applicable, is the hereditary monarchical system. It is a system of *mental levelling*. It indiscriminately admits every species of character to the same authority. Vice and virtue, ignorance and wisdom, in short, every quality, good or bad, is put on the same level. Kings succeed each other, not as rationals, but as animals. Can we then be surprised at the abject state of the human mind in monarchical countries, when the government itself is formed on such an abject levelling system ?—It has no fixed character. To-day it is one thing ; and to-morrow it is something else. It changes with the temper of every succeeding individual, and is subject to all the varieties of each. It is government through the medium of passions and accidents. It appears under all the various characters of childhood, decrepitude, dotage, a thing at nurse, in leading strings, or on crutches. It reverses the wholesome order of nature. It occasionally puts children over men, and the conceits of non-age over wisdom and experience. In short, we cannot conceive a more ridiculous figure of government, than hereditary succession, in all its cases, presents.

Could it be made a decree in nature, or an edict registered in heaven, and man could know it, that virtue and wisdom should invariably appertain to hereditary succession, the objections to it would be removed ; but when we see that nature acts as if she disowned and sported with the hereditary system ; that the mental characters of successors, in all countries, are below the average of human understanding; that one is a tyrant, another an idiot, a third insane, and some all three together, it is impossible to attach confidence to it, when reason in man has power to act.

It is not to the abbe Sieyes that I need apply this reasoning ; he has already saved me that trouble, by giving his own opinion upon the case. "If it be asked," says he, "what is my opinion with respect to hereditary right. I

answer, without hesitation, that, in good theory, an hereditary transmission of any power or office, can never accord
with the laws of true representation. Hereditaryship, is,
in this sense, as much an attaint upon principle, as an outrage upon society. But let us," continues he, " refer to
the history of all elective monarchies and principalities ;
is there one in which the elective mode is not worse than
the hereditary succession."

As to debating on which is the worst of the two, is admitting both to be bad ; and herein we are agreed. The
preference which the abbe has given, is a condemnation of
the thing he prefers. Such a mode of reasoning on such a
subject is inadmissible, because it finally amounts to an accusation of providence, as if she had left to man no other
choice with respect to government than between two evils,
the best of which he admits to be, " *an attaint upon principle,
and an outrage upon society.*"

Passing over, for the present, all the evils and mischiefs
which monarchy has occasioned in the world, nothing can
more effectually prove its uselessness in a state of *civil government*, than making it hereditary. Would we make any
office hereditary that required wisdom and abilities to fill it ?
And where wisdom and abilities are not necessary, such an
office, whatever it may be, is superfluous or insignificant.

Hereditary succession is a burlesque upon monarchy.
It puts it in the most ridiculous light, by presenting it as an
office which any child or ideot may fill. It requires some
talents, to be a common mechanic ; but, to be a king, requires only the animal figure of man—a sort of breathing
automaton. This sort of superstition may last a few years
more, but it cannot long resist the awakened reason and
interest of man.

As to Mr. Burke, he is a stickler for monarchy, not altogether as a pensioner, if he is one, which I believe, but as
a political man. He has taken up a contemptible opinion of mankind, who, in their turn, are taking up the same
of him. He considers them as a herd of beings that must
be governed by fraud, effigy, and show ; and an idol would
be as good a figure of monarchy with him, as a man. I
will, however, do him the justice to say, that, with respect
to America, he has been very complimentary. He always
contended, at least in my hearing, that the people of America were more enlightened than those of England, or of any

country in Europe; and that therefore the imposition of show was not necessary in their governments.

Though the comparison between hereditary and elective monarchy, which the abbe had made, is unnecessary to the case, because the representative system rejects both; yet were I to make the comparison, I should decide contrary to what he has done.

The civil wars which have originated from contested hereditary claims, are more numerous, and have been more dreadful, and of longer continuance, than those which have been occasioned by election. All the civil wars in France arose from the hereditary system : they were either produced by hereditary claims, or by the imperfection of the hereditary form, which admits of regencies, or monarchy at nurse. With respect to England, its history is full of the same misfortunes. The contests for succession between the houses of York and Lancaster, lasted a whole century ; and others of a similar nature, have renewed themselves since that period. Those of 1715 and 1745, were of the same kind. The succession-war for the crown of Spain, embroiled almost half of Europe. The disturbances in Holland are generated from the hereditaryship of the stadtholder. A government calling itself free, with an hereditary office, is like a thorn in the flesh, that produces a fermentation which endeavors to discharge it.

But I might go further, and place also foreign wars, of whatever kind, to the same cause. It is by adding the evil of hereditary succession to that of monarchy, that a permanent family interest is created, whose constant objects are dominion and revenue. Poland, though an elective monarchy, has had fewer wars than those which are hereditary ; and it is the only government that has made a voluntary essay, though but a small one, to reform the condition of the country.

Having thus glanced at a few of the defects of the old, or hereditary systems of government, let us compare it with the new, or representative system.

The representative system takes society and civilization for its basis ; nature, reason, and experience for its guide.

Experience, in all ages, and in all countries has demonstrated, that it is impossible to control nature in her distribution of mental powers. She gives them as she pleases. Whatever is the rule by which she, apparently to us, scatters them among mankind, that rule remains a secret to

man. It would be as ridiculous to attempt to fix the hereditaryship of human beauty, as of wisdom.

Whatever wisdom constituently is, it is like a seedless
plant; it may be reared when it appears; but it cannot be
voluntarily produced. There is always a sufficiency somewhere in the general mass of society for all purposes; but
with respect to the parts of society, it is continually changing its place. It rises in one to-day, in another to-morrow
and has most probably visited in rotation every family of
the earth, and again withdrawn.

As this is the order of nature, the order of government
must necessarily follow it, or government will, as we see it
does, degenerate into ignorance. The hereditary system,
therefore, is as repugnant to human wisdom, as to human
rights; and is as absurd, as it is unjust.

As the republic of letters brings forward the best literary
productions, by giving to genius a fair and universal chance;
so the representative system of government is calculated to
produce the wisest laws, by collecting wisdom where it can
be found. I smile to myself when I contemplate the ridiculous insignificance into which literature and all the sciences would sink, were they made hereditary; and I carry the same idea into governments. An hereditary governor is as inconsistent as an hereditary author. I know
not whether Homer or Euclid had sons; but I will venture
an opinion, that if they had, and had left their works un-
finished, those sons could not have completed them.

Do we need a stronger evidence of the absurdity of hereditary government, than is seen in descendants of those
men, in any line of life, who once were famous? Is there
scarcely an instance in which there is not a total reverse of
the character? It appears as if the tide of mental faculties flowed as far as it could in certain channels, and then
forsook its course, and arose in others. How irrational
then is the hereditary system which establishes channels
of power, in company with which wisdom refuses to flow!
By continuing this absurdity, man is perpetually in contradiction with himself; he accepts, for a king, or a chief
magistrate, or a legislator, a person whom he would not
elect for a constable.

It appears to general observation, that revolutions create
genius and talents; but those events do no more than bring
them forward. There exists in man, a mass of sense lying in a dormant state, and which, unless something excites

it to action, will descend with him, in that condition, to the grave. As it is to the advantage of society that the whole of its faculties should be employed, the construction of government ought to be such as to bring forward, by a quiet and regular operation, all that extent of capacity which never fails to appear in revolutions.

This cannot take place in the insipid state of hereditary government, not only because it prevents, but because it operates to benumb. When the mind of a nation is bowed down by any political superstition in its government, such as hereditary succession is, it loses a considerable portion of its powers on all other subjects and objects. Hereditary succession requires the same obedience to ignorance, as to wisdom; and when once the mind can bring itself to pay this indiscriminate reverence, it descends below the statute of mental manhood. It is fit to be great only in little things. It acts a treachery upon itself, and suffocates the sensations that urge to detection.

Though the ancient governments present to us a miserable picture of the condition of man, there is one which above all others exempts itself from the general description. I mean the democracy of the Athenians. We see more to admire and less to condemn, in that great, extraordinary people, than in any thing which history affords.

Mr. Burke is so little acquainted with constituent principles of government, that he confounds democracy and representation together. Representation was a thing unknown in the ancient democracies. In those the mass of the people met and enacted laws (grammatically speaking) in the first person. Simple democracy was no other than the common hall of the ancients. It signifies the *form*, as well as the public principle of the government. As these democracies increased in population, and the territory extended, the simple democratical form became unwieldly and impracticable; and as the system of representation was not known, the consequence was, they either degenerated convulsively into monarchies, or became absorbed into such as then existed. Had the system of representation been then understood, as it now is, there is no reason to believe that those forms of government, now called monarchical or aristocratical would ever have taken place. It was the want of some method to consolidate the parts of society, after it became too populous, and too extensive for the simple democratical form, and also the lax and solitary condition of shepherds and herdsmen in other parts of the world, that afforded opportunities to those unnatural modes of government to begin.

As it is necessary to clear away the rubbish of errors, into which the subject of government has been thrown, I shall proceed to remark on some others.

It has always been the political craft of courtiers and court governments, to abuse something which they called republicanism; but what republicanism was, or is, they never attempt to explain. Let us examine a little into this case.

The only forms of government are, the democratical, the aristocratical, the monarchical, and what is now called the representative.

What is called a *republic*, is not any *particular form* of government. It is wholly characteristical of the purport, matter, or object for which government ought to be instituted, and on which it is to be employed, *res-publica*, the public affairs, or the public good; or, literally translated, the *public thing*. It is a word of a good original, referring to what ought to be the character and business of government; and in this sense it is naturally opposed to the word *monarchy*, which has a base original signification. It means arbitrary power in an individual person; in the exercise of which, *himself*, and not the *res-publica*, is the object.

Every government that does not act on the principle of a republic, or, in other words, that deos not make the *res-publica* its whole and sole object, is not a good government. Republican government is no other than government established and conducted for the interest of the public, as well individually as collectively. It is not necessarily connected with any particular form, but it most naturally associates with the representative form, as being best calculated to secure the end for which a nation is at the expense of supporting it.

Various forms of government have affected to style themselves republics. Poland calls itself a republic, but is in fact an hereditary aristocracy, with what is called an elective monarchy. Holland calls itself a republic, which is chiefly aristocratical, with an hereditary stadtholdership. But the government of America, which is wholly on the system of representation, is the only real republic in character and practice, that now exists. Its government has no other object than the public business of the nation, and therefore it is properly a republic; and the Americans have taken care that *this*, and no other, shall be the object of their government, by their rejecting every thing hereditary, and establishing government on the system of representation only.

Those who have said that a republic is not a *form* of government calculated for countries of great extent, mistook, in the first place, the *business* of a government, for a *form* of government; for the *res-publica* equally appertains to every extent of territory and population. And, in the second place, if they meant any thing with respect to *form*, it was the simple democratical form, such as was the mode of government in the ancient democracies, in which there was no representation. The case, therefore, is not, that a republic cannot be extensive, but that it cannot be extensive on the simple democratic form; and the question naturally presents itself, *What is the best form of government for conducting the* RES-PUBLICA *or* PUBLIC BUSINESS *of a nation, after it becomes too extensive and populous for the simple democratical form?*

It cannot be monarchy, because monarchy is subject to an objection of the same amount to which the democratical form was subject.

It is possible that an individual may lay down a system of principles, on which government shall be constitutionally established to any extent of territory. This is no more than an operation of the mind, acting by its own powers. But the practice upon those principles, as applying to the various and numerous circumstances of a nation, its agriculture, manufactures, trade, commerce. &c. require a knowledge, of a different kind, and which can be had only from the various parts of society. It is an assemblage of practical knowledge, which no one individual can possess; and therefore the monarchical form is as much limited, in useful practice, from the incompetency of knowledge, as was the democratical form, from the multiplicity of population. The one degenerates, by extension, into confusion; the other, into ignorance and incapacity, of which all the great monarchies are an evidence. The monarchical form, therefore, could not be a substitute for the democratical, because it has equal inconveniences.

Much less could it when made hereditary. This is the most effectual of all forms to preclude knowledge. Neither could the high democratical mind have voluntarily yielded itself to be governed by children and ideots, and all the motley insignificance of character, which attends such a mere animal system, the disgrace and the reproach of reason and of man.

As to the aristocratical form, it has the same vices and defects with the monarchical, except that the chance of abilities is better from the proportion of numbers, but there is still no security for the right use and application of them.*

Referring, then, to the original simple democracy, it affords the true data from which government on a large scale can begin. It is incapable of extension, not from its principle, but from the inconvenience of its form; and monarchy and aristocracy from their incapacity. Retaining, then, democracy as the ground, and rejecting the corrupt systems of monarchy and aristocracy, the representative system naturally presents itself; remedying at once the defects of the simple democracy as to form, and the incapacity of the other two with regard to knowledge.

Simple democracy was society governing itself without the use of secondary means. By ingrafting representation upon democracy, we arrive at a system of government capable of embracing and confederating all the various interests and every extent of territory and population; and that also with advantages as much superior to hereditary government, as the republic of letters is to hereditary literature.

It is on this system that the American government is founded. It is representation ingrafted upon democracy. It has settled the form by a scale parallel in all cases to the extent of the principle. What Athens was in miniature, America will be in magnitude. The one was the wonder of the ancient world—the other is becoming the admiration and model of the present. It is the easiest of all the forms of government to be understood, and the most eligible in practice; and excludes at once the ignorance and insecurity of the hereditary mode, and the inconvenience of the simple democracy.

It is impossible to conceive a system of government capable of acting over such an extent of territory, and such a circle of interests, as is produced by the operation of

* For a character of aristocracy, the reader is referred to Rights of Man. part i. p. 84. et seq.

representation. France, great and populous as it is, is but a spot in the capaciousness of the system. It adapts itself to all possible cases. It is preferable to simple democracy even in small territories. Athens, by representation, would have surpassed her own democracy.

That which is called government, or rather that which we ought to conceive government to be, is no more than some common centre, in which all the parts of society unite. This cannot be established by any method so conducive to the various interests of the community, as by the representative system. It concentrates the knowledge necessary to the interests of the parts, and of the whole. It places government in a state of constant maturity. It is, as has been already observed, never young, never old. It is subject neither to nonage nor dotage. It is never in the cradle nor on crutches. It admits not of a separation between knowledge and power, and is superior, as government ought always to be, to all the accidents of individual man, and is therefore superior to what is called monarchy.

A nation is not a body, the figure of which is to be represented by the human body; but is like a body contained within a circle, having a common centre, in which every radius meets; and that centre is formed by representation. To connect representation with what is called monarchy, is eccentric government. Representation is of itself the delegated monarchy of a nation, and cannot debase itself by dividing it with another.

Mr. Burke has two or three times in his parliamentary speeches, and in his publications, made use of a jingle of words that convey no ideas. Speaking of government, he says, "It is better to have monarchy for its basis, and republicanism for its corrective, than republicanism for its basis, and monarchy for its corrective." If he means that it is better to correct folly with wisdom, than wisdom with folly, I will no otherwise contend with him, than to say, it would be much better to reject the folly altogether.

But what is this thing which Mr. Burke calls monarchy? Will he explain it: all mankind can understand what representation is; and that it must necessarily include a variety of knowledge and talents. But what security is there for the same qualities on the part of monarchy? Or, when this monarchy is a child, where then is the wisdom? What does it know about government? Who then is the monarch?

or where is the monarchy? If it is to be performed by regency, it proves it to be a farce. A regency is a mock
species of republic, and the whole of monarchy deserves
no better appellation. It is a thing as various as imagination can paint. It has none of the stable character that
government ought to possess. Every succession is a revolution, and every regency a counter-revolution. The whole
of it is a scene of perpetual court cabal and intrigue, of
which Mr. Burke is himself an instance.

Whether I have too little sense to see, or too much to be
imposed upon : whether I have too much or too little pride,
or of any thing else, I leave out of the question; but certain it is, that what is called monarchy, always appears to
me a silly, contemptible thing. I compare it to something
kept behind a curtain; about which there is a great deal of
bustle and fuss, and a wonderful air of seeming solemnity ;
but when, by any accident, the curtain happens to be open
and the company see what it is, they burst into laughter.

In the representative system of government, nothing like
this can happen. Like the nation itself, it possesses a perpetual stamina, as well of body as of mind, and presents
itself on the open theatre of the world in a fair and manly
manner. Whatever are its excellencies or its defects, they
are visible to all. It exists not by fraud and mystery; it
deals not in cant and sophistry ; but inspires a language,
that, passing from heart to heart, is felt and understood.

We must shut our eyes against reason, we must basely
degrade our understanding, not to see the folly of what is
called monarchy. Nature is orderly in all her works ; but
this is a mode of government that counteracts nature. It
turns the progress of the human faculties upside down.
It subjects age to be governed by children, and wisdom by
folly.

On the contrary, the representative system is always
parallel with the order and immutable laws of nature, and
meets the reason of man in every part. For example :

In the American federal government, more power is delegated to the president of the United States, than to any
other individual member of congress. He cannot, therefore, be elected to this office under the age of thirty-five
years. By this time the judgment of man becomes ma-
tured, and he has lived long enough to be acquainted with
men and things, and the country with him. But on the
monarchical plan (exclusive of the numerous chances there

are against every man born into the world, of drawing a prize in the lottery of human faculties,) the next in succession, whatever he may be, is put at the head of a nation, and of a government at the age of eighteen years. Does this appear like an act of wisdom? Is it consistent with the proper dignity and the manly character of a nation? Where is the propriety of calling such a lad the father of the people?—In all other cases, a person is a minor until the age of twenty-one years. Before this period, he is not trusted with the management of an acre of land, or with the heritable property of a flock of sheep, or an herd of swine; but wonderful to tell! he may at the age of eighteen years, be trusted with a nation.

That monarchy is all a bubble, a mere court artifice to procure money, is evident (at least to me,) in every character in which it can be viewed. It would be almost impossible, on the rational system of representative government, to make out a bill of expenses to such an enormous amount as this deception admits. Government is not of itself a very chargeable institution. The whole expense of the federal government of America, founded, as I have already said, on the system of representation, and extending over a country nearly ten times as large as England, is but six hundred thousand dollars, or one hundred and thirty thousand pounds sterling.

I presume that no man in his sober senses will compare the character of any of the kings of Europe, with that of general Washington. Yet, in France, and also in England, the expense of the civil list only, for the support of one man, is eight times greater than the whole expense of the federal government of America. To assign a reason for this, appears almost impossible. The generality of people in America, especially the poor, are more able to pay taxes, than the generality of people either in France or England.

But the case is, that the representative system diffuses such a body of knowledge throughout the nation, on the subject of government, as to explode ignorance and preclude imposition. The craft of courts cannot be acted on that ground. There is no place for mystery; no where for it to begin. Those who are not in the representation, know as much of the nature of business as those who are. An affectation of mysterious importance would there be scouted. Nations can have no secrets; and the secrets of courts, like those of individuals, are always their defects.

In the representative system, the reason for every thing must publicly appear. Every man is a proprietor in government, and considers it a necessary part of his business to understand. It concerns his interest because it affects his property. He examines the cost, and compares it with the advantages; and above all, he does not adopt the slavish custom of following what in other governments are called *leaders*.

It can only be by blinding the understanding of man, and making him believe that government is some wonderful mysterious thing, that excessive revenues are obtained. Monarchy is well calculated to ensure this end. It is the popery of government; a thing kept up to amuse the ignorant, and quiet them into paying taxes.

The government of a free country, properly speaking, is not in the persons, but in the laws. The enacting of those requires no great expense; and when they are administered, the whole of civil government is performed—the rest is all court contrivance.

CHAPTER IV.

ON CONSTITUTIONS.

THAT men mean distinct and separate things when they talk of constitutions and of governments, is evident; or, why are those terms distinctly and separately used? A constitution is not the act of a government, but of a people constituting a government; and government without a constitution, is power without a right.

All power exercised over a nation, must have some beginning. It must be either delegated, or assumed. There are no other sources. All delegated power is trust, and all assumed power is usurpation. Time does not alter the nature and quality of either.

In viewing this subject, the case and circumstances of America present themselves as in the beginning of a world; and our inquiry into the origin of government is shortened, by referring to the facts that have arisen in our day. We have no occasion to roam for information into the obscure field of antiquity, nor hazard ourselves upon conjecture. We are brought at once to the point of seeing government begin, as if we had lived in the beginning of time. The real volume, not of history, but of facts, is directly before us, unmutilated by contrivance, or the errors of tradition.

I will here concisely state the commencement of the American constitutions; by which the difference between constitutions and governments will sufficiently appear.

It may not be improper to remind the reader, that the United States of America consist of thirteen states, each of which established a government for itself, after the declaration of independence, of the fourth of July 1776. Each state acted independently of the rest, in forming its government; but the same general principle pervades the whole. When the several state governments were formed, they proceeded to form the federal government, that acts over the whole in all matters which concern the interest of the whole, or which relate to the intercourse of the several states with each other, or with foreign nations. I will begin with giving an instance from one of the state governments (that of Pennsylvania) and then proceed to thef ed-ral government.

The state of Pennsylvania, though nearly of the same extent of territory as England, was then divided into twelve counties. Each of those counties had elected a committee at the commencement of the dispute with the English government; and as the city of Philadelphia, which also had its committee, was the most central for intelligence, it became the centre of communication to the several county committees. When it became necessary to proceed to the formation of a government, the committee of Philadelphia proposed a conference of all the county committees, to be held in that city, and which met the latter end of July, 1776.

Though these committees had been elected by the people, they were not elected expressly for the purpose, nor invested with the authority of forming a constitution : and as they could not, consistently with the American idea of rights, assume such a power, they could only confer upon

the matter, and put it into a train of operation. The con-
ferees, therefore did no more than state the case, and recommend to the several counties to elect six representatives for each county, to meet in convention at Philadelphia,
with powers to form a constitution, and propose it for public consideration.

This convention, of which Benjamin Franklin was president, having met and deliberated, and agreed upon a constitution, they next ordered it to be published, not as a thing
established, but for the consideration of the whole people,
their approbation or rejection, and then adjourned to a
stated time. When the time of adjournment was expired,
the convention re-assembled; and as the general opinion
of the people in approbation of it was then known, the constitution was signed, sealed, and proclaimed on the *authority of the people*, and the original instrument deposited as a
public record. The convention then appointed a day for
the general election of the representatives who were to compose the government, and the time it should commence;
and having done this, they dissolved, and returned to their
several homes and occupations.

In this constitution were laid down, first, a declaration of
rights. Then followed the form which the government
should have, and the powers it should possess—the authority of the courts of judicature, and of juries—the manner in which elections should be conducted, and the proportion of representatives to the number of electors—the time
which each succeeding assembly should continue, which
was one year—the mode of levying, and of accounting for
the expenditure, of public money—of appointing public
officers, &c.

No article of this constitution could be altered or infringed at the discretion of the government that was to ensue.—
It was to that government a law. But as it would have
been unwise to preclude the benefit of experience, and in
order also to prevent the accumulation of errors, if any
should be found, and to preserve an unison of government
with the circumstances of the state at all times, the constitution provided, that, at the expiration of every seven
years, a convention should be elected; for the express purpose of revising the constitution, and making alterations,
additions, or abolitions therein, if any such should be found
necessary,

Here we see a regular process—a government issuing out of a constitution, formed by the people in their original character; and that constitution, serving, not only as an authority, but as a law of control to the government. It was the political bible of the state. Scarcely a family was without it. Every member of the government had a copy; and nothing was more common, when any debate arose on the principle of a bill, or on the extent of any species of authority, than for the members to take the printed constitution out of their pocket, and read the chapter with which such matter in debate was connected.

Having thus given an instance from one of the states, I will show the proceedings by which the federal constitution of the United States arose and was formed.

Congress, at its two first meetings, in September 1774, and May 1775, was nothing more than a deputation from the legislatures of the several provinces, afterwards states; and had no other authority than what arose from common consent, and the necessity of its acting as a public body. In every thing which related to the internal affairs of America, congress went no further than to issue recommendations, to the several provincial assemblies, who at discretion adopted them or not. Nothing on the part of congress was compulsive; yet, in this situation, it was more faithfully and affectionately obeyed, than was any government in Europe. This instance, like that of the national assembly of France, sufficiently shows, that the strength of government does not consist in any thing *within* itself, but in the attachment of a nation, and the interest which the people feel in supporting it. When this is lost, government is but a child in power; and though, like the old government of France, it may harass individuals for a while, it but facilitates its own fall.

After the declaration of independence, it became consistent with the principle on which representative government is founded, that the authority of congress should be defined and established. Whether that authority should be more or less than congress then discretionately exercised, was not then the question. It was merely the rectitude of the measure.

For this purpose the act, called the act of confederation (which was a sort of imperfect federal constitution) was proposed, and, after long deliberation, was concluded in the year 1781. It was not the act of congress. because it is repugnant to the principles of representative government that a body should give power to itself. Congress first informed the several states, of the powers which it conceived were necessary to be invested in the union, to enable it to perform the duties and services required from it; and the states severally agreed with each other, and concentrated in congress those powers.

It may not be improper to observe, that in both those instances (the one of Pennsylvania, and the other of the United States) there is no such thing as the idea of a compact between the people on one side, and the government on the other. The compact was that of the people with each other, to produce and constitute a government. To suppose that any government can be a party in a compact with the whole people, is to suppose it to have existence before it can have a right to exist. The only instance in which a compact can take place between the people and those who exercise the government, is, that the people shall pay them, while they choose to employ them.

Government is not a trade which any man or body of men has a right to set up and exercise for his own emolument, but is altogether a trust, in right of those by whom that trust is delegated, and by whom it is always resumable. It has of itself no rights; they are altogether duties.

Having thus given two instances of the original formation of a constitution, I will show the manner in which both have been changed since their first establishment.

The powers vested in the governments of the several states, by the state constitutions, were found, upon experience, to be too great; and those vested in the federal government, by the act of confederation, too little. The defect was not in the principle, but in the distribution of power.

Numerous publications, in pamphlets and in the newspapers, appeared on the propriety and necessity of new-modelling the federal government. After some time of public discussion, carried on through the channel of the press, and in conversations, the state of Virginia, experiencing some inconvenience with respect to commerce, proposed holding a continental conference; in consequence of which a deputation from five or six of the state assemblies met at Annapolis in Maryland, in 1786. This meeting, not conceiving itself sufficiently authorized to go into the business of a reform, did no more than state their

general opinions of the propriety of the measure, and recommend that a convention of all the states should be held
the year following.

This convention met at Philadelphia, in May 1787, of
which general Washington was elected president. He was
not at that time connected with any of the state governments, or with congress. He delivered up his commission when the war ended, and since then had lived a private citizen.

The convention went deeply into all the subjects; and
having, after a variety of debate and investigation, agreed
among themselves upon the several parts of a federal constitution, the next question was, the manner of giving it authority and practice.

For this purpose, they did not, like a cabal of courtiers,
send for a Dutch stadtholder, or a German elector; but
they referred the whole matter to the sense and interest of
the country.

They first directed, that the proposed constitution should
be published. Second, that each state should elect a convention, expressly for the purpose of taking it into consideration, and of ratifying or rejecting it; and that as soon
as the approbation and ratification of any nine states
should be given, that those states should proceed to the
election of their proportion of members to the new federal
government; and that the operation of it should then begin, and the former federal government cease.

The several states proceeded accordingly to elect their
conventions; some of those conventions ratified the constitution by very large majorities, and two or three unanimously. In others there were much debate and division
of opinion. In the Massachusetts convention, which met
at Boston, the majority was not above nineteen or twenty,
in about three hundred members; but such is the nature
of representative government, that it quietly decides all
matters by majority. After the debate in the Massachusetts convention was closed, and the vote taken, the ob-
jecting members rose, and declared, " *That though they had
argued and voted against it, because certain parts appeared to
them in a different light to what they appeared to other members;
yet, as the vote had been decided in favor of the constitution as
proposed, they should give it the same practical support as if they
had voted for it.*"

As soon as nine states had concurred, (and the rest followed in the order their conventions were elected) the old fabric of the federal government was taken down, and a new one erected, of which general Washington is president. In this place I cannot help remarking, that the character and services of this gentleman are sufficient to put all those men called kings to shame. While they are receiving from the sweat and labors of mankind, a prodigality of pay, to which neither their abilities nor their services can entitle them, he is rendering every service in his power, and refusing every pecuniary reward. He accepted no pay as commander-in-chief; he accepts none as president of the United States.

After the new federal constitution was established, the state of Pennsylvania, conceiving that some parts of its own constitution required to be altered, elected a convention for that purpose. The proposed alterations were published, and the people concurring therein, they were established.

In forming those constitutions, or in altering them, little or no inconvenience took place. The ordinary course of things was not interrupted, and the advantages have been much. It is always the interest of a far greater number of people in a nation to have things right, than to let them remain wrong; and when public matters are open to debate, and the public judgment free, it will not decide wrong, unless it decides too hastily.

In the two instances of changing the constitutions, the government then in being were not actors either way.— Government has no right to make itself a party in any debate respecting the principles or modes of forming, or of changing constitutions. It is not for the benefit of those who exercise the powers of government, that constitutions, and the governments issuing from them, are established. In all those matters, the right of judging and acting are in those who pay, and not in those who receive.

A constitution is the property of a nation, and not of those who exercise the government. All the constitutions of America are declared to be established on the authority of the people. In France, the word nation is used instead of the people; but in both cases, a constitution is a thing antecedent to the government, and always distinct therefrom.

In England, it is not difficult to perceive that every thing has a constitution, except the nation. Every society and association that is established, first agreed upon a number of original articles, digested into form, which are its constitution. It then appointed its officers, whose powers and authorities are described in that constitution, and the government of that society then commenced. Those officers, by whatever name they are called, have no authority to add to, alter, or abridge the original articles. It is only to the constituting power that this right belongs.

From the want of understanding the difference between a constitution and a government, Dr. Johnson, and all writers of his description, have always bewildered themselves. They could not but perceive, that there must necessarily be a *controlling* power existing somewhere, and they placed this power in the discretion of the persons exercising the government, instead of placing it in a constitution formed by the nation. When it is in a constitution, it has the nation for its support, and the natural and the political controlling powers are together. The laws which are enacted by governments, control men only as individuals, but the nation, through its constitution, controls the whole government, and has a natural ability so to do.— The final controlling power, therefore, and the original constituting power, are one and the same power.

Dr. Johnson could not have advanced such a position in any country where there was a constitution ; and he is himself an evidence, that no such thing as a constitution exists in England. But it may be put as a question, not improper to be investigated, that if a constitution does not exist, how came the idea of its existence so generally established ?

In order to decide this question, it is necessary to consider a constitution in both its cases : 1st, as creating a government and giving it powers : 2d, as regulating and restraining the powers so given.

If we begin with William of Normandy, we find that the government of England was originally a tyranny, founded on an invasion and conquest of the country. This being admitted, it will then appear that the exertion of the nation, at different periods, to abate that tyranny, and render it less intolerable, has been credited for a constitution.

Magna Charta, as it was called, (it is now like an almanac of the same date) was no more than compelling the government to renounce a part of its assumptions. It did

not create and give powers to government in the manner
a constitution does; but was, as far as it went, of the nature of a re-conquest, and not of a constitution; for, could
the nation have totally expelled the usurpation, as France
has done its despotism, it would then have had a constitution to form.

The history of the Edwards and the Henries, and up to
the commencement of the Stuarts, exhibits as many instances of tyranny as could be acted within the limits to
which the nation had restricted it. The Stuarts endeavored to pass those limits, and their fate is well known. In
all those instances we see nothing of a constitution, but only
of restrictions on assumed power.

After this, another William, descended from the same
stock, and claiming from the same origin, gained possession; and of the two evils, James and William, the nation
preferred what it thought the least; since, from the circumstances, it must take one. The act, called the Bill of
Rights, comes here into view. What is it but a bargain,
which the parts of the government made with each other
to divide power, profit, and privileges? You shall have so
much, and I will have the rest; and with respect to the
nation, it said, for *your share*, *you* *shall have the right of petitioning*. This being the case, the bill of rights is more
properly a bill of wrongs, and of insult. As to what is
called the convention-parliament, it was a thing that made
itself, and then made the authority by which it acted. A
few persons got together, and called themselves by that
name. Several of them had never been elected, and none
of them for the purpose.

From the time of William, a species of government arose,
issuing out of this coalition bill of rights; and more so,
since the corruption introduced at the Hanover succession,
by the agency of Walpole: that can be described by no
other name than a despotic legislation. Though the parts
may embarrass each other, the whole has no bounds; and
the only right it acknowledges out of itself, is the right of
petitioning. Where then is the constitution that either
gives or restrains power?

It is not because a part of the government is elective,
that makes it less a despotism, if the persons so elected,
possess afterwards, as a parliament, unlimited powers.
Election, in this case, becomes separated from representation, and the candidates are candidates for despotism.

I cannot believe that any nation, reasoning on its own rights, would have thought of calling those things a *constitution*, if the cry of constitution had not been set up by the government. It has got into circulation like the words *bore*, and *quiz*, by being chalked up in speeches of parliament, as those words were on window-shutters and door posts; but whatever the constitution may be in other respects, it has undoubtedly been *the most productive machine for taxation that was ever invented*. The taxes in France, under the new constitution, are not quite thirteen shillings per head,* and the taxes in England, under what is called its present constitution, are forty-eight shillings and sixpence per head, men, women, and children, amounting to nearly seventeen millions sterling, besides the expense of collection, which is upwards of a million more.

In a country like England, where the whole of the civil government is executed by the people of every town and county, by means of parish officers, magistrates, quarterly sessions, juries, and assize, without any trouble to what is called government, or any other expense to the revenue than the salary of the judges, it is astonishing how such a mass of taxes can be employed. Not even the internal defence of the country is paid out of the revenue. On all occasions, whether real or contrived, recourse is continually had to new loans and to new taxes. No wonder then, that a machine of government so advantageous to the advocates of a court, should be so triumphantly extolled! No wonder that St. James's or St. Stephen's should echo with the continual cry of constitution! No wonder that the French revolution should be reprobated, and the *res-publica* treated with reproach! The *red book* of England, like the red book of France, will explain the reason.†

I will now, by way of relaxation, turn a thought or two to Mr. Burke. I ask his pardon for neglecting him so long.

* The whole amount of the assessed taxes of France, for the present year, is three hundred millions of francs, which is twelve millions and a half sterling; and the incidental taxes are estimated at three millions, making in the whole fifteen millions and an half; which among twenty-four millions of people, is not quite thirty shillings per head. France has lessened her taxes since the revolution, nearly nine millions sterling annually. Before the revolution, the city of Paris paid a duty of upwards of thirty per cent. on all articles brought into the city. This tax was collected at the city gates. It was taken off on the first of last May, and the gates taken down.

† What was called the *livre rouge*, or the red book, in France, was not exactly similar to the court calendar in England; but it sufficiently showed how a great part of the taxes were lavished.

" America," says he, (in his speech on the Canada constitution bill) " never dreamed of such absurd doctrine as
the Rights of Man."

Mr. Burke is such a bold presumer, and advances his
assertions and premises with such a deficiency of judgment,
that, without troubling ourselves about principles of philosophy or politics, the mere logical conclusions they produce, are ridiculous.   For instance :

If governments, as Mr. Burke asserts, are not founded
on the rights of *man*, and are founded on *any rights* at all,
they consequently must be founded on the rights of *something* that is *not man*.   What, then, is that something?

Generally speaking, we know of no other creatures that
inhabit the earth than man and beast; and in all cases,
where only two things offer themselves, and one must be
admitted, a negation proved on any one, amounts to an af-
firmative on the other ; and therefore, Mr. Burke, by proving against the rights of *man*, proves in behalf of the *beast* ;
and consequently, proves that government is a beast: and
as difficult things sometimes explain each other, we now
see the origin of keeping wild beasts in the Tower; for
they certainly can be of no other use than to show the origin of the government.   They are in the place of a constitution.   O! John Bull, what honors thou hast lost by not
being a wild beast.   Thou mightest, on Mr. Burke's system, have been in the Tower for life.

If Mr. Burke's arguments have not weight enough to
keep one serious, the fault is less mine than his ; and as I
am willing to make an apology to the reader for the liberty
I have taken, I hope Mr. Burke will also make his for giving
the cause.

Having thus paid Mr. Burke the compliment of remem-
bering him, I return to the subject.

From the want of a constitution in England, to restrain
and regulate the wild impulse of power, many of the laws
are irrational and tyrannical, and the administration of
them vague and problematical.

The attention of the government of England (for I rather
choose to call it by this name, than the English government) appears, since its political connexion with Germany,
to have been so completely engrossed and absorbed by foreign affairs, and the means of raising taxes, that it seems
to exist for no other purposes.   Domestic concerns are

neglected; and, with respect to regular law, there is scarcely such a thing.

Almost every case must now be determined by some precedent, be that precedent good or bad, or whether it properly applies or not; and the practice is become so general, as to suggest a suspicion, that it proceeds from a deeper policy than at first sight appears.

Since the revolution of America, and more so since that of France, this preaching up the doctrine of precedents, drawn from times and circumstances antecedent to those events, has been the studied practice of the English government. The generality of those precedents are founded on principles and opinions, the reverse of what they ought to be; and the greater distance of time they are drawn from, the more they are to be suspected. But by associating those precedents with a superstitious reverence for ancient things, as monks show relics and call them holy, the generality of mankind are deceived into the design. Governments now act as if they were afraid to awaken a single reflection in man. They are softly leading him to the sepulchre of precedents, to deaden his faculties and call his attention from the scene of revolutions. They feel that he is arriving at knowledge faster than they wish, and their policy of precedents is the barometer of their fears. This political popery, like the ecclesiastical popery of old, has had its day, and is hastening to its exit. The ragged relic and the antiquated precedent, the monk and the monarch, will moulder together.

Government by precedent, without any regard to the principle of the precedent, is one of the vilest systems that can be set up. In numerous instances, the precedent ought to operate as a warning, and not as an example, and requires to be shunned instead of imitated; but instead of this, precedents are taken in the lump and put at once for constitution and for law.

Either the doctrine of precedent is policy to keep a man in a state of ignorance, or it is a practical confession that wisdom degenerates in governments as governments increase in age, and can only hobble along by the stilts and crutches of precedents. How is it that the same persons who would proudly be thought wiser than their predecessors, appear at the same time only as the ghosts of departed wisdom? How strangely is antiquity treated! To answer some purposes it is spoken of as the times of darkness and ignorance, and to answer others it is put for the light of the world.

If the doctrine of precedents is to be followed, the expenses of government need not continue the same. Why pay men extravagantly, who have but little to do? If every thing that can happen is already in precedent, legislation is at an end, and precedent, like a dictionary, determines every case. Either, therefore, government has arrived at its dotage, and requires to be renovated, or all the occasions for exercising its wisdom have occurred.

We now see all over Europe, and particularly in England, the curious phenomenon of a nation looking one way, and a government the other; the one forward, and the other backward. If governments are to go on by precedent, while nations go on by improvement, they must at last come to a final separation, and the sooner, and the more civilly, they determine this point, the better it will be for them.*

Having thus spoken of constitutions generally, as things distinct from actual governments, let us proceed to consider the parts of which a constitution is composed.

Opinions differ more on this subject, than with respect to the whole. That a nation ought to have a constitution, as a rule for the conduct of its government, is a simple question in which all men, not directly courtiers, will agree. It is only on the component parts that questions and opinions multiply.

But this difficulty, like every other, will diminish when put into a train of being rightly understood.

The first thing is, that a nation has a right to establish a constitution.

Whether it exercises this right in the most judicious manner at first, is quite another case. It exercises it agreeably to the judgment it possesses; and by continuing to do so, all errors will at last be exploded.

* In England, the improvements in agriculture, useful arts, manufactures, and commerce, have been made in opposition to the genius of its government, which is that of following precedents. It is from the enterprise and industry of the individuals, and their numerous associations, in which, tritely speaking, government is neither pillow nor bolster, that these improvements have proceeded. No man thought about the government, or who was in, or who was out, when he was planning or executing those things : and all he had to hope, with respect to government, was, that it would let him alone. Three or four very silly ministerial newspapers are continually offending against the spirit of national improvement, by ascribing it to a minister.— They may with as much truth ascribe this book to a minister.

When this right is established in a nation, there is no fear that it will be employed to its own injury. A nation can have no interest in being wrong.

Though all the constitutions of America are on one general principle, yet no two of them are exactly alike in their component parts, or in the distribution of the powers which they give to the actual governments. Some are more, and others less complex.

In forming a constitution, it is first necessary to consider what are the ends for which government is necessary : secondly, what are the best means, and the least expensive, for accomplishing those ends.

Government is nothing more than a national association ; and the object of this association is the good of all, as well individually as collectively. Every man wishes to pursue his occupation, and to enjoy the fruits of his labors, and the produce of his property in peace and safety, and with the least possible expense. When these things are accomplished, all the objects for which government ought to be established are answered.

It has been customary to consider government under three distinct general heads. The legislative, the executive, and the judicial.

But if we permit our judgment to act unincumbered by the habit of multiplied terms, we can perceive no more than two divisions of power, of which civil government is composed, namely, that of legislating or enacting laws, and that of executing or administering them. Every thing, therefore, appertaining to civil government, classes itself under one or other of these two divisions.

So far as regards the execution of the laws, that which is called the judicial power, is strictly and properly the executive power of every country. It is that power to which every individual has an appeal, and which causes the laws to be executed ; neither have we any other clear idea with respect to the official execution of the laws. In England, and also in America and France, this power begins with the magistrate, and proceeds up through all the courts of judicature.

I leave to courtiers to explain what is meant by calling monarchy the executive power. It is merely a name in which acts of government are done ; and any other, or none at all, would answer the same purpose. Laws have neither more nor less authority on this account. It must

be from the justness of their principles, and the interest
which a nation feels therein, that they derive support; if
they require any other than this, it is a sign that something in the system of government is imperfect. Laws difficult to be executed cannot be generally good.

With respect to the organization of the *legislative power*,
different modes have been adopted in different countries.
In America it is generally composed of two houses. In
France it consists but of one, but in both countries it is
wholly by representation.

The case is, that mankind (from the long tyranny of assumed power) have had so few opportunities of making
the necessary trials on modes and principles of government, in order to discover the best, *that government is but
now beginning to be known*, and experience is yet wanting to
determine many particulars.

The objections against two houses are, first, that there
is an inconsistency in any part of a whole legislature, coming to a final determination by vote on any matter, whilst
that matter with respect to *that whole*, is yet only in a train
of deliberation, and consequently open to new illustrations.

2d, That by taking the vote on each, as a separate body,
it always admits of the possibility, and is often the case in
practice, that the minority governs the majority, and that,
in some instances, to a great degree of inconsistency.

3d, That two houses arbitrarily checking or controlling
each other, is inconsistent; because it cannot be proved,
on the principles of just representation, that either should
be wiser, or better than the other. They may check in the
wrong as well as in the right; and therefore, to give the
power where we cannot give the wisdom to use it, nor be
assured of its being rightly used, renders the hazard at
least equal to the precaution.*

---

* With respect to the two houses, of which the English parliament is composed, they appear to be effectually influenced into one, and, as a legislature,
to have no temper of its own. The minister, whoever he at any time may
be, touches it as with an opium wand, and it sleeps obedience.

But if we look at the distinct abilities of the two houses, the difference will
appear so great, as to show the inconsistency of placing power where there
can be no certainty of the judgment to use it. Wretched as the state of representation is in England, it is manhood compared with what is called the
house of lords; and so little is this nick-named house regarded, that the
people scarcely inquire at any time what it is doing. It appears also to be
most under influence, and the furthest removed from the general interest
of the nation. In the debate on engaging in the Russian and Turkish war,
the majority in the house of peers in favor of it was upwards of ninety, when
in the other house, which is more than double its numbers, the majority was
sixty-three.

The objection against a single house is, that it is always in a condition of committing itself too soon. But it should at the same time be remembered that when there is a constitution which defines the power, and establishes the principles within which a legislature shall act, there is already a more effectual check provided, and more powerfully operating, than any other check can be. For example,

Were a bill to be brought into any of the American legislatures, similar to that which was passed into an act by the English parliament, at the commencement of the reign of George I. to extend the duration of the assemblies to a longer period than they now sit, the check is in the constitution, which in effect says, *thus far shalt thou go and no further.*

But in order to remove the objection against a single house (that of acting with too quick an impulse) and at the same time to avoid the inconsistencies, in some cases absurdities, arising from the two houses, the following method has been proposed as an improvement on both.

1st, To have but one representation.

2d, To divide that representation, by lot, into two or three parts.

3d, That every proposed bill shall first be debated in those parts, by succession, that they may become hearers of each other, but without taking any vote. After which the whole representation to assemble, for a general debate and determination, by vote.

To this proposed improvement has been added another, for the purpose of keeping the representation in a state of constant renovation ; which is, that one third of the representation of each county shall go out at the expiration of one year, and the number be replaced by new elections. Another third at the expiration of the second year, replaced in like manner, and every third year to be a general election.*

The proceedings on Mr. Fox's bill, respecting the rights of juries, merits also to be noticed. The persons called the peers, were not the objects of that bill. They are already in possession of more privileges than that bill gave to others. They are their own jury, and if any one of that house were prosecuted for a libel, he would not suffer, even upon conviction, for the first offence. Such inequality in laws ought not to exist in any country. The French constitution says, that *the law is the same to every individual, whether to protect or to punish. All are equal in its sight.*

* As to the state of representation in England, it is too absurd to be reasoned upon. Almost all the represented parts are decreasing in population, and the unrepresented parts are increasing. A general convention of the nation is necessary to take the whole state of its government into consideration.

But in whatever manner the separate parts of a constitution may be arranged, there is one general principle that distinguishes freedom from slavery, which is, that all *hereditary government over a people is to them a species of slavery, and representative government is freedom.*

Considering government in the only light in which it should be considered, that of a NATIONAL ASSOCIATION, it ought to be so constructed as not to be disordered by any accident happening among the parts ; and therefore, no extraordinary power, capable of producing such an effect, should be lodged in the hands of any individual. The death, sickness, absence, or defection, of any one individual in a government, ought to be a matter of no more consequence, with respect to the nation, than if the same circumstance had taken place in a member of the English parliament, or the French national assembly.

Scarcely any thing presents a more degrading character of national greatness, than its being thrown into confusion by any thing happening to, or acted by an individual ; and the ridiculousness of the scene is often increased by the natural insignificance of the person by whom it is occasioned. Were a government so constructed, that it could not go on unless a goose or a gander were present in the senate, the difficulties would be just as great and as real on the flight or sickness of the goose or the gander, as if they were called a king. We laugh at individuals for the silly difficulties they make to themselves, without perceiving that the greatest of all ridiculous things are acted in governments.*

All the constitutions of America are on a plan that excludes the childish embarrassments which occur in monarchical countries. No suspension of government can there

---

* It is related, that in the canton of Berne, in Switzerland, it had been customary, from time immemorial, to keep a bear at the public expense, and the people had been taught to believe, that if they had not a bear, they should all be undone. It happened some years ago, that the bear, then in being, was taken sick, and died too suddenly to have his place immediately supplied with another. During the interregnum the people discovered, that the corn grew and the vintage flourished, and the sun and moon continued to rise and set, and every thing went on the same as before, and, taking courage from these circumstances, they resolved not to keep any more bears : for, said they, " a bear is a very voracious, expensive animal, and we were obliged to pull out his claws, lest he should hurt the citizens."

The story of the bear of Berne was related in some of the French newspapers, at the time of the flight of Louis XVI. and the application of it to monarchy could not be mistaken in France ; but it seems, that the aristocracy of Berne applied it to themselves, and have since prohibited the reading of French newspapers.

take place for a moment, from any circumstance whatever. The system of representation provides for every thing, and is the only system in which nations and governments can always appear in their proper character.

As extraordinary power ought not be lodged in the hands of any individual, so ought there to be no appropriations of public money to any person beyond what his services in a state may be worth. It signifies not whether a man be called a president, a king, an emperor, a senator, or by any other name, which propriety or folly may devise, or arrogance assume; it is only a certain service he can perform in the state; and the service of any such individual in the routine of office, whether such office be called monarchical, presidential, senatorial, or by another name or title, can never exceed the value of ten thousand pounds a-year. All the great services that are done in the world are performed by volunteer characters, who accept no pay for them; but the routine of office is always regulated to such a general standard of abilities as to be within the compass of numbers in every country to perform, and therefore cannot merit very extraordinary recompense. *Government*, says Swift, *is a plain thing, and fitted to the capacity of many heads.*

It is inhuman to talk of a million sterling a-year, paid out of the public taxes of any country, for the support of any individual, whilst thousands who are forced to contribute thereto are pining with want, and struggling with misery. Government does not consist in a contrast between prisons and palaces, between poverty and pomp; it is not instituted to rob the needy of his mite, and increase the wretchedness of the wretched.—But of this part of the subject I shall speak hereafter, and confine myself at present to political observations.

When extraordinary power and extraordinary pay are allotted to any individual in a government, he becomes the centre, round which every kind of corruption generates and forms. Give to any man a million a-year, and add thereto the power of creating and disposing of places, at the expense of a country, and the liberties of that country are no longer secure. What is called the splendor of a throne, is no other than the corruption of the state. It is made up of a band of parasites, living in luxurious indolence, out of the public taxes.

When once such a vicious system is established, it becomes the guard and protection of all inferior abuses. The man who is in the receipt of a million a-year is the last person to promote a spirit of reform, lest, in the event, it should reach to himself. It is always his interest to defend inferior abuses, as so many out-works to protect the citadel; and in this species of political fortification, all the parts have such a common dependance, that it is never to be expected they will attack each other.*

Monarchy would not have continued so many ages in the world had it not been for the abuses it protects. It is the master-fraud, which shelters all others. By admitting a participation of the spoil, it makes itself friends; and when it ceases to do this, it will cease to be the idol of courtiers.

As the principle on which constitutions are now formed, rejects all hereditary pretensions to government, it also rejects all that catalogue of assumptions known by the name of prerogatives.

If there is any government where prerogatives might with apparent safety be intrusted to any individual, it is in the federal government of America. The president of the United States of America is elected only for four years. He is not only responsible in the general sense of the word, but a particular mode is laid down in the constitution for trying him. He cannot be elected under thirty-five years of age; and he must be a native of the country.

---

* It is scarcely possible to touch on any subject, that will not suggest an allusion to some corruption in governments. The simile of "*fortifications*," unfortunately involves with it a circumstance, which is directly in point with the matter above alluded to.

Among the numerous instances of abuse which have been acted or protected by governments, ancient or modern, there is not a greater than that of quartering a man and his heirs upon the public, to be maintained at its expense.

Humanity dictates a provision for the poor—but by what right, moral or political, does any government assume to say, that the person called the duke of Richmond, shall be maintained by the public? Yet, if common report is true, not a beggar in London can purchase his wretched pittance of coal, without paying towards the civil list of the duke of Richmond. Were the whole produce of this imposition but a shilling a-year, the iniquitous principle would be still the same—but when it amounts, as it is said to do, to not less than twenty thousand pounds per ann. the enormity is too serious to be permitted to remain.—This is one of the effects of monarchy and aristocracy.

In stating this case, I am led by no personal dislike. Though I think it mean in any man to live upon the public, the vice originates in the government: and so general is it become, that whether the parties are in the ministry or in the opposition, it makes no difference; they are sure of the guarantee of each other.

In a comparison of these cases with the government of England, the difference when applied to the latter, amounts to an absurdity. In England, the person who exercises the prerogative is often a foreigner; always half a foreigner, and always married to a foreigner. He is never in full natural or political connexion with the country, is not responsible for any thing, and becomes of age at eighteen years; yet such a person is permitted to form foreign alliances, without even the knowledge of the nation ; and to make war and peace without its consent.

But this is not all. Though such a person cannot dispose of the government, in the manner of a testator, he dictates the marriage connexions, which, in effect, accomplishes a great part of the same end. He cannot directly bequeath half the government to Prussia, but he can form a marriage partnership that will produce the same effect. Under such circumstances, it is happy for England that she is not situated on the continent, or she might, like Holland, fall under the dictatorship of Prussia. Holland, by marriage, is as effectually governed by Prussia, as if the old tyranny of bequeathing the government had been the means.

The presidency in America (or, as it is sometimes called, the executive) is the only office from which a foreigner is excluded; and in England it is the only one to which he is admitted. A foreigner cannot be a member of parliament, but he may be what is called a king. If there is any reason for excluding foreigners, it ought to be from those offices where most mischief can be acted, and where, by uniting every bias of interest and attachment, the trust is best secured.

But as nations proceed in the great business of forming constitutions, they will examine with more precision into the nature and business of that department which is called the executive. What the legislative and judicial departments are, every one can see; but with respect to what, in Europe, is called the executive, as distinct from those two, it is either a political superfluity or a chaos of unknown things.

Some kind of official department, to which reports shall be made from different parts of the nation, or from abroad, to be laid before the national representatives, is all that is necessary ; but there is no consistency in calling this the executive; neither can it be considered in any other light than as inferior to the legislature. The sovereign authority in any country is the power of making laws, and every thing else is an official department.

Next to the arrangement of the principles and the organization of the several parts of a constitution, is the provision to be made for the support of the persons to whom the nation shall confide the administration of the constitutional powers.

A nation can have no right to the time and services of any person at his own expense, whom it may choose to employ or intrust in any department whatever; neither can any reason be given for making provision for the support of any one part of the government and not for the other.

But, admitting that the honor of being intrusted with any part of a government, is to be considered a sufficient reward, it ought to be so to every person alike. If the members of the legislature of any country are to serve at their own expense, that which is called the executive, whether monarchical, or by any other name, ought to serve in like manner. It is inconsistent to pay the one, and accept the service of the other gratis.

In America every department in the government, is decently provided for; but no one is extravagantly paid. Every member of congress, and of the state assemblies, is allowed a sufficiency for his expenses. Whereas in England, a most prodigal provision is made for the support of one part of the government, and none for the other; the consequence of which is, that the one is furnished with the means of corruption, and the other is put into the condition of being corrupted. Less than a fourth part of such expense, applied as it is in America, would remedy a great part of the corruption.

Another reform in the American constitutions, is the exploding all oaths of personality. The oath of allegiance is to the nation only. The putting any individual as a figure for a nation is improper. The happiness of a nation is the first object, and therefore the intention of an oath of allegiance ought not to be obscured by being figuratively taken, to, or in the name of, any person. The oath, called the civic oath, in France, *viz.* the "*nation, the law, and the king,*" is improper. If taken at all, it ought to be as in America, to the nation only. The law may or may not be good; but, in this place, it can have no other meaning, than as being conducive to the happiness of the nation, and therefore is included in it. The remainder of the oath is improper, on the ground that all personal oaths ought to be abolished. They are the remains of tyranny on one part, and slavery on the other; and the name of the Creator ought not to be introduced to witness the degradation of his creation; or if taken, as is already mentioned, as figurative of the nation, it is in this place redundant. But whatever apology may be made for oaths at the first establishment of a government, they ought not to be permitted afterwards. If a government requires the support of oaths, it is a sign that it is not worth supporting, and ought not to be supported. Make government what it ought to be, and it will support itself.

To conclude this part of the subject. One of the greatest improvements that has been made for the perpetual security and progress of constitutional liberty, is the provision which the new constitutions make for occasionally revising, altering and amending them.

The principle upon which Mr. Burke formed his political creed, that " *of binding and controlling posterity to the end of time, and renouncing and abdicating the rights of all posterity for ever,*" is now become too detestable to be made a subject of debate; and, therefore, I pass it over with no other notice than exposing it.

Government is but now beginning to be known. Hitherto it has been the mere exercise of power, which forbad all effectual inquiry into rights, and grounded itself wholly on possession. While the enemy of liberty was its judge, the progress of its principles must have been small indeed.

The constitutions of America, and also that of France, have either fixed a period for their revision, or laid down the mode by which improvements shall be made. It is perhaps impossible to establish any thing that combines principles with opinions and practice, which the progress of circumstances, through a length of years, will not in some measure derange, or render inconsistent; and, therefore, to prevent inconveniences accumulating, till they discourage reformations or provoke revolutions, it is best to regulate them as they occur. The rights of man are the rights of all generations of men, and cannot be monopolized by any. That which is worth following, will be followed for the sake of its worth; and it is in this that its security lies, and not in any conditions with which it may be incumbered. When a man leaves property to his heirs, he does not connect it with an obligation that they shall accept it. Why then should we do otherwise with respect to constitutions?

The best constitution that could now be devised, consistent with the condition of the present moment, may be far short of that excellence which a few years may afford. There is a morning of reason rising upon man, on the subject of government, that has not appeared before. As the barbarism of the present old governments expires, the moral condition of nations, with respect to each other, will be changed. Man will not be brought up with the savage idea of considering his species as enemies, because the accident of birth gave the individuals existence in countries distinguished by different names; and as constitutions have always some relation to external as well as to domestic circumstances, the means of benefiting by every change, foreign or domestic, should be a part of every constitution.

We already see an alteration in the national disposition of England and France towards each other, which, when we look back only a few years, is itself a revolution. Who could have foreseen, or who would have believed, that a French national assembly would ever have been a popular toast in England, or that a friendly alliance of the two nations should become the wish of either? It shows, that man, were he not corrupted by governments, is naturally the friend of man, and that human nature is not of itself vicious. That spirit of jealousy and ferocity, which the governments of the two countries inspired, and which they rendered subservient to the purpose of taxation, is now yielding to the dictates of reason, interest, and humanity. The trade of courts is beginning to be understood, and the affectation of mystery, with all the artificial sorcery by which they imposed upon mankind, is on the decline. It has received its death wound; and though it may linger, it will expire.

Government ought to be as much open to improvement as any thing which appertains to man, instead of which it has been monopolized from age to age, by the most ignorant and vicious of the human race. Need we any other proof of their wretched management, than the excess of debts and taxes with which every nation groans, and the quarrels into which they have precipitated the world?

Just emerging from such a barbarous condition, it is too soon to determine to what extent of improvement government may yet be carried. For what we can foresee, all Europe may form but one great republic, and man be free of the whole.

CHAPTER V.

WAYS AND MEANS OF IMPROVING THE CONDITION OF EUROPE: INTERSPERSED WITH MISCELLANEOUS OBSERVATIONS.

In contemplating a subject that embraces with equatorial magnitude the whole region of humanity, it is impossible to confine the pursuit in any one single direction. It takes ground on every character and condition that appertains to man, and blends the individual, the nation, and the world.

From a small spark, kindled in America, a flame has arisen, not to be extinguished. Without consuming, like the *ultima ratio regum*, it winds its progress from nation to nation, and conquers by a silent operation. Man finds himself changed, he scarcely perceives how. He acquires a knowledge of his rights by attending justly to his interest, and discovers in the event that the strength and powers of despotism consist wholly in the fear of resisting it, and that, in order " *to be free, it is sufficient that he wills it.*"

Having in all the preceding parts of this work endeavored to establish a system of principles as a basis on which governments ought to be erected, I shall proceed in this, to the ways and means of rendering them into practice. But in order to introduce this part of the subject with more propriety, and stronger effect, some preliminary observations, deducible from, or connected with, those principles, are necessary.

Whatever the form or constitution of government may be, it ought to have no other object than the general happiness. When, instead of this, it operates to create and increase wretchedness in any of the parts of society, it is on a wrong system, and reformation is necessary.

Customary language has classed the condition of man under the two descriptions of civilized and uncivilized life. To the one it has ascribed felicity and affluence; to the other, hardship and want. But however our imagination may be impressed by painting and comparison, it is nevertheless true, that a great portion of mankind, in what are called civilized countries, are in a state of poverty and wretchedness far below the condition of an Indian. I speak not of one country, but of all. It is so in England, it is so all over Europe. Let us inquire into the cause.

It lies not in any natural defect in the principles of civilization, but in preventing those principles having an universal operation; the consequence of which is, a perpetual system of war and expense, that drains the country and defeats the general felicity of which civilization is capable.

All the European governments (France now excepted,) are constructed, not on the principle of universal civilization, but on the reverse of it. So far as those governments relate to each other, they are in the same condition as we conceive of savage uncivilized life; they put themselves beyond the law as well of God as of man, and are, with respect to principle and reciprocal conduct, like so many individuals in a state of nature.

The inhabitants of every country, under the civilization of laws, easily associate together; but governments being in an uncivilized state and almost continually at war, they pervert the abundance which civilized life produces, to carry on the uncivilized part to a greater extent. By thus ingrafting the barbarism of government upon the internal civilization of a country, it draws from the latter, and more especially from the poor, a great portion of those earnings which should be applied to their own subsistence and comfort. Apart from all reflections of morality and philosophy, it is a melancholy fact, that more than one fourth of the labor of mankind is annually consumed by this barbarous system.

What has served to continue this evil, is the pecuniary advantage, which all the governments of Europe have found in keeping up this state of uncivilization. It affords to them pretences for power and revenue, for which there would be neither occasion nor apology, if the circle of civilization were rendered complete. Civil government alone, or the government of laws, is not productive of pretences for many taxes; it operates at home, directly under the eye of the country, and precludes the possibility of much imposition. But when the scene is laid in the uncivilized contention of governments, the field of pretences is enlarged, and the country, being no longer a judge, is open to every imposition which governments please to act.

Not a thirtieth, scarcely a fortieth, part of the taxes which are raised in England, are either occasioned by, or applied to, the purposes of civil government. It is not difficult to see, that the whole which the actual government does in this respect, is to enact laws, and that the country administers and executes them, at its own expense, by means of magistrates, juries sessions, and assize, over and above the taxes which it pays.

In this view of the case, we have two distinct characters of government; the one, the civil government, or the government of laws, which operates at home; the other, the court or cabinet government, which operates abroad on the rude plan of uncivilized life; the one attended with little charge, the other with boundless extravagance; and so distinct are the two, that if the latter were to sink, as it were by a sudden opening of the earth, and totally disappear, the former would not be deranged. It would still proceed because it is the common interest of the nation that it should, and all the means are in practice.

Revolutions, then, have for their object, a change in the moral condition of governments, and with this change the burden of public taxes will lessen, and civilization will be left to the enjoyment of that abundance, of which it is now deprived.

In contemplating the whole of this subject, I extend my views into the department of commerce. In all my publications, where the matter would admit, I have been an advocate for commerce, because I am a friend to its effects. It is a pacific system, operating to unite mankind, by rendering nations, as well as individuals, useful to each other. As to mere theoretical reformation, I have never preached it up. The most effectual process is that of improving the condition of man by means of his interest; and it is on this ground that I take my stand.

If commerce were permitted to act to the universal extent it is capable of, it would extirpate the system of war, and produce a revolution in the uncivilized state of governments. The invention of commerce has arisen since those governments began, and is the greatest approach towards universal civilization, that has yet been made by any means not immediately flowing from moral principles.

Whatever has a tendency to promote the civil intercourse of nations, by an exchange of benefits, is a subject as worthy of philosophy as of politics. Commerce is no other than the traffic of two persons, multiplied on a scale of numbers; and by the same rule that nature intended the intercourse of two, she intended that of all. For this purpose she has distributed the materials of manufactures and commerce, in various and distant parts of a nation and of the world; and as they cannot be procured by war so cheaply or so commodiously as by commerce, she has rendered the latter the means of extirpating the former.

As the two are nearly the opposites of each other, consequently, the uncivilized state of European governments is injurious to commerce. Every kind of destruction or embarrassment serves to lessen the quantity, and it matters but little in what part of the commercial world the reduction begins. Like blood, it cannot be taken from any of the parts, without being taken from the whole mass in circulation, and all partake of the loss. When the ability in any nation to buy is destroyed, it equally involves the seller. Could the government of England destroy the commerce of all other nations, she would most effectually ruin her own.

It is possible that a nation may be the carrier for the world, but she cannot be the merchant. She cannot be the seller and the buyer of her own merchandize. The ability to buy must reside out of herself; and, therefore, the prosperity of any commercial nation is regulated by the prosperity of the rest. If they are poor, she cannot be rich; and her condition, be it what it may, is an index of the height of the commercial tide in other nations.

That the principles of commerce, and its universal operation may be understood, without understanding the practice, is a position that reason will not deny; and it is on this ground only that I argue the subject. It is one thing in the counting-house, in the world it is another. With respect to its operation, it must necessarily be contemplated as a reciprocal thing, that only one half its powers resides within the nation, and that the whole is as effectually destroyed by destroying the half that resides without, as if the destruction had been committed on that which is within, for neither can act without the other.

When in the last, as well as in former wars, the commerce of England sunk, it was because the general quantity was lessened every where; and it now rises because commerce is in a rising state in every nation. If England at this day, imports and exports more than at any other period, the nation with which she trades must necessarily do the same ; her imports are their exports, and *vice versa*.

There can be no such thing as a nation flourishing alone in commerce; she can only participate ; and the destruction of it in any part must necessarily affect all. When, therefore, governments are at war, the attack is made upon the common stock of commerce, and the consequence is the same as if each had attacked his own.

The present increase of commerce is not to be attributed to ministers, or to any political contrivances, but to its own natural operations in consequence of peace. The regular markets had been destroyed, the channels of trade broken up, and the high road of the seas infested with robbers of every nation, and the attention of the world called to other objects. Those interruptions have ceased, and peace has restored the deranged condition of things to their proper order.*

It is worth remarking, that every nation reckons the balance of trade in its own favor; and therefore something must be irregular in the common ideas upon this subject.

The fact, however, is true, according to what is called a balance ; and it is from this cause that commerce is universally supported. Every nation feels the advantage, or it would abandon the practice : but the deception lies in the mode of making up the accounts, and in attributing what are called profits to a wrong cause.

Mr. Pitt has sometimes amused himself, by showing what he called a balance of trade from the custom-house books. This mode of calculation, not only affords no rule that is true, but one that is false.

---

* In America the increase of commerce is greater in proportion than in England It is, at this time, at least one half more than at any period prior to the revolution. The greatest number of vessels cleared out of the port of Philadelphia, before the commencement of the war, was between eight and nine hundred. In the year 1788, the number was upwards of twelve hundred. As the state of Pennsylvania is estimated as an eighth part of the United States in population, the whole number of vessels must now be nearly ten thousand.

In the first place, every cargo that departs from the custom-house, appears on the books as an export; and according to the custom-house balance, the losses at sea, and by foreign failures, are all reckoned on the side of the profit, because they appear as exports.

Second, Because the importation by the smuggling trade does not appear on the custom-house books, to arrange against the exports.

No balance, therefore, as applying to superior advantages, can be drawn from these documents; and if we examine the natural operation of commerce, the idea is fallacious; and if true, would soon be injurious. The great support of commerce consists in the balance being a level of benefits among all nations.

Two merchants of different nations trading together, will both become rich, and each makes the balance in his own favor; consequently, they do not get rich out of each other; and it is the same with respect to the nations in which they reside. The case must be, that each nation must get rich out of its own means, and increase that riches by something which it procures from another in exchange.

If a merchant in England sends an article of English manufacture abroad, which costs him a shilling at home, and imports something which sells for two, he makes a balance of one shilling in his own favor: but this is not gained out of the foreign nation or the foreign merchant, for he also does the same by the article he receives, and neither has a balance of advantage upon the other. The original value of the two articles in their proper countries were but two shillings; but by changing their places, they acquire a new idea of value, equal to double what they had at first, and that increased value is equally divided.

There is no otherwise a balance on foreign than on domestic commerce. The merchants of London and Newcastle trade on the same principle, as if they resided in different nations, and make their balances in the same manner: yet London does not get rich out of Newcastle, any more than Newcastle out of London: but coals, the merchandize of Newcastle, have an additional value at London, and London merchandize has the same at Newcastle.

Though the principle of all commerce is the same, the domestic, in a national view, is the part the most beneficial; because the whole of the advantages, on both sides, rest within the nation; whereas, in foreign commerce, it is only a participation of one half.

The most unprofitable of all commerce is that connected with foreign dominion. To a few individuals it may be beneficial, merely because it is commerce; but to the nation it is a loss. The expense of maintaining dominion more than absorbs the profits of any trade. It does not increase the general quantity in the world, but operates to lessen it; and as a greater mass would be afloat by relinquishing dominion, the participation without the expense would be more valuable than a greater quantity with it.

But it is impossible to engross commerce by dominion; and therefore it is still more fallacious. It cannot exist in confined channels, and necessarily breaks out by regular or irregular means that defeat the attempt and to succeed would be still worse. France, since the revolution, has been more than indifferent as to foreign possessions; and other nations will become the same, when they investigate the subject with respect to commerce.

To the expense of dominion is to be added that of navies, and when the amount of the two is subtracted from the profits of commerce, it will appear, that what is called the balance of trade, even admitting it to exist, is not enjoyed by the nation, but absorbed by the government.

The idea of having navies for the protection of commerce, is delusive. It is putting the means of destruction for the means of protection. Commerce needs no other protection than the reciprocal interest which every nation feels in supporting it—it is common stock—it exists by a balance of advantages to all; and the only interruption it meets, is from the present uncivilized state of governments, and which is its common interest to reform.*

Quitting this subject, I now proceed to other matters.— As it is necessary to include England in the prospect of a general reformation, it is proper to inquire into the defects of its government. It is only by each nation reforming its own, that the whole can be improved, and the full benefit

* When I saw Mr. Pitt's mode of estimating the balance of trade, in one of his parliamentary speeches, he appeared to me to know nothing of the nature and interest of commerce; and no man has more wantonly tortured it than himself. During a period of peace, it has been shackled with the calamities of war. Three times has it been thrown into stagnation, and the vessels unmanned by impressing, within less than four years of peace.

of reformation enjoyed. Only partial advantages can flow from partial reforms.

France and England are the only two countries in Europe where a reformation in government could have successfully begun. The one secure by the ocean, and the other by the immensity of its internal strength, could defy the malignancy of foreign despotism. But it is with revolutions as with commerce, the advantages increase by their becoming general, and double to either what each would receive alone.

As a new system is now opening to the view of the world, the European courts are plotting to counteract it.— Alliances, contrary to all former systems, are agitating, and a common interest of courts is forming against the common interest of man. The combination draws a line that runs throughout Europe, and presents a cause so entirely new, as to exclude all calculations from former circumstances. While despotism warred with despotism, man had no interest in the contest; but in a cause that unites the soldier with the citizen, and nation with nation, the despotism of courts, though it feels the danger, and meditates revenge is afraid to strike.

No question has arisen within the records of history that pressed with the importance of the present. It is not whether this or that party shall be in or out, or whig or tory, or high or low shall prevail; but whether man shall inherit his rights, and universal civilization take place?— Whether the fruits of his labor shall be enjoyed by himself, or consumed by the profligacy of governments?— Whether robbery shall be banished from courts, and wretchedness from countries?

When, in countries that are called civilized, we see age going to the work-house, and youth to the gallows, something must be wrong in the system of government. It would seem, by the exterior appearance of such countries, that all was happiness; but there lies hidden from the eye of common observation, a mass of wretchedness that has scarcely any other chance, than to expire in poverty or infamy. Its entrance into life is marked with the presage of its fate; and until this is remedied, it is in vain to punish.

Civil government does not exist by executions; but in making that provision for the instruction of youth, and the support of age, as to exclude, as much as possible, profli-

gacy from the one, and despair from the other. Instead
of this, the resources of a country are lavished upon kings,
upon courts, upon hirelings, impostors and prostitutes; and
even the poor themselves, with all their wants upon them,
are compelled to support the fraud that oppresses them.

Why is it, that scarcely any are executed but the poor?
The fact is a proof, among other things, of a wretchedness
in their condition. Bred up without morals, and cast upon
the world without a prospect, they are the exposed sacrifice of vice and legal barbarity. The millions that are su-
perfluously wasted upon governments are more than sufficient to reform those evils, and to benefit the condition of
every man in a nation, not included within the purlieus of
a court. This I hope to make appear in the progress of
this work.

It is the nature of compassion to associate with misfortune. In taking up this subject I seek no recompense—I
fear no consequences. Fortified with that proud integrity,
that disdains to triumph or to yield, I will advocate the
rights of man.

At an early period, little more than sixteen years of age,
raw and adventurous, and heated with the false heroism of
a master* who had served in a man of war, I began the
carver of my own fortune, and entered on board the privateer Terrible, captain Death. From this adventure I
was happily prevented by the affectionate and moral re-
monstrance of a good father, who, from his own habits of
life, being of the Quaker profession, must have begun to
look upon me as lost. But the impression, much as it effected at the time, began to wear away, and I entered
afterwards in the privateer, King of Prussia, captain Men-
dez, and went in her to sea. Yet, from such a beginning,
and with all the inconveniences of early life against me, I
am proud to say, that with a perseverance undismayed by
difficulties, a disinterestedness that compels respect, I have
not only contributed to raise a new empire in the world,
founded on a new system of government, but I have arrived at an eminence in political literature, the most difficult
of all lines to succeed and excel in, which aristocracy,
with all its aids, has not been able to reach or to rival.

Knowing my own heart, and feeling myself, as I now do,
superior to all the skirmish of party, the inveteracy of

* Rev. William Knowles, master of the grammar school of Thetford, in
Norfolk.

interested or mistaken opponents, I answer not to falsehood
or abuse, but proceed to the defects of the English government.*

* Politics and self-interest have been so uniformly connected, that the
world, from being so often deceived, has a right to be suspicious of public
characters; but with regard to myself, I am perfectly easy on this head. I
did not, at my first setting out in public life, nearly seventeen years ago, turn
my thoughts to subjects of government from motives of interest—and my
conduct from that moment to this, proves the fact. I saw an opportunity in
which I thought I could do some good, and I followed exactly what my heart
dictated. I neither read books, nor studied other people's opinions. I
thought for myself. The case was this:

During the suspension of the old governments in America, both before and
at the breaking out of hostilities, I was struck with the order and decorum
with which every thing was conducted; and impressed with the idea, that a
little more than what society naturally performed, was all the government
that was necessary, and that monarchy and aristocracy were frauds and im-
positions upon mankind. On these principles I published the pamphlet Common Sense. The success it met with was beyond any thing since the invention of printing. I gave a copy-right to every state in the union, and the demand ran to not less than one hundred thousand copies. I continued the
subject in the same manner, under the title of The Crisis, till the complete
establishment of the revolution.

After the declaration of independence, congress unanimously, and unknown
to me, appointed me secretary in the foreign department. This was agreeable to me, because it gave me the opportunity of seeing into the abilities of
foreign courts, and their manner of doing business. But a misunderstanding
arising between congress and me, respecting one of their commissioners, then
in Europe, Mr. Silas Deane, I resigned the office.

When the war ended I went from Philadelphia to Bordentown, on the east
bank of the Delaware, where I have a small place. Congress was at this time
at Princeton, fifteen miles distant; and general Washington's head-quarters
were at Rocky-hill, within the neighborhood of congress, for the purpose of
resigning his commission (the object for which he accepted it being accomplished) and of retiring to private life. While he was on this business, he
wrote me the letter which I here subjoin.

                                        Rocky-Hill, Sept. 10, 1783.

I have learned since I have been at this place, that you are at Bordentown.
Whether for the sake of retirement or economy, I know not. Be it for either, for both, or whatever it may, if you will come to this place, and partake with me, I shall be exceedingly happy to see you.

Your presence may remind congress of your past services to this country;
and if it is in my power to impress them, command my best exertions with
freedom, as they will be rendered cheerfully by one, who entertains a lively
sense of the importance of your works, and who, with much pleasure, sub-
scribes himself,

              Your sincere friend,

                              G. WASHINGTON.

During the war, in the latter end of the year 1780, I formed to myself the
design of coming over to England, and communicated it to general Greene,
who was then in Philadelphia, on his route to the southward, general Washington being then at too great a distance to communicate with immediately,
I was strongly impressed with the idea, that if I could get over to England,
without being known, and only remain in safety till I could get out a publication, I could open the eyes of the country with respect to the madness
and stupidity of its government. I saw that the parties in parliament had
pitted themselves as far as they could go, and could make no new impressions
on each other. General Greene entered fully into my views, but the affair

I begin with charters and corporations.

It is a perversion of terms to say, that a charter gives rights. It operates by a contrary effect, that of taking rights away. Rights are inherently in all the inhabitants; but charters, by annulling those rights in the majority, leave the right by exclusion in the hands of a few. If charters were constructed so as to express in direct terms, *" that every inhabitant, who is not a member of a corporation, shall not exercise the right of voting,"* such charters would in the face be charters, not of rights, but of exclusion. The effect is the same under the form they now stand; and the only persons on whom they operate, are the persons whom they exclude. Those whose rights are guaranteed, by not being taken away, exercise no other rights, than as members of the community they are entitled to without a charter; and therefore, all charters have no other than an indirect negative operation. They do not give rights to A, but they make a difference in favor of A, by taking away the rights of B, and consequently are instruments of injustice.

But charters and corporations have a more extensive evil effect than what relates merely to elections. They are sources of endless contention in the places where they ex-

---

of Arnold and Andre happening just after, he changed his mind, and, under strong apprehensions for my safety, wrote to me very pressingly from Annapolis, in Maryland, to give up the design, which, with some reluctance, I did. Soon after this I accompanied colonel Laurens (son of Mr. Laurens, who was then in the Tower) to France, on business from congress. We landed at l'Orient, and while I remained there, he being gone forward, a circumstance occurred, that renewed my former design. An English packet from Falmouth to New-York, with government despatches on board, was brought into l'Orient. That a packet should be taken, is no very extraordinary thing; but that the despatches should be taken with it will scarcely be credited, as they are always slung at the cabin window, in a bag loaded with cannon ball, and ready to be sunk in a moment. The fact, however, is as I have stated it, for the despatches came into my hands, and I read them. The capture, as I was informed, succeeded by the following stratagem:—the captain of the privateer Madame, who spoke English, on coming up with the packet, passed himself for the captain of an English frigate, and invited the captain of the packet on board, which, when done, he sent some of his hands and aud secured the mail. But be the circumstances of the capture what they may, I speak with certainty as to the despatches. They were sent up to Paris, to count Vergennes, and when colonel Laurens and myself returned to America, we took the originals to congress.

By these despatches I saw further into the stupidity of the English cabinet than I otherwise could have done, and I renewed my former design. But colonel Laurens was so unwilling to return alone, more especially, as among other matters, we had a charge of upwards of two hundred thousand pounds sterling in money, that I gave into his wishes, and finally gave up my plan. But I am now certain, that if I could have executed it, it would not have been altogether unsuccessful.

ist; and they lessen the common rights of national society. A native of England, under the operation of these charters and corporations, cannot be said to be an Englishman in the full sense of the word. He is not free of the nation, in the same manner that a Frenchman is free of France, and an American of America. His rights are circumscribed to the town, and, in some cases, to the parish of his birth; and in all other parts, though in his native land, he must undergo a local naturalization by purchase, or he is forbidden or expelled the place. This species of feudality is kept up to aggrandize the corporations to the ruin of the towns; and the effect is visible.

The generality of corporation towns are in a state of solitary decay, and prevented from further ruin only by some circumstances in their situation, such as a navigable river, or a plentiful surrounding country. As population is one of the chief sources of wealth, (for without it land itself has no value) every thing which operates to prevent it must lessen the value of property; and as corporations have not only this tendency, but directly this effect, they cannot but be injurious. If any policy were to be followed, instead of that of general freedom, to every person to settle where he chose, (as in France or America) it would be more consistent to give encouragement to new comers, than to preclude their admission by exacting premiums from them.*

The persons most immediately interested in the abolition of corporations, are the inhabitants of the towns where corporations are established. The instances of Manchester, Birmingham, and Sheffield, show, by contrast, the injury which those Gothic institutions are to property and commerce. A few examples may be found, such as that of London, whose natural and commercial advantages, owing to its situation on the Thames, is capable of bearing up against the political evils of a corporation; but in almost

---

* It is difficult to account for the origin of charter and corporation towns, unless we suppose them to have arisen out of, or having been connected with, some species of garrison services. The times in which they began justify this idea. The generality of those towns have been garrisons and the corporations were charged with the care of the gates of the towns, when no military garrison was present. Their refusing or granting admission to strangers, which has produced the custom of giving, selling and buying freedom, has more of the nature of garrison authority than civil government. Soldiers are free of all corporations throughout the nation, by the same propriety that every soldier is free of every garrison, and no other persons are. He can follow any employment, with the permission of his officers, in any corporation town throughout the nation.

all other cases the fatality is too visible to be doubted or denied.

Though the whole nation is not so directly affected by the depression of property in corporation towns as the inhabitants themselves, it partakes of the consequences. By lessening the value of property, the quantity of national commerce is curtailed. Every man is a customer in proportion to his ability; and as all parts of a nation trade with each other, whatever affects any of the parts, must necessarily communicate to the whole.

As one of the houses of the English parliament is, in a great measure, made up by elections from these corporations; and as it is unnatural that a pure stream would flow from a foul fountain, its vices are but a continuation of the vices of its origin. A man of moral honor and good political principles, cannot submit to the mean drudgery and disgraceful arts, by which such elections are carried. To be a successful candidate, he must be destitute of the qualities that constitute a just legislator: and being thus disciplined to corruption by the mode of entering into parliament, it is not to be expected that the representative should be better than the man.

Mr. Burke, in speaking of the English representation, has advanced as bold a challenge as ever was given in the days of chivalry. " Our representation," says he, " has been found *perfectly adequate to all the purposes* for which a representation of the people can be desired or devised. I defy," continues he, " the enemies of our constitution to show the contrary." This declaration from a man, who has been in constant opposition to all the measures of parliament the whole of his political life, a year or two excepted, is most extraordinary; and comparing him with himself, admits of no other alternative, than that he acted against his judgment as a member, or has declared contrary to it as an author.

But it is not in the representation only that the defects lie, and therefore I proceed in the next place to aristocracy.

What is called the house of peers, is constituted on a ground very similar to that, against which there is a law in other cases. It amounts to a combination of persons in one common interest. No reason can be given, why an house of legislation should be composed entirely of men whose occupation consists in letting landed property, than

why it should be composed of those who hire, or of brew⁹
ers, or bakers, or any other separate class of men.

Mr. Burke calls this house, " *the great ground and pillar
of security to the landed interest.*"   Let us examine this idea.

What pillar of security does the landed interest require
more than any other interest in the state, or what right
has it to a distinct and separate representation from the
general interest of a nation?   The only use to be made of
this power, (and which it has always made,) is to ward off
taxes from itself, and throw the burden upon such articles
of consumption by which itself would be least affected.

That this has been the consequence (and will always be
the consequence of constructing governments on combina-
tions,) is evident with respect to England, from the history
of its taxes.

Notwithstanding taxes have increased and multiplied
upon every article of common consumption, the land-tax,
which more particularly affects this " pillar," has diminished. In 1788, the amount of the land-tax was 1,950,000*l.*
which is half a million less than it produced almost an
hundred years ago, notwithstanding the rentals are in
many instances doubled since that period.

Before the coming of the Hanoverians, the taxes were
divided in nearly equal proportions between the land and
articles of consumption, the land bearing rather the largest
share; but since that era, nearly thirteen millions annually
of new taxes have been thrown upon consumption. The
consequence of which has been a constant increase in the
number and wretchedness of the poor, and in the amount
of the poor-rates.   Yet here again the burden does not
fall in equal proportions on the aristocracy with the rest
of the community.   Their residences, whether in town or
country, are not mixed with the habitations of the poor.—
They live apart from distress, and the expense of relieving
it.   It is in manufacturing towns and laboring villages that
those burdens press the heaviest; in many of which it is
one class of poor supporting another.

Several of the most heavy and productive taxes are so
contrived, as to give an exemption to this pillar, thus standing in its own defence.   The tax upon beer brewed for
sale does not affect the aristocracy, who brew their own
beer free of this duty.   It falls only on those who have not
conveniency or ability to brew, and who must purchase it
in small quantities.   But what will mankind think of the

justice of taxation, when they know, that this tax alone, from which the aristocracy are from circumstances exempt, is nearly equal to the whole of the land-tax, being in the year 1788, and it is not less now, 1,666,152*l.* and with its proportion of the taxes on malt and hops, it exceeds it. That a single article, thus partially consumed, and that chiefly by the working part, should be subject to a tax, equal to that on the whole rental of a nation, is, perhaps, a fact not to be paralleled in the history of revenues.

This is one of the consequences resulting from an house of legislation, composed on the ground of a combination of common interest; for whatever their separate politics as to parties may be, in this they are united. Whether a combination acts to raise the price of any article for sale, or the rate of wages; or whether it acts to throw taxes from itself upon another class of the community, the principle and the effect are the same: and if the one be illegal, it will be difficult to show that the other ought to exist.

It is no use to say, that taxes are first proposed in the house of commons; for as the other house has always a negative, it can always defend itself; and it would be ridiculous to suppose that its acquiescence in the measures to be proposed were not understood beforehand. Besides which, it has obtained so much influence by borough-traffic, and so many of its relations and connexions are distributed on both sides of the commons, as to give it, besides an absolute negative in the house, a preponderancy in the other, in all matters of common concern.

It is difficult to discover what is meant by the *landed interest*, if it does not mean a combination of aristocratical land-holders, opposing their own pecuniary interest to that of the farmer, and every branch of trade, commerce, and manufacture. In all other respects it is the only interest that needs no partial protection. It enjoys the general protection of the world. Every individual, high or low, is interested in the fruits of the earth; men, women, and children, of all ages and degrees, will turn out to assist the farmer, rather than a harvest should not be got in; and they will not act thus by any other property. It is the only one for which the common prayer of mankind is put up, and the only one that can never fail from the want of means. It is the interest, not of the policy, but of the existence of man, and when it ceases, he must cease to be.

No other interest in a nation stands on the same united support. Commerce, manufactures, arts, sciences, and every thing else, compared with this, are supported but in parts. Their prosperity or their decay has not the same universal influence. When the vallies laugh and sing, it is not the farmer only, but all creation that rejoices. It is a prosperity that excludes all envy; and this cannot be said of any thing else.

Why then does Mr. Burke talk of his house of peers, as the pillar of the landed interest? Were that pillar to sink into the earth, the same landed property would continue, and the same ploughing, sowing, and reaping would go on. The aristocracy are not the farmers who work the land, and raise the produce, but are the mere consumers of the rent; and when compared with the active world, are the drones, a seraglio of males, who neither collect the honey nor form the hive, but exist only for lazy enjoyment.

Mr. Burke, in his first essay, called aristocracy, " *the corinthian capital of polished society.*" Towards completing the figure, he has now added the *pillar ;* but still the base is wanting; and whenever a nation chooses to act a Sampson, not blind, but bold, down go the temple of Dagon, the lords and the Philistines.

If a house of legislation is to be composed of men of one class, for the purpose of protecting a distinct interest, all the other interests should have the same. The inequality as well as the burden of taxation, arises from admitting it in one case, and not in all. Had there been a house of farmers, there had been no game laws; or a house of merchants and manufacturers, the taxes had neither been so unequal nor so excessive. It is from the power of taxation being in the hands of those who can throw so great a part of it from their own shoulders, that it has raged without a check.

Men of small or moderate estates, are more injured by the taxes being thrown on articles of consumption, than they are eased by warding it from landed property, for the following reasons :

1st, They consume more of the productive taxable articles, in proportion to their property, than those of large estates.

2d, Their residence is chiefly in towns, and their property in houses; and the increase of the poor-rates, occasioned by taxes on consumption, is in much greater proportion than the land-tax has been favored. In Birmingham, the poor-rates are not less than seven shillings in the pound. From this, as is already observed, the aristocracy are in a great measure exempt.

These are but a part of the mischiefs flowing from the wretched scheme of an house of peers.

As a combination, it can always throw a considerable portion of taxes from itself ; as an hereditary house, accountable to nobody, it resembles a rotten borough, whose consent is to be courted by interest. There are but few of its members, who are not in some mode or other participators, or disposers of the public money. One turns a candle-holder, or a lord in waiting ; another a lord of the bedchamber, a groom of the stole, or any insignificant nominal office, to which a salary is annexed, paid out of the public taxes, and which avoids the direct appearance of corruption. Such situations are derogatory to the character of man ; and where they can be submitted to, honor cannot reside.

To all these are to be added the numerous dependants, the long list of the younger branches and distant relations, who are to be provided for at the public expense : in short were an estimation to be made of the charge of the aristocracy to a nation, it will be found nearly equal to that of supporting the poor. The duke of Richmond alone (and there are cases similar to his) takes away as much for himself, as would maintain two thousand poor and aged persons. Is it, then, any wonder, that under such a system of government taxes and rates have multiplied to their present extent?

In stating these matters, I speak an open and disinterested language, dictated by no passion but that of humanity. To me, who have not only refused offers, because I thought them improper, but have declined rewards I might with reputation have accepted, it is no wonder that meanness and imposition appear disgusting. Independence is my happiness, and I view things as they are, without regard to place or person ; my country is the world, and my religion is to do good.

Mr. Burke, in speaking of the aristocratical law of primogeniture, says, " It is the standing law of our landed inheritance ; and which without question, has a tendency, and I think," continues, he, " a happy tendency, to preserve a character of weight and consequence."

Mr. Burke may call this law what he pleases, but humanity and impartial reflection will pronounce it a law of brutal injustice. Were we not accustomed to the daily practice, and did we only hear of it as the law of some distant part of the world, we should conclude that the legislators of such countries had not arrived at a state of civilization.

As to preserving a character of *weight and consequence*, the case appears to me directly the reverse. It is an attaint upon character; a sort of privateering on family property. It may have weight among dependant tenants, but it gives none on a scale of national, and much less of universal character. Speaking for myself, my parents were not able to give me a shilling, beyond what they gave me in education; and to do this they distressed themselves; yet, I possess more of what is called consequence, in the world, than any one in Mr. Burke's catalogue of aristocrats.

Having thus glanced at some of the defects of the two houses of parliament, I proceed to what is called the crown, upon which I shall be very concise.

It signifies a nominal office of a million sterling a-year, the business of which consists in receiving the money. Whether the person be wise or foolish, sane or insane, a native or a foreigner, matters not. Every ministry acts upon the same idea that Mr. Burke writes, namely, that the people must be hoodwinked, and held in superstitious ignorance by some bugbear or other; and what is called the crown answers this purpose, and therefore it answers all the purposes to be expected from it. This is more than can be said of the other two branches.

The hazard to which this office is exposed in all countries, is not from any thing that can happen to the man, but from what may happen to the nation; the danger of its coming to its senses.

It has been customary to call the crown the executive power, and the custom is continued, though the reason has ceased.

It was called the *executive*, because he whom it signified, used formerly to sit in the character of a judge, in administering or executing the laws. The tribunals were then a part of the court. The power, therefore, which is now called the judicial, was what is called the executive; and, consequently, one or the other of the terms is redundant, and one of the offices useless. When we speak of the crown now, it means nothing; it signifies neither a judge nor a general: besides which it is the laws that govern, and not the man. The old terms are kept up, and give an appearance of consequence to empty forms: and the only effect they have is that of increasing expenses.

Before I proceed to the means of rendering governments more conducive to the general happiness of mankind, than they are at present, it will not be improper to take a review of the progress of taxation in England.

It is a general idea, that when taxes are once laid on, they are never taken off. However true this may have been of late, it was not always so. Either, therefore, the people of former times were more watchful over government than those of the present, or government was administered with less extravagance.

It is now seven hundred years since the Norman conquest, and the establishment of what is called the crown. Taking this portion of time in seven separate periods of one hundred years each, the amount of the annual taxes, at each period will be as follows:

Annual amount of taxes levied by William the
conqueror, beginning in the year 1066, 400,000*l.*
Annual amount of taxes at one hundred years
from the conquest, (1166) - - - 200,000
Annual amount of taxes at two hundred years
from the conquest, (1266) - - - 150,000
Annual amount of taxes at three hundred years
from the conquest, (1366) - - - 130,000
Annual amount of taxes at four hundred years
from the conquest, (1466) - - - 100,000

These statements, and those which follow, are taken from sir John Sinclair's History of the Revenue; by which it appears, that taxes continued decreasing for four hundred years, at the expiration of which time they were reduced three-fourths, *viz.* from four hundred thousand pounds to one hundred thousand. The people of England of the present day, have a traditionary and historical idea of the bravery of their ancestors; but whatever their virtues or vices might have been, they certainly were a people who would not be imposed upon, and who kept government in awe as to taxation, if not as to principle. Though they were not able to expel the monarchical usurpation, they restricted it to a public economy of taxes.

Let us now review the remaining three hundred years.
Annual amount of taxes at five hundred years
   from the conquest, (1566)   -   -   500,000*l.*
Annual amount of taxes at six hundred years
   from the conquest, (1666)   .   -   -   1,800,000
Annual amount of taxes at the present time,
   (1791)   -   .   -   -   -   -   17,000,000

The difference between the first four hundred years
and the last three, is so astonishing, as to warrant an opinion, that the national character of the English has changed.
It would have been impossible to have dragooned the former English into the excess of taxation that now exists; and
when it is considered that the pay of the army, the navy,
and of all the revenue-officers, is the same now as it was
above a hundred years ago, when the taxes were not above
a tenth part of what they are at present, it appears impossible to account for the enormous increase and expenditure, on any other grounds than extravagance, corruption,
and intrigue.*

* Several of the court newspapers have of late made frequent mention of
Wat Tyler. That his memory should be traduced by court sycophants, and
all those who live on the spoil of a public, is not to be wondered at. He was,
however, the means of checking the rage and injustice of taxation in his time,
and the nation owed much to his valor. The history is concisely this :—in
the time of Richard II. a poll-tax was levied, of one shilling per head upon
every person in the nation, of whatever class or condition, on poor as well as
rich, above the age of fifteen years. If any favor was shown in the law, it was
to the rich rather than the poor ; as no person could be charged more than
twenty shillings for himself, family and servants, though ever so numerous—
while all other families, under the number of twenty, were charged per head.
Poll-taxes had always been odious—but this being also oppressive and unjust,
it excited, as it naturally must, universal detestation among the poor and
middle classes. The person known by the name of Wat Tyler, and whose
proper name was Walter, and a tyler by trade, lived at Deptford. The gatherer of the poll-tax, on coming to his house, demanded a tax for one of his
daughters, whom Tyler declared was under the age of fifteen. The tax-
gatherer insisted on satisfying himself, and began an indecent examination of
the girl, which enraging the father, he struck him with a hammer, that brought
him to the ground, and was the cause of his death.

This circumstance served to bring the discontents to an issue. The inhabitants of the neighborhood espoused the cause of Tyler, who, in a few days
was joined, according to some historians, by upwards of fifty thousand men,
and chosen their chief. With this force he marched to London, to demand
an abolition of the tax, and a redress of other grievances. The court, finding
itself in a forlorn condition, and unable to make resistance, agreed, with Richard at its head, to hold a conference with Tyler in Smithfield, making many
fair professions, courtier-like, of its disposition to redress the oppressions.
While Richard and Tyler were in conversation on these matters, each being
on horseback, Walworth, then mayor of London, and one of the creatures of
the court, watched an opportunity, and like a cowardly assassin, stabbed Tyler with a dagger—and two or three others falling upon him, he was instantly
sacrificed.

With the revolution of 1688, and more so since the Hanover succession, came the destructive system of continental intrigues, and the rage for foreign wars and foreign dominion; systems of such secure mystery, that the expenses admit of no accounts; a single line stands for millions. To what excess taxation might have extended, had not the French revolution contributed to break up the system, and put an end to pretences, is impossible to say. Viewed, as that revolution ought to be, as the fortunate means of lessening the load of taxes of both countries, it is of as much importance to England as to France; and, if properly improved to all the advantages of which it is capable, and to which it leads, deserves as much celebration in one country as the other.

In pursuing this subject, I shall begin with the matter that first presents itself, that of lessening the burden of taxes; and shall then add such matters and propositions, respecting the three countries of England, France and America, as the present prospect of things appear to justify; I mean an alliance of the three, for the purposes that will be mentioned in their proper places.

What has happened may happen again. By the statement before shown, of the progress of taxation, it is seen, that taxes have been lessened to a fourth part of what they had formerly been. Though the present circumstances do not admit of the same reduction, yet they admit of such a beginning, as may accomplish that end in a less time, than in the former case.

The amount of taxes for the year, ending at Michaelmas, 1778, was as follows:

Land tax	1,950,000*l.*
Customs	3,789,274
Excise (including old and new malt)	6,751,727
Stamps	1,278,214
Miscellaneous taxes and incidents	1,803,755
	15,572,970*l.*

Tyler appears to have been an intrepid, disinterested man, with respect to himself. All his proposals made to Richard, were on a more just and public ground, than those which had been made to John by the barons; and notwithstanding the sycophancy of historians, and men like Mr. Burke, who seek to gloss over a base action of the court by traducing Tyler, his fame will outlive their falsehood. If the barons merited a monument to be erected in Runneymede, Tyler merits one in Smithfield.

Since the year 1788, upwards of one million, new taxes have been laid on, besides the produce of the lotteries; and as the taxes have in general been more productive since than before, the amount may be taken, in round numbers, at 17,000,000*l.*

N. B. The expense of collection and the drawbacks, which together amount to nearly two millions, are paid out of the gross amount; and the above is the net sum paid into the exchequer.

The sum of seventeen millions is applied to two different purposes; the one to pay the interest of the national debt, the other to pay the current expenses of each year. About nine millions are appropriated to the former; and the remainder, being nearly eight millions, to the latter. As to the million, said to be applied to the reduction of the debt, it is so much like paying with one hand and taking out with the other, as not to merit much notice.

It happened, fortunately for France, that she possessed national domains for paying off her debt, and thereby lessening her taxes; but as this is not the case in England, her reduction of taxes can only take place by reducing the current expenses, which may now be done to the amount of four or five millions annually, as will hereafter appear. When this is accomplished, it will more than counterbalance the enormous charge of the American war; and the saving will be from the same sources from whence the evil arose.

As to the national debt, however heavy the interest may be in taxes, yet, as it seems to keep alive a capital, useful to commerce, it balances by its effects a considerable part of its own weight; and as the quantity of gold and silver in England is, by some means or other, short of its proper proportion,* (being not more than twenty millions, whereas it should be sixty) it would, besides the injustice, be bad policy to extinguish a capital that serves to supply that defect. But with respect to the current expense, whatever is saved therefrom is gain. The excess may serve to keep corruption alive, but it has no reaction on credit and commerce, like the interest of the debt.

It is now very probable, that the English government (I do not mean the nation) is unfriendly to the French revo-

---

* Foreign intrigues, foreign wars, and foreign dominions, will in a great measure account for the deficiency.

lution.   Whatever serves to expose the intrigue and lessen
the influence of courts, by lessening taxation, will be unwelcome to those who feed upon the spoil.   Whilst the
clamor of French intrigue, arbitrary power, popery, and
wooden shoes could be kept up, the nations were easily
allured and alarmed into taxes.   Those days are now past;
deception, it is to be hoped, has reaped its last harvest, and
better times are in prospect for both countries, and for the
world.

Taking it for granted, that an alliance may be formed
between England, France, and America, for the purposes
hereafter to be mentioned, the national expenses of France
and England may consequently be lessened.   The same
fleets and armies will no longer be necessary to either, and
the reduction can be made ship for ship on each side.   But
to accomplish these objects, the governments must necessarily be fitted to a common correspondent principle.
Confidence can never take place, while an hostile disposition remains in either, or where mystery and secrecy on
one side, is opposed to candor and openness on the other.

These matters admitted, the national expenses might be
put back, *for the sake of a precedent*, to what they were at
some period when France and England were not enemies.
This, consequently, must be prior to the Hanover succession, and also to the revolution of 1688.*   The first instance that presents itself, antecedent to those dates, is in
the very wasteful and profligate time of Charles II. at
which time England and France acted as allies.   If I have
chosen a period of great extravagance, it will serve to
show modern extravagance in a still worse light; especially as the pay of the navy, the army, and the revenue-
officers has not increased since that time.

* I happened to be in England at the celebration of the centenary of the
revolution of 1688.   The characters of William and Mary have always appeared to me detestable;   the one seeking to destroy his uncle, and the other
her father, to get possession of power themselves : yet, as the nation was disposed to think something of that event, I felt hurt at seeing it ascribe the
whole reputation of it to a man who had undertaken it as a job, and who, besides what he otherwise got, charged six hundred thousand pounds for the
expense of the little fleet that brought him from Holland.   George I. acted
the same close-fisted part as William had done, and bought the duchy of Bre-
men with the money he got from England, two hundred and fifty thousand
pounds over and above his pay as king ; and having thus purchased it at the
expense of England, added it to his Hanoverian dominions for his own private benefit.   In fact every nation that does not govern itself, is governed as
a job.   England has been the prey of jobs ever since the revolution.

The peace establishment was then as follows: See sir John Sinclair's History of the Revenue.

Navy	-	-	-	-	300,000*l.*
Army	-	-	-	-	212,000
Ordnance	-	-	-		40,000
Civil List	-	-	-	-	462,115

1,014,115*l.*

The parliament, however, settled the whole annual peace establishment at 1,200,000.* If we go back to the time of Elizabeth, the amount of all the taxes was but half a million, yet the nation sees nothing during that period, that reproaches it with want of consequence.

All circumstances then taken together, arising from the French revolution, from the approaching harmony and reciprocal interest of the two nations, the abolition of court intrigue on both sides, and the progress of knowledge in the science of government, the annual expenditure might be put back to one million and a half, *viz.*

Navy	-	-	-	-	500,000*l.*
Army	-	-	-	500,000
Expenses of government			500,000

1,500,000*l.*

Even this sum is six times greater than the expenses of government are in America, yet the civil internal government of England (I mean that administered by means of quarter sessions, juries, and assize, and which, in fact, is nearly the whole, and is performed by the nation,) is less expense upon the revenue, than the same species and portion of government is in America.

It is time that nations should be rational, and not be governed like animals for the pleasure of their riders. To read the history of kings, a man would be almost inclined to suppose that government consisted in stag-hunting, and that every nation paid a million a-year to the huntsman. Man ought to have pride, or shame enough to blush at being thus imposed upon, and when he feels his proper character, he will. Upon all subjects of this nature, there is often passing in the mind a train of ideas he has not yet

---

* Charles, like his predecessors and successors, finding that war was the harvest of governments, engaged in a war with the Dutch, the expense of which increased the annual expenditure to 1,800,000*l.* as stated under the date of 1666 ; but the peace establishment was but 1,200,000*l.*

accustomed himself to encourage and communicate. Restrained by something that puts on the character of prudence, he acts the hypocrite to himself as well as to others. It is, however, curious to observe how soon this spell can be dissolved. A single expression, boldly conceived and uttered, will sometimes put a whole company into their proper feelings, and whole nations are acted upon in the same manner.

As to the offices of which any civil government may be composed, it matters but little by what names they are described. In the routine of business, as before observed, whether a man be styled a president, a king, an emperor, a senator, or any thing else, it is impossible that any service he can perform, can merit from a nation more than ten thousand pounds a-year; and as no man should be paid beyond his services, so every man of a proper heart will not accept more. Public money ought to be touched with the most scrupulous consciousness of honor. It is not the produce of riches only, but of the hard earnings of labor and poverty. It is drawn even from the bitterness of want and misery. Not a beggar passes, or perishes in the streets, whose mite is not in that mass.

Were it possible that the congress of America, could be so lost to their duty, and to the interest of their constituents, as to offer general Washington, as president of America, a million a-year, he would not, and he could not, accept it. His sense of honor is of another kind. It has cost England almost seventy millions sterling, to maintain a family imported from abroad, of very inferior capacity to thousands in the nation ; and scarcely a year has passed that has not produced some mercenary application. Even the physicians' bills have been sent to the public to be paid. No wonder that jails are crowded, and taxes and poor-rates increased. Under such systems, nothing is to be looked for but what has already happened ; and as to reformation, whenever it comes, it must be from the nation, and not from the government.

To show that the sum of five hundred thousand pounds is more than sufficient to defray all the expenses of government, exclusive of navies and armies, the following estimate is added for any country, of the same extent as England.

In the first place three hundred representatives, fairly elected, are sufficient for all the purposes to which legisla-

tion can apply, and preferable to a larger number. They
may be divided into two, or three houses, or meet in one,
as in France, or in any manner a constitution shall direct.

As representation is always considered, in free countries, as the most honorable of all stations, the allowance
made to it is merely to defray the expense which the representatives incur by that service, and not to it as an office.

If an allowance, at the rate of five hundred pounds per annum be made to every representative, deducting for non-attendance, the expense, if the whole number attended for six months each year would be	75,000*l.*
The official departments cannot reasonably exceed the following number, with the salaries annexed:	
Three offices, at ten thousand pounds each	30,000
Ten ditto, at five thousand pounds each	50,000
Twenty ditto, at two thousand pounds each	40,000
Forty ditto, at one thousand pounds each	40,000
Two hundred do. at five hundred pounds each	100,000
Three hundred ditto, at two hundred pounds each - - - - - -	60,000
Five hundred ditto, at one hundred pounds each - - - - - -	50,000
Seven hundred ditto, at seventy-five pounds each - - - - - -	52,500
	497,500*l.*

If a nation chooses, it can deduct four per cent. from all
offices, and make one of twenty thousand per annum.

All revenue-officers are paid out of the monies they collect and therefore, are not included in this estimation.

The foregoing is not offered as an exact detail of offices,
but to show the number and rate of salaries which five
hundred thousand pounds will support; and it will, on experience, be found impracticable to find business sufficient
to justify even this expense. As to the manner in which
office-business is now performed, the chiefs, in several
offices, such as the post-office, and certain offices in the exchequer, &c. do little more than sign their names three or
four times a year; and the whole duty is performed by
under clerks.

Taking, therefore, one million and an half as a sufficient
peace establishment for all the honest purposes of govern-

ment, which is three hundred thousand pounds more than the peace establishment in the profligate and prodigal times of Charles II. (notwithstanding, as has been already observed, the pay and salaries of the army, navy, and revenue-officers, continue the same as at that period,) there will remain a surplus of upwards of six millions out of the present current expenses. The question then will be, how to dispose of this surplus.

Whoever has observed the manner in which trade and taxes twist themselves together, must be sensible of the impossibility of separating them suddenly.

1st, Because the articles now on hand are already charged with the duty, and the reduction cannot take place on the present stock.

2d. Because, on all those articles on which the duty is charged in the gross, such as per barrel, hogshead, hundred weight, or ton, the abolition of the duty does not admit of being divided down so as fully to relieve the consumer, who purchases by the pint, or the pound. The last duty laid on strong beer and ale, was three shillings per barrel, which, if taken off, would lessen the purchase only half a farthing per pint, and consequently, would not reach to practical relief.

This being the condition of a greater part of the taxes, it will be necessary to look for such others as are free from this embarrassment, and where the relief will be direct and visible, and capable of immediate operation.

In the first place, then, the poor-rates are a direct tax which every housekeeper feels, and who knows also, to a farthing, the sum which he pays. The national amount of the whole of the poor-rates is not positively known, but can be procured. Sir John Sinclair, in his History of the Revenue, has stated it at 2,100,587*l*. A considerable part of which is expended in litigations, in which the poor, instead of being relieved, are tormented. The expense, however, is the same to the parish from whatever cause it arises.

In Birmingham, the amount of the poor-rates is fourteen thousand pounds a-year. This, though a large sum, is moderate, compared with the population. Birmingham is said to contain seventy thousand souls, and on a proportion of seventy thousand to fourteen thousand pounds poor-rates, the national amount of poor-rates, taking the population of England at seven millions, would be but one million four hundred thousand pounds. It is, therefore, most probable, that the population of Birmingham is over-rated. Fourteen thousand pounds is the proportion upon fifty thousand souls, taking two millions of poor-rates as the national amount.

Be it, however, what it may, it is no other than the consequence of the excessive burden of taxes, for, at the time when the taxes were very low, the poor were able to maintain themselves; and there were no poor-rates.* In the present state of things, a laboring man, with a wife and two or three children, does not pay less than between seven and eight pounds a year in taxes. He is not sensible of this, because it is disguised to him in the articles which he buys, and he thinks only of their dearness; but as the taxes take from him, at least, a fourth part of his yearly earnings, he is consequently disabled from providing for a family, especially if himself, or any of them, are afflicted with sickness.

The first step, therefore, of practical relief would be to abolish the poor-rates entirely, and in lieu thereof, to make a remission of taxes to the poor to double the amount of the present poor-rates, viz. four millions annually out of the surplus taxes. By this measure, the poor would be benefited two millions, and the housekeepers two millions. This alone would be equal to a reduction of one hundred and twenty millions of the national debt, and consequently equal to the whole expense of the American war.

It will then remain to be considered which is the most effectual mode of distributing the remission of four millions.

It is easily seen, that the poor are generally composed of large families of children, and old people unable to labor. If these two classes are provided for, the remedy will so far reach to the full extent of the case, that what remains will be incidental, and, in a great measure, fall within the compass of benefit clubs, which though of humble invention, merit to be ranked amongst the best of modern institutions.

Admitting England to contain seven millions of souls; if one fifth thereof are of that class of poor which need support, the number will be one million four hundred thousand. Of this number, one hundred and forty thousand

* Poor-rates began about the time of Henry VIII. when the taxes began to increase, and they have increased as the taxes increased ever since.

will be aged poor, as will be hereafter shown, and for which a distinct provision will be proposed.

There will then remain one million two hundred and sixty thousand, which, at five souls to each family, amount to two hundred and fifty-two thousand families, rendered poor from the expense of children and the weight of taxes.

The number of children under fourteen years of age, in each of those families, will be found to be five to every two families; some having two, others three; some one, and others four; some none, and others five; but it rarely happens that more than five are under fourteen years of age, and after this age they are capable of service, or of being apprenticed.

Allowing five children (under fourteen years) to every two families.

The number of children will be   630,000

The number of parents, were they all living, would be   504,000

It is certain that if the children are provided for, the parents are relieved of consequence, because it is from the expense of bringing up children that their poverty arises.

Having thus ascertained the greatest number that can be supposed to need support on account of young families, I proceed to the mode of relief, or distribution which is,

To pay as a remission of taxes to every poor family, out of the surplus taxes, and in room of poor-rates, four pounds a-year for every child under fourteen years of age ; enjoining the parents of such children to send them to school, to learn reading, writing, and common arithmetic ; the ministers of every parish, of every denomination, to certify jointly to an office, for this purpose, that the duty is performed.

The amount of this expense will be, for six hundred and thirty thousand children, at 4*l.* each per ann.   2,520,000*l.*

By adopting this method, not only the poverty of the parents will be relieved, but ignorance will be banished from the rising generation, and the number of poor will hereafter become less, because their abilities, by the aid of education, will be greater. Many a youth, with good natural genius, who is apprenticed to a mechanical trade, such as a carpenter, wheelwright, blacksmith, &c. is prevented getting forward the whole of his life, from the want of a little common education when a boy.

I now proceed to the case of the aged.

I divide age into two classes. 1st, the approach of old age, beginning at fifty : 2d, old age commencing at sixty.

At fifty, though the mental faculties of man are in full vigor, and his judgment better than at any preceding date, the bodily powers are on the decline. He cannot bear the same quantity of fatigue as at an earlier period. He begins to earn less, and is less capable of enduring the wind and weather; and in those retired employments where much sight is required, he fails apace, and feels himself like an old horse, beginning to be turned adrift.

At sixty, his labor ought to be over, at least from direct necessity. It is painful to see old age working itself to death, in what are called civilized countries, for its daily bread.

To form some judgment of the number of those above fifty years of age, I have several times counted the persons I met in the streets of London, men, women, and children, and have generally found that the average is about one in sixteen or seventeen. If it be said that aged persons do not come much into the streets, so neither do infants; and a great proportion of grown children are in schools, and in the work-shops as apprentices. Taking then sixteen for a divisor, the whole number of persons, in England, of fifty years and upwards, of both sexes, rich and poor, will be four hundred and twenty thousand.

The persons to be provided for out of this gross number will be, husbandmen, common laborers, journeymen of every trade and their wives, sailors, and disbanded soldiers, worn out servants of both sexes, and poor widows.

There will be also a considerable number of middling tradesmen, who, having lived decently in the former part of life, begin, as age approaches, to lose their business, and at last fall into decay.

Besides these, there will be constantly thrown off from the revolutions of that wheel, which no man can stop, nor regulate, a number from every class of life connected with commerce and adventure.

To provide for all those accidents, and whatever else may befal, I take the number of persons, who at one time or other of their lives, after fifty years of age, may feel it necessary or comfortable to be better supported, than they can support themselves, and that not as a matter of grace and favor, but of right, at one third of the whole number, which is one hundred and forty thousand, as stated p. 228, and for whom a distinct provision was proposed to be made. If there be more, society, notwithstanding the show and pomposity of government, is in a deplorable condition in England.

Of this one hundred and forty thousand, I take one half, seventy thousand, to be of the age of fifty and under sixty, and the other half to be sixty years and upwards.—Having thus ascertained the probable proportion of the number of aged persons, I proceed to the mode of rendering their condition comfortable, which is,

To pay to every such person of the age of fifty years, and until he shall arrive at the age of sixty, the sum of six pounds per ann. out of the surplus taxes; and ten pounds per ann. during life, after the age of sixty. The expense of which will be,

Seventy thousand persons at 6*l.* per ann.　420,000*l.*
Seventy thousand persons at 10　per ann.　700,000

　　　　　　　　　　　　　　　　　　1,120,000*l.*

This support as already remarked, is not of the nature of charity, but of a right. Every person in England, male and female, pays on an average in taxes, two pounds eight shillings and sixpence per ann. from the day of his (or her) birth; and if the expense of collection be added, he pays two pounds eleven shillings and sixpence; consequently, at the end of fifty years he has paid one hundred and twenty-eight pounds fifteen shillings; and at sixty, one hundred and fifty-four pounds ten shillings. Converting, therefore, his (or her) individual tax into a tontine, the money he shall receive after fifty years, is but little more than the legal interest of the net money he has paid; the rest is made up from those whose circumstances do not require them to draw such support, and the capital in both cases defrays the expenses of government. It is on this ground that I have extended the probable claims to one third of the number of aged persons in the nation.—Is it then better that the lives of one hundred and forty thousand aged persons be rendered comfortable, or that a million a-year of public money be expended on any one individual and he often of the most worthless and insignificant character? Let reason and justice, let honor and humanity, let even hypocrisy, sycophancy and Mr. Burke, let George, let Louis, Leopold, Frederic, Catherine, Cornwallis, or Tippoo Saib, answer the question.*

The sum thus remitted to the poor will be,

To two hundred and fifty-two thousand poor families, containing six hundred and thirty thousand children, - - - -	2,520,000l.
To one hundred and forty thousand aged persons, - - - - - -	1,120,000
	3,640,000l.

There will then remain three hundred and sixty thousand pounds out of the four millions, part of which may be applied as follows :

After all the above cases are provided for, there will still be a number of families who, though not properly of the class of poor, yet find it difficult to give education to their children ; and such children, under such a case, would be in a worse condition than if their parents were actually poor. A nation under a well regulated government, should permit none to remain uninstructed. It is monarchical and aristocratical governments only that require ignorance for their support.

Suppose then four hundred thousand children to be in this condition, which is a greater number than ought to be supposed, after the provisions already made, the method will be,

To allow for each of those children ten shillings a-year for the expense of schooling, for six years each, which will give them six months schooling each year, and half a crown a-year for paper and spelling books.

* Reckoning the taxes by families, five to a family, each family pays on an average, 12l. 17s. and 6d. per ann. to this sum are to be added the poor-rates. Though all pay taxes in the articles they consume, all do not pay poor-rates. About two millions are exempted, some as not being housekeepers, others as not being able, and the poor themselves who receive the relief. The average, therefore of poor-rates on the remaining number, is forty shillings for every family of five persons, which makes the whole average amount of taxes and rates, 14l. 17s. 6d. for six persons, 17l. 17s.—for seven persons, 20l. 16s. 6d.

The average of taxes in America, under the new or representative system of government, including the interest of the debt contracted in the war, and taking the population at four millions of souls, which it now amounts to, and is daily increasing, is five shillings per head, men, women, and children. The difference, therefore, between the two governments, is as under,

	England.	America.
For a family of five persons	14l. 17s. 6d.	1l. 5s. 0d.
For a family of six persons	17 17 0	1 10 0
For a family of seven persons	20 16 6	1 15 0

The expense of this will be annually* 250,000*l.*

There will then remain one hundred and ten thousand pounds.

Notwithstanding the great modes of relief which the best instituted and best principled government may devise, there will still be a number of smaller cases, which it is good policy as well as beneficence in a nation to consider.

Were twenty shillings to be given to every woman immediately on the birth of a child, who should make the demand, and none will make it whose circumstances do not require it, it might relieve a great deal of instant distress.

There are about two hundred thousand births yearly in England; and if claimed by one fourth,

The amount would be   -   -   -   -   50,000*l.*

And twenty shillings to every new married couple who should claim in like manner. This would not exceed the sum of   -   -   -   -   -   -   20,000*l.*

Also twenty thousand pounds to be appropriated to defray the funeral expenses of persons, who, travelling for work, may die at a distance from their friends. By relieving parishes from this charge, the sick stranger will be better treated.

I shall finish this part of my subject with a plan adapted to the particular condition of a metropolis, such as London.

Cases are continually occurring in a metropolis different from those which occur in the country, and for which a different, or rather an additional mode, of relief is necessary. In the country, even in large towns, people have a knowledge of each other, and distress never rises to that extreme height it sometimes does in a metropolis. There is no such thing in the country as persons, in the literal sense of the word, starved to death, or dying with cold

---

* Public schools do not answer the general purpose of the poor. They are chiefly in corporation-towns, from which the country towns and villages are excluded—or if admitted the distance occasions a great loss of time. Education, to be useful to the poor, should be on the spot—and the best method, I believe, to accomplish this, is to enable the parents to pay the expense themselves. There are always persons of both sexes to be found in every village, especially when growing into years, capable of such an undertaking. Twenty children, at ten shillings each (and that not more than six months in each year,) would be as much as some livings amount to in the remote parts of England—and there are often distressed clergymen's widows to whom such an income would be acceptable. Whatever is given on this account to children answers two purposes, to them it is education, to those who educate them it is a livelihood.

from the want of a lodging. Yet such cases, and others equally as miserable, happen in London.

Many a youth comes up to London full of expectations, and little or no money, and unless he gets employment he is already half undone ; and boys bred up in London without any means of a livelihood, and as it often happens, of dissolute parents, are in a still worse condition, and servants long out of place are not much better off. In short, a world of little cases are continually arising, which busy or affluent life knows not of, to open the first door to distress. Hunger is not among the postponable wants, and a day, even a few hours, in such a condition, is often the crisis of a life of ruin.

These circumstances, which are the general cause of the little thefts and pilferings that lead to greater, may be prevented. There yet remain twenty thousand pounds out of the four millions of surplus taxes, which with another fund hereafter to be mentioned, amounting to about twenty thousand pounds more, cannot be better applied than to this purpose. The plan then will be,

1st, To erect two or more buildings, or take some already erected, capable of containing at least six thousand persons, and to have in each of these places as many kinds of employment as can be contrived, so that every person who shall come may find something which he or she can do.

2d. To receive all who shall come, without inquiring who or what they are. The only condition to be, that for so much, or so many hours work, each person shall receive so many meals of wholesome food, and a warm lodging, at least as good as a barrack. That a certain portion of what each person's work shall be worth shall be reserved, and given to him, or her, on their going away ; and that each person shall stay as long, or as short time, or come as often as he choose, on these conditions.

If each person staid three months, it would assist by rotation twenty-four thousand persons annually, though the real number, at all times, would be but six thousand. By establishing an asylum of this kind, such persons to whom temporary distresses occur, would have an opportunity to recruit themselves, and be enabled to look out for better employment.

Allowing that their labor paid but one half the expense of supporting them, after reserving a portion of their earnings for themselves, the sum of forty thousand pounds additional would defray all other charges for even a greater number than six thousand.

The fund very properly convertible to this purpose, in addition to the twenty thousand pounds, remaining of the former fund, will be the produce of the tax upon coals, and so iniquitously and wantonly applied to the support of the duke of Richmond. It is horrid that any man, more especially at the price coals now are, should live on the distresses of a community; and any government permitting such an abuse deserves to be dissolved. This fund is said to be about twenty thousand pounds per annum.

I shall now conclude this plan with enumerating the several particulars, and then proceed to other matters.

The enumeration is as follows:

1st, Abolition of two millions poor-rates.

2d, Provision for two hundred and fifty-two thousand poor families.

3d, Education for one million and thirty thousand children.

4th, Comfortable provision for one hundred and forty thousand aged persons.

5th, Donation of twenty shillings each for fifty thousand births.

6th, Donation of twenty shillings each for twenty thousand marriages.

7th, Allowance of twenty thousand pounds for the funeral expenses of persons travelling for work, and dying at a distance from their friends.

8th. Employment, at all times, for the casual poor in the cities of London and Westminster.

By the operation of this plan, the poor laws, those instruments of civil torture, will be superseded, and the wasteful expense of litigation prevented. The hearts of the humane will not be shocked by ragged and hungry children, and persons of seventy and eighty years of age begging for bread. The dying poor will not be dragged from place to place to breath their last, as a reprisal of parish upon parish. Widows will have a maintenance for their children, and not be carted away, on the death of their husbands, like culprits and criminals; and children will no longer be considered as increasing the distresses of their parents. The haunts of the wretched will be known, because it will be to their advantage; and the number of petty crimes, the offspring of distress and poverty, will be lessened.

The poor, as well as the rich, will then be interested in the support of government, and the cause and apprehension of riots and tumults will cease. Ye who sit in ease, and solace yourselves in plenty, and such there are in Turkey and Russia, as well as in England, and who say to yourselves, "are we not well off," have ye thought of these things? When ye do, ye will cease to speak and feel for yourselves alone.

The plan is easy in practice. It does not embarrass trade by a sudden interruption in the order of taxes, but effects the relief by changing the application of them; and the money necessary for the purpose can be drawn from the excise collections, which are made eight times a-year in every market town in England.

Having now arranged and concluded this subject, I proceed to the next.

Taking the present current expenses at seven millions and an half, which is the least amount they are now at, there will remain (after the sum of one million and an half be taken for the new current expenses, and four millions for the beforementioned service) the sum of two millions, part of which to be applied as follows:

Though fleets and armies, by an alliance with France, will, in a great measure, become useless, yet the persons who have devoted themselves to those services, and have thereby unfitted themselves for other lines of life, are not to be sufferers by the means that make others happy.— They are a different description of men to those who form or hang about a court.

A part of the army will remain at least for some years, and also of the navy, for which a provision is already made in the former part of this plan of one million, which is almost half a million more than the peace establishment of the army and navy in the prodigal times of Charles II.

Suppose then fifteen thousand soldiers to be disbanded, and to allow to each of those men three shillings a week during life, clear of all deductions, to be paid in the same manner as the Chelsea college pensioners are paid, and for them to return to their trades and their friends; and also to add fifteen thousand sixpences per week to the pay of the soldiers who shall remain; the annual expense will be;

To the pay of fifteen thousand disbanded soldiers, at three shillings per week,	117,000*l.*
Additional pay to the remaining soldiers,	19,500
Suppose that the pay to the officers of the disbanded corps be of the same amount as the sum allowed to the men	117,000
	253,500*l.*
To prevent bulky estimations, admit the same sum to the disbanded navy as to the army, and the same increase of pay	253,500*l.*
Total,	507,000*l.*

Every year some part of this sum of half a million (I omit the odd seven thousand pounds, for the purpose of keeping the account unembarrassed) will fall in, and the whole of it in time, as it is on the ground of life annuities, except the increased pay of thirty-nine thousand pounds. As it falls in, a part of the taxes may be taken off; for instance, when thirty thousand pounds fall in, the duty on hops may be wholly taken off; and as other parts fall in, the duties on candles and soap may be lessened, till at last they totally cease.

There now remains at least one million and an half of surplus taxes.

The tax on houses and windows is one of those direct taxes, which, like the poor-rates, is not confounded with trade; and when taken off, the relief will be instantly felt. This tax falls heavy on the middle class of people,

The amount of this tax by the returns of 1788,

	l.	*s.*	*d.*
was,			
Houses and windows by the act of 1766	385,459	11	7
do. do. by the act of 1779	130,739	14	5½
Total,	516,199	6	0½

If this tax be struck off, there will then remain about one million of surplus taxes, and as it is always proper to keep a sum in reserve, for incidental matters, it may be best not to extend reductions further, in the first instance, but to consider what may be accomplished by other modes of reform.

Among the taxes most heavily felt is the commutation tax. I shall, therefore, offer a plan for its abolition, by substituting another in its place, which will effect three objects at once :

1st, That of removing the burden to where it can best be borne.

2d, Restoring justice among families by a distribution of property.

3d, Extirpating the overgrown influence arising from the unnatural law of primogeniture, and which is one of the principal sources of corruption at elections.

The amount of the commutation tax by the re-
turns of 1788, was,   -   -   -   771.657*l.*

When taxes are proposed, the country is amused by the plausible language of taxing luxuries. One thing is called a luxury at one time, and something else at another; but the real luxury does not consist in the article, but in the means of procuring it, and this is always kept out of sight.

I know not why any plant or herb of the field should be a greater luxury in one country than another, but an overgrown estate in either is a luxury at all times, and as such is the proper object of taxation. It is, therefore, right to take those kind tax-making gentlemen up on their own word, and argue on the principle themselves have laid down, that of *taxing luxuries.* If they, or their champion, Mr. Burke, who, I fear, is growing out of date like the man in armor, can prove that an estate of twenty, thirty or forty thousand pounds a-year is not a luxury, I will give up the argument.

Admitting that any annual sum, say, for instance, one thousand pounds, is necessary or sufficient for the support of a family, consequently the second thousand is of the nature of a luxury, the third still more so, and by proceeding on, we shall at last arrive at a sum that may not improperly be called a prohibitable luxury. It would be impolitic to set bounds to property acquired by industry, and therefore it is right to place the prohibition beyond the probable acquisition to which industry can extend; but there ought to be a limit to property, or the accumulation of it by bequest. It should pass in some other line. The richest in every nation have poor relations, and those often very near in consanguinity.

The following table of progressive taxation is constructed on the above principles, and as a substitute for the commutation tax. It will reach the point of prohibition by a

regular operation, and thereby supersede the aristocratical law of primogeniture.

TABLE I.

A tax on all estates of the clear yearly value of fifty
pounds, after deducting the land tax, and up

To 500*l.*	-	-	-	-	0	3*d.* per pound
From 500 to 1000		-	-	0	6	" "
On the 2d thousand	-	-	0	9	" "
On the 3d ditto	-	-	-	1*s.* 0	" "
On the 4th ditto	-	-	-	1 6	" "

And so on, adding 1*s.* per pound on every additional thousand.

At the twenty-third thousand the tax becomes twenty
shillings in the pound, and consequently every thousand
beyond that sum can produce no profit but by dividing the
estate. Yet formidable as this tax appears, it will not, I
believe, produce so much as the commutation tax; should
it produce more, it ought to be lowered to that amount
upon estates under two or three thousand a-year.

On small and middling estates it is lighter (as it is intended to be) than the commutation tax. It is not till after
seven or eight thousand a-year, that it begins to be heavy.
The object is not so much the produce of the tax as the
justice of the measure. The aristocracy has screened itself too much, and this serves to restore a part of the lost
equilibrium.

As an instance of its screening itself, it is only necessary
to look back to the first establishment of the excise laws,
at what is called the revolution, or the coming of Charles
II. The aristocratical interest then in power, commuted
the feudal services itself was under, by laying a tax on
beer brewed for *sale;* that is, they compounded with
Charles for an exemption from those services for themselves and their heirs, by a tax to be paid by other people.
The aristocracy do not purchase beer brewed for sale, but
brew their own beer free of the duty, and if any commutation at that time was necessary, it ought to have been at
the expense of those for whom the exemptions from those
services were intended;* instead of which it was thrown
on an entire different class of men.

* The tax on beer brewed for sale, from which the aristocracy are exempt
is almost one million more than the present commutation tax, being by the

But the chief object of this progressive tax (besides the justice of rendering taxes more equal than they are) is, as already stated, to extirpate the overgrown influence arising from the unnatural law of primogeniture, and which is one of the principle sources of corruption at elections.

It would be attended with no good consequences to inquire how such vast estates as thirty, forty, or fifty thousand a-year could commence, and that at a time when commerce and manufactures were not in a state to admit of such acquisitions. Let it be sufficient to remedy the evil by putting them in a condition of descending again to the community by the quiet means of apportioning them among all the heirs and heiresses of those families. This will be the more necessary because hitherto the aristocracy have quartered their younger children and connexions upon the public, in useless posts, places, and offices, which when abolished will leave them destitute, unless the law of primogeniture be also abolished or superseded.

A progressive tax will in a great measure, effect this object, and that as a matter of interest to the parties most immediately concerned, as will be seen by the following table; which shows the nett produce upon every estate, after subtracting the tax. By this it will appear, that after an estate exceeds thirteen or fourteen thousand a-year, the remainder produces but little profit to the holder, and consequently, will either pass to the younger children, or to other kindred.

returns of 1788, 1,666,152*l*—and consequently they ought to take on themselves the amount of the commutation tax, as they are already exempted from one which is almost a million greater.

TABLE II.

Showing the nett produce of every estate, from one thousand to twenty-three thousand pounds a-year.

No. of thousands per ann.	Total tax subtracted.	Nett produce.
1000*l.*	21*l.*	979*l.*
2000	59	1941
3000	109	2891
4000	184	3861
5000	284	4716
6000	434	5566
7000	634	6366
8000	880	7120
9000	1180	7820
10,000	1530	8470
11,000	1930	9070
12,000	2380	9620
13,000	2880	10,120
14,000	3430	10,570
15,000	4030	10,970
16,000	4680	11,320
17,000	5380	11,620
18,000	6130	11,870
19,000	6930	12,170
20,000	7780	12,220
21,000	8680	12,320
22,000	9630	12,370
23,000	10,630	12,370

N. B. The odd shillings are dropped in this table.

According to this table, an estate cannot produce more than 12,370*l.* clear of the land tax and the progressive tax, and therefore the dividing such estates will follow as a matter of family interest. An estate of 23,000*l.* a-year divided into five estates of four thousand each and one of three, will be charged only 1129*l.* which is but five per cent. but if held by any one possessor will be charged 10,630*l.*

Although an inquiry into the origin of those estates be unnecessary, the continuation of them in their present state is another subject. It is a matter of national concern. As hereditary estates, the law has created the evil, and it ought also to provide the remedy. Primogeniture ought to be abolished, not only because it is unnatural and unjust, but because the country suffers by its operation. By cutting off (as before observed) the younger children from their proper portion of inheritance, the public is loaded with the expense of maintaining them; and the freedom of elections violated by the overbearing influence which this unjust monopoly of family property produces. Nor is this all. It occasions a waste of national property. A considerable part of the land of the country is rendered unproductive, by the great extent of parks and chases which this law serves to keep up, and this at a time when the annual production of grain is not equal to the national consumption.*—In short, the evils of the aristocratical system are so great and numerous, so inconsistent with every thing that is just, wise, natural and beneficent, that when they are considered, there ought not to be a doubt that many, who are now classed under that description, will wish to see such a system abolished.

What pleasure can they derive from contemplating the exposed condition, and almost certain beggary of their younger offspring? Every aristocratical family has an appendage of family beggars hanging round it, which in a few ages, or a few generations, are shook off, and console themselves with telling their tale in alms-houses, workhouses, and prisons. This is the natural consequence of aristocracy. The peer and the beggar are often of the same family. One extreme produces the other: to make one rich many must be made poor; neither can the system be supported by other means.

There are two classes of people to whom the laws of England are particularly hostile, and those the most helpless; younger children and the poor. Of the former I have just spoken; of the latter I shall mention one instance out of the many that might be produced, and with which I shall close this subject.

Several laws are in existence for regulating and limiting workmen's wages. Why not leave them as free to make their own bargains, as the law-makers are to let their farms and houses? Personal labor is all the property they have. Why is that little, and the little freedom they enjoy to be infringed? But the injustice will appear stronger, if we consider the operation and effect of such laws. When wages are fixed by what is called a law, the legal wages remain stationary, while every thing else is in progression:

* See the Reports on the Corn Trade.

and as those who make that law, still continue to lay on new taxes by other laws, they increase the expense of living by one law, and take away the means by another.

But if these gentlemen law-makers and tax-makers thought it right to limit the poor pittance which personal labor can produce, and on which a whole family is to be supported, they certainly must feel themselves happily indulged in a limitation on their own part, of not less than twelve thousand a-year, and that of property they never acquired (nor probably any of their ancestors) and of which they have made so ill a use.

Having now finished this subject, I shall bring the several particulars into one view, and then proceed to other matters.

The first eight articles are brought forward from p. 235.

1. Abolition of two millions poor-rates.

2. Provision for two hundred and fifty-two thousand poor families, at the rate of four pounds per head for each child under fourteen years of age; which, with the addition of two hundred and fifty thousand pounds, provides also education for one million and thirty thousand children.

3. Annuity of six pounds per ann. each for all poor persons, decayed tradesmen and others, supposed seventy thousand, of the age of fifty years, and until sixty.

4. Annuity of ten pounds each for life for all poor persons, decayed tradesmen, and others, supposed seventy thousand, of the age of sixty years.

5. Donation of twenty shillings each for fifty thousand births.

6. Donation of twenty shillings each for twenty thousand marriages.

7. Allowance of twenty thousand pounds for the funeral expenses of persons travelling for work, and dying at a distance from their friends.

8. Employment at all times for the casual poor in the cities of London and Westminster.

Second enumeration.

9. Abolition of the tax on houses and windows.

10. Allowance of three shillings per week for life to fifteen thousand disbanded soldiers, and a proportionate allowance to the officers of the disbanded corps.

11. Increase of pay to the remaining soldiers of 19,500l. annually.

12. The same allowance to the disbanded navy, and the same increase of pay, as to the army.

13. Abolition of the commutation tax.

14. Plan of a progressive tax, operating to extirpate the unjust and unnatural law of primogeniture, and the vicious influence of the aristocratical system.*

There yet remains, as already stated, one million of surplus taxes. Some part of this will be required for circumstances that do not immediately present themselves, and such part as shall not be wanted, will admit of a further reduction of taxes equal to that amount.

Among the claims that justice requires to be made, the condition of the inferior revenue-officers will merit attention. It is a reproach to any government to waste such an immensity of revenue in sinecures and nominal and unnecessary places and offices, and not allow even a decent livelihood to those on whom the labor falls. The salary of the inferior officers of the revenue has stood at the petty pittance of less than fifty pounds a-year, for upwards of one hundred years. It ought to be seventy. About one hundred and twenty thousand pounds applied to this purpose, will put all those salaries in a decent condition.

This was proposed to be done almost twenty years ago, but the treasury board then in being, startled at it, as it might lead to similar expectations from the army and navy; and the event was, that the king, or somebody for him, applied to parliament to have his own salary raised an hun-

---

* When inquiries are made into the condition of the poor, various degrees of distress will most probably be found, to render a different arrangement preferable to that which is already proposed. Widows with families will be in greater want than where there are husbands living. There is also a difference in the expense of living in different counties—and more so in fuel.

Suppose fifty thousand extraordinary cases, at the rate of ten pounds per family per ann.

100,000 families, at 8*l.* per family per ann.	500,000*l.*
100,000 families, at 7*l.* per " "	800,000
100,000 families, at 5*l.* per " "	700,000
And instead of ten shillings per head for the education of other children, to allow fifty shillings per family for that purpose to fifty thousand families	520,000
	250,000
	2,770,000
140,000 aged persons as before,	1,120,000
	3,890,000*l.*

This arrangement amounts to the same sum as stated in p. 232. including the 250,000*l.* for education: but it provides (including the aged people) for four hundred and four thousand families, which is almost one third of all the families in England.

dred thousand pounds a-year, which, being done, every thing else was laid aside.

With respect to another class of men, the inferior clergy, I forbear to enlarge on their condition; but all partialities and prejudices for, or against, different modes and forms of religion aside, common justice will determine, whether there ought to be an income of twenty or thirty pounds a year to one man, and of ten thousand to another. I speak on this subject with the more freedom, because I am known not to be a Presbyterian; and therefore the cant cry of court sycophants, about church and meeting, kept up to amuse and bewilder the nation, cannot be raised against me.

Ye simple men on both sides the question, do you not see through this courtly craft? If ye can be kept disputing and wrangling about church and meeting, ye just answer the purpose of every courtier, who lives the while on the spoil of the taxes, and laughs at your credulity.— Every religion is good that teaches man to be good; and I know of none that instructs him to be bad.

All the beforementioned calculations, suppose only sixteen millions and an half of taxes paid into the exchequer, after the expense of collection and drawbacks at the custom-house and excise-office are deducted; whereas the sum paid into the exchequer is very nearly, if not quite, seventeen millions. The taxes raised in Scotland and Ireland are expended in those countries, and therefore their savings will come out of their own taxes; but if any part be paid into the English exchequer, it might be remitted.— This will not make one hundred thousand pounds a-year difference.

There now remains only the national debt to be considered. In the year 1789, the interest, exclusive of the tontine, was 9,150,138*l*. How much the capital has been reduced since that time the minister best knows. But after paying the interest, abolishing the tax on houses and windows, the commutation tax and the poor-rates; and making all the provisions for the poor, for the education of children, the support of the aged, the disbanded part of the army and navy, and increasing the pay of the remainder, there will be a surplus of one million.

The present scheme of paying off the national debt appears to me, speaking as an indifferent person, to be an ill concerted, if not a fallacious job. The burden of the national debt consists not in its being so many millions, or so many hundred millions, but in the quantity of taxes collected every year to pay the interest. If this quantity continues the same, the burden of the national debt is the same to all intents and purposes, be the capital more or less.—— The only knowledge which the public can have of the reduction of the debt, must be through the reduction of taxes for paying the interest. The debt, therefore, is not reduced one farthing to the public by all the millions that have been paid; and it would require more money now to purchase up the capital, than when the scheme began.

Digressing for a moment at this point, to which I shall return again, I look back to the appointment of Mr. Pitt, as minister.

I was then in America. The war was over; and though resentment had ceased, memory was still alive.

When the news of the coalition arrived, though it was a matter of no concern to me as a citizen of America, I felt it as a man. It had something in it which shocked, by publicly sporting with decency, if not with principle. It was impudence in lord North; it was a want of firmness in Mr. Fox.

Mr. Pitt was, at that time, what may be called a maiden character in politics. So far from being hackneyed, he appeared not to be initiated into the first mysteries of court intrigue. Every thing was in his favor. Resentment against the coalition served as friendship to him, and his ignorance of vice was credited for virtue. With the return of peace, commerce and prosperity would rise of itself; yet even this increase was thrown to his account.

When he came to the helm, the storm was over, and he had nothing to interrupt his course. It required even ingenuity to be wrong, and he succeeded. A little time showed him the same sort of man as his predecessors had been. Instead of profiting by those errors which had accumulated a burden of taxes unparalleled in the world, he sought, I might almost say, he advertised for enemies, and provoked means to increase taxation. Aiming at something, he knew not what, he ransacked Europe and India for adventures, and abandoning the fair pretensions he began with, became the knight-errant of modern times.

It is unpleasant to see character throw itself away. It is more so to see one's self deceived. Mr. Pitt had merited nothing, but he promised much. He gave symptoms

of a mind superior to the meanness and corruption of
courts. His apparent candor encouraged expectations;
and the public confidence, stunned, wearied, and confounded by a chaos of parties, revived and attached itself to
him. But mistaking, as he has done, the disgust of the nation against the coalition, for merit in himself, he has rushed into measures, which a man less supported would not
have presumed to act.

All this seems to show that change of ministers amounts
to nothing. One goes out, another comes in, and still the
same measures, vices, and extravagance are pursued. It
signifies not who is minister. The defect lies in the system. The foundation and the superstructure of the government is bad. Prop it as you please, it continually sinks
into court government, and ever will.

I return, as I promised, to the subject of the national
debt, that offspring of the Dutch-Anglo revolution, and its
handmaid the Hanover succession.

But it is now too late to inquire how it began. Those
to whom it is due have advanced the money; and whether
it was well or ill spent, or pocketed, is not their crime.—
It is, however, easy to see, that as the nation proceeds in
contemplating the nature and principles of government and
to understand taxes, and make comparisons between those
of America, France and England, it will be next to impossible to keep it in the same torpid state it has hitherto
been. Some reform must, from the necessity of the case,
soon begin. It is not whether these principles press with
little or much force in the present moment. They are out.
They are abroad in the world, and no force can stop
them. Like a secret told, they are beyond recal; and
he must be blind indeed that does not see that a change is
already beginning.

Nine millions of dead taxes is a serious thing; and this
not only for bad, but in a great measure for foreign government. By putting the power of making war into the
hands of the foreigners who came for what they could get,
little else was to be expected than what has happened.

Reasons are already advanced in this work, showing
that whatever the reforms in the taxes may be, they ought
to be made in the current expenses of government, and not
in the part applied to the interest of the national debt.—
By remitting the taxes of the poor, *they* will be totally relieved and all discontent will be taken away; and by strik-

ing off such of the taxes as are already mentioned, the nation will more than recover the whole expense of the mad American war.

There will then remain only the national debt as a subject of discontent, and in order to remove, or rather to prevent this, it would be good policy in the stockholders themselves to consider it as property, subject like all other property, to bear some portion of the taxes. It would give to it both popularity and security, and as a great part of its present inconvenience is balanced by the capital which it keeps alive, a measure of this kind would so far add to that balance as to silence objections.

This may be done by such gradual means as to accomplish all that is necessary with the greatest ease and convenience.

Instead of taxing the capital, the best method would be to tax the interest by some progressive ratio, and to lessen the public taxes in the same proportion as the interest diminished.

Suppose the interest was taxed one halfpenny in the pound the first year, a penny more the second, and to proceed by a certain ratio to be determined upon, always less than any other tax upon property. Such a tax would be subtracted from the interest at the time of payment, without any expense of collection.

One halfpenny in the pound would lessen the interest and consequently the taxes, twenty thousand pounds. The tax on wagons amounts to this sum, and this tax might be taken off the first year. The second year the tax on female servants, or some other of the like amount might also be taken off, and by proceeding in this manner, always applying the tax raised from the property of the debt towards its extinction, and not carrying it to the current services, it would liberate itself.

The stockholders, notwithstanding this tax, would pay less taxes than they do now. What they would save by the extinction of the poor-rates, and the tax on houses and windows, and the commutation tax, would be considerably greater than what this tax, slow, but certain in its operation, amounts to.

It appears to me to be prudence to look out for measures that may apply under any circumstance that may approach. There is, at this moment, a crisis in the affairs of Europe that requires it. Preparation now is wisdom.

If taxation be once let loose, it will be difficult to rein-state it; neither would the relief be so effectual, as if it pro-ceeded by some certain and gradual reduction.

The fraud, hypocrisy, and imposition of governments, are now beginning to be too well understood to promise them any longer career. The farce of monarchy and aris-tocracy, in all countries, is following that of chivalry, and Mr. Burke is dressing for the funeral. Let it then pass quietly to the tomb of all other follies, and the mourners be comforted.

The time is not very distant when England will laugh at itself for sending to Holland, Hanover, Zell, or Bruns-wick for men, at the expense of a million a-year, who un-derstood neither her laws, her language, nor her interest, and whose capacities would scarcely have fitted them for the office of a parish constable. If government could be trusted to such hands, it must be some easy and simple thing indeed, and materials fit for all the purposes may be found in every town and village in England.

When it shall be said in any country in the world, my poor are happy: neither ignorance nor distress is to be found among them; my jails are empty of prisoners, my streets of beggars; the aged are not in want, the taxes are not oppressive; the rational world is my friend, because I am the friend of its happiness: when these things can be said, then may that country boast of its constitution and its government.

Within the space of a few years we have seen two revo-lutions, those of America and France. In the former, the contest was long and the conflict severe; in the latter, the nation acted with such a consolidated impulse, that having no foreign enemy to contend with, the revolution was com-plete in power the moment it appeared. From both those instances it is evident, that the greatest forces that can be brought into the field of revolutions, are reason and com-mon interest. Where these can have the opportunity of acting, opposition dies with fear, or crumbles away by con-viction. It is a great standing which they have now uni-versally obtained; and we may hereafter hope to see rev-olutions, or changes in governments, produced with the same quiet operation by which any measure, determinable by reason and discussion, is accomplished.

When a nation changes its opinion and habits of think-ing, it is no longer to be governed as before; but it would

of taxes, but be in a condition of getting rid of a considerable part of their present burdens, as has been already
stated. Long experience however, has shown, that reforms
of this kind are not those which old governments wish to
promote, and therefore, it is to nations, and not to such
governments, that these matters present themselves.

In the preceding part of this work, I have spoken of an
alliance between England, France, and America, for purposes that were to be afterwards mentioned. Though I
have no direct authority on the part of America, I have
good reason to conclude that she is disposed to enter into
a consideration of such a measure, provided that the governments with which she might ally, acted as national governments, and not as courts enveloped in intrigue and mystery. That France as a nation and a national government,
would prefer an alliance with England, is a matter of certainty. Nations, like individuals who have long been enemies, without knowing each other, or knowing why, become better friends when they discover the errors and im-
positions under which they had acted.

Admitting, therefore, the probability of such a connexion, I will state some matters by which such an alliance,
together with that of Holland, might render service, not
only to the parties immediately concerned, but to all parts
of Europe.

It is, I think, quite certain, that if the fleets of England,
France, and Holland were confederated, they could propose, with effect, a limitation to, and a general dismantling
of, all the navies in Europe, to a certain proportion to be
agreed upon.

1st, That no new ship of war shall be built by any power
in Europe, themselves included.

2d, That all the navies now in existence shall be put
back, supposed to one tenth of their present force. This
will save to France and England, each, at least two millions annually, and their relative force be in the same proportion as it is now. If men will permit themselves to
think, as rational beings ought to think, nothing can appear more ridiculous and absurd, exclusive of all moral
reflections, than to be at the expense of building navies,
filling them with men, and then hauling them into the ocean,
to try which can sink each other fastest. Peace, which
costs nothing, is attended with infinitely more advantage,
than any victory with all its expense. But this, though it

best answers the purpose of nations, does not that of court
governments, whose habitual policy is pretence for taxation, places, and offices.

It is, I think, also certain, that the above confederated
powers, together with that of the United States of America,
can propose, with effect, to Spain, the independence of
South-America, and the opening those countries of immense
extent and wealth to the general commerce of the world,
as North-America now is.

With how much more glory, and advantage to itself,
does a nation act, when it exerts its powers to rescue the
world from bondage, and to create to itself friends, than
when it employs those powers to increase ruin, desolation,
and misery. The horrid scene that is now acting by the
English government in the East-Indies, is fit only to be
told of Goths and Vandals, who, destitute of principle,
robbed and tortured the world which they were incapable
of enjoying.

The opening of South-America would produce an immense field for commerce, and a ready money market for
manufactures, which the eastern world does not. The
East is already a country of manufactures, the importation of which is not only an injury to the manufactures of
England, but a drain upon its specie. The balance against
England by this trade is regularly upwards of half a million annually sent out in the East-India ships in silver; and
this is the reason, together with German intrigue, and German subsidies, that there is so little silver in England.

But any war is harvest to such governments, however
ruinous it may be to a nation. It serves to keep up deceit-
ful expectations, which prevent people from looking into
the defects and abuses of government. It is the *lo here!*
and the *lo there!* that amuses and cheats the multitude.

Never did so great an opportunity offer itself to England,
and to all Europe, as is produced by the two revolutions of
America and France. By the former, freedom has a national champion in the western world; and by the latter, in
Europe. When another nation shall join France, despotism and bad government will scarcely dare to appear.
To use a trite expression, the iron is becoming hot all over
Europe. The insulted German and the enslaved Spaniard,
the Russ and the Pole, are beginning to think. The present
age will hereafter merit to be called the Age of Reason,

not only be wrong, but bad policy, to attempt by force what ought to be accomplished by reason. Rebellion consists in forcibly opposing the general will of a nation, whether by a party or by a government. There ought, therefore, to be in every nation a method of occasionally ascertaining the state of public opinion with respect to government. On this point the old government of France was superior to the present government of England, because, on extraordinary occasions, recourse could be had to what was then called the states-general. But in England there are no such occasional bodies; and as to those who are now called representatives, a great part of them are mere machines of the court, placemen and dependants.

I presume, that though all the people of England pay taxes, not an hundredth part of them are electors, and the members of one of the houses of parliament represent nobody but themselves. There is, therefore, no power but the voluntary will of the people that has a right to act in any matter respecting a general reform; and by the same right that two persons can confer on such a subject, a thousand may. The object, in all such preliminary proceedings, is to find out what the general sense of a nation is, and to be governed by it. If it prefer a bad or defective government to a reform, or choose to pay ten times more taxes than there is any occasion for, it has a right so to do; and so long as the majority do not impose conditions on the minority, different from what they impose upon themselves, though there may be much error, there is no injustice. Neither will the error continue long. Reason and discussion will soon bring things right, however wrong they may begin. By such a process no tumult is to be apprehended. The poor, in all countries, are naturally both peaceable and grateful in all reforms in which their interest and happiness are included. It is only by neglecting and rejecting them that they become tumultuous.

The objects that now press on the public attention are, the French revolution, and the prospect of a general revolution in governments. Of all nations in Europe there is none so much interested in the French revolution as England. Enemies for ages, and that at a vast expense, and without any national object, the opportunity now presents itself of amicably closing the scene, and joining their efforts to reform the rest of Europe. By doing this they will not only prevent the further effusion of blood, and increase and the present generation will appear to the future as the Adam of a new world.

When all the governments of Europe shall be established on the representative system, nations will become acquainted, and the animosities and prejudices fomented by the intrigues and artifice of courts, will cease. The oppressed soldier will become a freeman; and the tortured sailor, no longer dragged through the streets like a felon, will pursue his mercantile voyage in safety. It would be better that nations should continue the pay of their soldiers during their lives, and give them their discharge and restore them to freedom and their friends, and cease recruiting, than retain such multitudes at the same expense, in a condition useless to society and to themselves. As soldiers have hitherto been treated in most countries, they might be said to be without a friend. Shunned by the citizen on an apprehension of their being enemies to liberty, and too often insulted by those who commanded them, their condition was a double oppression. But where genuine principles of liberty pervade a people, every thing is restored to order; and the soldier civilly treated, returns the civility.

In contemplating revolutions, it is easy to perceive that they may arise from two distinct causes; the one, to avoid or get rid of some great calamity, the other, to obtain some great and positive good; and the two may be distinguished by the names of active and passive revolutions. In those which proceed from the former cause, the temper becomes incensed and soured; and the redress, obtained by danger, is too often sullied by revenge. But in those which proceed from the latter, the heart, rather animated than agitated, enters serenely upon the subject. Reason and discussion, persuasion and conviction, become the weapons in the contest, and it is only when those are attempted to be suppressed that recourse is had to violence. When men unite in agreeing that a *thing is good*, could it be obtained, such for instance as relief from a burden of taxes and the extinction of corruption, the object is more than half accomplished. What they approve as the end, they will promote in the means.

Will any man say in the present excess of taxation, falling so heavily on the poor, that a remission of five pounds annually of taxes to one hundred and four thousand poor families is not a *good thing*? Will he say that a remission of seven pounds annually to one hundred thousand other

poor families; of eight pounds annually to another hundred thousand poor families, and of ten pounds annually to
fifty thousand poor and widowed families, are not *good
things ?* And, to proceed a step further in this climax, will
he say, that to provide against the misfortunes to which all
human life is subject, by securing six pounds annually for
all poor, distressed, and reduced persons of the age of fifty
and until sixty, and of ten pounds annually after sixty, is
not a *good thing ?*

Will he say, that an abolition of two millions of poor-
rates to the housekeepers, and of the whole of the house
and window-light tax and of the commutation tax is not a
good thing ? Or will he say, that to abolish corruption is a
bad thing ?

If, therefore, the good to be obtained be worthy of a passive, rational, and costless revolution, it would be bad policy to prefer waiting for a calamity that should force a violent one. I have no idea, considering the reforms which
are now passing and spreading throughout Europe, that
England will permit herself to be the last; and where the
occasion and the opportunity quietly offer, it is better than
to wait for a turbulent necessity. It may be considered as
an honor to the animal faculties of man to obtain redress
by courage and danger, but it is far greater honor to the
rational faculties to accomplish the same object by reason,
accommodation and general consent.*

As reforms, or revolutions, call them which you please,
extend themselves among nations, those nations will form
connexions and conventions, and when a few are thus confederated, the progress will be rapid, till despotism and
corrupt government be totally expelled, at least out of two

---

* I know it is the opinion of many of the most enlightened characters in
France (there always will be those who see further into events than others,)
not only among the general mass of citizens, but of many of the principal
members of the national assembly, that the monarchical plan will not continue many years in that country. They have found out, that as wisdom cannot be hereditary, power ought not—and that for a man to merit a million sterling a-year from a nation, he ought to have a mind capable of comprehending
from an atom to a universe, which, if he had he would be above receiving the
pay. But they wished not to appear to lead the nation faster than its own
reason and interest dictated. In all the conversations where I have been
present upon this subject, the idea always was, that when such a time, from
the general opinion of the nation, shall arrive, that the honorable and liberal
method would be, to make a handsome present in fee simple to the person,
whoever he may be, that shall then be in the monarchical office, and for him
to retire to the enjoyment of private life, possessing his share of general rights
and privileges, and to be no more accountable to the public for his time and
his conduct than any other citizen.

quarters of the world, Europe and America. The Algerine piracy may then be commanded to cease, for it is only by the malicious policy of old governments, against each other that it exists.

Throughout this work, various and numerous as the subjects are, which I have taken up and investigated, there is only a single paragraph upon religion, *viz. "that every religion is good that teaches man to be good."*

I have carefully avoided to enlarge upon the subject, because I am inclined to believe, that what is called the present ministry, wish to see contentions about religion kept up to prevent the nation turning its attention to subjects of government. It is, as if they were to say, *"look that way, or any way but this."*

But as religion is very improperly made a political machine, and the reality of it is thereby destroyed, I will conclude this work with stating in what light religion appears to me.

If we suppose a large family of children, who, on any particular day, or particular occasion, made it a custom to present to their parents some token of their affection and gratitude, each of them would make a different offering, and most probably in a different manner. Some would pay their congratulations in themes of verse and prose, by some little devices, as their genius dictated, or according to what they thought would please; and, perhaps, the least of all, not able to do any of those things, would ramble into the garden, or the field, and gather what it thought the prettiest flower it could find, though, perhaps, it might be but a simple weed. The parents would be more gratified, by such a variety, than if the whole of them had acted on a concerted plan, and each had made exactly the same offering. This would have the cold appearance of contrivance, or the harsh one of control. But of all unwelcome things, nothing would more afflict the parent than to know, that the whole of them had afterwards gotten together by the ears, boys and girls, fighting, reviling, and abusing each other about which was the best or the worst present.

Why may we not suppose, that the great Father of all is pleased with variety of devotion; and that the greatest offence we can act, is that by which we seek to torment and render each other miserable? For my own part, I am fully satisfied that what I am now doing, with an endeavor to conciliate mankind, to render their condition happy, to

unite nations that have hitherto been enemies, and to extirpate the horrid practice of war, and break the chains of
slavery and oppression, is acceptable in his sight, and being the best service I can perform, I act it cheerfully.

I do not believe that any two men, on what are called
doctrinal points, think alike who think at all. It is only
those who have not thought that appear to agree. It is in
this case as with what is called the British constitution.
It has been taken for granted to be good, and encomiums
have supplied the place of proof. But when the nation
comes to examine into principles and the abuses it admits,
it will be found to have more defects than I have pointed
out in this work and the former.

As to what are called national religions, we may, with
as much propriety, talk of national gods. It is either political craft or the remains of the pagan system, when every
nation had its separate particular deity. Among all the
writers of the English church clergy, who have treated on
the general subject of religion, the present bishop of Landaff, has not been excelled, and it is with much pleasure
that I take this opportunity of expressing this token of respect. I have now gone through the whole of the subject
at least, as far as it appears to me at present. It has been
my intention for the five years I have been in Europe to
offer an address to the people of England on the subject of
government, if the opportunity presented itself before I returned to America. Mr. Burke has thrown it in my way,
and I thank him. On a certain occasion, three years ago,
I pressed him to propose a national convention, to be fairly elected, for the purpose of taking the state of the nation
into consideration ; but I found that however strongly the
parliamentary current was then setting against the party
he acted with, their policy was to keep every thing within
that field of corruption, and trust to accidents. Long experience had shown that parliaments would follow any
change of ministers, and on this they rested their hopes
and their expectations.

Formerly, when divisions arose respecting governments,
recourse was had to the sword, and a civil war ensued.
That savage custom is exploded by the new system, and
reference is had to national conventions. Discussion and
the general will arbitrates the question, and to this, private
opinion yields with a good grace, and order is preserved
uninterrupted.

Some gentlemen have affected to call the principles upon which this work and the former part of the Rights of Man are founded, "a new fangled doctrine." The question is not whether these principles are new or old, but whether they are right or wrong. Suppose the former, I will show their effect by a figure easily understood.

It is now towards the middle of February. Were I to take a turn into the country, the trees would present a leafless, wintery appearance. As people are apt to pluck twigs as they go along, I perhaps might do the same, and by chance might observe, that a *single bud* on that twig had begun to swell. I should reason very unnaturally, or rather not reason at all, to suppose *this* was the *only* bud in England which had this appearance. Instead of deciding thus I should instantly conclude, that the same appearance was beginning, or about to begin, every where; and though the vegetable sleep will continue longer on some trees and plants than on others, and though some of them may not *blossom* for two or three years, all will be in leaf in the summer, except those which are *rotten*. What pace the political summer may keep with the natural, no human foresight can determine. It is, however, not difficult to perceive that the spring is begun. Thus wishing, as I sincerely do, freedom and happiness to all nations, I close the SECOND PART.

APPENDIX.

As the publication of this work has been delayed beyond the time intended, I think it not improper, all circumstances considered, to state the causes that have occasioned that delay.

The reader will probably observe, that some parts in the plan contained in this work for reducing the taxes, and certain parts in Mr. Pitt's speech at the opening of the present session, Tuesday, January 31, are so much alike, as to induce a belief, that either the author had taken the hint from Mr. Pitt, or Mr. Pitt from the author.—I will first point out the parts that are similar, and then state such circumstances as I am acquainted with, leaving the reader to make his own conclusion.

Considering it as almost an unprecedented case, that taxes should be proposed to be taken off, it is equally extraordinary that such a measure should occur to two persons at the same time; and still more so (considering the vast variety and multiplicity of taxes) that they should hit on the same specific taxes. Mr. Pitt has mentioned, in his speech, the tax on *carts* and *wagons;* that on *female servants;* the lowering the tax on *candles,* and the taking off the tax of three shillings on *houses* having under seven windows.

Every one of those specific taxes are a part of the plan contained in this work, and proposed also to be taken off. Mr. Pitt's plan, it is true, goes no further than to a reduction of three hundred and twenty thousand pounds; and the reduction proposed in this work, to nearly six millions. I have made my calculations on only sixteen millions and an half of revenue, still asserting that it was very nearly, if not quite, seventeen millions. Mr. Pitt states it at 16,690,000*l.* I know enough of the matter to say, that he has not *overstated* it. Having thus given the particulars, which correspond in this work and his speech, I will state a chain of circumstances that may lead to some explanation.

The first hint for lessening the taxes, and that as a consequence flowing from the French revolution, is to be found in the Address and Declaration of the gentlemen who met at the Thatched-House tavern, August 20, 1791. Among many other particulars stated in that address, is the following, put as an interrogation to the government opposers of the French revolution. "*Are they sorry that the pretence for new oppressive taxes, and the occasion for continuing many old taxes will be at an end?*"

It is well known, that the persons who chiefly frequent the Thatched-House tavern, are men of court connexions, and so much did they take this address and declaration respecting the French revolution and the reduction of taxes in disgust, that the landlord was under the necessity of informing the gentlemen, who composed the meeting of the 20th of August, and who proposed holding another meeting, that he could not receive them.*

* The gentleman who signed the address and declaration as chairman of the meeting, Mr. Horne Tooke, being generally supposed to be the person

What was only hinted in the address and declaration respecting taxes and principles of government, will be found reduced to a regular system in this work. But as Mr. Pitt's speech contains some of the same things respecting taxes, I now come to give the circumstances before alluded to.

The case is this: this work was intended to be published just before the meeting of parliament, and for that purpose a considerable part of the copy was put into the printer's hands in September, and all the remaining copy, as far as page 160, which contains the part to which Mr. Pitt's speech is similar, was given to him full six weeks before the meeting of parliament, and he was informed of the time at which it was to appear. He had composed nearly the whole about a fortnight before the time of parliament's meeting, and had printed as far as page 112, and had given me a proof of the next sheet, up to page 128. It was then in sufficient forwardness to be out at the time proposed, as two other sheets were ready for striking off. I had before told him, that if he thought he should be straitened for time, I could get part of the work done at another press, which he desired me not to do. In this manner the work stood on the Tuesday fortnight, preceding the meeting of parliament, when all at once, without any previous intimation, though I had been with him the evening before, he sent me by one of his workmen, all the remaining copy, from page 112, declining to go on with the work *on any consideration.*

To account for this extraordinary conduct I was totally at a loss, as he stopped at the part where the arguments on systems and principles of government closed, and where the plan for the reduction of taxes, the education of children, and the support of the poor and the aged begins;

who drew it up, and having spoken much in commendation of it, has been jocularly accused of praising his own work. To free him from this embarrassment, and to save him the repeated trouble of mentioning the author, as he has not failed to do, I make no hesitation in saying, that as the opportunity of benefiting by the French revolution easily occurred to me, I drew up the publication in question, and showed it to him and some other gentlemen : who, fully approving it, held a meeting for the purpose of making it public, and subscribed to the amount of fifty guineas to defray the expense of advertising. I believe there are at this time in England a greater number of men acting on disinterested principles, and determined to look into the nature and practices of government themselves, and not blindly trust, as has hitherto been the case, either to government generally, or to parliaments, or to parliamentary opposition, than at any former period. Had this been done a century ago, corruption and taxation had not arrived to the height they are now at.

and still more especially, as he had, at the time of his beginning to print, and before he had seen the whole copy,
offered a thousand pounds for the copy-right, together with
the future copy-right of the former part of the Rights of
Man. I told the person who brought me this offer that I
should not accept it, and wished it not to be renewed, giving him as my reason, that though I believed the printer
to be an honest man, I would never put it in the power of
any printer or publisher to suppress or alter a work of
mine, by making him master of the copy, or give to him
the right of selling it to any minister, or to any other person, or to treat as a mere matter of traffic, that which I intended should operate as a principle.

His refusal to complete the work (which he could not
purchase) obliged me to seek for another printer, and this
of consequence would throw the publication back till after
the meeting of parliament, otherwise it would have appeared that Mr. Pitt had only taken up a part of the plan which
I had more fully stated.

Whether that gentleman, or any other, had seen the
work or any part of it, is more than I have authority to
say. But the manner in which the work was returned,
and the particular time at which this was done, and that
after the offers he had made, are suspicious circumstances.
I know what the opinion of booksellers and publishers
is upon such a case, but as to my own opinion, I choose to
make no declaration. There are many ways by which
proof sheets may be procured by other persons before a
work publicly appears; to which I shall add a certain circumstance, which is,

A ministerial bookseller in Piccadilly who has been employed, as common report says, by a clerk of one of the
boards closely connected with the ministry (the board of
trade and plantation of which Hawkesbury is president) to
publish what he calls my Life. (I wish his own life and
those of the cabinet were as good) used to have his books
printed at the same printing-office that I employed; but
when the former part of the Rights of Man came out, he
took his work away in dudgeon; and about a week or ten
days before the printer returned my copy, he came to
make him an offer of his work again, which was accepted.
This would consequently give him admission into the printing-office where the sheets of this work were then lying;
and as booksellers and printers are free with each other.

he would have the opportunity of seeing what was going on. Be the case however as it may, Mr. Pitt's plan, little and diminutive as it is, would have made a very awkward appearance, had this work appeared at the time the printer had engaged to finish it.

I have now stated the particulars which occasioned the delay, from the proposal to purchase, to the refusal to print. If all the gentlemen are innocent, it is very unfortunate for them that such a variety of suspicious circumstances should, without any design, arrange themselves together.

Having now finished this part, I will conclude with stating another circumstance.

About a fortnight or three weeks before the meeting of parliament, a small addition, amounting to about twelve shillings and sixpence a year, was made to the pay of the soldiers, or rather, their pay was docked so much less.— Some gentlemen who knew in part, that this work would contain a plan of reforms respecting the oppressed condition of soldiers, wished me to add a note to the work, signifying that the part upon that subject had been in the printer's hands some weeks before that addition of pay was proposed. I declined doing this, lest it should be interpreted into an air of vanity, or an endeavor to excite suspicion (for which perhaps there might be no grounds) that some of the government gentlemen, had, by some means or other, made out what this work would contain; and had not the printing been interrupted so as to occasion a delay beyond the time fixed for publication, nothing contained in this appendix would have appeared.

THOMAS PAINE.

END OF THE RIGHTS OF MAN.

AUTHORS OF THE "REPUBLICAN."

———

GENTLEMEN,

M. DUCHASTELET has mentioned to me the intention of some persons to commence a work under the title of "The Republican."

As I am a citizen of a country which knows no other majesty than that of the people ; no other government than that of the representative body ; no other sovereignty than that of the laws, and which is attached to *France* both by alliance and by gratitude, I voluntarily offer you my services in support of principles as honorable to a nation as they are adapted to promote the happiness of mankind. I offer them to you with the more zeal, as I know the moral, literary, and political character of those who are engaged in the undertaking, and find myself honored in their good opinion.

But I must at the same time observe, that from ignorance of the French language, my works must necessarily undergo a translation ; they can of course be of but little utility, and my offering must consist more of wishes than services ; I must add, that I am obliged to pass a part of this summer in England and Ireland.

As the public has done me the unmerited favor of recognizing me under the appellation of Common Sense, which is my usual signature, I shall continue it in this publication to avoid mistakes, and to prevent my being supposed the author of works not my own. As to my political principles, I shall endeavor, in this letter, to trace their general features in such a manner, as that they cannot be misunderstood.

It is desirable in most instances to avoid that, which may give even the least suspicion as to the part meant to be adopted, and particularly on the present occasion, where a perfect clearness of expression is necessary to the avoidance of any possible misinterpretation. I am happy, therefore, to find, that the work in question is entitled "The Republican." This word expresses perfectly the idea which we ought to have of government in general—*res-republica*—the public affairs of a nation.

As to the word *monarchy*, though the address and intrigue of courts have rendered it familiar, it does not contain the less of reproach or of insult to a nation. The word, in its immediate and original sense, signifies *the absolute power of a single individual*, who may prove a fool, an hypocrite, or a tyrant. The appellation admits of no other interpretation than that which is here given. France is therefore not a *monarchy*; it is insulted when called by that name. The servile spirit which characterizes this species of government is banished from France, and this country, like America, can now afford to monarchy no more than a glance of disdain.

Of the errors which monarchical ignorance or knavery has spread through the world, the one which bears the marks of the most dexterous invention, is the opinion that the system of *republicanism* is only adapted to a small country, and that a *monarchy* is suited, on the contrary, to those of greater extent. Such is the language of courts, and the sentiments which they have caused to be adopted in monarchical countries; but the opinion is contrary at the same time to principle and to experience.

The government, to be of real use, should possess a complete knowledge of all the parties; all the circumstances, and all the interests of a nation. The monarchical system, in consequence, instead of being suited to a country of great extent, would be more admissible in a small territory where an individual may be supposed to know the affairs and the interests of the whole. But when it is attempted to extend this individual knowledge to the affairs of a great country, the capacity of knowing bears no longer any proportion to the extent or multiplicity of the objects which ought to be known, and the government inevitably falls from ignorance into tyranny. For the proof of this position we need only look to Spain, Russia, Germany, Turkey, and the whole of the eastern continent—Countries for the deliverance of which I offer my most sincere wishes.

On the contrary, the true *republican* system, by election and representation, offers the only means which are known and in my opinion the only means which are possible of proportioning the wisdom and the information of a government to the extent of a country.

The system of *representation* is the strongest and most powerful centre that can be devised for a nation. Its attraction acts so powerfully, that men give it their approbation even without reasoning on the cause; and France, however distant its several parts, finds itself at this moment *an whole*, in its *central* representation. The citizen is assured that his rights are protected, and the soldier feels that he is no longer the slave of a despot, but that he is become one of the nation, and interested of course in its defence.

The states at present styled *republican*, as Holland, Genoa, Venice, Berne, &c. are not only unworthy the name, but are actually in opposition to every principle of a *republican* government, and the countries submitted to their power are, truly speaking, subject to an *aristocratic* slavery!

It is, perhaps, impossible in the first steps which are made in a revolution to avoid all kind of error, in principle or in practice, or in some instances to prevent the combination of both. Before the sense of a nation is sufficiently enlightened, and before men have entered into the habits of a free communication with each other of their natural thoughts, a certain reserve—a timid prudence seizes on the human mind, and prevents it from attaining its level—with that vigor and promptitude that belongs to *right*—An example of this influence discovers itself in the commencement of the present revolution: but happily this discovery has been made before the constitution was completed, and in time to provide a remedy.

The *hereditary succession* can never exist as a matter of *right*; it is a *nullity*—a *nothing*. To admit the idea, is to regard man as a species of property belonging to some individuals, either born or to be born! It is to consider our descendants, and all posterity, as mere animals without a right or a will! It is in fine, the most base and humiliating idea that ever degraded the human species, and which, for the honor of humanity, should be destroyed for ever.

The idea of hereditary succession is so contrary to the rights of man, that if we were ourselves to be recalled to existence, instead of being replaced by our posterity, we should not have the right of depriving ourselves beforehand of those rights which would then properly belong to us. On what ground, then, or by what authority, do we dare to deprive of their rights those children who will soon be men? Why are we not struck with the injustice which we perpetrate on our descendants, by endeavoring to transmit them as a vile herd, to masters whose vices are all that can be foreseen.

Whenever the French constitution shall be rendered conformable to its declaration of rights, we shall then be enabled to give to France, and with justice, the appellation of a *civic empire*; for its government will be the empire of laws, founded on the great republican principles of *elective representation*, and the rights of man—But monarchy and hereditary succession are incompatible with the *basis* of its constitution.

I hope that I have at present sufficiently proved to you that I am a good republican; and I have such a confidence in the truth of the principles, that I doubt not they will soon be as universal in France as in America. The pride of human nature will assist their evidence, will contribute to their establishment, and men will be ashamed of monarchy.

I am, with respect,

Gentlemen,

Your friend,

THOMAS PAINE.

Paris, June, 1791.

ABBE SIEYES.

Sir,

At the moment of my departure for England, I read, in the Moniteur of Tuesday last, your letter, in which you give the challenge on the subject of government, and offer to defend what is called the *monarchical opinion* against the republican system.

I accept of your challenge with pleasure; and I place such a confidence in the superiority of the republican system over that nullity of a system, called *monarchy*, that I engage not to exceed the extent of fifty pages, and to leave you the liberty of taking as much latitude as you may think proper.

The respect which I bear your moral and literary reputation, will be your security for my candor in the course of this discussion; but, notwithstanding that I shall treat the subject seriously and sincerely, let me premise, that I consider myself at liberty to ridicule, as they deserve, monarchical absurdities, whensoever the occasion shall present itself.

By republicanism, I do not understand what the name signifies in Holland, and in some parts of Italy. I understand simply a government by representation—a government founded upon the principles of the declaration of rights; principles to which several parts of the French constitution arise in contradiction. The declarations of the rights of France and America are but one and the same thing in principles, and almost in expressions; and this is the republicanism which I undertake to defend against what is called *monarchy* and *aristocracy.*

I see with pleasure, that in respect to one point, we are already agreed; and *that is the extreme danger of a civil list of thirty millions.* I can discover no reason why one of the parts of the government should be supported with so extravagant a profusion, whilst the other scarcely receives what is sufficient for its common wants.

This dangerous and dishonorable disproportion, at once supplies the one with the means of corrupting, and throws the other into the predicament of being corrupted. In America there is but little difference, with regard to this point, between the legislative and the executive part of our government; but the first is much better attended to than it is in France.*

In whatsoever manner, sir, I may treat the subject of which you have proposed the investigation, I hope, that you will not doubt my entertaining for you the highest esteem. I must also add, that I am not the personal enemy of kings. Quite the contrary. No man more heartily wishes than myself to see them all in the happy and honorable state of private individuals; but, I am the avowed, open and intrepid enemy of what is called monarchy; and I am such by principles which nothing can either alter or corrupt—by my attachment to humanity; by the anxiety which I feel within myself, for the dignity and the honor of the human race; by the disgust which I experience, when I observe men directed by children, and governed by brutes; by the horror which all the evils that monarchy has spread over the earth excite within my breast; and by those sentiments which make me shudder at the calamities, the exactions, the wars, and the massacres with which monarchy has crushed mankind: in short, it is against all the hell of monarchy that I have declared war.

THOMAS PAINE.

* A deputy to the congress receives about a guinea and a half daily : and provisions are cheaper in America than in France.

ADDRESS TO THE ADDRESSERS,

ON THE LATE PROCLAMATION.

ADDRESS TO THE ADDRESSERS.

Could I have commanded circumstances with a wish, I know not of any that would have more generally promoted the progress of knowledge, than the late proclamation, and the numerous rotten-borough and corporation addresses thereon. They have not only served as advertisements, but they have excited a spirit of inquiry into principles of government, and a desire to read the Rights of Man, in places, where that spirit and that work were before unknown.

The people of England, wearied and stunned with parties, and alternately deceived by each, had almost resigned the prerogative of thinking. Even curiosity had expired, and a universal languor had spread itself over the land. The opposition was visibly no other than a contest for power, whilst the mass of the nation stood torpidly by as the prize.

In this hopeless state of things, the first part of the Rights of Man made its appearance. It had to combat with a strange mixture of prejudice and indifference; it stood exposed to every species of newspaper abuse; and besides this, it had to remove the obstructions which Mr. Burke's rude and outrageous attack on the French revolution had artfully raised.

But how easy does even the most illiterate reader distinguish the spontaneous effusions of the heart, from the labored productions of the brain! Truth, whenever it can fully appear, is a thing so naturally familiar to the mind, that an acquaintance commences at first sight. No artificial light, yet discovered, can display all the properties of daylight; so neither can the best invented fiction fill the mind with every conviction which truth begets.

To overthrow Mr. Burke's fallacious book was scarcely the operation of a day. Even the phalanx of placemen and pensioners, who had given the tone to the multitude, by clamoring forth his political fame, became suddenly silent; and the final event to himself has been, that as he rose like a rocket, he fell like the stick.

It seldom happens, that the mind rests satisfied with the simple detection of error or imposition. Once put in motion, *that* motion soon becomes accelerated; where it had intended to stop, it discovers new reasons to proceed, and renews and continues the pursuit far beyond the limits it first prescribed to itself. Thus it has happened to the people of England. From a detection of Mr. Burke's incoherent rhapsodies, and distorted facts, they began an inquiry into the first principles of government, whilst himself, like an object left far behind, became invisible and forgotten.

Much as the first part of the Rights of Man impressed at its first appearance, the progressive mind soon discovered that it did not go far enough. It detected errors; it exposed absurdities; it shook the fabric of political superstition; it generated new ideas; but it did not produce a regular system of principles in the room of those which it displaced. And, if I may guess at the mind of the government party, they beheld it as an unexpected gale that would soon blow over, and they forbore, like sailors in threatening weather, to whistle, lest they should increase the wind. Every thing, on their part, was profound silence.

When the second part of the Rights of Man, *combining principles and practice*, was preparing to appear, they affected, for a while, to act with the same policy as before; but finding their silence had no more influence in stifling the progress of the work, than it would have in stopping the progress of time, they changed their plan, and affected to treat it with clamorous contempt. The speech-making placemen and pensioners, and place expectants, in both houses of parliament, the *outs* as well as *ins*, represented it as a silly, insignificant performance; as a work incapable of producing any effect; as something, which they were sure the good sense of the people would either despise or indignantly spurn; but such was the overstrained awkwardness with which they harangued and encouraged each other, that in the very act of declaring their confidence they betrayed their fears.

As most of the rotten-borough addressers are obscured in holes and corners throughout the country, and to whom a newspaper arrives as rarely as an almanac, they most probably have not had an opportunity of knowing how far this part of the farce (the original prelude to all the addresses) has been acted. For *their* information, I will suspend a while the more serious purpose of my letter, and entertain them with two or three speeches in the last session of parliament, which will serve them for politics till parliament meets again.

You must know, gentlemen, that the second part of the Rights of Man (the part against which you have been presenting addresses. though it is most probable that many of you did not know it) was to have come out precisely at the time that parliament last met. It happened not to be published till a few days after. But as it was well known that the book would shortly appear, the parliamentary orators entered into a very cordial coalition to cry the book down, and they began their attack by crying up the *blessings* of the constitution.

Had it been your fate to have been there, it would have been impossible not to have been moved at the heart-and-pockets-felt congratulations that passed between all the parties on this subject of *blessings;* for the *buts* enjoy places and pensions and sinecures as well as the *ins*, and are as devoutly attached to the firm of the house.

One of the most conspicuous of this motley groupe is the clerk of the court of king's bench, who calls himself lord Stormont. He is also called justice-general of Scotland, and keeper of Scoon, (an opposition man) and he draws from the public for these nominal offices, not less, as I am informed, than six thousand pounds a-year, and he is, most probably, at the trouble of counting the money, and signing a receipt, to show, perhaps, that he is qualified to be clerk as well as justice. He spoke as follows.*

" That *we* shall *all* be unanimous in expressing *our* attachment to the constitution of these realms, *I am confident.*

---

* See his speech in the Morning Chronicle of Feb. 1.

It is a subject upon which there can be *no* divided opinion *in this house*. I do not pretend to be deep read in the knowledge of the constitution, but I take upon me to say, that from the extent of *my* knowledge [for I have so many thousands a-year for nothing] it appears to *me* that from the period of the revolution, for it was by no means created then, it has been, both in *theory* and *practice*, the *wisest* system that ever was formed. I never was [he means he never was *till now*] a dealer in *political cant*. My life has not been occupied in *that way*, but the speculations of late years *seem to have taken a turn, for which I cannot account.* When I came into public life, the political pamphlets of the time, however they might be charged with the heat and violence of parties, were agreed in extolling the radical beauties of the constitution itself. I remember [he means he has forgotten] a most captivating eulogium on its *charms*, by lord Bolingbroke, where he recommends his readers to contemplate it in all respects, with the assurance that it would be found more estimable the more it was *seen*. I do *not recollect* his precise words, but I wish that men who write upon these subjects would take *this for their model*, instead of the political pamphlets, which, I am told, are now in circulation; [such, I suppose, as the Rights of Man] pamphlets which I have *not read*, and whose purport I know only by *report*. [he means, perhaps, by the *noise* they make] This, however, I am sure, that pamphlets tending to unsettle the public reverence for the constitution, will have very little influence. They can do very little harm; for [by the way, he is no dealer in political cant] *the English are a sober thinking people, and are more intelligent, more solid, more steady in their opinions, than any people I ever had the fortune to see.* [This is pretty well laid on, though, for a new beginner.] But if there should ever come a time when the propagation of those doctrines should agitate the public mind, I am *sure* for *every one* of your lordships, that no attack will be made on the constitution, from which it is truly said that *we* derive *all our* prosperity, without raising *every one* of your lordships to its support. It will then be found that there is no difference among *us*, but that *we* are *all* determined to *stand* or *fall* together, in defence of the inestimable system"—of places and pensions.

After Stormont, on the opposition side, sat down, up rose *another noble lord!* on the ministerial side, Grenville. This man ought to be as strong in the back as a mule, or the *sire* of a mule, or it would crack with the weight of places and offices. He rose, however, without feeling any incumbrance, full master of his weight; and thus said *this* noble lord to *t'other* noble lord!

" The *patriotic* and *manly* manner in which the noble lord has declared *his* sentiments on the subject of the constitution, demands *my cordial* approbation. The noble viscount has *proved*, that however we may differ on *particular measures*, amidst all the jars and dissonance of *parties*, we are unanimous in *principle*. There is a perfect and entire consent [between *us*] in the love and maintenance of the constitution as *happily subsisting*. It must undoubtedly give your lordships *concern*, to find that the *time is come!* [heigh ho!] when there is *propriety* in these expressions of regard to [o! o! o!] THE CONSTITUTION. And that there are men [confound—their—politics] who disseminate doctrines *hostile* to the *genuine spirit* of our *well-balanced system* [it is certainly a well-balanced system when both sides hold places and pensions at once.] I agree with the noble viscount that they have not [I hope] much success. I am convinced that there is no danger to be apprehended from their attempts: but it is *truly* important and *consolatory* [to us placemen, I suppose] to know, that if ever there should arise a serious alarm, there is but one *spirit, one sense* [and that sense I presume is not *common sense*] and *one* determination in *this house*"—which undoubtedly is to hold all their places and pensions as long as they can.

Both those speeches (except the parts enclosed in brackets, which are added for the purpose of *illustration*) are copied *verbatim* from the Morning Chronicle of the 1st of February last; and when the situation of the speakers is considered, the one in the opposition, and the other in the ministry, and both of them living at the public expense, by sinecure, or nominal places and offices, it required a very unblushing front to be able to deliver them. Can those men seriously suppose any nation to be so completely blind as not to see through them? Can Stormont imagine that the *political cant*, with which he has larded his harangue, will conceal the craft? Does he not know that there never was a cover large enough to conceal *itself?* Or can Grenville believe, that his credit with the public increases with his avarice for places?

But, if these orators will accept a service from me, in return for the allusions they have made to the Rights of

Man, I will make a speech for either of them to deliver, on the excellence of the constitution, that shall be as much to the purpose as what they have spoken, or as Bolingbroke's captivating eulogium. Here it is.

"That we shall all be unanimous in expressing our attachment to the constitution, I am confident. It is, my lords, incomprehensibly good : but the great wonder of all is the wisdom; for it is, my lords, *the wisest system that ever was formed.*

"With respect to us, noble lords, though the world does not know it, it is very well known to us, that we have more wisdom than we know what to do with ; and what is still better, my lords, we have it all in stock. I defy your lordships to prove, that a tittle of it has been used yet; and if we but go on, my lords, with the frugality we have hitherto done, we shall leave to our heirs and successors, when we go out of the world, the whole stock of wisdom *untouched,* that we brought in; and there is no doubt but they will follow our example. This, my lords, is one of the blessed effects of the hereditary system ; for we can never be without wisdom so long as we keep it by us, and do not use it.

"But, my lords, as all this wisdom is hereditary property, for the sole benefit of us and our heirs, and it is necessary that the people should know where to get a supply for their own use, the excellence of our constitution has provided us a king for this very purpose, and for *no other.* But, my lords, I perceive a defect to which the constitution is subject, and which I propose to remedy by bringing a bill into parliament for that purpose.

"The constitution, my lords, out of delicacy, I presume, has left it as a matter of *choice* to a king whether he will be wise or not. It has not, I mean, my lords, insisted upon it as a constitutional point, which, I conceive it ought to have done; for I pledge myself to your lordships to prove, and that with *true patriotic boldness,* that he has *no choice in the matter.* This bill, my lords, which I shall bring in, will be to declare, that the constitution, according to the true intent and meaning thereof, does not invest the king with this choice; our ancestors were too wise to do that ; and, in order to prevent any doubts that might otherwise arise, I shall prepare, my lords, an enacting clause, to fix the wisdom of kings, by act of parliament; and then, my lords, our constitution will be the wonder of the world!

" Wisdom, my lords, is the one thing needful; but that there may be no mistake in this matter, and that we may proceed consistently with the true wisdom of the constitution, I shall propose a *certain criterion* whereby the *exact quantity of wisdom* necessary for a king may be known.— [Here should be a cry of—Hear him! Hear him!]

" It is recorded, my lords, in the Statutes at large of the Jews, 'a book, my lords, which I have not read, and whose purport I know only by report,' *but perhaps the bench of bishops can recollect something about it*, that Saul gave the most convincing proofs of royal wisdom before he was made a king, *for he was sent to seek his father's asses and he could not find them.*

" Here, my lords, we have, most happily for us, a case in point: this precedent ought to be established by act of parliament; and every king, before he be crowned, should be sent to seek his father's asses, and if he cannot find them, he shall be declared wise enough to be king, according to the true meaning of our excellent constitution.   All, therefore, my lords, that will be necessary to be done, by the enacting clause that I shall bring in, will be to invest the king beforehand with the quantity of wisdom necessary for this purpose, lest he should happen not to possess it; and this, my lords, we can do without making use of any of our own.

" We further read, my lords, in the said Statutes at large of the Jews, that Samuel, who certainly was as mad as any man-of-rights now-a-days, (hear him! hear him!) was displeased, and even exasperated, at the proposal of the Jews to have a king, and he warned them against it with all that assurance and impudence of which he was master.   I have been, my lords, at the trouble of going all the way to Paternoster-row, to procure an extract from the printed copy.   I was told that I should meet with it there, or in Amen-corner, for I was then going, my lords, to rummage for it among the curiosities of the Antiquarian society.   I will read the extract to your lordships, to show how little Samuel knew of the matter.

" The extract, my lords, is from 1 Sam. chap viii.

" ' And Samuel told all the words of the Lord unto the people that asked of him a king.

" ' And he said, This will be the manner of the king that shall reign over you.   He will take your sons and appoint them for himself, for his chariots, and to be his horsemen ; and some shall run before his chariots.

" ' And he will appoint him captains over thousands, and captains over fifties, and will set them to ear his ground and to reap his harvest, and to make his instruments of war, and instruments of his chariots.

" ' And he will take your daughters to be confectionaries, and to be cooks, and to be bakers.

" ' And he will take your fields, and your vineyards, and your olive-yards, even the best of them, and give them to his servants.

" ' And he will take the tenth of your seed, and of your vineyards, and give to his officers, and to his servants.

" ' And he will take your men-servants, and your maid-servants, and your goodliest young men, and your asses, and put them to his work.

" ' And he will take the tenth of your sheep, and ye shall be his servants.

" ' And ye shall cry out in that day, because of your king, which ye shall have chosen you ; and the lord will not hear you in that day.' "

" Now, my lords, what can we think of this man Samuel? Is there a word of truth, or any thing like truth, in all that he has said? He pretended to be a prophet, or a wise man, but has not the event proved him to be a fool, or an incendiary? Look around you, my lords, and see if any thing has happened that he pretended to foretel?— Has not the most profound peace reigned throughout the world ever since kings were in fashion? Are not, for example, the present kings of Europe the most peaceable of mankind, and the empress of Russia the very milk of human kindness? It would not be worth having kings, my lords, if it were not that they never go to war.

" If we look at home, my lords, do we not see the same things here as are seen every where else? Are our young men taken to be horsemen, or foot soldiers, any more than in Germany or in Prussia, or in Hanover or in Hesse? Are not our sailors as safe on land as at sea? Are they ever dragged from their homes, like oxen to the slaughter-house, to serve on board ships of war? When they return from the perils of a long voyage with the merchandize of distant countries, does not every man sit down under his own vine and his own fig-tree, in perfect security? Is the tenth of our seed taken by tax-gatherers, or is any part of it given to the king's servants? In short, *is not every thing as free from taxes as the light from Heaven?*

" Ah ! my lords, do we not see the blessed effect of having kings in every thing we look at ?   Is not the G. R. or the broad R. stamped upon every thing ?   Even the shoes, the gloves, and the hats that we wear, are enriched with the impression, and all our candles blaze a burnt-offering.

" Besides these blessings, my lords, that cover us from the sole of the foot to the crown of the head, do we not see a race of youths growing up to be kings, who are the very paragons of virtue ?   There is not one of them, my lords, but might be trusted with untold gold, as safely as the other.   Are they not '*more sober, intelligent, more solid, more steady,*' and withal, more learned, more wise, more every thing, than any youths '*we ever had the fortune to see.*'   Ah ! my lords, they are a *hopeful family.*

" The blessed prospect of succession, which the nation has at this moment before its eyes, is a most undeniable proof of the excellence of our constitution, and of the blessed hereditary system ; for nothing, my lords, but a constitution founded on the truest and purest wisdom could admit such heaven-born and heaven-taught characters into the government.   Permit me now, my lords, to recal your attention to the libellous chapter I have just read about kings.   I mention this, my lords, because it is my intention to move for a bill to be brought into parliament to expunge that chapter from the Bible, and that the lord chancellor, with the assistance of the prince of Wales, the duke of York, and the duke of Clarence, be requested to write a chapter in the room of it ; and that Mr. Burke do see that it be truly canonical, and faithfully inserted."—*Finis.*

If the clerk of the court of king's bench should choose to be the author of this luminous encomium on the constitution, I hope he will get it well by heart before he attempts to deliver it, and not have to apologize to parliament, as he did in the case of Bolingbroke's encomium, for forgetting his lesson ; and, with this admonition I leave him.

Having thus informed the addressers of what passed at the meeting of parliament, I return to take up the subject at the part where I broke off in order to introduce the preceding speeches.

I was then stating, that the first policy of the government party was silence, and the next, clamorous contempt; but as people generally choose to read and judge for themselves, the work still went on, and the affectation of contempt, like the silence that preceded it, passed for nothing.

Thus foiled in their second scheme, their evil genius, like a will-with-a-wisp, led them to a third; when all at once, as if it had been unfolded to them by a fortune-teller, Mr. Dundas had discovered it by second sight, this once harmless, insignificant book, without undergoing the alteration of a single letter, became a most wicked and dangerous libel. The whole cabinet, like a ship's crew, became alarmed; all hands were piped upon deck, as if a conspiracy of elements was forming around them, and out came the proclamation and the prosecution; and addresses supplied the place of prayers.

Ye silly swains, thought I to myself, why do you torment yourselves thus? The Rights of Man is a book calmly and rationally written; why then are you so disturbed? Did you see how little or how suspicious such conduct makes you appear, even cunning alone, had you no other faculty, would hush you into prudence. The plans, principles, and arguments, contained in that work, are placed before the eyes of the nation, and of the world, in a fair, open, and manly manner, and nothing more is necessary than to refute them. Do this, and the whole is done; but if ye cannot, so neither can ye suppress the reading, nor convict the author; for the law, in the opinion of all good men, would convict itself, that should condemn what cannot be refuted.

Having now shown the addressers the several stages of the business, prior to their being called upon, like Cæsar in the Tyber, crying to Cassius, " *help, Cassius, or I sink!*" I next come to remark on the policy of the government, in promoting addresses; on the consequences naturally resulting therefrom ; and on the conduct of the persons concerned.

With respect to the policy, it evidently carries with it every mark and feature of disguised fear. And it will hereafter be placed in the history of extraordinary things, that a pamphlet should be produced by an individual, unconnected with any sect or party, and not seeking to make any, and almost a stranger in the land, that should completely frighten a whole government, and that in the midst

of its triumphant security. Such a circumstance cannot
fail to prove, that either the pamphlet has irresistible powers, or the government very extraordinary defects, or both.
The nation exhibits no signs of fear at the Rights of Man;
why then should the government, unless the interest of the
two are really opposite to each other, and the secret is beginning to be known? That there are two distinct classes
of men in the nation, those who pay taxes, and those who
receive and live upon the taxes, is evident at first sight;
and when taxation is carried to excess, it cannot fail to
disunite those two, and something of this kind is now beginning to appear.

It is also curious to observe, amidst all the fume and
bustle about proclamations and addresses, kept up by a
few noisy and interested men, how little the mass of the nation seem to care about either. They appear to me, by
the indifference they show, not to believe a word the proclamation contains: and as to the addresses, they travel to
London with the silence of a funeral, and having announc-
ed their arrival in the Gazette, are deposited with the ashes
of their predecessors, and Mr. Dundas writes their *hic
jacent.*

One of the best effects which the proclamation, and its
echo the addresses have had, has been that of exciting and
spreading curiosity; and it requires only a single reflection to discover, that the object of all curiosity is knowledge. When the mass of the nation saw that placemen,
pensioners, and borough-mongers, were the persons that
stood forward to promote addresses, it could not fail to
create suspicions that the public good was not their object; that the character of the books, or writings, to which
such persons obscurely alluded, not daring to mention
them, was directly contrary to what they described them
to be, and that it was necessary that every man, for his
own satisfaction, should exercise his proper right, and read
and judge for himself.

But how will the persons who have been induced to read
the Rights of Man, by the clamor that has been raised
against it, be surprised to find, that, instead of a wicked, in-
flammatory work, instead of a licentious and profligate performance, it abounds with principle of governments that are
uncontrovertible—with arguments which every reader will
feel, are unanswerable—with plans for the increase of commerce and manufactures—for the extinction of war—for

the education of the children of the poor—for the comfortable support of the aged and decayed persons of both sexes—for the relief of the army and navy, and, in short, for
the promotion of every thing that can benefit the moral,
civil and political condition of man.

Why, then, some calm observer will ask, why is the work
prosecuted, if these be the goodly matters it contains? I
will tell thee, friend; it contains also a plan for the reduction of taxes, for lessening the immense expenses of government, for abolishing places and pensions; and it proposes
applying the redundant taxes, that shall be saved by these
reforms, to the purposes mentioned in the former paragraph,
instead of applying them to the support of idle and profligate placemen and pensioners.

Is it, then, any wonder that placemen and pensioners,
and the whole train of court expectants, should become the
promoters of addresses, proclamations, and prosecutions?
Or, is it any wonder, that corporations and rotten-boroughs,
which are attacked and exposed, both in the first and second parts of the Rights of Man, as unjust monopolies and
public nuisances, should join in the cavalcade? Yet these
are the sources from which addresses have sprung. Had
not such persons came forward to oppose the Rights of
Man, I should have doubted the efficacy of my own writings: but those opposers have now proved to me, that the
blow was well directed, and they have done it justice, by
confessing the smart.

The principal deception in this business of addresses has
been, that the promoters of them have not come forward
in their proper characters. They have assumed to pass
themselves upon the public, as a part of the public, bearing
a share of the burden of taxes, and acting for the public
good; whereas, they are in general that part of it that adds
to the public burden, by living on the produce of the public taxes. They are to the public what the locusts are to
the tree: the burden would be less, and the prosperity
would be greater, if they were shaken off.

" I do not come here," said Onslow, at the Surry county meeting "as the lord lieutenant and custos rotulorum of
the county, but I come here as a plain country gentleman."
The fact is, that he came there as what he was, and as no
other, and consequently he came as one of the class I have
been describing. If it be the character of a gentleman to
be fed by the public, as a pauper is by the parish, Onslow

has a fair claim to the title; and the same description will suit the duke of Richmond, who led the address at the Sussex meeting. He also may set up for a gentleman.

As to the meeting in the next adjoining county (Kent) it was a scene of disgrace. About two hundred persons met, when a small part of them drew privately away from the rest, and voted an address: the consequence of which was that they got together by the ears, and produced a riot in the very act of producing an address to prevent riots.

That the proclamation and the addresses have failed of their intended effect, may be collected from the silence which the government party itself observes. The number of addresses has been weekly retailed in the Gazette; but the number of addressers has been concealed. Several of the addresses have been voted by not more than ten or twelve persons; and a considerable number of them by not more than thirty. The whole number of addresses presented at the time of writing this letter is three hundred and twenty (rotten-boroughs, and corporations included) and even admitting, on an average, one hundred addressers to each address. the whole number of addressers would be but thirty-two thousand, and nearly three months have been taken up in procuring this number. That the success of the proclamation has been less than the success of the work it was intended to discourage, is a matter within my own knowledge; for a greater number of the cheap edition of the first and second parts of the Rights of Man has been sold in the space of one month, than the whole number of addresses (admitting them to be thirty-two thousand) have amounted to in three months.

It is a dangerous attempt in any government to say to a nation, " *thou shalt not read.*" This is now done in Spain, and was formerly done under the old government of France; but it served to procure the downfal of the latter, and is subverting that of the former; and it will have the same tendency in all countries; because *thought* by some means or other, is got abroad in the world, and cannot be restrained though reading may.

If the Rights of Man were a book that deserved the vile description which the promoters of the addresses have given of it, why did not these men prove their charge, and satisfy the people, by producing it, and reading it publicly? This most certainly ought to have been done, and would also have been done, had they believed it would have answered their purpose. But the fact is, that the book contains truths, which those time-servers dreaded to hear, and dreaded that the people should know; and it is now following up the addresses in every part of the nation, and convicting them of falsehoods.

Among the unwarrantable proceedings to which the proclamation has given rise, the meetings of the justices in several of the towns and counties ought to be noticed. Those men have assumed to re-act the farce of general warrants, and to suppress by their own authority, whatever publications they please. This is an attempt at power, equalled only by the conduct of the minor despots of the most despotic governments in Europe, and yet those justices affect to call England a free country. But even this, perhaps, like the scheme for garrisoning the country, by building military barracks, is necessary to awaken the country to a sense of its rights, and, as such, it will have a good effect.

Another part of the conduct of such justices has been, that of threatening to take away the licenses from taverns and public-houses, where the inhabitants of the neighborhood associated to read and discuss the principles of government, and to inform each other thereon. This, again, is similar to what is doing in Spain and Russia; and the reflection which it cannot fail to suggest is, that the principles and conduct of any government must be bad, when that government dreads and startles at discussion, and seeks security by a prevention of knowledge.

If the government, or the constitution, or by whatever name it be called, be that miracle of perfection which the proclamation and the addresses have trumpeted it forth to be, it ought to have defied discussion and investigation, instead of dreading it. Whereas, every attempt it makes, either by proclamation, persecution, or address, to suppress investigation, is a confession that it feels itself unable to bear it. It is error only, and not truth, that shrinks from inquiry. All the numerous pamphlets, and all the newspaper falsehood and abuse, that have been published against the Rights of Man, have fallen before it like pointless arrows; and, in like manner, would any work have fallen before the constitution, had the constitution, as it is called, been founded on as good political principles as those on which the Rights of Man is written?

It is a good constitution for courtiers, placemen, pensioners, borough-holders, and the leaders of parties, and these are the men that have been the active leaders of addresses; but it is a bad constitution for at least ninety-nine parts of the nation out of an hundred, and this truth is every day making its way.

It is bad, first, because it entails upon the nation the unnecessary expense of supporting three forms and systems of government at once, namely the monarchical, the aristocratical, and the democratical.

Secondly, because it is impossible to unite such a discordant composition by any other means than perpetual corruption; and therefore the corruption so loudly and so universally complained of, is no other than the natural consequence of such an unnatural compound of governments; and in this consists that excellence which the numerous herd of placemen and pensioners so loudly extol and which at the same time, occasions that enormous load of taxes under which the rest of the nation groans.

Among the mass of national delusions calculated to amuse and impose upon the multitude, the standing one has been that of flattering them into taxes, by calling the government (or as they please to express it, the English constitution) *"the envy and admiration of the world."* Scarcely an address has been voted in which some of the speakers have not uttered this hackneyed nonsensical falsehood.

Two revolutions have taken place, those of America and France, and both of them have rejected the unnatural compounded system of the English government; America has declared against all hereditary government, and established the representative system of government only. France has entirely rejected the aristocratical part, and is now discovering the absurdity of the monarchical, and is approaching fast to the representative system. On what ground then, do these men continue a declaration, respecting what they call the *envy and admiration of other nations,* which the voluntary practice of such nations, as have had the opportunity of establishing governments, contradicts and falsifies. Will such men never confine themselves to truth? Will they be for ever the deceivers of the people?

But I will go further, and show, that were government now to begin in England, the people could not be brought to establish the same system they now submit to.

In speaking upon this subject (or on any other) *on the pure ground of principle*, antiquity and precedent cease to be authority, and hoary-headed error loses its effect. The reasonableness and propriety of things must be examined abstractedly from custom and usage; and in this point of view, the right which grows into practice to-day is as much a right, and as old in principle and theory, as if it had the customary sanction of a thousand ages. Principles have no connexion with time, nor characters with names.

To say that the government of this country is composed of king, lords, and commons, is the mere phraseology of custom. It is composed of men; and whoever the men be to whom the government of any country is intrusted, they ought to be the best and wisest that can be found, and if they are not so, they are not fit for the station. A man derives no more excellence from the change of a name, or calling him king, or calling him lord, than I should do by changing my name from Thomas to George, or from Paine to Guelph. I should not be a whit the more able to write a book, because my name was altered; neither would any man, now called a king or a lord, have a whit the more sense than he now has, were he to call himself Thomas Paine.

As to the word "commons," applied as it is in England, it is a term of degradation and reproach, and ought to be abolished. It is a term unknown in free countries.

But to the point. Let us suppose that government was now to begin in England, and that the plan of government, offered to the nation for its approbation or rejection, consisted of the following parts:

1st, That some one individual should be taken from all the rest of the nation, and to whom all the rest should swear obedience, and never be permitted to sit down in his presence, and that they should give him one million sterling a-year. That the nation should never after have power or authority to make laws but with his express consent, and that his sons and his sons' sons, whether wise or foolish, good men or bad, fit or unfit, should have the same power, and also the same money annually paid to them for ever.

2d, That there should be two houses of legislators to assist in making laws, one of which should, in the first instance, be entirely appointed by the aforesaid person, and that their sons and their sons' sons, whether wise or foolish, good men or bad, fit or unfit, should for ever after be hereditary legislators.

3d. That the other house should be chosen in the same manner as the house now called the house of commons is chosen, and should be subject to the control of the two aforesaid hereditary powers in all things.

It would be impossible to cram such a farrago of imposition and absurdity down the throat of this or any other nation, that was capable of reasoning upon its rights and its interest.

They would ask, in the first place, on what ground of right, or on what principle, such irrational and preposterous distinctions could, or ought to be made; and what pretensions any man could have, or what services he could render, to entitle him to a million a-year? They would go further, and revolt at the idea of consigning their children and their children's children, to the domination of persons hereafter to be born, who might, for any thing they could foresee, turn out to be knaves or fools; and they would finally discover, that the project of hereditary governors and legislators *was a treasonable usurpation over the rights of posterity.* Not only the calm dictates of reason, and the force of natural affection, but the integrity of manly pride, would impel men to spurn such proposals.

From the grosser absurdities of such a scheme, they would extend their examination to the practical defects; they would soon see that it would end in tyranny, accomplished by fraud. That in the operation of it, it would be two to one against them, because the two parts that were to be made hereditary, would form a common interest, and stick to each other; and that themselves and representatives would become no better than hewers of wood and drawers of water for the other parts of the government.— Yet call one of those powers king, the other lords, and the third, the commons, and it gives the model of what is called the English government.

I have asserted, and have shown, both in the first and second parts of the Rights of Man, that there is no such thing as an English constitution, and that the people have yet a constitution to form. *A constitution is a thing antecedent to a government; it is the act of the people creating a government and giving it powers, and defining the limits and exercise of the powers so given.* But when did the people of

England, acting in their original constituent character, by
a delegation elected for that express purpose, declare and
say, " *We the people of this land, do constitute and appoint this
to be our system and form of government?*"   The government
has assumed to constitute itself, but it never was constituted by the people, in whom alone the right of constituting
resides.

I will here recite the preamble to the federal constitution of the United States of America.   I have shown in
the second part of the Rights of Man, the manner by which
the constitution was formed and afterwards ratified ; and
to which I refer the reader.   The preamble is in the following words :

" WE, THE PEOPLE, of the United States, in order to form
a more perfect union, establish justice, insure domestic
tranquillity, provide for common defence, promote the general welfare, and secure the blessings of liberty to ourselves and our posterity, DO ORDAIN AND ESTABLISH THIS CON-
STITUTION for the United States of America."

Then follow the several articles which appoint the manner in which the several component parts of the government, legislative and executive, shall be elected, and the
period of their duration, and the powers they shall have :
also, the manner by which future additions, alterations, or
amendments, shall be made to the constitution.   Consequently, every improvement that can be made in the science of government, follows in that country as a matter of
order.   It is only in governments founded on assumption
and false principles, that reasoning upon, and investigating systems and principles of government, and showing
their several excellencies and defects, are termed libellous
and seditious.   These terms were made part of the charge
brought against Locke, Hampden, and Sydney, and will
continue to be brought against all good men, so long as
bad governments shall continue.

The government of this country has been ostentatiously
giving challenges for more than an hundred years past,
upon what it called its own excellence and perfection.—
Scarcely a king's speech, or a parliamentary speech, has
been uttered, in which this glove has not been thrown, till
the world has been insulted with their challenges.   But it
now appears that all this was vapor and vain-boasting, or
that it was intended to conceal abuses and defects, and
hush the people into taxes.   I have taken the challenge

up, and in behalf of the public have shown, in a fair, open,
and candid manner, both the radical and practical defects
of the system ; when, lo! those champions of the civil list
have fled away, and sent the attorney-general to deny the
challenge, by turning the acceptance of it into an attack,
and defending their places and pensions by a prosecution.

I will here drop this part of the subject, and state a few
particulars respecting the prosecution now pending, by
which the addressers will see that they have been used as
tools to the prosecuting party and their dependants. The
case is as follows :

The original edition of the first and second part of the
Rights of Man, having been expensively printed (in the
modern style of printing pamphlets, that they might be
bound up with Mr. Burke's reflections on the French revolution,) the high price precluded the generality of people
from purchasing ; and many applications were made to
me from various parts of the country to print the work in
a cheaper manner. The people of Sheffield requested
leave to print two thousand copies for themselves, with
which request I immediately complied. The same request came to me from Rotherham, from Leicester, from
Chester, from several towns in Scotland ; and Mr. James
Mackintosh, author of Vindiciæ Galliciæ, brought me a request from Warwickshire, for leave to print ten thousand
copies in that county. I had already sent a cheap edition
to Scotland; and finding the applications increase, I concluded that the best method of complying therewith, would
be to print a very numerous edition in London, under
my own direction, by which means the work would be
more perfect, and the price be reduced lower than it could
be by printing small editions in the country, of only a few
thousands each.

The cheap edition of the first part was begun about the
middle of last April, and from that moment, and not before,
I expected a prosecution, and the event has proved that I
was not mistaken. I had then occasion to write to Mr.
Thomas Walker of Manchester, and after informing him
of my intention of giving up the work for the purpose of
general information, I informed him of what I apprehended would be the consequence ; that while the work was at
a price that precluded an extensive circulation, the government party, not able to controvert the plans, arguments,
and principles it contained, had chosen to remain silent :

but that I expected they would make an attempt to deprive
the mass of the nation, and especially the poor, of the
right of reading, by the pretence of prosecuting either the
author or the publisher, or both. They chose to begin
with the publisher.

Nearly a month, however, passed, before I had any information given me of their intentions. I was then at
Bromley, in Kent, upon which I came immediately to town
(May 14) and went to Mr. Jordan, the publisher of the
original edition. He had that evening been served with a
summons, to appear at the court of king's bench on the
Monday following, but for what purpose was not stated.
Supposing it to be on account of the work, I appointed a
meeting with him on the next morning, which was accordingly had, when I provided an attorney, and took the expense of the defence on myself. But finding afterwards
that he absented himself from the attorney employed, and
had engaged another, and that he had been closeted with
the solicitors of the treasury, I left him to follow his own
choice, and he chose to plead guilty. This he might do
if he pleased ; and I make no objection against him for it.
I believe that his idea by the word *guilty*, was no other
than declaring himself to be the publisher, without any regard to the merits or demerits of the work ; for were it to
be construed otherwise, it would amount to the absurdity
of converting a publisher into a jury, and his confession
into a verdict upon the work itself. This would be the
highest possible refinement upon packing of juries.

On the 21st of May, they commenced their prosecution
against me as the author, by leaving a summons at my lodg-
ings in town, to appear at the court of king's bench on the
8th of June, following ; and on the same day (May 21) *they
issued also their proclamation.* Thus the court of St. James
and the court of king's bench, were playing into each other's hands at the same instant of time, and the farce of addresses brought up the rear ; and this mode of proceeding
is called by the prostituted name of law. Such a thundering rapidity, after a ministerial dormancy of almost a year
and an half, can be attributed to no other cause than their
having gained information of the forwardness of the cheap
edition, and the dread they felt at the progressive increase
of political knowledge.

I was strongly advised by several gentlemen, as well
those in the practice of the law, as others, to prefer a bill

of indictment against the publisher of the proclamation, as a publication tending to influence, or rather to dictate the verdict of a jury on the issue of a matter then pending; but it appeared to me much better to avail myself of the opportunity which such a precedent justified me in using, by meeting the proclamation and the addresses on their own ground, and publicly defending the work which had been thus unwarrantably attacked and traduced. And conscious as I now am, that the work entitled, Rights of Man, so far from being, as has been maliciously or erroneously represented, a false, wicked and seditious libel, is a work abounding with unanswerable truths, with principles of the purest morality and benevolence, and with arguments not to be controverted. Conscious, I say, of these things, and having no object in view but the happiness of mankind, I have now put the matter to the best proof in my power, by giving to the public a cheap edition of the first and second parts of that work. Let every man read and judge for himself, not only of the merits or demerits of the work, but of the matters therein contained, which relate to his own interest and happiness.

If, to expose the fraud and imposition of monarchy, and every species of hereditary government; to lessen the oppression of taxes; to propose plans for the education of helpless infancy, and the comfortable support of the aged and distressed; to endeavor to conciliate nations to each other; to extirpate the horrid practice of war; to promote universal peace, civilization, and commerce; and to break the chains of political superstition, and raise degraded man to his proper rank;—if these things be libellous, let me live the life of a libeller, and let the name of *libeller* be engraved on my tomb.

Of all the weak and ill-judged measures which fear, ignorance, or arrogance could suggest, the proclamation, and the project for addresses are the two worst. They served to advertise the work which the promoters of those measures wished to keep unknown; and in doing this they offered violence to the judgment of the people, by calling on them to condemn what they forbad them to know; and put the strength of their party to that hazardous issue that prudence would have avoided. The county meeting for Middlesex was attended by only one hundred and eighteen addressers. They, no doubt, expected, that thousands would flock to their standard, and clamor against the

Rights of Man. But the case most probably is, that men are not so blind to their rights and their interests, as governments believe.

Having thus shown the extraordinary manner in which the government party commenced their attack, I proceed to offer a few observations on the prosecution, and on the mode of trial by special jury.

In the first place, I have written a book; and if it cannot be refuted, it cannot be condemned. But I do not consider the prosecution as particularly levelled against me, but against the general right, or the right of every man, of investigating systems and principles of government, and showing their several excellencies or defects. If the press be free only to flatter government, as Burke has done, and to cry up and extol what certain court sycophants are pleased to call a "glorious constitution," and not free to examine into its errors or abuses, or whether a constitution really exist or not, such freedom is no other than that of Spain, Turkey or Russia; and a jury in this case, would not be a jury to try, but an inquisition to condemn.

I have asserted, and by fair and open argument maintained, the right of every nation at all times to establish such a system and form of government for itself as best accords with its disposition, interest and happiness; and to change and alter it as it sees occasion. Will any jury deny to the nation this right? If they do, they are traitors, and their verdict would be null and void. And if they admit the right, the means must be admitted also; for it would be the highest absurdity to say, that the right existed, but the means did not. The question then is, What are the means by which the possession and exercise of this national right are to be secured? The answer will be, that of maintaining, inviolably, the right of investigation; for investigation always serves to detect error, and to bring forth truth.

I have, as an individual, given my opinion upon what I believe to be not only the best, but the true system of government, which is the representative system, and I have given reasons for that opinion.

1st, Because in the representative system, no office of very extraordinary power, or extravagant pay, is attached to any individual; and consequently there is nothing to excite those national contentions and civil wars, with which countries under monarchical governments are frequently convulsed, and of which the history of England exhibits such numerous instances.

2d, Because the representative is a system of government always in maturity; whereas monarchical government fluctuates through all the stages, from nonage to dotage.

3d, Because the representative system admits of none but men, properly qualified, into the government, or removes them if they prove to be otherwise. Whereas in the hereditary system, a nation may be encumbered with a knave or an ideot for a whole life-time, and not be benefited by a successor.

4th. Because there does not exist a right to establish hereditary government; or, in other words, hereditary successors; because hereditary government always means a government yet to come, and the case always is, that those who are to live afterwards have the same right to establish government for themselves, as the people had who lived before them; and, therefore, all laws attempting to establish hereditary government, are founded on assumption and political fiction.

If these positions be truths, and I challenge any man to prove the contrary; if they tend to instruct and enlighten mankind, and to free them from error, oppression, and political superstition, which are the objects I have in view in publishing them, that jury would commit an act of injustice to their country, and to me, if not an act of perjury, that should call them *false, wicked,* and *malicious.*

Dragonetti, in his treatise, On Virtues and Rewards, has a paragraph worthy of being recorded in every country in the world—"The science, (says he) of the politician, consists in fixing the true point of happiness and freedom. Those men deserve the gratitude of ages, who should discover a mode of government that contained the greatest sum of *individual happiness* with the least *national expense.*" But if juries are to be made use of to prohibit inquiry, to suppress truth, and to stop the progress of knowledge, this boasted palladium of liberty becomes the most successful instrument of tyranny.

Among the arts practised at the bar, and from the bench, to impose upon the understanding of a jury, and to obtain a verdict where the consciences of men could not otherwise consent, one of the most successful has been that of calling truth a libel, and of insinuating, that the words "falsely, wickedly, and maliciously," though they are made the formidable and high sounding part of the charge, are not matters for consideration with a jury. For what purpose, then, are they retained, unless it be for that of imposition and wilful defamation?

I cannot conceive a greater violation of order, nor a more abominable insult upon morality, and upon human understanding, than to see a man sitting in the judgment seat, affecting by an antiquated foppery of dress to impress the audience with awe; then causing witnesses and jury to be sworn to truth and justice, himself having officially sworn the same; then causing to be read a prosecution against a man, charging him with having *wickedly and maliciously written and published a certain false, wicked and seditious book*; and having gone through all this with a show of solemnity, as if he saw the eye of the Almighty darting through the roof of the building like a ray of light, turn in an instant, the whole into a farce, and in order to obtain a verdict that could not otherwise be obtained, tell the jury that the charge of *falsely, wickedly, and seditiously*, meant nothing, that *truth* was out of the question; and that whether the person accused spoke truth or falsehood, or intended *virtuously or wickedly*, was the same thing; and finally conclude the wretched inquisitorial scene, by stating some antiquated precedent, equally as abominable as that which is then acting; or giving some opinion of his own, and *falsely calling the one and the other—law*. It was, most probably, to such a judge as this, that the most solemn of all reproofs was given—" *The Lord will smite thee, thou whitened wall.*"

I now proceed to offer some remarks on what is called a special jury. As to what is called a special verdict, I shall make no other remark upon it, than that it is in reality *not* a verdict. It is an attempt on the part of the jury to delegate, or of the bench to obtain, the exercise of that right, which is committed to the jury only.

With respect to special juries, I shall state such matters as I have been able to collect, for I do not find any uniform opinion concerning the mode of appointing them.

In the first place, the mode of trial is but of modern invention, and the origin of it, as I am told, is as follows:

Formerly, when disputes arose between merchants, and were brought before a court, the case was that the nature of their commerce, and the method of keeping merchants' accounts not being sufficiently understood by persons out of their own line, it became necessary to depart from the common mode of appointing juries, whose *practical knowledge* would enable them justly to decide upon the case. From this introduction, special juries became more general, but some doubts having arisen as to their legality, an act was passed in the 3d of George II. to establish them as legal, and also to extend them to all cases, not only between individuals, but in cases where *the government itself should be the prosecutor*. This most probably gave rise to the suspicion so generally entertained of packing a jury; because by this act, when the crown as it is called, is the prosecutor, the master of the crown-office, who holds his office under the crown, is the person who either wholly nominates, or has great power in nominating the jury, and therefore it has greatly the appearance of the prosecuting party selecting a jury.

The process is as follows:

On motion being made in court, by either the plaintiff or defendant, for a special jury, the court grants it or not, at its own discretion.

If it be granted, the solicitor of the party that applied for the special jury, gives notice to the solicitor of the adverse party, and a day and hour are appointed for them to meet at the office of the master of the crown-office. The master of the crown-office sends to the sheriff or his deputy, who attends with the sheriff's book of freeholders. Forty-eight names are taken, and a copy thereof given to each of the parties; and on a future day, notice is again given, and the solicitors meet a second time, and each strikes out twelve names. The list being thus reduced from forty-eight to twenty four, the first twelve that appear in court and answer to their names, is the special jury for that cause. The first operation, that of taking the forty-eight names, is called nominating the jury; and the reducing them to twenty-four is called striking the jury.

Having thus stated the general process, I come to particulars; and the first question will be, how are the forty-eight names, out of which the jury is to be struck, obtained from the sheriff's book? For herein lies the principle ground of suspicion, with respect to what is understood by packing of juries.

Either they must be taken by some rule agreed upon between the parties, or by some common rule known and established beforehand, or at the discretion of some person.

who, in such a case, ought to be perfectly disinterested in the issue, as well officially as otherwise.

In the case of merchants, and in all cases between individuals, the master of the office, called the crown-office, is officially an indifferent person, and as such may be a proper person to act between the parties, and present them with a list of forty-eight names, out of which each party is to strike twelve. But the case assumes an entire difference of character, when the government itself is the prosecutor. The master of the crown-office is then an officer holding his office under the prosecutor; and it is therefore no wonder, that the suspicion of packing juries should, in such cases, have been so prevalent.

This will apply with additional force, when the prosecution is commenced against the author or publisher of such works as treat of reforms, and of the abolition of superfluous places and offices, &c. because in such cases every person holding an office, subject to that suspicion, becomes interested as a party; and the office, called the crown-office, may, upon examination, be found to be of this description.

I have heard it asserted, that the master of the crown-office is to open the sheriff's book as it were per hazard, and take thereout forty-eight *following* names, to which the word merchant or esquire is affixed. The former of these are certainly proper, when the case is between merchants, and has reference to the origin of the custom, and to nothing else. As to the word esquire, every man is an esquire who pleases to call himself esquire; and the sensible part of mankind are leaving it off. But the matter for inquiry is, whether there be any existing law to direct the mode by which the forty-eight names shall be taken, or whether the mode be merely that of custom which the office has created; or whether the selection of the forty-eight be wholly at the discretion and choice of the master of the crown-office? One or other of the two latter appears to be the case, because the act already mentioned, of the 3d of George II. lays down no rule or mode, nor refers to any preceding law—but says only, that special juries shall hereafter be struck, "*in such manner as special juries have been and are usually struck.*"

This act appears to have been what is generally understood by a "*deep take in.*" It was fitted to the spur of the moment in which it was passed, 3d of George II. when parties ran high, and it served to throw into the hands of Walpole, who was then minister, the management of juries in crown prosecutions, by making the nomination of the forty-eight persons, from whom the jury was to be struck, follow the precedent established by custom between individuals, and by this means it slipped into practice with less suspicion. Now, the manner of obtaining special juries through the medium of an officer of the government, such, for instance, as a master of the crown-office, may be impartial in the case of merchants, or other individuals, but it becomes highly improper and suspicious in cases where the government itself is one of the parties. And it must, upon the whole, appear a strange inconsistency, that a government should keep one officer to nominate the forty-eight persons from whom the jury is to be struck, both of whom are *officers of the civil list*, and yet continue to call this by the pompous name of *the glorious right of trial by jury!*

In the case of the king against Jordan, for publishing the Rights of Man, the attorney-general moved for the appointment of a special jury, and the master of the crown-office nominated the forty-eight persons himself, and took them from such part of the sheriff's book as he pleased.

The trial did not come on, occasioned by Jordan withdrawing his plea; but if it had, it might have afforded an opportunity of discussing the subject of special juries; for though such discussion might have had no effect in the court of king's bench it would, in the present disposition for inquiry, have had a considerable effect upon the country; and in all national reforms, this is the proper point to begin at. Put a country right, and it will soon put government right. Among the improper things acted by the government in the case of special juries, on their own motion, one has been that of treating the jury with a dinner, and afterwards giving each juryman two guineas, if a verdict be found for the prosecution, and only one if otherwise; and it has been long observed, that in London and Westminster there are persons who appear to make a trade of serving, by being so frequently seen upon special juries.

Thus much for special juries. As to what is called a *common jury*, upon any government prosecution against the author or publisher of the Rights of Man, during the time of the *present sheriffry*, I have one question to offer, which is, *whether the present sheriffs of London, having publicly prejudged*

*the case, by the part they have taken in procuring an address
from the county of Middlesex, (however diminutive and insignificant the number of addressers were, being only one hundred and
eighteen) are eligible or proper persons to be intrusted with the
power of returning a jury to try the issue of any such prosecution.*

But the whole matter appears, at least to me, to be worthy of a more extensive consideration than what relates to
any jury, whether special or common; for the case is,
whether any part of a whole nation, locally selected as a
jury of twelve men always is, be competent to judge and
determine for the whole nation, on any matter that relates
to systems and principles of government, and whether it
be not applying the institution of juries to purposes for
which such institutions were not intended? For example,

I have asserted, in the work Rights of Man, that as every
man in the nation pays taxes, so has every man a right to
a share in government, and consequently that the people
of Manchester, Birmingham, Sheffield, Leeds, Halifax, &c.
have the same right as those of London. Shall then twelve
men, picked out between Temple-bar and Whitechapel, because the book happened to be first published there, decide upon the rights of the inhabitants of those towns, or
of any other town or village in the nation?

Having thus spoken of juries, I come next to offer a few
observations on the matter contained in the information or
prosecution.

The work, Rights of Man, consists of part the first, and
part the second. The first the prosecutor has thought it
most proper to let alone; and from the second part he has
selected a few short paragraphs, making in the whole not
quite two pages of the same printing as in the cheap edition. Those paragraphs relate chiefly to certain facts,
such as the revolution of 1688, and the coming of George
I. commonly called of the house of Hanover, or the
house of Brunswick, or some such house. The arguments,
plans and principles contained in the work, the prosecutor
has not ventured to attack. They are beyond his reach.

The act which the prosecutor appears to rest most upon
for the support of the prosecution, is the act, entitled " An
act, declaring the rights and liberties of the subject and
settling the succession of the crown," passed in the first
year of William and Mary, and more commonly known
by the name of the " bill of rights."

I have called this bill *"A bill of wrongs and of insult."*
My reasons, and also my proofs, are as follow:

The method and principle which this bill takes for declaring rights and liberties, are in direct contradiction to
rights and liberties; it is an assumed attempt to take them
wholly from posterity—for the declaration in the said bill
is as follows:

"The lords spiritual and temporal, and commons, do, in
the name of all the people, most humbly and faithfully *submit
themselves, their heirs, and posterity forever;"* that is, to William and Mary his wife, their heirs and successors. This
is a strange way of declaring rights and liberties. But
the parliament who made this declaration in the name,
and on the part of the people, had no authority from them
for so doing; and with respect to *posterity for ever*, they had
no right or authority whatever in the case. It was assumption and usurpation. I have reasoned very exten-
sively against the principle of this bill, in the first part of
the Rights of Man; the prosecutor has silently admitted
that reasoning, and he now commences a prosecution on
the authority of the bill, after admitting the reasoning
against it.

It is also to be observed, that the declaration in this bill,
abject and irrational as it is, had no other intentional operation than against the family of the Stuarts, and their
abettors. The idea did not then exist, that in the space
of an hundred years, posterity might discover a different
and much better system of government, and that every
species of hereditary government might fall as popes and
monks had fallen before. This, I say, was not then thought
of, and therefore the application of the bill, in the present
case, is a new, erroneous, and illegal application, and is
the same as creating a new bill *ex post facto*.

It has ever been the craft of courtiers, for the purpose
of keeping up an expensive and enormous civil list, and a
mummery of useless and antiquated places and offices at
the public expense, to be continually hanging England
upon some individual or other, called *king*, though the man
might not have capacity to be a parish constable. The
folly and absurdity of this, is appearing more and more
every day; and still those men continue to act as if no alteration in the public opinion had taken place. They hear
each other's nonsense, and suppose the whole nation talks
the same gibberish.

Let such men cry up the house of Orange, or the house of Brunswick, if they please. They would cry up any other house if it suited their purpose, and give as good reasons for it. But what is this house, or that house, or any other house to a nation ? " *For a nation to be free, it is sufficient that she wills it.*" Her freedom depends wholly upon herself, and not on any house, nor on any individual. I ask not in what light this cargo of foreign houses appears to others, but I will say in what light it appears to me. It was like the trees of the forest, saying unto the bramble, come thou and reign over us.

Thus much for both their houses. I now come to speak of two other houses, which are also put into the information, and those are the house of lords, and the house of commons. Here, I suppose, the attorney-general intends to prove me guilty of speaking either truth or falsehood ; for, according to the modern interpretation of libels, it does not signify which, and the only improvement necessary to show the complete absurdity of such doctrine, would be, to prosecute a man for uttering a most *false and wicked truth.*

I will quote the part I am going to give, from the office copy, with the attorney-general's innuendoes, enclosed in parentheses, as they stand in the information, and I hope that civil list officer will caution the court not to laugh when he reads them, and also to take care not to laugh himself.

The information states, That *Thomas Paine, being a wicked, malicious, seditious, and evil disposed person, hath, with force and arms, and most wicked cunning, written and published a certain false, scandalous, malicious, and seditious libel ; in one part thereof, to the tenor and effect following, that is to say :*

" With respect to the two houses, of which the English parliament (*meaning the parliament of this kingdom*) is composed, they appear to be effectually influenced into one, and, as a legislature, to have no temper of its own. The minister (*meaning the minister employed by the king of this realm, in the administration of the government thereof*) whoever he, at any time may be, touches it (*meaning the two houses of parliament of this kingdom*) as with an opium wand, and it (*meaning the two houses of parliament of this kingdom*) sleeps obedience. As I am not malicious enough to disturb their repose, though it be time they should awake, I leave the

two houses and the attorney-general, to the enjoyment of
their dreams, and proceed to a new subject."

The gentlemen, to whom I shall next address myself, are
those who have styled themselves "*friends of the people,*"
holding their meeting at the Freemason's tavern, London.

One of the principal members of this society, is Mr.
Grey, who, I believe, is also one of the most independent
members in parliament. I collect this opinion from what
Mr. Burke formerly mentioned to me, rather than from
any knowledge of my own. The occasion was as follows:

I was in England at the time the bubble broke forth
about Nootka Sound; and the day after the king's message, as it is called, was sent to parliament; I wrote a note
to Mr. Burke, that upon the condition the French revolution should not be a subject (for he was then writing the
book I have since answered) I would call on him the next
day, and mention some matters I was acquainted with, respecting the affair; for it appeared to me extraordinary,
that any body of men, calling themselves representatives,
should commit themselves so precipitately, or, "sleep
obedience," as parliament was then doing, and run a nation into expense, and, perhaps a war, without so much as
inquiring into the case, or the subject, of both which I had
some knowledge.

When I saw Mr. Burke, and mentioned the circumstances to him, he particularly spoke of Mr. Grey, as the
fittest member to bring such matters forward; for, said
Mr. Burke, "*I am not the proper* person to do it, as I am in
a treaty with Mr. Pitt about Mr. Hastings' trial." I hope
the attorney-general will allow, that Mr. Burke was then
sleeping his obedience. But to return to the society.

I cannot bring myself to believe, that the general motive of this society is any thing more than that by which
every former parliamentary opposition has been governed, and by which the present is sufficiently known. Fail-
ing in their pursuit of power and place within doors, they
have now (and that in not a very mannerly manner) endeavored to possess themselves of that ground out of doors,
which, had it not been made by others, would not have
been made by them. They appear to me to have watched, with more cunning than candor, the progress of a certain publication, and when they saw it had excited a spirit
of inquiry, and was rapidly spreading, they stepped forward to profit by the opportunity, and Mr. Fox *then* called

it a libel. In saying this, he libelled himself. Politicians of this cast, such, I mean, as those who trim between parties, and lie by for events, are to be found in every country, and it never yet happened that they did not do more harm than good. They embarrass business, fritter it to nothing, perplex the people, and the event to themselves generally is, that they go just far enough to make enemies of the few, without going far enough to make friends of the many.

Whoever will read the declarations of this society, of the 25th of April, and 5th of May, will find a studied reserve upon all the points that are real abuses. They speak not once of the extravagance of government, of the abominable list of unnecessary and sinecure places and pensions, of the enormity of the civil list, of the excess of taxes, nor of any one matter that substantially affects the nation; and from some conversation that has passed in that society, it does not appear to me that it is any part of their plan, to carry this class of reforms into practice. No opposition party ever did, when it gained possession.

In making these free observations, I mean not to enter into contention with this society; their incivility towards me is what I should expect from place-hunting reformers. They are welcome, however, to the ground they have advanced upon, and I wish that every individual among them may act in the same upright, uninfluenced, and public spirited manner that I have done. Whatever reforms may be obtained, and by whatever means, they will be for the benefit of others, and not of me. I have no other interest in the cause than the interest of my heart. The part I have acted has been wholly that of a volunteer, unconnected with party; and when I quit, it shall be as honorably as I began.

I consider the reform of parliament, by an application to parliament, as proposed by the society, to be a worn out hacknied subject, about which the nation is tired, and the parties are deceiving each other. It is not a subject that is cognizable before parliament, because no government has a right to alter itself, either in whole or in part. The right, and the exercise of that right, appertains to the nation only, and the proper means is by a national convention, elected for the purpose, by all the people. By this, the will of the nation whether to reform or not, or what the reform shall be, or how far it shall extend, will be known,

and it cannot be known by any other means.   Partial addresses, or separate associations, are not testimonies of the
general will.

It is, however, certain, that the opinions of men, with respect to systems and principles of government, are changing fast in all countries.   The alteration in England, within the space of little more than a year, is far greater than
could have been believed, and it is daily and hourly increasing.   It moves along the country with the silence of
thought.   The enormous expense of government, has provoked men to think, by making them feel ; and the proclamation has served to increase jealousy and disgust.   To
prevent, therefore, those commotions which too often and
too suddenly arise from suffocated discontents, it is best
that the general WILL should have the full and free opportunity of being publicly ascertained and known.

Wretched as the state of representation is in England, it
is every day becoming worse, because the unrepresented
parts of the nation are increasing in population and property, and the represented parts are decreasing. It is, therefore, no ill grounded estimation to say, that as not one person in seven is represented, at least fourteen millions of
taxes, out of the seventeen millions, are paid by the unrepresented part; for although copyholds and leaseholds are
assessed to the land tax, the holders are unrepresented.
Should then a general demur take place as to the obligation
of paying taxes, on the ground of not being represented, it
is not the representatives of rotten-boroughs, nor special
juries, that can decide the question.   This is one of the
possible cases that ought to be foreseen, in order to prevent the inconveniencies that might arise to numerous individuals, by provoking it.

I confess I have no idea of petitioning for rights. Whatever the rights of people are, they have a right to them, and
nobody has a right either to withhold them, or to grant
them.   Government ought to be established on such principles of justice as to exclude the occasion of all such applications ; for wherever they appear, they are virtually
accusations.

I wish that Mr. Grey, since he has embarked in the business, would take the whole of it into consideration.   He
will then see, that the right of reforming the state of the
representation does not reside in parliament, and that the
only motion he could consistently make would be, that

parliament should *recommend* the election of a convention of the people, because all pay taxes. But whether parliament recommended it or not, the right of the nation would neither be lessened nor increased thereby.

As to petitions from the unrepresented part, they ought not to be looked for. As well might it be expected that Manchester, Sheffield, &c. should petition the rotten-boroughs, as that they should petition the representatives of those boroughs. Those two towns alone pay far more taxes than all the rotten-boroughs put together, and it is scarcely to be expected they should pay their court either to the boroughs, or the borough-mongers.

It ought also to be observed, that what is called parliament, is composed of two houses that have always declared against the right of each other to interfere in any matter that related to the circumstances of either, particularly that of election. A reform, therefore in the representation cannot, on the ground they have individually taken, become the subject of an act of parliament, because such a mode would include the interference, against which the commons on their part have protested; but must, as well on the ground of formality, as on that of right, proceed from a national convention.

Let Mr. Grey or any other man, sit down and endeavor to put his thoughts together, for the purpose of drawing up an application to parliament for a reform of parliament, and he will soon convince himself of the folly of the attempt. He will find that he cannot get on; that he cannot make his thoughts join, so as to produce any effect; for whatever formality of words he may use, they will unavoidably include two ideas directly opposed to each other; the one in setting forth the reasons, the other in praying for relief, and the two when placed together, would stand thus : "*The representation in parliament is so very corrupt, that we can no longer confide in it,—and therefore, confiding in the justice and wisdom of parliament, we pray,*" &c.

The heavy manner in which every former proposed application to parliament has dragged, sufficiently shows, that though the nation might not exactly see the awkwardness of the measure, it could not clearly see its way, by those means. To this also may be added another remark, which is, that the worse parliament is, the less will be the inclination to petition it. This indifference, viewed as it ought to be, is one of the strongest censures the public express. It is as if they were to say to them, "Ye are not worth reforming."

Let any man examine the court-calendar of placemen in both houses, and the manner in which the civil list operates, and he will be at no loss to account for this indifference and want of confidence on one side, nor of the opposition to reforms on the other.

Who would have supposed that Mr. Burke, holding forth as he formerly did against secret influence, and corrupt majorities, should become a concealed pensioner? I will now state the case, not for the little purpose of exposing Mr. Burke, but to show the inconsistency of any application to a body of men, more than half of whom, as far as the nation can at present know, may be in the same case with himself.

Towards the end of lord North's administration, Mr. Burke brought a bill into parliament, generally known by the name of Mr. Burke's reform bill; in which, among other things, it is enacted, "That no pension exceeding the sum of three hundred pounds a-year, shall be granted to any one person, and that the whole amount of the pensions granted in one year shall not exceed six hundred thousand pounds;" a list of which, "together with the *names of the persons* to whom the same are granted, shall be laid before parliament in twenty days after the beginning of each session, until the whole pension list shall be reduced to ninety thousand pounds." A provisory clause is afterwards added, "That it shall be lawful for the first commissioner of the treasury, to return into the exchequer, any pension or annuity, *without a name*, on his making oath that such pension or annuity is not directly or indirectly for the benfit, use, or behoof of any member of the house of commons."

But soon after that administration ended, and the party Mr. Burke acted with, came into power. it appears from the circumstances I am going to relate, that Mr. Burke became himself a pensioner in disguise; in a similar manner, as if a pension had been granted in the name of John Nokes to be privately paid to and enjoyed by Tom Stiles. The name of Edmund Burke does not appear in the original transaction: but after the pension was obtained, Mr. Burke wanted to make the most of it at once, by selling or mortgaging it; and the gentleman, in whose name the pension stands, applied to one of the public offices for that purpose. This unfortunately brought forth the name of *Edmund Burke*, as the real pensioner of 1,500*l.* per annum. When men trumpet forth what they call the blessings of the constitution, it ought to be known what sort of blessings they allude to.

As to the civil list, of a million a-year, it is not to be supposed that any one man can eat, drink, or consume the whole upon himself. The case is, that above half the sum is annually apportioned among courtiers, and court members of both houses, in places and offices, altogether insignificant and perfectly useless, as to every purpose of civil, rational, and manly government. For instance,

Of what use in the science and system of government, is what is called a lord chamberlain, a master and mistress of the robes, a master of the horse, a master of the hawks, and an hundred other such things? Laws derive no additional force, nor additional excellence from such mummery.

In the disbursements of the civil list for the year 1786 (which may be seen in Sir John Sinclair's History of the Revenue) are four separate charges for this mummery office of chamberlain:

1st,	-	-	-	-	-	33,770*l.* 17*s.*	—
2d,	-	-	-	-	-	3,000	—
3d,	-	-	-	-	-	24,069 19	—
4th,	-	-	-	-	-	10,000 19	3*d.*

75,849*l.* 14*s.* 3*d.*

Besides 1,110*l.* charged for alms.

From this sample the rest may be guessed at. As to the master of the hawks (there are no hawks kept, and if there were, it is no reason the people should pay the expense of feeding them, many of whom are put to it to get bread for their children) his salary is 1,372*l.* 10*s.*

And besides a list of items of this kind, sufficient to fill a quire of paper, the pension lists alone are 107,404*l.* 13*s.* 4*d.* which is a greater sum than all the expenses of the federal government in America amount to.

Among the items, there are two, that I had no expectation of finding, and which, in this day of inquiry after civil list influence, ought to be exposed. The one is an annual payment of one thousand seven hundred pounds to the dissenting ministers in England, and the other, eight hundred pounds to those in Ireland.

This is the fact, and the distribution, as I am informed, is as follows : the whole sum of 1,700*l.* is paid to one person, a dissenting minister in London, who divides it among eight others; and those eight among such others as they please. The lay-body of the dissenters, and many of their principal ministers, have long considered it as dishonorable and have endeavored to prevent it, but still it continues to be secretly paid; and as the world has sometimes seen very fulsome addresses from parts of that body, it may naturally be supposed that the receivers, like bishops and other court-clergy, are not idle in promoting them. How the money is distributed in Ireland, I know not.

To recount all the secret history of the civil list, is not the intention of this publication. It is sufficient in this place to expose its general character, and the mass of influence it keeps alive. It will necessarily become one of the objects of reform; and therefore enough is said to show, that under its operation, no application to parliament can be expected to succeed, nor can consistently be made.

Such reforms will not be promoted by the party that is in possession of those places, nor by the opposition who are waiting for them ; and as to a *mere reform*, in the state of the representation, under the idea that another parliament, differently elected from the present, but still a component third part of the same system, and subject to the control of the other two parts, will abolish those abuses, is altogether delusion; because it is not only impracticable on the ground of formality, but is unwisely exposing another set of men to the same corruptions that have tainted the present.

Were all the objects that require a reform accomplishable by a mere reform in the state of representation, the persons who compose the present parliament might, with rather more propriety be asked to abolish all the abuses themselves, than be applied to as the mere instruments of doing it by a future parliament. If the virtue be wanting to abolish the abuse, it is also wanting to act as the means, and the nation must, from necessity, proceed by some other plan.

Having thus endeavored to show what the abject condition of parliament is, and the impropriety of going a second time over the same ground that has before miscarried, I come to the remaining part of the subject.

There ought to be, in the constitution of every country, a mode of referring back, on any extraordinary occasion, to the sovereign and original constituent power, which is the nation itself. The right of altering any part of a government, cannot, as already observed, reside in the government, or that government might make itself what it pleased.

It ought also to be taken for granted, that though a nation may feel inconveniencies, either in the excess of taxation, or in the mode of expenditure, or in any thing else, it may not at first be sufficiently assured in what part of its government the defect lies, or where the evil originates. It may be supposed to be in one part, and on inquiry be found to be in another; or partly in all. This obscurity is naturally interwoven with what are called mixed governments.

Be, however, the reform to be accomplished whatever it may, it can only follow in consequence of obtaining a full knowledge of all the causes that have rendered such reform necessary, and every thing short of this is guess-work or frivolous cunning. In this case, it cannot be supposed that any application to parliament can bring forward this knowledge. The body is itself the supposed cause, or one of the supposed causes, of the abuses in question; and cannot be expected, and ought not to be asked, to give evidence against itself. The inquiry, therefore, which is of necessity the first step in the business, cannot be trusted to parliament, but must be undertaken by a distinct body of men, separated from every suspicion of corruption or influence.

Instead, then, of referring to rotten-boroughs and absurd corporations for addresses, or hawking them about the country to be signed by a few dependant tenants, the real and effectual mode would be to come at once to the point, and to ascertain the sense of the nation by electing a national convention. By this method, as already observed, the general WILL, whether to reform or not, or what the reform shall be, or how far it shall extend, will be known, and it cannot be known by any other means. Such a body, empowered and supported by the nation, will have authority to demand information upon all matters necessary to be inquired into; and no minister, nor any person, will dare to refuse it. It will then be seen whether seventeen millions of taxes are necessary, and for what purposes they are expended. The concealed pensioners will then be obliged to unmask; and the source of influence and corruption, if any such there be, will be laid open to the nation, not for the purpose of revenge, but of redress.

By taking this public and national ground, all objections against partial addresses on the one side, or private associations on the other, will be done away, *the nation will declare its own reforms;* and the clamor about party and faction, or ins or outs, will become ridiculous.

The plan and organization of a convention is easy in practice.

In the first place, the number of inhabitants in every county can be sufficiently ascertained, from the number of houses assessed to the house and window-light tax in each county. This will give the rule for apportioning the number of members to be elected to the national convention in each of the counties.

If the total number of inhabitants in England be seven millions, and the total number of members to be elected to the convention be one thousand, the number of members to be elected in a county, containing one hundred and fifty thousand inhabitants, will be twenty-one, and in like proportion for any other county.

As the election of a convention must, in order to ascertain the general sense of the nation, go on grounds different from that of parliamentary elections, the mode that best promises this end will have no difficulties to combat with from absurd customs and pretended rights. The right of every man will be the same, whether he lives in a city, a town, or a village. The custom of attaching rights to *place,* or in other words to inanimate matter, instead of to *persons,* independently of place, is too absurd to make any part of a rational argument.

As every man in the nation, of the age of twenty-one years, pays taxes, either out of the property he possesses, or out of the product of his labor, which is property to him; and is amenable in his own person to every law of the land; so has every one the same equal right to vote, and no one part of a nation, nor any individual, has a right to dispute the right of another. The man who should do this, ought to forfeit the exercise of his *own* right for a term of years. This would render the punishment consistent with the crime.

When a qualification to vote is regulated by years, it is placed on the firmest possible ground; because the quali-

fication is such, as nothing but dying before the time can
take away; and the equality of rights, as a principle, is
recognized in the act of regulating the exercise. But
when rights are placed upon, or made dependant upon
property, they are on the most precarious of all tenures:
" Riches make themselves wings, and fly away," and the
rights fly with them; and thus they become lost to the
man when they would be of most value.

It is from a strange mixture of tyranny and cowardice,
that exclusions have been set up and continued. The
boldness to do wrong at first, changes afterwards into cowardly craft, and at last into fear. The representatives in
England appear now to act as if they were afraid to do
right, even in part, lest it should awaken the nation to a
sense of all the wrongs it has endured. This case serves
to show, that the same conduct that best constitutes the
safety of an individual, namely, a strict adherence to principle, constitutes also the safety of a government, and that
without it safety is but an empty name. When the rich
plunder the poor of his rights, it becomes an example to
the poor to plunder the rich of his property; for the rights
of the one are as much property to him, as wealth is property to the other, and the *little all* is as dear as the *much*.

It is only by setting out on just principles that men are
trained to be just to each other; and it will always be
found, that when the rich protect the rights of the poor,
the poor will protect the property of the rich. But the
guarantee, to be effectual, must be parliamentarily reciprocal.

Exclusions are not only unjust, but they frequently operate as injuriously to the party who monopolizes, as to
those who are excluded. When men seek to exclude others
from participating in the exercise of any right, they should,
at least, be assured, that they can effectually perform the
whole of the business they undertake; for unless they do
this, themselves will be losers by the monopoly. This has
been the case with respect to the monopolized right of
election. The monopolizing party has not been able to
keep the parliamentary representation, to whom the power
of taxation was entrusted, in the state it ought to have
been, and have thereby multiplied taxes upon themselves
equally with those who were excluded.

A great deal has been, and will continue to be said,
about disqualifications, arising from the commission of

offences; but were this subject urged to its full extent, it
would disqualify a great number of the present electors,
together with their representatives; for, of all offences,
none are more destructive to the morals of society than
bribery and corruption. It is, therefore, civility to such
persons to pass this subject over, and to give them a fair
opportunity of recovering, or rather of creating character.

Every thing, in the present mode of electioneering in
England, is the reverse of what it ought to be, and the vul-
garity that attends elections is no other than the natural
consequence of inverting the order of the system.

In the first place, the candidate seeks the elector, instead
of the elector seeking for a representative; and the electors are advertised as being in the interest of the candidate,
instead of the candidate being in the interest of the electors. The candidate pays the elector for his vote, instead
of the nation paying the representative for his time and attendance on public business. The complaint for an un-
due election is brought by the candidate; as if he, and not
the electors, were the party aggrieved; and he takes on
himself at any period of the election, to break it up, by
declining, as if the election was in his right and not in
theirs.

The compact that was entered into at the last Westminster election between two of the candidates (Mr. Fox and
lord Hood) was an indecent violation of the principles of
election. The candidates, assumed, in their own persons,
the rights of the electors; for it was only in the body of
the electors, and not at all in the candidates, that the right
of making any such compact or compromise could exist.
But the principle of election and representation is so completely done away, in every stage thereof, that inconsistency has no longer the power of surprising.

Neither from elections thus conducted, nor from rotten-
borough addressers, nor from county meetings, promoted
by placemen and pensioners. can the sense of the nation
be known. It is still corruption appealing to itself. But
a convention of a thousand persons, fairly elected, would
bring every matter to a decided issue.

As to county meetings, it is only persons of leisure, or
those who live near to the place of meeting, that can attend, and the number on such occasions is but like a drop
in the bucket compared with the whole. The only consistent service which such meetings could render, would

be that of apportioning the county into convenient dis-
tricts, and when this is done, each district might, according
to its number of inhabitants, elect its quota of county members to the national convention; and the vote of each
elector might be taken in the parish where he resided,
either by ballot or by voice, as he should choose to give it.

A national convention thus formed, would bring together
the sense and opinions of every part of the nation, fairly
taken. The science of government, and the interest of
the public, and of the several parts thereof would then, undergo an ample and rational discussion, freed from the language of parliamentary disguise.

But in all deliberations of this kind, though men have a
right to reason with, and endeavor to convince each other,
upon any matter that respects their common good, yet, in
point of practice, the majority of opinions, when known,
forms a rule for the whole, and to this rule every good
citizen practically conforms.

Mr. Burke, as if he knew (for every concealed pensioner has the opportunity of knowing) that the abuses acted
under the present system, are too flagrant to be palliated,
and that the majority of opinions, whenever such abuses
should be made public. would be for a general and effectual
reform, has endeavored to preclude the event, by sturdily
denying the right of a majority of a nation to act as a
whole. Let us bestow a thought upon this case.

When any matter is proposed as a subject for consulta-
tion, it necessarily implies some mode of decision. Common consent, arising from absolute necessity, has placed
this in a majority of opinions; because without it there
can be no decision, and consequently no order. It is perhaps the only case in which mankind however various in
their ideas upon other matters, can consistently be unanimous; because it is a mode of decision derived from the
primary original right of every individual concerned; *that*
right being first individually exercised in giving an opinion, and whether that opinion shall arrange with the minority or the majority, is a subsequent accidental thing
that neither increases nor diminishes the individual original
right itself. Prior to any debate, inquiry or investigation,
it is not supposed to be known on which side the majority
of opinions will fall, and therefore whilst this mode of decision secures to every one the right of giving an opinion,
it admits to every one an equal chance in the ultimate event.

Among the matters that will present themselves to the consideration of a national convention, there is one, wholly of a domestic nature, but so marvellously loaded with confusion, as to appear at first sight, almost impossible to be reformed. I mean the condition of what is called law.

But, if we examine into the cause from whence this confusion, now so much the subject of universal complaint, is produced, not only the remedy will immediately present itself, but with it, the means of preventing the like case hereafter.

In the first place, the confusion has generated itself from the absurdity of every parliament assuming to be eternal in power, and the laws partake in a similar manner of this assumption. They have no period of legal or natural expiration; and, however absurd in principle, or inconsistent in practice, many of them have become, they still are, if not especially repealed, considered as making a part of the general mass. By this means the body of what is called law, is spread over a space of *several hundred years*, comprehending laws obsolete, laws repugnant, laws ridiculous, and every other kind of laws forgotten or remembered; and what renders the case still worse, is, that the confusion multiplies with the progress of time.*

To bring this misshapen monster into form, and to prevent its lapsing again into a wilderness state, only two things, and those very simple, are necessary.

The first is, to review the whole mass of laws, and to bring forward such only as are worth retaining, and let all the rest drop; and to give to the laws so brought forward a new era, commencing from the time of such reform.

Secondly, that at the expiration of every twenty-one years (or any other stated period) a like review shall again be taken, and the laws, found proper to be retained, be again carried forward, commencing with that date, and the useless laws dropped and discontinued.

By this means there can be no obsolete laws, and scarcely such a thing as laws standing in direct or equivocal contradiction to each other, and every person will know the period of time to which he is to look back for all the laws in being.

* In the time of Henry IV. a law was passed, making it felony " to multiply gold or silver, or to make use of the craft of multiplication," and this law remained two hundred and eighty-five years upon the statute books. It was then repealed as being ridiculous and injurious.

It is worth remarking that whilst every other branch of science is brought within some commodious system, and the study of it simplified by easy methods, the laws take the contrary course, and become every year more complicated, entangled, confused, and obscure.

Among the paragraphs which the attorney-general has taken from the Rights of Man, and put into his information, one is, that where I have said, " that with respect to regular law, there is *scarcely such a thing*."

As I do not know whether the attorney-general means to show this expression to be libellous, because it is *true*, or because it is *false*, I shall make no other reply to him in this place, than by remarking, that if almanac-makers had not been more judicious than law-makers, the study of almanacs would by this time have become as abstruse as the study of the law, and we should hear of a library of almanacs as we now do of statutes; but by the simple operation of letting the obsolete matter drop, and carrying forward that only which is proper to be retained, all that is necessary to be known, is found within the space of a year, and laws also admit of being kept within some given period.

I shall here close this letter, so far as it respects the addressers, the proclamation, and the prosecution ; and shall offer a few observations to the society, styling itself " The Friends of the People."

That the science of government is beginning to be better understood than in former times, and that the age of fiction and political superstition, and of craft and mystery is passing away, are matters which the experience of every day proves to be true, as well in England as in other countries.

As therefore it is impossible to calculate the silent progress of opinion, and also impossible to govern a nation after it has changed its habits of thinking, by the craft or policy that it was governed by before, the only true method to prevent popular discontents and commotions is, to throw, by every fair and rational argument, all the light upon the subject that can possibly be thrown ; and at the same time, to open the means of collecting the general sense of the nation ; and this cannot, as already observed, be done by any plan so effectually as a national convention. Here individual opinion will quiet itself by having a centre to rest upon.

The society already mentioned (which is made up of men of various descriptions, but chiefly of those called Foxites) appears to me, either to have taken wrong grounds from want of judgment, or to have acted with cunning reserve. It is now amusing the people with a new phrase, namely, that of " a temperate and moderate reform," the interpretation of which is, *a continuance of the abuses as long as possible. If we cannot hold all let us hold some.*

Who are those that are frightened at reforms? Are the public afraid that their taxes should be lessened too much? Are they afraid that sinecure places and pensions should be abolished too fast? Are the poor afraid that their condition should be rendered too comfortable? Is the worn-out mechanic, or the aged and decayed tradesman, frightened at the prospect of receiving ten pounds a-year out of the surplus taxes? Is the soldier frightened at the thoughts of his discharge, and three shillings per week during life? Is the sailor afraid that press-warrants will be abolished? The society mistakes the fears of borough-mongers, placemen and pensioners, for the fears of the people; and the *temperate and moderate reform* it talks of, is calculated to suit the condition of the former.

Those words, " temperate and moderate," are words either of political cowardice, or of cunning, or seduction. A thing, moderately good, is not so good as it ought to be. Moderation in temper, is always a virtue; but moderation in principle, is a species of vice. But who is to be the judge of what is a temperate and moderate reform? The society is the representative of nobody; neither can the unrepresented part of the nation commit this power to those in parliament, in whose election they had no choice; and therefore, even upon the ground the society has taken, recourse must be had to a national convention.

The objection which Mr. Fox made to Mr. Grey's proposed motion for a parliamentary reform was, that it contained no plan. It certainly did not. But the plan very easily presents itself; and whilst it is fair for all parties, it prevents the dangers that might otherwise arise from private or popular discontent.

THOMAS PAINE.

LORD ONSLOW,

Lord lieutenant of the county of Surry; on the subject of the late excellent PROCLAMATION :—*or the* CHAIRMAN *who shall preside at the meeting to be held at Epsom, June 18.*

LONDON, JUNE 17, 1792.

SIR,

I HAVE seen in the public newspapers the following advertisement, to wit—

"To the nobility, gentlemen clergy, freeholders, and other inhabitants of the county of Surry.

"At the requisition and desire of several of the freeholders of the county, I am, in the absence of the sheriff, to desire the favor of your attendance, at a meeting to be held at Epsom, on Monday, the 18th instant, at 12 o'clock at noon, to consider of an humble address to his MAJESTY, to express our grateful approbation of his MAJESTY's paternal, and well-timed attendance to the public welfare, in his late most gracious proclamation against the enemies of our happy constitution.

(Signed)   ONSLOW CRANLEY."

Taking it for granted, that the aforesaid advertisement, equally as obscure as the proclamation to which it refers, has nevertheless some meaning, and is intended to effect some purpose; and as a prosecution (whether wisely or unwisely, justly or unjustly) is commenced against a work entitled the RIGHTS OF MAN, of which I have the honor and happiness to be the author; I feel it necessary to address this letter to you, and to request that it may be read

publicly to the gentlemen who shall meet at Epsom in consequence of the advertisement.

The work now under prosecution is, I conceive, the same
work which is intended to be suppressed by the aforesaid
proclamation. Admitting this to be the case, the gentlemen
of the county of Surry are called upon by somebody to condemn a work, and they are at the same time forbidden by
the proclamation to know what that work is; and they are
further called upon to give their aid and assistance to prevent other people from knowing it also.—It is therefore necessary that the author, for his own justification, as well as to
prevent the gentlemen who shall meet from being imposed
upon by misrepresentation, should give some outlines of the
principles and plans which that work contains.

The work, sir, in question contains, first, an investigation
of general principles of government.

It also distinguishes government into two classes or
systems, the one the hereditary system; the other the
representative system; and it compares these two systems
with each other.

It shows, that what is called hereditary government cannot exist as a matter of right; because hereditary government always means a government yet to come; and the case
always is, that those who are to live afterwards have always
the same right to establish a government for themselves as
the people who had lived before them.

It also shows the defect to which hereditary government
is unavoidably subject: that it must, from the nature of it,
throw government into the hands of men totally unworthy
of it from the want of principle, or unfitted for it from want
of capacity. James II. and many others are recorded in
the English history, as proofs of the former of those cases,
and instances are to be found all over Europe, to prove the
truth of the latter.

It then shows that the representative system is the only
true system of government; that it is also the only system
under which the liberties of any people can be permanently secure; and further, that it is the only one that can continue the same equal probability at all times of admitting
of none but men properly qualified, both by principles and
abilities, into government, and of excluding such as are
otherwise.

The work shows also, by plans and calculations not
hitherto denied nor controverted, not even by the prosecu-

tion that is commenced, that the taxes now existing may be reduced at least six millions, that taxes may be entirely taken off from the poor, who are computed at one third of the nation ; and that taxes on the other two thirds may be considerably reduced ; that the aged poor may be comfortably provided for, and the children of poor families properly educated ; that fifteen thousand soldiers. and the same number of sailors may be allowed three shillings per week during life out of the surplus taxes ; and also that a proportionate allowance may be made to the officers, and the pay of the remaining soldiers and sailors be raised ; and that it is better to apply the surplus taxes to those purposes than to consume them upon lazy and profligate placemen and pensioners ; and that the revenue, said to be twenty thousand pounds per annum, raised by a tax upon coals, and given to the duke of Richmond, is a gross imposition upon all the people of London, and ought to be instantly abolished.

This, sir, is a concise abstract of the principles and plans contained in the work that is now prosecuted, and for the suppression of which the proclamation appears to be intended ; but as it is impossible that I can, in the compass of a letter, bring into view all the matters contained in the work, and as it is proper that the gentlemen who may compose that meeting should know what the merits or demerits of it are, before they come to any resolutions, either directly or indirectly relating thereto, I request the honor of presenting them with one hundred copies of the second part of the Rights of Man, and also one thousand copies of my letter to Mr. Dundas, which I have directed to be sent to Epsom for that purpose ; and I beg the favor of the chairman to take the trouble of presenting them to the gentlemen who shall meet on that occasion, with my sincere wishes for their happiness, and for that of the nation in general.

Having now closed thus much of the subject of my letter. I next come to speak of what has relation to me personally. I am well aware of the delicacy that attends it, but the purpose of calling the meeting appears to me so inconsistent with that justice that is always due between man and man, that it is proper I should (as well on account of the gentlemen who may meet, as on my own account) explain myself fully and candidly thereon.

I have already informed the gentlemen, that a prosecution is commenced against a work of which I have the honor and happiness to be the author; and I have good reasons for believing that the proclamation which the gentlemen are called to consider, and to present an address upon, is purposely calculated to give an impression to the jury before whom that matter is to come. In short, that it is dictating a verdict by proclamation; and I consider the instigators of the meeting to be held at Epsom, as aiding and abetting the same improper, and, in my opinion, illegal purpose, and that in a manner very artfully contrived, as I shall now show.

Had a meeting been called of the freeholders of the county of Middlesex, the gentlemen who had composed that meeting would have rendered themselves objectionable as persons to serve on a jury before whom the judicial case was afterwards to come. But by calling a meeting out of the county of Middlesex, that matter is artfully avoided, and the gentlemen of Surry are summoned, as if it were intended thereby to give a tone to the sort of verdict which the instigators of the meeting no doubt wish should be brought in, and to give countenance to the jury in so doing.

I am, sir,

With much respect to the

Gentlemen who shall meet,

Their and your obedient and humble servant,

THOMAS PAINE.

LETTER II.

TO THE SAME.

LONDON, JUNE, 21, 1792.

SIR,

WHEN I wrote you the letter which Mr. Horne Tooke did me the favor to present to you, as chairman of the meeting held at Epsom, Monday, June 18, it was not with much expectation that you would do me the justice of permitting, or recommending it to be publicly read. I am well aware that the signature of Thomas Paine has something in it dreadful to sinecure placemen and pensioners;

and when you, on seeing the letter opened, informed the meeting that it was signed Thomas Paine, and added in a note of exclamation, "the common enemy of us all," you spoke one of the greatest truths you ever uttered, if you confine the expression to men of the same description with yourself; men living in indolence and luxury, on the spoil and labors of the public.

The letter has since appeared in the Argus, and probably in other papers. It will justify itself; but if any thing on that account hath been wanting, your conduct at the meeting would have supplied the omission. You there sufficiently proved that I was not mistaken in supposing that the meeting was called to give an indirect aid to the prosecution commenced against a work, the reputation of which will long outlive the memory of the pensioner I am writing to.

When meetings, sir, are called by the partisans of the court, to preclude the nation the right of investigating systems and principles of government, and of exposing errors and defects under the pretence of prosecuting any individual—it furnishes an additional motive for maintaining sacred that violated right.

The principles and arguments contained in the work in question, Rights of Man, have stood, and they now stand, and I believe ever will stand, unrefuted. They are stated in a fair and open manner to the world, and they have already received the public approbation of a greater number of men, of the best of characters, of every denomination of religion, and of every rank in life (placemen and pensioners excepted,) than all the juries that shall meet in England, for ten years to come, will amount to; and I have moreover good reasons for believing that the approvers of that work, as well private as public, are already more numerous than all the present electors throughout the nation.

Not less than forty pamphlets, intended as answers thereto, have appeared, and as suddenly disappeared; scarcely are the titles of any of them remembered, notwithstanding their endeavors have been aided by all the daily abuse which the court and ministerial newspapers, for almost a year and a half, could bestow, both upon the work and the author; and now that every attempt to refute, and every abuse has failed, the invention of calling the work a libel has been hit upon, and the discomfited party has pusillanimously retreated to prosecution and a jury, and obscure addresses.

As I well know that a long letter from me will not be agreeable to you, I will relieve your uneasiness by making it as short as I conveniently can; and will conclude it with taking up the subject at that part where Mr. Horne Tooke was interrupted from going on when at the meeting.

That gentleman was stating, that the situation you stood in rendered it improper for you to appear *actively* in a scene in which your private interest was too visible; that you were a bedchamber lord at a thousand a-year, and a pensioner at three thousand pounds a-year more; and here he was stopped by the little, but noisy circle you had collected round. Permit me then, sir, to add an explanation to his words, for the benefit of your neighbors, and with which, and a few observations, I shall close my letter.

When it was reported in the English newspapers, some short time since, that the empress of Russia had given to one of her minions a large tract of country, and several thousands of peasants as property, it very justly provoked indignation and abhorrence in those who heard it. But if we compare the mode practised in England, with that which appears to us so abhorrent in Russia, it will be found to amount to very near the same thing; for example—

As the whole of the revenue in England is drawn by taxes from the pockets of the people, those things called gifts and grants (of which kind are all pensions and sinecure places) are paid out of that stock. The difference, therefore, between the two modes is, that in England the money is collected by the government, and then given to the pensioner, and in Russia he is left to collect it for himself. The smallest sum which the poorest family in a county so near London as Surry, can be supposed to pay annually of taxes, is not less than five pounds; and as your sinecure of one thousand, and pension of three thousand per annum, are made up of taxes paid by eight hundred such poor families, it comes to the same thing as if the eight hundred families had been given to you, as in Russia, and you had collected the money on your account. Were you to say that you are not quartered particularly on the people of Surry, but on the nation at large, the objection would amount to nothing; for as there are more pensioners than counties, every one may be considered as quartered on that in which he lives.

What honor or happiness you can derive from being the *principal pauper* of the neighborhood, and occasioning a greater expense than the poor, the aged, and the infirm, for ten miles round you, I leave you to enjoy. At the same time I can see that it is no wonder you should be strenuous in suppressing a book which strikes at the root of those abuses. No wonder that you should be against reforms, against the freedom of the press, and the right of investigation. To you, and to others of your description, these are dreadful things; but you should also consider, that the motives which prompt you to *act*, ought, by reflection to compel you to be *silent*.

Having now returned your compliment, and sufficiently tired your patience, I take my leave of you with mentioning, that if you had not prevented my former letter from being read at the meeting, you would not have had the trouble of reading this; and also with requesting, that the next time you call me " *a common enemy*," you would add, " *of us sinecure placemen and pensioners*."

I am, Sir,

&c. &c. &c.

THOMAS PAINE.

DISSERTATION

ON

FIRST PRINCIPLES OF GOVERNMENT.

THERE is no subject more interesting to every man than the subject of government. His security, be he rich or poor, and, in a great measure, his prosperity, is connected therewith; it is therefore his interest as well as his duty to make himself acquainted with its principles, and what the practice ought to be.

Every art and science, however imperfectly known at first, has been studied, improved, and brought to what we call perfection, by the progressive labors of succeeding generations; but the science of government has stood still. No improvement has been made in the principle, and scarcely any in the practice, till the American revolution began. In all the countries of Europe (except in France) the same forms and systems that were erected in the remote ages of ignorance, still continue, and their antiquity is put in the place of principle; it is forbidden to investigate their origin or by what right they exist. If it be asked how has this happened, the answer is easy; they are established on a principle that is false, and they employ their power to prevent detection.

Notwithstanding the mystery with which the science of government has been enveloped, for the purpose of enslaving, plundering and imposing upon mankind, it is of all things the least mysterious and the most easy to be understood. The meanest capacity cannot be at a loss, if it begins its inquiries at the right point. Every art and science

has some point, or alphabet, at which the study of that art
or science begins, and by the assistance of which the progress is facilitated. The same method ought to be observed with respect to the science of government.

Instead then of embarrassing the subject in the outset
with the numerous subdivisions, under which different
forms of government have been classed, such as aristocracy, democracy, oligarchy, monarchy, &c. the better
method will be to begin with what may be called primary
divisions, or those under which all the several subdivisions
will be comprehended.

The primary divisions are but two.

1st, Government by election and representation.

2d. Government by hereditary succession.

All the several forms and systems of government, however numerous or diversified, class themselves under one
or other of those primary divisions; for either they are
on the system of representation, or on that of hereditary
succession. As to that equivocal thing called mixed government, such as the late government of Holland, and the
present government of England, it does not make an ex-
ception to the general rule, because the parts separately
considered are either representative or hereditary.

Beginning then our inquiries at this point, we have first
to examine into the nature of those two primary divisions.
If they are equally right in principle, it is mere matter of
opinion which we prefer. If the one be demonstratively
better than the other, that difference directs our choice;
but if one of them should be so absolutely false as not to
have a right to existence, the matter settles itself at once;
because a negative proved on one thing, where two only
are offered, and one must be accepted, amounts to an af-
firmative on the other.

The revolutions that are now spreading themselves in the
world have their origin in this state of the case, and the
present war is a conflict between the representative system, founded on the rights of the people, and the hereditary system, founded in usurpation. As to what are called monarchy, royalty, and aristocracy, they do not, either
as things or as terms, sufficiently describe the hereditary
system; they are but secondary things or signs of the
hereditary system, and which fall of themselves if that
system has not a right to exist. Were there no such terms
as monarchy, royalty, and aristocracy, or were other terms

substituted in their place, the hereditary system, if it continued, would not be altered thereby. It would be the same system under any other titulary name as it is now.

The character therefore of the revolutions of the present day distinguishes itself most definitely by grounding itself on the system of representative government, in opposition to the hereditary. No other distinction reaches the whole of the principle.

Having thus opened the case generally, I proceed, in the first place, to examine the hereditary system, because it has the priority in point of time. The representative system is the invention of the modern world; and that no doubt may arise as to my own opinion, I declare it before hand, which is, *that there is not a problem in Euclid more mechanically true, than that hereditary government has not a right to exist. When therefore we take from any man the exercise of hereditary power, we take away that which he never had the right to possess, and which no law or custom could, or ever can, give him a title to.*

The arguments that have hitherto been employed against the hereditary system have been chiefly founded upon the absurdity of it, and its incompetency to the purposes of good government. Nothing can present to our judgment, or to our imagination, a figure of greater absurdity than that of seeing the government of a nation fall, as it frequently does, into the hands of a lad necessarily destitute of experience, and often little better than a fool. It is an insult to every man of years, of character, and of talents, in a country. The moment we begin to reason upon the hereditary system, it falls into derision; let but a single idea begin, and a thousand will soon follow. Insignificance, imbecility, childhood, dotage, want of moral character; in fine, every defect, serious or laughable, unite to hold up the hereditary system as a figure of ridicule.— Leaving however the ridiculousness of the thing to the reflections of the reader, I proceed to the more important part of the question, namely, whether such a system has a right to exist?

To be satisfied of the right of a thing to exist, we must be satisfied that it had a right to begin. If it had not a right to begin, it has not a right to continue. By what right then did the hereditary system begin? Let a man but ask himself this question, and he will find that he cannot satisfy himself with an answer.

The right which any man. or any family had to set himself up at first to govern a nation. and to establish itself
hereditarily, was no other than the right which Robespierre had to do the same thing in France. If he had
none, they had none. If they had any, he had as much:
for it is impossible to discover superiority of right in any
family, by virtue of which hereditary government could
begin. The Capets, the Guelphs, the Robespierres, the
Marats, are all on the same standing as to the question of
right. It belongs exclusively to none.

It is one step towards liberty, to perceive that hereditary government could not begin as an exclusive right in
any family. The next point will be, whether, having once
began, it could grow into a right by the influence of time?

This would be supposing an absurdity ; for either it is
putting time in the place of principle, or making it superior
to principle ; whereas no time has more connexion with, or
influence upon principle, than principle has upon time.——
The wrong which began a thousand years ago, is as much
a wrong as if it began to-day ; and the right which originates to-day, is as much a right as if it had the sanction of
a thousand years. Time with respect to principles is an
eternal *now :* it has no operation upon them : it changes
nothing of their nature and qualities. But what have we
to do with a thousand years? Our life-time is but a short
portion of that period, and if we find the wrong in existence
as soon as we begin to live, that is the point of time at
which it begins to us ; and our right to resist it, is the same
as if it never existed before.

As hereditary government could not begin as a natural
right in any family, nor derive after its commencement any
right from time, we have only to examine whether there exists in a nation a right to set it up, and establish it by what is
called law, as has been done in England? I answer *no ;*
and that any law or any constitution made for that purpose
is an act of treason against the right of every minor in the
nation, at the time it is made, and against the rights of all
succeeding generations. I shall speak upon each of those
cases. First. of the minor, at the time such law is made.
Secondly, of the generations that are to follow.

A nation, in a collective sense, comprehends all the individuals of whatever age, from those just born to those
just dying. Of these, one part will be minors, and the
other aged. The average of life is not exactly the same

in every climate and country, but in general the minority in years are the majority in numbers, that is, the number of persons under twenty-one years, is greater than the number of persons above that age. This difference in number is not necessary to the establishment of the principle I mean to lay down, but it serves to show the justice of it more strongly. The principle would be equally as good, if the majority in years were also the majority in numbers.

The rights of minors are as sacred as the rights of the aged. The difference is altogether in the different ages of the two parties, and nothing in the nature of the rights; the rights are the same rights; and are to be preserved inviolate for the inheritance of the minors when they shall come of age. During the minority of minors their rights are under the sacred guardianship of the aged. The minor cannot surrender them; the guardian cannot dispossess him; consequently, the aged part of a nation, who are the law-makers for the *time being*, and who, in the march of life, are but a few years ahead of those who are yet minors, and to whom they must shortly give place, have not, and cannot have the right to make a law to set up and establish hereditary government, or, to speak more distinctly, *an hereditary succession of governors;* because it is an attempt to deprive every minor in the nation, at the time such a law is made, of his inheritance of rights when he shall come of age, and to subjugate him to a system of government, to which, during his minority, he could neither consent nor object.

If a person, who is a minor at the time such a law is proposed, had happened to have been born a few years sooner, so as to be of the age of twenty-one years at the time of proposing it, his right to have objected against it, to have exposed the injustice and tyrannical principles of it, and to have voted against it, will be admitted on all sides. If, therefore, the law operates to prevent his exercising the same rights after he comes of age as he would have had a right to exercise had he been of age at the time, it is, undeniably, a law to take away and annul the rights of every person in the nation who shall be a minor at the time of making such a law, and consequently the right to make it cannot exist.

I come now to speak of government by hereditary succession as it applies to succeeding generations; and to show

that in this case, as in the case of minors, there does not
exist in a nation a right to set it up.

A nation, though continually existing, is continually in a
state of renewal and succession. It is never stationary.
Every day produces new births, carries minors forward to
maturity, and old persons from the stage. In this ever-run-
ning flood of generations there is no part superior in authority to another. Could we conceive an idea of superiority in any, at what point of time, or in what century of
the world, are we to fix it? To what cause are we to ascribe
it? By what evidence are we to prove it? By what criterion are we to know it? A single reflection will teach us
that our ancestors, like ourselves, were but tenants for life
in the great freehold of rights. The fee-absolute was not
in them, it is not in us, it belongs to the whole family of
man, through all ages. If we think otherwise than this,
we think either as slaves or as tyrants. As slaves, if we
think that any former generation had a right to bind us;
as tyrants, if we think that we have authority to bind the
generations that are to follow.

It may not be inapplicable to the subject, to endeavor to
define what is to be understood by a generation in the sense
of the word as here used.

As a natural term its meaning is sufficiently clear. The
father, the son, the grandson, are so many distinct generations. But when we speak of a generation as describing
the persons in whom legal authority resides, as distinct from
another generation of the same description who are to succeed them, it comprehends all those who are above the
age of twenty-one years, at the time that we count from ;
and a generation of this kind will continue in authority between fourteen and twenty-one years, that is, until the number of minors, who shall have arrived at age, shall be
greater than the number of persons remaining of the former stock.

For example; if France, at this or any other moment,
contains twenty-four millions of souls, twelve millions will
be males, and twelve females. Of the twelve millions of
males, six millions will be of the age of twenty-one years,
and six will be under, and the authority to govern will reside in the first six. But every day will make some alteration, and in twenty-one years every one of those minors
who survives will have arrived at age, and the greater part
of the former stock will be gone ; the majority of persons

then living, in whom the legal authority resides, will be composed of those who, twenty-one years before, had no legal existence. Those will be fathers and grandfathers in their turn, and in the next twenty-one years, (or less,) another race of minors, arrived at age, will succeed them, and so on.

As this is ever the case, and as every generation is equal in rights to another, it consequently follows, that there cannot be a right in any to establish government by hereditary succession, because it would be supposing itself possessed of a right superior to the rest, namely that of commanding by its own authority how the world shall be hereafter governed, and who shall govern it. Every age and generation is and must be (as a matter of right) as free to act for itself in all cases, as the age and generation that preceded it. The vanity and presumption of governing beyond the grave is the most ridiculous and insolent of all tyrannies. Man has no property in man, neither has one generation a property in the generations that are to follow.

In the first part of the Rights of Man I have spoken of government by hereditary succession; and I will here close the subject with an extract from that work, which states it under the two following heads.

" 1st, Of the right of any family to establish itself with hereditary powers.

" 2d, Of the right of a nation to establish a particular family.

" With respect to the first of those heads, that of a family establishing itself with hereditary powers on its own authority, independent of the nation, all men will concur in calling it despotism, and it would be trespassing on their understanding to attempt to prove it.

" But the second head, that of a nation, that is, of a generation for the time being, establishing a particular family with hereditary powers, it does not present itself as despotism on the first reflection; but if men will permit a second reflection to take place, and carry that reflection forward, even but one remove out of their own persons to that of their offspring, they will then see, that hereditary succession becomes the same despotism to others, which the first persons reprobated for themselves. It operates to preclude the consent of the succeeding generation, and the preclusion of consent is despotism.

" In order to see this matter more clearly, let us consider the generation which undertakes to establish a family with hereditary powers, separately from the generations which are to follow.

" The generation which first selects a person and puts him at the head of its government, either with the title of king, or any other nominal distinction, acts its own choice as a free agent for itself, be that choice wise or foolish. The person so set up is *not hereditary*, but selected and appointed ; and the generation which sets him up does not live under an hereditary government, but under a government of its own choice. Were the person so set up, and the generation who sets him up, to live for ever, it never could become hereditary succession, and of consequence, hereditary succession could only follow on the death of the first parties.

" As therefore hereditary succession is out of the question with respect to the first generation, we have next to consider the character in which that generation acts towards the commencing generation, and to all succeeding ones.

" It assumes a character to which it has neither right nor title ; for it changes itself from a legislator to a testator, and affects to make a will and testament which is to have operation, after the demise of the makers, to bequeath the government ; and it not only attempts to bequeath, but to establish on the succeeding generation a new and different form of government under which itself lived. Itself, as already observed, lived not under an hereditary government, but under a government of its own choice ; and it now attempts by virtue of a will and testament, which it has not authority to make, to take from the commencing generation and from all the future ones, the right and free agency by which itself acted.

" In whatever light hereditary succession, as growing out of the will and testament of some former generation, presents itself, it is both criminal and absurd. A cannot make a will to take from B his property and give it to C ; yet this is the manner in which what is called hereditary succession by law operates. A certain generation makes a will, under the form of a law, to take away the rights of the commencing generation, and of all future generations, and convey those rights to a third person, who afterwards comes forward and assumes the government in consequence of that illicit conveyance."

The history of the English parliament furnishes an example of this kind; and which merits to be recorded, as being the greatest instance of legislative ignorance and want of principle that is to be found in any country. The case is as follows:

The English parliament of 1688, imported a man and his wife from Holland, William and Mary, and made them king and queen of England. Having done this, the said paliament made a law to convey the government of the country to the heirs of William and Mary, in the following words: " We, the lords spiritual and temporal, and commons, do, in the name of the people of England, most humbly and faithfully submit *ourselves, our heirs, and posterities*, to William and Mary, *their heirs and posterities*, for ever." And in a subsequent law, as quoted by Edmund Burke, the said parliament, in the name of the people of England then living, *binds the said people, their heirs and posterities, to William and Mary, their heirs and posterities to the end of time.*

It is not sufficient that we laugh at the ignorance of such law-makers, it is necessary that we reprobate their want of principle. The constituent assembly of France, (1789) fell into the same vice as the parliament of England had done, and assumed to establish an hereditary succession in the family of the Capets, as an act of the constitution of that year. That every nation, *for the time being*, has a right to govern itself as it pleases, must always be admitted, but government by hereditary succession is government for another race of people, and not for itself; and as those on whom it is to operate are not yet in existence, or are minors, so neither is the right in existence to set it up for them, and to assume such a right is treason against the rights of posterity.

I here close the arguments on the first head, that of government by hereditary succession; and proceed to the second, that of government by election and representation; or, as it may be concisely expressed, *representative government*, in contradistinction to *hereditary government.*

Reasoning by exclusion, if *hereditary government* has not a right to exist, and that it has not is proveable, *representative government* is admitted of course.

In contemplating government by election and representation, we amuse not ourselves in inquiring when or how, or by what right it began. Its origin is ever in view. Man is himself the origin and the evidence of the right.— It appertains to him in right of his existence, and his person is the title-deed.

The true and only true basis of representative government is equality of rights. Every man has a right to one vote, and no more, in the choice of representatives. The rich have no more right to exclude the poor from the right of voting or of electing and being elected than the poor have to exclude the rich; and wherever it is attempted, or proposed, on either side, it is a question of force, and not of right. Who is he that would exclude another? That other has a right to exclude him.

That which is now called aristocracy implies an inequality of rights; but who are the persons that have a right to establish this inequality? Will the rich exclude themselves? No! Will the poor exclude themselves? No! By what right then can any be excluded? It would be a question, if any man, or class of men, have a right to exclude themselves; but be this as it may, they cannot have the right to exclude another. The poor will not delegate such a right to the rich, nor the rich to the poor, and to assume it is not only to assume arbitrary power, but to assume a right to commit robbery. Personal rights, of which the right of voting for representatives is one, are a species of property of the most sacred kind; and he that would employ his pecuniary property, or presume upon the influence it gives him, to dispossess or rob another of his property of rights, uses that pecuniary property as he would use fire-arms, and merits to have it taken from him.

Inequality of rights is created by a combination in one part of the community to exclude another part from its rights. Whenever it may be made an article of a constitution, or a law, that the right of voting, or of electing and being elected, shall appertain exclusively to persons possessing a certain quantity of property, be it little or much, it is a combination of the persons possessing that quantity, to exclude those who do not possess the same quantity. It is investing themselves with powers as a self-created part of society, to the exclusion of the rest.

It is always to be taken for granted, that those who oppose an equality of rights, never mean the exclusion should take place on themselves; and in this view of the case, pardoning the vanity of the thing, aristocracy is a subject of laughter. This self-soothing vanity is encouraged by another idea not less selfish, which is, that the opposers conceive they are playing a safe game, in which there is a chance to gain and none to lose; that at any rate the doctrine of equality includes *them*, and that if they cannot get more rights than those whom they oppose and would exclude, they shall not have less. This opinion has already been fatal to thousands who, not contented with *equal rights*, have sought more till they lost all, and experienced in themselves the degrading *inequality* they endeavored to fix upon others.

In any view of the case it is dangerous and impolitic, sometimes ridiculous, and always unjust, to make property the criterion of the right of voting. If the sum, or value of the property upon which the right is to take place be considerable, it will exclude a majority of the people, and unite them in a common interest against the government and against those who support it, and as the power is always with the majority, they can overturn such a government and its supporters whenever they please.

If, in order to avoid this danger, a small quantity of property be fixed, as the criterion of the right, it exhibits liberty in disgrace, by putting it in competition with accident and insignificance. When a brood-mare shall fortunately produce a foal or a mule, that by being worth the sum in question, shall convey to its owner the right of voting, or by its death take it from him, in whom does the origin of such a right exist? Is it in the man, or in the mule? When we consider how many ways property may be acquired without merit, and lost without a crime, we ought to spurn the idea of making it a criterion of rights.

But the offensive part of the case is, that this exclusion from the right of voting implies a stigma on the moral character of the persons excluded; and this is what no part of the community has a right to pronounce upon another part. No external circumstance can justify it; wealth is no proof of moral character; nor poverty the want of it. On the contrary, wealth is often the presumptive evidence of dishonesty; and poverty the negative evidence of innocence. If, therefore, property, whether little or much, be made a criterion, the means by which that property has been acquired, ought to be made a criterion also.

The only ground upon which exclusion from the right of voting is consistent with justice, would be to inflict it as a punishment for a certain time, upon those who should propose to take away that right from others. The right of voting for representatives is the primary right by which other rights are protected. To take away this right is to reduce a man to slavery, for slavery consists in being subject to the will of another, and he that has not a vote in the election of representatives, is in this case. The proposal, therefore, to disfranchise any class of men is as criminal as the proposal to take away property. When we speak of right, we ought always to unite with it the idea of duties: rights become duties by reciprocity. The right which I enjoy it becomes my duty to guarantee to another, and he to me; and those who violate the duty justly incur a forfeiture of the right.

In a political view of the case, the strength and permanent security of government is in proportion to the number of people interested in supporting it. The true policy therefore is to interest the whole by an equality of rights, for the danger arises from exclusions. It is possible to exclude men from the right of voting, but it is impossible to exclude them from the right of rebelling against that exclusion; and when all other rights are taken away, the right of rebellion is made perfect.

While men could be persuaded they had no rights, or that rights appertained only to a certain class of men, or that government was a thing existing in right of itself, it was not difficult to govern them authoritatively. The ignorance in which they were held, and the superstition in which they were instructed, furnished the means of doing it; but when the ignorance is gone, and the superstition with it; when they perceive the imposition that has been acted upon them: when they reflect that the cultivator and the manufacturer are the primary means of all the wealth that exists in the world, beyond what nature spontaneously produces; when they begin to feel their consequence by their usefulness, and their right as members of society. it is then no longer possible to govern them as before. The fraud once detected cannot be reacted. To attempt it is to provoke derision or invite destruction.

That property will ever be unequal is certain. Industry, superiority of talents, or dexterity of management, extreme frugality, fortunate opportunities, or the opposite, or the

mean of those things, will ever produce that effect without
having recourse to the harsh, ill-sounding names of avarice and oppression; and besides this, there are some
men who, though they do not despise wealth, will not stoop
to the drudgery of the means of acquiring it, nor will be
troubled with it beyond their wants or their independence;
whilst in others there is an avidity to obtain it by every
means not punishable; it makes the sole business of their
lives, and they follow it as a religion.   All that is required
with respect to property is to obtain it *honestly*, and not
employ it *criminally;* but it is always criminally employed,
when it is made the criterion for exclusive rights.

In institutions that are purely pecuniary, such as that of
a bank or a commercial company, the rights of the members composing that company are wholly created by the
property they invest therein; and no other rights are represented in the government of that company, than what
arise out of that property; neither has that government
cognizance of *any thing but property.*

But the case is totally different with respect to the institution of civil government, organized on the system of representation.   Such a government has cognizance of *every
thing*, and of *every man* as a member of the national society,
whether he has property or not; and therefore the principle requires that every man and *every kind of right* be represented, of which the right to acquire and to hold property
is but one, and that not of the most essential kind.   The protection of a man's person is more sacred than the protection of property; and besides this, the faculty of performing any kind of work or services by which he acquires a
livelihood, or maintaining his family, is of the nature of
property.   It is property to him; he has acquired it; and
it is as much the object of his protection, as exterior property, possessed without that faculty, can be the object of
protection to another person.

I have always believed that the best security for property, be it much or little, is to remove from every part of
the community, as far as can possibly be done, every cause
of complaint, and every motive to violence; and this can
only be done by an equality of rights.   When rights are
secure, property is secure in consequence.   But when
property is made a pretence for unequal or exclusive
rights, it weakens the right to hold the property, and pro-
vokes indignation and tumult; for it is unnatural to believe

that property can be secure under the guarantee of a society injured in its rights by the influence of that property.

Next to the injustice and ill policy of making property a pretence for exclusive rights, is the unaccountable absurdity of giving to mere *sound* the idea of property, and annexing to it certain rights ; for what else is a *title* but sound? Nature is often giving to the world some extraordinary men, who arrive at fame by merit and universal consent, such as Aristotle, Socrates, Plato, &c. They were truly great or noble. But when government sets up a manufactory of nobles, it is as absurd, as if she undertook to manufacture wise men. *Her nobles are all counterfeits.*

As property, honestly obtained, is best secured by an equality of rights, so ill-gotten property depends for protection on a monopoly of rights. He who has robbed another of his property, will next endeavor to disarm him of his rights, to secure that property ; for when the robber becomes the legislator he believes himself secure. That part of the government of England that is called the house of lords, was originally composed of persons who had committed the robberies of which I have been speaking. It was an association for the protection of the property they had stolen.

But besides the criminality of the origin of aristocracy, it has an injurious effect on the moral and physical character of man. Like slavery it debilitates the human faculties ; for as the mind, bowed down by slavery, loses in silence its elastic powers, so, in the contrary extreme, when it is buoyed up by folly, it becomes incapable of exerting them, and dwindles into imbecility. It is impossible that a mind employed upon ribands and titles can ever be great. The childishness of the objects consumes the man.

It is at all times necessary, and more particularly so during the progress of a revolution, and until right ideas confirm themselves by habit, that we frequently refresh our patriotism by reference to first principles. It is by tracing things to their origin that we learn to understand them : and it is by keeping that line and that origin always in view that we never forget them.

An inquiry into the origin of rights will demonstrate to us that *rights* are not *gifts* from one man to another, nor from one class of men to another ; for who is he who could be the first giver, or by what principle, or on what authority, could he possess the right of giving? A declaration of rights is not a creation of them, nor a donation of them. It is a manifest of the principle by which they exist, followed by a detail of what the rights are; for every civil right has a natural right for its foundation, and it includes the principle of a reciprocal guarantee of those rights from man to man. As, therefore, it is impossible to discover any origin of rights otherwise than in the origin of man, it consequently follows, that rights appertain to man in right of his existence only, and must therefore be equal to every man. The principle of an *equality of rights* is clear and simple. Every man can understand it, and it is by understanding his rights that he learns his duties; for where the rights of men are equal, every man must finally see the necessity of protecting the rights of others as the most effectual security for his own. But if in the formation of a constitution we depart from the principle of equal rights, or attempt any modification of it, we plunge into a labyrinth of difficulties from which there is no way out but by retreating. Where are we to stop? Or by what principle are we to find out the point to stop at, that shall discriminate between men of the same country, part of whom shall be free, and the rest not? If property is to be made the criterion, it is a total departure from every moral principle of liberty, because it is attaching rights to mere matter, and making man the agent of that matter. It is moreover holding up property as an apple of discord, and not only exciting but justifying war against it; for I maintain the principle that when property is used as an instrument to take away the rights of those who may happen not to possess property, it is used to an unlawful purpose, as firearms would be in a similar case.

In a state of nature all men are equal in rights, but they are not equal in power; the weak cannot protect themselves against the strong. This being the case, the institution of civil society is for the purpose of making an equalization of powers that shall be parallel to, and a guarantee of, the equality of rights. The laws of a country, when properly constructed, apply to this purpose. Every man takes the arm of the law for his protection as more effectual than his own; and therefore every man has an equal right in the formation of the government and of the laws by which he is to be governed and judged. In extensive countries and societies, such as America and France, this right in the individual can only be exercised by delegation, that is, by election and representation; and hence it is that the institution of representative government arises.

Hitherto, I have confined myself to matters of principle only. First, that hereditary government has not a right to exist; that it cannot be established on any principle of right; and that it is a violation of all principle. Secondly, that government by election and representation has its origin in the natural and eternal rights of man; for whether a man be his own lawgiver, as he would be in a state of nature; or whether he exercises his portion of legislative sovereignty in his own person, as might be the case in small democracies where all could assemble for the formation of the laws by which they were to be governed; or whether he exercises it in the choice of persons to represent him in a national assembly of representatives, the origin of the right is the same in all cases. The first, as is before observed, is defective in power; the second, is practicable only in democracies of small extent; the third, is the greatest scale upon which human government can be instituted.

Next to matters of *principle*, are matters of *opinion*, and it is necessary to distinguish between the two. Whether the rights of men shall be equal is not a matter of opinion but of right, and consequently of principle; for men do not hold their rights as grants from each other, but each one in right of himself. Society is the guardian but not the giver. And, as in extensive societies, such as America and France, the right of the individual in matters of government, cannot be exercised but by election and representation, it consequently follows, that the only system of government, consistent with principle, where simple democracy is impracticable, is the representative system. But as to the organical part, or the manner in which the several parts of government shall be arranged and composed, it is altogether *matter of opinion*. It is necessary that all the parts be conformable with the *principle of equal rights*; and so long as this principle be religiously adhered to, no very material error can take place, neither can any error continue long in that part that falls within the province of opinion.

In all matters of opinion, the social compact, or the principle by which society is held together, requires that the majority of opinions becomes the rule for the whole, and that the minority yields practical obedience thereto. This is perfectly conformable to the principle of equal rights; for, in the first place, every man has a *right to give an opinion*, but no man has a right that his own should govern the rest. In the second place, it is not supposed to be known beforehand on which side of any question, whether for or against, any man's opinion will fall. He may happen to be in a majority upon some questions, and in a minority upon others; and by the same rule that he expects obedience in the one case, he must yield it in the other. All the disorders that have arisen in France during the progress of the revolution have had their origin, not in the *principle of equal rights*, but in the violation of that principle. The principle of equal rights has been repeatedly violated, and that not by the majority, but by the minority, and *that minority has been composed of men possessing property, as well as of men without property; property, therefore, even upon the experience already had, is no more a criterion of character than it is of rights.* It will sometimes happen that the minority are right, and the majority are wrong, but as soon as experience proves this to be the case, the minority will increase to a majority, and the error will reform itself by the tranquil operation of freedom of opinion and equality of rights. Nothing therefore can justify an insurrection, neither can it ever be necessary, where rights are equal and opinions free.

Various methods will present themselves upon a question of this kind, and though experience is yet wanting to determine which is the best, it has, I think, sufficiently decided which is the worst. That is the worst, which in its deliberations and decisions is subject to the precipitancy and passion of an individual; and when the whole legislature is crowded into one body, it is an individual in mass. In all cases of deliberation it is necessary to have a corps of reserve, and it would be better to divide the representation by lot into two parts, and let them revise and correct each other, than that the whole should sit together, and debate at once.

Representative government is not necessarily confined to any one particular form. The principle is the same in all the forms under which it can be arranged. The equal rights of the people is the root from which the whole springs, and the branches may be arranged as present opinion or future experience shall best direct. As to that *hospital of incurables* (as Chesterfield calls it) the British house of peers, it is an excrescence growing out of corruption; and there is no more affinity or resemblance between any of the branches of a legislative body originating from the right of the people, and the aforesaid house of peers, than between a regular member of the human body and an ulcerated wen.

As to that part of government that is called the *executive*, it is necessary in the first place to fix a precise meaning to the word.

There are but two divisions into which power can be arranged. First, that of willing or decreeing the laws; secondly, that of executing or putting them in practice. The former, corresponds to the intellectual faculties of the human mind, which reasons and determines what shall be done; the second to the mechanical powers of the human body that puts that determination into practice. If the former decides, and the latter does not perform, it is a state of imbecility; and if the latter acts without the predetermination of the former, it is a state of lunacy. The executive department is, therefore, official, and is subordinate to the legislative, as the body is to the mind, in a state of health; for, it is impossible to conceive the idea of two sovereignties, a sovereignty to *will*, and a sovereignty to *act*. The executive is not invested with the power of deliberating whether it shall act or not; it has no discretionary authority in the case; for it can *act no other thing* than what the laws decree, and it is *obliged* to act conformably thereto; and in this view of the case, the executive is made up of all the official departments that execute the laws of which, that which is called the judiciary is the chief.

But mankind have conceived an idea that *some kind of authority* is necessary to *superintend* the execution of the laws and to see that they are faithfully performed; and it is by confounding this superintending authority with the official execution that we get embarrassed about the term *executive power.*—All the parts in the governments of the United States of America that are called THE EXECUTIVE, are no other than authorities to superintend the execution of the laws; and they are so far independent of the legislative, that they know the legislative only through the laws, and cannot be controlled or directed by it, through any other medium.

In what manner this superintending authority shall be appointed, or composed, is a matter that falls within the province of opinion. Some may prefer one method and some another; and in all cases, where opinion only, and not principle is concerned, the majority of opinions forms the rule for all. There are, however, some things deducible from reason, and evidenced by experience, that serve to guide our decision upon the case. The one is, never to invest any individual with extraordinary power; for besides his being tempted to misuse it, it will excite contention and commotion in the nation for the office. Secondly, never to invest power long in the hands of any number of individuals. The inconveniencies that may be supposed to accompany frequent changes, are less to be feared than the dangers that arises from long continuance.

I shall conclude this discourse with offering some observations on the means of *preserving liberty ;* for it is not only necessary that we establish it, but that we preserve it.

It is, in the first place, necessary that we distinguish between the means made use of to overthrow despotism, in order to prepare the way for the establishment of liberty, and the means to be used after despotism is overthrown.

The means made use of in the first case are justified by necessity. Those means are, in general, insurrections; for whilst the established government of despotism continues in any country, it is scarcely possible that any other means can be used. It is also certain that in the commencement of a revolution, the revolutionary party permit to themselves a *discretionary exercise of power* regulated more by circumstances than by principle, which, were the practice to continue, liberty would never be established, or if established, would soon be overthrown. It is never to be expected in a revolution that every man is to change his opinion at the same moment. There never yet was any truth or any principle so irresistibly obvious, that all men believed it at once. Time and reason must co-operate with each other to the final establishment of any principle; and therefore those who may happen to be first convinced have not a right to persecute others, on whom conviction operates more slowly. The moral principle of revolutions is to instruct, not to destroy.

Had a constitution been established two years ago (as ought to have been done) the violences that have since desolated France and injured the character of the revolution, would, in my opinion, have been prevented. The nation would then have had a bond of union, and every individual would have known the line of conduct he was to follow. But instead of this, a revolutionary government, a thing without either principle or authority, was substituted in its place; virtue and crime depended upon accident; and that which was patriotism one day, became treason the next. All these things have followed from the want of a constitution; for it is the nature and intention of a constitution to *prevent governing by party*, by establishing a common principle that shall limit and control the power and impulse of party, and that says to all parties, *thus far shalt thou go and no further.* But in the absence of a constitution men look entirely to party; and instead of principle governing party, party governs principle.

An avidity to punish is always dangerous to liberty. It leads men to stretch, to misinterpret, and to misapply even the best of laws. He that would make his own liberty secure, must guard even his enemy from oppression; for if he violates this duty, he establishes a precedent that will reach to himself.

THOMAS PAINE.

Paris, July 1795.

SPEECH,

AS DELIVERED IN THE FRENCH NATIONAL CONVENTION, JULY 7, 1795, WHEREIN HE ALLUDES TO THE PRECEDING WORK.

ON the motion of Lanthenas. "That permission be granted to Thomas Paine, to deliver his sentiments on the declaration of rights and the constitution," Thomas Paine ascended the tribune; and no opposition being made to the motion, one of the secretaries, who stood by Mr. Paine, read his speech, of which the following is a literal translation:

CITIZENS, The effects of a malignant fever, with which I was afflicted during a rigorous confinement in the Luxembourg, have thus long prevented me from attending at my post in the bosom of the convention, and the magnitude of the subject under discussion, and no other consideration on earth, could induce me now to repair to my station.

A recurrence to the vicissitudes I have experienced, and the critical situations in which I have been placed in consequence of the French revolution, will throw upon what I now propose to submit to the convention, the most unequivocal proofs of my integrity, and the rectitude of those principles which have uniformly influenced my conduct.

In England I was proscribed for having vindicated the French revolution, and I have suffered a rigorous imprisonment in France for having pursued a similar mode of conduct. During the reign of terrorism, I was a close prisoner for eight long months, and remained so above three months after the era of the 10th Thermidor. I ought, however, to state, that I was not persecuted by the *people* either of England or France. The proceedings in both countries were the effects of the despotism existing in their respective governments. But, even if my persecution had originated in the people at large, my principles and conduct would still have remained the same. Principles which are influenced and subject to the control of tyranny have not their foundation in the heart.

A few days ago I transmitted to you, by the ordinary mode of distribution, a short treatise, entitled "Dissertation on the First Principles of Government." This little work I did intend to have dedicated to the people of Holland, who, about the time I began to write it, were determined to accomplish a revolution in their government, rather than to the people of France, who had long before effected that glorious object. But there are, in the constitution which is about to be ratified by the convention, certain articles, and in the report which preceded it, certain points, so repugnant to reason, and incompatible with the true principles of liberty, as to render this treatise, drawn up for another purpose, applicable to the present occasion, and under this impression I presumed to submit it to your consideration.

If there be faults in the constitution, it were better to expunge them now, than to abide the event of their mischievous tendency; for certain it is, that the plan of the constitution which has been presented to you is not consistent with the grand object of the revolution, nor congenial to the sentiments of the individuals who accomplished it.

To deprive half the people in a nation of their rights as citizens, is an easy matter in theory or on paper, but it is a most dangerous experiment, and rarely practicable in the execution.

I shall now proceed to the observations I have to offer on this important subject; and I pledge myself that they shall be neither numerous nor diffusive.

In my apprehension, a constitution embraces two distinct parts or objects, the *principle* and the *practice;* and it is not only an essential, but an indispensable provision, that the practice should emanate from, and accord with, the principle. Now I maintain, that the converse of this proposition is the case in the plan of the constitution under discussion. The first article, for instance, of the *political state* of citizens, (v. Title ii. of the Constitution) says :

" Every man born and resident in France, who, being twenty-one years of age, has inscribed his name on the civic register of his canton, and who has lived afterwards one year on the territory of the republic, and who pays any direct contribution whatsoever, real or personal, is a French citizen."

I might here ask, if those only who come under the above description are to be considered as citizens, what designation do you mean to give the rest of the people? I allude to that portion of the people on whom the principal part of the labor falls, and on whom the weight of indirect taxation will in the event chiefly press. In the structure of the social fabric, this class of people are infinitely superior to that privileged order, whose only qualification is their wealth or territorial possessions. For what is trade without merchants? What is land without cultivation? And what is the produce of the land without manufactures? But to return to the subject.

In the first place, this article is incompatible with the three first articles of the declaration of rights, which precede the constitutional act.

The first article of the declaration of rights says :

" The end of society is the public good ; and the institution of government is to secure to every individual the enjoyment of his rights."

But the article of the constitution to which I have just adverted, proposes as the object of society, not the public good, or in other words, the good of *all*, but a partial good, or the good only of a *few;* and the constitution provides solely for the rights of this few, to the exclusion of the many.

The second article of the declaration of rights says :

" The rights of man in society, are liberty, equality, and security of his person and property."

But the article alluded to in the constitution has a direct tendency to establish the converse of this position, inasmuch as the persons excluded by this *inequality* can neither be said to possess liberty, nor security against oppression. They are consigned totally to the caprice and tyranny of the rest.

The third article of the declaration of rights says :

" Liberty consists in such acts of volition, as are not injurious to others."

But the article of the constitution, on which I have observed, breaks down this barrier. It enables the liberty of one part of society to destroy the freedom of the other.

Having thus pointed out the inconsistency of this article to the declaration of rights I shall proceed to comment on that part of the same article which makes a direct contribution a necessary qualification to the right of citizenship.

A modern refinement on the object of public revenue has divided the taxes or contributions into two classes, the *direct* and the *indirect*, without being able to define precisely the distinction, or difference between them, because the effect of both is the same.

Those are designated indirect taxes which fall upon the consumers of certain articles, on which the tax is imposed, because the tax being included in the price, the consumer pays it without taking notice of it.

The same observation is applicable to the territorial tax. The land proprietors, in order to reimburse themselves, will rack-rent their tenants : the farmer, of course, will transfer the obligation to the miller, by enhancing the price of grain; the miller to the baker, by increasing the price of flour; and the baker to the consumer, by raising the price of bread. The territorial tax, therefore, though called *direct*, is in its consequences *indirect*.

To this tax the land proprietor contributes only in proportion to the quantity of bread and other provisions that are consumed in his own family. The deficit is furnished by the great mass of the community, which comprehends every individual of the nation.

From the logical distinction between the direct and indirect taxation, some emolument may result, I allow, to auditors of public accounts, &c. but to the people at large I deny that such a distinction (which by the way is without a difference) can be productive of any practical benefit. It ought not, therefore, to be admitted as a principle in the constitution.

Besides this objection, the provision in question does not affect to define, secure, or establish the right of citizenship. It consigns to the caprice or discretion of the legislature the power of pronouncing who shall, or shall not, exercise the functions of a citizen ; and this may be done effectually, either by the imposition of a *direct* or *indirect* tax, according to the selfish views of the legislators, or by the mode of collecting the taxes so imposed.

Neither a tenant who occupies an extensive farm, nor a merchant or manufacturer, who may have embarked a large capital in their respective pursuits, can ever, according to this system, attain the pre-emption of a citizen. On the other hand, any upstart, who has by succession or management, got possession of a few acres of land, or a miserable tenement, may exultingly exercise the functions of a citizen, although perhaps neither possesses a hundredth part of the worth or property of a simple mechanic, nor contributes in any proportion to the exigences of the state.

The contempt in which the old government held mercantile pursuits, and the obloquy that attached on merchants and manufacturers, contributed not a little to its embarrassments, and its eventual subversion ; and, strange to tell, though the mischiefs arising from this mode of conduct are so obvious, yet an article is proposed for your adoption, which has a manifest tendency to restore a defect inherent in the monarchy.

I shall now proceed to the second article of the same title, with which I shall conclude my remarks.

The second article says, " Every French soldier, who shall have served one or more campaigns in the cause of liberty, is deemed a citizen of the republic, without any respect or reference to other qualifications."

It should seem, that in this article, the committee were desirous of extricating themselves from a dilemma into which they had been plunged by the preceding article. When men depart from an established principle, they are compelled to resort to trick and subterfuge, always shifting their means to preserve the unity of their objects ; and as it rarely happens that the first expedient makes amends for the prostitution of principle, they must call in aid a second of a more flagrant nature to supply the deficiency of the former. In this manner legislators go on accumulating error upon error, and artifice upon artifice, until the mass becomes so bulky and incongruous, and their embarrassment so desperate, that they are compelled, as their last expedient, to resort to the very principle they had violated. The committee were precisely in this predicament, when they framed this article ; and to me, I confess, their conduct appears specious rather than efficacious.

It was not for himself alone, but for his family, that the French citizen, at the dawn of the revolution (for then indeed every man was considered a citizen) marched soldier-like to the frontiers, and repelled a foreign invasion. He had it not in his contemplation, that he should enjoy liberty for the residue of his earthly career, and by his own act preclude his offspring from that inestimable blessing. No! He wished to leave it as an inheritance to his children, and that they also might hand it down to their latest posterity. If a Frenchman, who united in his person the character of a soldier and a citizen, was now to return from the army to his peaceful habitation, he must address his family in this manner:

" Sorry I am, that I cannot leave to you a small portion of what I have acquired by exposing my person to the ferocity of our enemies, and defeating their machinations. I have helped to establish the republic, and, painful the reflection, all the laurels which I have won in the field are blasted, and all the privileges to which my exertions have entitled me, extend not beyond the period of my own existence!" Thus the measure that has been adopted by way of subterfuge, falls short of what the framers of it speculated upon; for in conciliating the affections of the *soldier*, they have subjected the *father* to the most pungent sensations, by obliging him to adopt a generation of slaves.

Citizens, a great deal has been urged respecting insurrections. I am confident that no man has a greater abhorrence of them than myself, and I am sorry that any insinuations should have been thrown out against me, as a promoter of violence of any kind. The whole tenor of my life and conversation gives the lie to those calumnies, and proves me to be a friend to order, truth and justice.

I hope you will attribute this effusion of my sentiments to my anxiety for the honor and success of the revolution. I have no interest distinct from that which has a tendency to meliorate the condition of mankind. The revolution, as far as it respects myself, has been productive of more loss and persecution than it is possible for me to describe, or for you to indemnify. But with respect to the subject under consideration, I could not refrain from declaring my sentiments.

In my opinion, if you subvert the basis of the revolution, if you dispense with principles, and substitute expedients, you will extinguish that enthusiasm and energy which have hitherto been the life and soul of the revolution ; and you will substitute in its place nothing but a cold indifference and self-interest, which will again degenerate into intrigue, cunning, and effeminacy.

But to discard all considerations of a personal and subordinate nature, it is essential to the well-being of the republic, that the practical or organic part of the constitution should correspond with its principles ; and as this does not appear to be the case in the plan that has been presented to you, it is absolutely necessary that it should be submitted to the revision of a committee, who should be instructed to compare it with the declaration of rights, in order to ascertain the difference between the two, and to make such alterations as shall render them perfectly consistent and compatible with each other.

MR. SECRETARY DUNDAS.

———

LONDON, JUNE 6, 1792.

SIR,

As you opened the debate in the house of commons, May 25th, on the proclamation for suppressing publications, which that proclamation (without naming any) calls wicked and seditious; and as you applied those opprobious epithets to the works entitled Rights of Man, I think it unnecessary to offer any other reason for addressing this letter to you.

I begin, then, at once, by declaring, that I do not believe there are to be found in the writings of any author, ancient or modern, on the subject of government, a spirit of greater benignity, and a stronger inculcation of moral principles than in those which I have published. They come, sir, from a man, who, by having lived in different countries, and under different systems of government, and who, being intimate in the construction of them, is a better judge of the subject than it is possible that you, from the want of those opportunities can be : and besides this, they come from a heart that knows not how to beguile.

I will further say, that when that moment arrives in which the best consolation that shall be left, will be looking back on some past actions, more virtuous and more meritorious than the rest, I shall then with happiness remember, among other things, that I have written the Rights of Man. As to what proclamations, or prosecutions, or placemen, and place expectants; those who possess, or those who are gaping for office, may say of them, it will not alter their character, either with the world or with me.

Having, sir, made this declaration, I shall proceed to remark, not particularly on your speech, but on any one to which your motion gave rise. To begin with Mr. Adam.

He accuses me of not having done the very thing that I have done.

In his speech, (see the Morning Chronicle of May 26) he says, "that he had well considered the subject of constitutional publications, and was by no means ready to say that books of science upon government though recommending a doctrine, or system different from the form of our constitution were fit objects of prosecution; that if he did, he must condemn Harrington for his Oceana, Sir Thomas More for his Utopia, and Hume for his Idea of a Perfect Commonwealth. But the publication of Mr. Paine reviled what was most sacred in the constitution, destroyed every principle of subordination, and established nothing in their room."

I readily saw that Mr. Adam had not read the second part of the Rights of Man; and I am put under the necessity either of submitting to an erroneous charge, or of justifying myself against it; and certainly shall prefer the latter. If, then, I shall prove to Mr. Adam, that in my reasoning upon systems of government, in the second part of the Rights of Man, I have shown, I think, as clearly as words can convey ideas, a certain system of government; and that not existing in theory only, but already in established practice, and systematically and practically free from all the vices and defects of the English government, and capable of producing more happiness to the people; and that also with an eightieth part of the taxes, which the present English system of government consumes; I hope he will do me the justice when he next goes to the house, to acknowledge he had been mistaken in saying, that I had established nothing, and had destroyed every principle of subordination. I now come to the point.

In the second part of the Rights of Man I have distinguished government into two classes or systems; the hereditary and the representative systems.

In the first part of the Rights of Man, I have shown, and it cannot be refuted, that there does not exist a right to establish hereditary government.

In the second part of the Rights of Man I have not repeated those arguments, because they are irrefutable, but have confined myself to show the defects of hereditary government, or hereditary succession, that it must, from the nature of it, throw government into the hands of men unworthy of it, either from want of principle or capacity.

To show the absurdity of the hereditary system still more strongly, I will now put the following case : take any fifty men promiscuously, and it will be very extraordinary, if, out of that number, more than one man should be found, whose principles and talents taken together (for some might have principles, and others have talents) would render him a person truly fitted to fill any very extraordinary office of national trust. If then such a fitness of character could not be expected to be found in more than one person out of fifty, it would happen but once in a thousand years to the eldest son of any one family, admitting each on an average, to hold the office twenty years. Mr. Adam talks of something in the constitution which he calls most sacred : but I hope he does not mean hereditary succession, a thing which appears to me a violation of every order of nature and of common sense.

When I look into history and see the multitudes of men, otherwise virtuous, who have died and whose families have been ruined, in defence of knaves and fools, and which they would not have done had they reasoned at all upon the system ; I do not know a greater good that an individual can render to mankind, than to endeavor to break the chains of political superstition. Those chains are now dissolving fast, and proclamations and prosecutions will serve but to hasten that dissolution.

Having thus spoken of the hereditary system as a bad system, and subject to every possible defect, I now come to the representative system ; and this Mr. Adam will find stated in the second part of the Rights of Man, not only as the best, but as the only theory of government under which the liberties of a people can be permanently secure.

But it is needless now to talk of mere theory since there is already a government in full practice, established upon that theory ; or in other words, upon the rights of man, and has been so for almost twenty years. Mr. Pitt, in a speech of his some short time since, said " That there never did, and never could exist a government established upon those rights, and that if it began at noon, it would end at night." Mr. Pitt has not yet arrived at the degree of a school boy in this species of knowledge. His practice has been confined to means of extorting the revenue, and his boast has been—how much ? Whereas the boast of the system of government that I am speaking of, is not how much, but how little.

The system of government purely representative, un-
mixed with any thing of hereditary nonsense, began in
America. I will now compare the effects of that system of
government, with the system of government in England,
both during and since the close of the war.

So powerful is the representative system ; first, by combining and consolidating all the parts of a country together,
however great the extent ; and, secondly, by admitting of
none but men properly qualified into the government, or
dismissing them if they prove otherwise, that America was
enabled thereby totally to defeat and overthrow all the
schemes and projects of the hereditary government of England against her. As the establishment of the revolution
and independence of America is a proof of this fact, it is
needless to enlarge upon it.

I now come to the comparative effect of the two systems
since the close of the war, and I request Mr. Adam to attend to it.

America had internally sustained the ravage of upwards
of seven years of war, which England had not. England
sustained only the expense of the war : whereas America
sustained not only the expense, but the destruction of property committed by both armies. Not a house was built
during that period, and many thousands were destroyed.

The farms and plantations along the coast of the country,
for more than a thousand miles, were laid waste. Her
commerce was annihilated. Her ships were either taken
or had rotted within her own harbors. The credit of her
funds had fallen upwards of ninety per cent. that is, an
original hundred pounds would not sell for ten pounds. In
short she was apparently put back an hundred years when
the war closed ; which was not the case with England.

But such was the event, that the same representative
system of government, though since better organized, which
enabled her to conquer, enabled her also to recover, and
she now presents a more flourishing condition, and a more
happy and harmonized society under that system of government, than any country in the world can boast under
any other. Her towns are rebuilt much better than before ;
her farms and plantations are in higher improvement than
ever : her commerce is spread over the world, and her
funds have risen from less than ten pounds the hundred to
upwards of one hundred and twenty. Mr. Pitt and his col-
leagues, talk of the things that have happened in his

boyish administration, without knowing what greater things
have happened elsewhere, and under other systems of government.

I next come to state the expense of the two systems,
as they now stand in each of the countries; but it may
first be proper to observe, that government in America is
what it ought to be, a matter of honor and trust, and not
made a trade of for the purpose of lucre.

The whole amount of nett taxes in England (exclusive of
the expense of collections, of drawbacks, of seizures and
condemnations, of fines and penalties, of fees of office, of
litigations and informers, which are some of the blessed
means of enforcing them) is seventeen millions. Of this
sum, about nine millions go for the payment of the interest
of the national debt, and the remainder, being about eight
millions, is for the current annual expenses. Thus much
for one side of the case. I now come to the other.

The expense of the several departments of the general
representative government of the United States of America,
extending over a space of country nearly ten times larger
than England, is two hundred and ninety-four thousand
five hundred and fifty-eight dollars, which at 4s. 6d. per
dollar, is 66,305l. 11s. sterling, and is thus apportioned:

Expense of the Executive Department.

The office of president, for which the president receives nothing for himself	5,625l. 0s.
Vice-president	1,125 0
Chief-justice	900 0
Five associate justices	3,937 10
Nineteen judges of districts and the attorney-general	6,873 15

Legislative Department.

Members of congress at 6 dolls. (1l. 7s.) per day, their secretaries, clerks, chaplains, messengers, door-keepers, &c.	25,515l. 0

Treasury Department.

Secretary, assistant, comptroller, auditor, treasurer, register, and loan-office keeper in each state, together with all necessary clerks, office keepers, &c.	12,825 0

Amount carried forward 56,801l. 5s.

Amount bro't forward   56,301*l.*   5*s.*

Department of State, including Foreign Affairs.

Secretary, clerks, &c. -   -   -   -   1,406   5

Department of War.

Secretary, clerks, paymasters, commissioners.
&c.   -   -   -   -   -   -   1,462   10

Commissioners for settling old accounts.

The whole board, clerks, &c.   -   -   2,598   15

Incidental and contingent expenses.

For fire-wood, stationary, printing, &c. -   4,036   16

66,305*l.* 11*s.*

On account of the incursions of the Indians on the back
settlements, congress is obliged at this time to keep six
thousand militia in pay, in addition to a regiment of foot,
and a battalion of artillery, which it always keeps; and this
increases the expense of the war-department to 390,000
dollars, which is 87,795*l.* sterling, but when peace shall be
concluded with the Indians, the greatest part of this expense will cease, and the total amount of the expense of
government, including that of the army, will not amount to
100,000*l.* which, as has been already stated, is but an
eightieth part of the expenses of the English government.

I request Mr. Adam and Mr. Dundas, and all those who
are talking of constitutions, and blessings, and kings, and
lords, and the Lord knows what, to look at this statement.
Here is a form and system of government, that is better
organized and better administered than any government in
the world, and that for less than one hundred thousand
pounds per annum, and yet every member of congress receives, as a compensation for his time and attendance on
public business, one pound seven shillings per day, which
is at the rate of nearly five hundred pounds a-year.

This is a government that has nothing to fear. It needs
no proclamations to deter people from writing and reading. It needs no political superstition to support it. It
was by encouraging discussion and rendering the press
free upon all subjects of government, that the principles of
government became understood in America, and the people are now enjoying the present blessings under it. You
hear of no riots, tumults and disorders in that country; because there exists no cause to produce them. Those things

are never the effect of freedom, but of restraint, oppression and excessive taxation.

In America, there is not that class of poor and wretched people that are so numerously dispersed all over England, who are to be told by a proclamation, that they are happy; and this is in a great measure to be accounted for, not by the difference of proclamations, but by the difference of governments and the difference of taxes between that country and this. What the laboring people of that country earn, they apply to their own use, and to the education of their children, and do not pay it away in taxes as fast as they earn it, to support court extravagance, and a long enormous list of placemen and pensioners; and besides this, they have learned the manly doctrine of reverencing themselves, and consequently of respecting each other; and they laugh at those imaginary beings called kings and lords, and all the fraudulent trumpery of courts.

When placemen and pensioners, or those who expect to be such, are lavish in praise of a government, it is not a sign of its being a good one. The pension-list alone in England (see sir John Sinclair's History of the Revenue, p. 6, of the Appendix) is one hundred and seven thousand four hundred and four pounds, which is more than the expenses of the whole government of America amount to; and I am now more convinced than before, that the offer that was made to me of a thousand pounds for the copyright of the second part of the Rights of Man, together with the remaining copy-right of the first part, was to have effected, by a quick suppression, what is now attempted to be done by a prosecution. The connexion which the person who made that offer has with the king's printing-office, may furnish part of the means of inquiring into this affair, when the ministry shall please to bring their prosecution to issue. But to return to my subject.

I have said, in the second part of the Rights of Man, and I repeat it here, that the service of any man, whether called king, president, senator, legislator or any thing else, cannot be worth more to any country, in the regular routine of office, than ten thousand pounds per annum. We have a better man in America, and more of a gentleman than any king I ever knew of, who does not occasion even half that expense; for though the salary is fixed at 5625*l.* he does not accept it, and it is only the incidental expenses that are paid out of it. The name by which a man is called, is, of itself, but an empty thing. It is worth and character alone which can render him valuable, for without this, kings and lords, and presidents, are but jingling names.

But without troubling myself about constitutions of government, I have shown in the second part of the Rights of Man, that an alliance may be formed between England, France and America, and that the expenses of government in England may be put back to one million and an half, viz.

Civil expense of government				500,000*l.*
Army	-	-	-	500,000
Navy	-	-	-	500,000

1,500,000*l.*

And even this sum is fifteen times greater than the expenses of government are in America; and it is also greater than the whole peace establishment of England amounted to, about an hundred years ago. So much has the weight and oppression of taxes increased since the revolution, and especially since the year 1714.

To show that the sum of 500,000*l.* is sufficient to defray all the civil expenses of government, I have, in that work annexed the following estimate for any country of the same extent as England.

In the first place, three hundred representatives, fairly elected, are sufficient for all the purposes to which legislation can apply, and preferable to a larger number.

If, then, an allowance, at the rate of 500*l.* per annum be made to every representative, deducting for non-attendance, the expense, if the whole number attended six months each year, would be   75,000*l.*

The official departments could not exceed the following number, with their salaries, viz.

Three officers	at	10,000*l.*	each	30,000
Ten ditto	at	5,000	"	50,000
Twenty ditto	at	2,000	"	40,000
Forty ditto	at	1,000	"	40,000
Two hundred ditto	at	500	"	100,000
Three hundred ditto	at	200	"	60,000
Five hundred ditto	at	100	"	50,000
Seven hundred ditto	at	75	"	52,500

497,500*l.*

if a nation chose, it might deduct four per cent. from all the offices, and make one of twenty thousand pounds per annum, and style the person who should fill it, king or majesty, or give him any other title.

Taking, however, this sum of one million and an half, as an abundant supply for all the expenses of government under any form whatever, there will remain a surplus of nearly six millions and an half out of the present taxes, after paying the interest of the national debt; and I have shown in the second part of the Rights of Man what appears to me, the best mode of applying the surplus money; for I am now speaking of expenses and savings, and not of systems of government.

I have in the first place, estimated the poor rates at two millions annually, and shown that the first effectual step would be to abolish the poor rates entirely (which would be a saving of two millions to the housekeepers,) and to remit four millions out of the surplus taxes to the poor, to be paid to them in money in proportion to the number of children in each family, and the number of aged persons.

I have estimated the number of persons of both sexes in England of fifty years of age and upwards at 420,000, and have taken one third of this number, viz. 140,000 to be poor people.

To save long calculations, I have taken 70,000 of them to be fifty years of age, and under sixty; and the others to be sixty years and upwards; and to allow six pounds per annum to the former class, and ten pounds per annum to the latter. The expense of which will be,

Seventy thousand persons at 6l. per annum   420,000l.
Seventy thousand persons at 10l. per annum   700,000

1,120,000l.

There will then remain of the four millions, two millions eight hundred and eighty thousand pounds. I have stated two different methods of appropriating this money. The one is to pay it in proportion to the number of children in each family at the rate of three or four pounds per annum for each child; the other is to apportion it according to the expense of living in different counties: but in either of these cases it would together with the allowance to be made to the aged, completely take off taxes from one third of all the families in England, besides relieving all the other families from the burden of poor rates.

The whole number of families in England, lotting five souls to each family, is one million four hundred thousand, of which take one third, *viz.* 466,666 to be poor families, who now pay four millions of taxes, and that the poorest pays at least four guineas a-year; and that the other thirteen millions are paid by the other two-thirds. The plan, therefore, as stated in the work, is first, to remit or pay, as is already stated, this sum of four millions to the poor, because it is impossible to separate them from the others in the present mode of collecting taxes on articles of consumption : and, secondly, to abolish the poor rates, the house and window-light tax, and to change the commutation tax into a progressive tax, on large estates, the particulars of all which are set forth in the work.

I will conclude this part of my letter with an extract from the second part of the Rights of Man, which Mr. Dundas (a man rolling in luxury at the expense of the nation) has branded with the epithet of "wicked."

"By the operation of this plan, the poor laws, those instruments of civil torture, will be superseded, and the wasteful expense of litigation prevented. The hearts of the humane will not be shocked by ragged and hungry children, and persons of seventy and eighty years of age, begging for bread. The dying poor will not be dragged from place to place, to breathe their last, as a reprisal of parish upon parish. Widows will have a maintenance for their children, and not be carted away, on the death of their husbands, like culprits and criminals, and children will no longer be considered as increasing the distresses of their parents. The haunts of the wretched will be known, because it will be to their advantage, and the number of petty crimes, the offspring of poverty and distress, will be lessened. The poor, as well as the rich, will then be interested in the support of government, and the cause and apprehension of riots and tumults will cease. Ye, who sit in ease, and solace yourselves in plenty, and such there are in Turkey and Russia, as well as in England, and who say to yourselves, *are we not well off?* have ye thought of these things? when ye do, ye will cease to speak and feel for yourselves alone." Rights of Man, part ii.

After this remission of four millions be made, and the poor rates and houses and window-light tax be abolished, and the commutation tax changed, there will still remain

nearly one million and an half of surplus taxes; and as by
an alliance between England, France and America, armies
and navies will, in a great measure, be rendered unnecessary, and as men who have either been brought up in, or
long habited to, those lines of life, are still citizens of a nation in common with the rest, and have a right to participate in all plans of national benefit, it is proposed in that
work (Rights of Man, part ii.) to apply annually 507,000*l.*
out of the surplus taxes to this purpose, in the following
manner :

To fifteen thousand disbanded soldiers, 3*s.* per
   week, clear of deductions, during life   117,000*l.*
Additional pay to the remaining soldiers per
   annum   19,500
To the officers of the disbanded corps, during
   life, the sum of   117,000
To fifteen thousand disbanded sailors, 3*s.* per
   week during life   117,000
Additional pay to the remaining sailors   19,500
To the officers of the disbanded part of the
   navy, during life   117,000
                                         —————

                                   507,000*l.*

The limits to which it is proper to confine this letter, will
not admit of my entering into further particulars. I address it to Mr. Dundas because he took the lead in the debate, and he wishes, I suppose, to appear conspicuous ;
but the purport of it is to justify myself from the charge
which Mr. Adam has made.

This gentleman, as has been observed in the beginning
of this letter, considers the writings of Harrington, More
and Hume, as justifiable and legal publications, because
they reasoned by comparison, though in so doing they
showed plans and systems of government, not only different from, but preferable to, that of England, and he accuses
me of endeavoring to confuse, instead of producing a system in the room of that which I had reasoned by comparison of the representative system against the hereditary
system ; but I have gone further ; for I have produced an
instance of a government established entirely on the representative system, under which greater happiness is enjoyed, much fewer taxes required, and much higher credit
is established, than under the system of government in
England. The funds in England have arisen since the

war only from 54*l.* to 97*l.* and they have been down since
the proclamation, to 87*l.* whereas the funds in America
rose in the mean time from 10*l.* to 120*l.*

His charge against me of " destroying every principle of
subordination," is equally as groundless; which even a
single paragraph from the work will prove, and which I
shall here quote :

" Formerly, when divisions arose respecting government,
recourse was had to the sword, and a civil war ensued.
That savage custom is exploded by the new system, and
recourse is had to a national convention. Discussion, and
the general will, arbitrates the question, and to this private
opinion yields with a good grace, and order is preserved
uninterrupted." Rights of Man, part ii.

That two different charges should be brought at the same
time, the one by a member of the legislature, for not doing
a certain thing, and the other by the attorney-general for
doing it, is a strange jumble of contradiction. I have now
justified myself, or the work rather, against the first by
stating the case in this letter, and the justification of the
other will be undertaken in its proper place. But in any
case the work will go on.

I shall now conclude this letter, with saying, that the
only objection I found against the plan and principles contained in the second part of the Rights of Man when I had
written the book, was, that they would beneficially interest
at least ninety-nine persons out of every hundred throughout the nation, and therefore would not leave sufficient
room for men to act from the direct and disinterested principles of honor; but the prosecution now commenced has
fortunately removed that objection, and the approvers and
protectors of that work now feel the immediate impulse of
honor, added to that of national interest.

> I am, Mr. Dundas,
>> Not your obedient humble servant,
>>> But to the contrary,
>>>> THOMAS PAINE.

DECLINE AND FALL

ENGLISH SYSTEM OF FINANCE.

———

"On the verge, nay even in the gulf of bankruptcy."
Debates in Parliament.

NOTHING, they say, is more certain than death, and nothing more uncertain than the time of dying; yet we can always fix a period beyond which man cannot live, and within some moment of which he will die. We are enabled to do this, not by any spirit of prophecy, or foresight into the event, but by observation of what has happened in all cases of human or animal existence. If then any other subject, such, for instance, as a system of finance, exhibits in its progress a series of symptoms indicating decay, its final dissolution is certain, and the period of it can be calculated from the symptoms it exhibits.

Those who have hitherto written on the English system of finance, (the funding system) have been uniformly impressed with the idea that its downfal would happen *some time or other*. They took, however, no data for their opinion, but expressed it predictively, or merely as opinion, from a conviction that the perpetual duration of such a system was a natural impossibility. It is in this manner that Dr. Price has spoken of it; and Smith, in his Wealth of Nations, has spoken in the same manner; that is, merely as opinion without data. "The progress," says Smith,

" of the enormous debts, which at present oppress, and will in the long run *most probably ruin*, all the great nations of Europe, (he should have said *government*) has been pretty uniform." But this general manner of speaking, though it might make some impression, carried with it no conviction.

It is not my intention to predict any thing; but I will show from data already known, from symptoms and facts which the English funding system has already exhibited publicly, that it will not continue to the end of Mr. Pitt's life, supposing him to live the usual age of a man. How much sooner it may fall, I leave to others to predict.

Let financiers diversify systems of credit as they will, it is nevertheless true, that every system of credit is a system of paper money. Two experiments have already been had upon paper money; the one in America, the other in France. In both those cases the whole capital was emitted, and that whole capital, which in America was called continental money, and in France assignats, appeared in circulation; the consequence of which was that the quantity became so enormous, and so disproportioned to the quantity of population, and to the quantity of objects upon which it could be employed, that the market, if I may so express it, was glutted with it, and the value of it fell. Between five and six years determined the fate of those experiments. The same fate would have happened to gold and silver, could gold and silver have been issued in the same abundant manner as paper had been, and confined within the country as paper money always is, by having no circulation out of it; or to speak on a larger scale, the same thing would happen in the world, could the world be glutted with gold and silver, as America and France has been with paper.

The English system differs from that of America and France in this one particular, that its capital is kept out of sight; that is, it does not appear in circulation. Were the whole capital of the national debt, which at the time I write this, is almost one hundred millions of pounds sterling, to be emitted in assignats or bills, and that whole quantity put into circulation, as was done in America and in France, those English assignats, or bills, would soon sink in value as those of America and France have done; and that in a greater degree, because the quantity of them would be more disproportioned to the quantity of population in England, than was the case in either of the other two countries. A nominal pound sterling in such bills would not be worth one penny.

But though the English system, by thus keeping the capital out of sight, is preserved from hasty destruction, as in the case of America and France, it nevertheless approaches the same fate, and will arrive at it with the same certainty, though by a slower progress. The difference is altogether in the degree of speed by which the two systems approach their fate, which, to speak in round numbers, is as twenty is to one; that is, the English system, that of funding the capital instead of issuing it, contained within itself a capacity of enduring twenty times longer than the systems adopted by America and France; and at the end of that time it would arrive at the same common grave, the Potter's Field, of paper money.

The datum, I take for this proposition of twenty to one, is the difference between a capital and the interest at five per cent. Twenty times the interest is equal to the capital. The accumulation of paper money in England is in proportion to the accumulation of the interest upon every new loan; and therefore the progress to the dissolution is twenty times slower than if the capital were to be emitted and put into circulation immediately. Every twenty years in the English system is equal to one year in the French and American systems.

Having thus stated the duration of the two systems, that of funding upon interest, and that of emitting the whole capital without funding, to be as twenty to one, I come to examine the symptoms of decay, approaching to dissolution, that the English system has already exhibited, and to compare them with similar systems in the French and American systems.

The English funding system began one hundred years ago; in which time there has been six wars, including the war that ended in 1697.

1. The war that ended, as I have just said, in 1697.
2. The war that began in 1702.
3. The war that began in 1739.
4. The war that began in 1756.
5. The American war, that began in 1775.
6. The present war, that began in 1793.

The national debt, at the conclusion of the war, which ended in 1697, was twenty-one millions and an half. (See Smith's Wealth of Nations, chapter on public debts.) We now see it approaching fast to four hundred millions. If between these two extremes of twenty-one millions and four hundred millions, embracing the several expenses of all the including wars, there exists some common ratio that will ascertain arithmetically the amount of the debts at the end of each war, as certainly as the fact is known to be, that ratio will in like manner determine what the amount of the debt will be in all future wars, and will ascertain the period within which the funding system will expire in a bankruptcy of the government; for the ratio I allude to is the ratio which the nature of the thing has established for itself.

Hitherto no idea has been entertained that any such ratio existed, or could exist, that could determine a problem of this kind, that is, that could ascertain, without having any knowledge of the fact, what the expense of any former war had been, or what the expense of any future war would be; but it is nevertheless true that such a ratio does exist, as I shall show, and also the mode of applying it.

The ratio I allude to is not in Arithmetical progression like the numbers

$$2, 3, 4, 5, 6, 7, 8, 9;$$

nor yet in geometrical progression, like the numbers

$$2, 4, 8, 16, 32, 64, 128, 256;$$

but it is in the series of one half upon each preceding number; like the numbers

$$8, 12, 18, 27, 40, 60. 90, 135.$$

Any person can perceive that the second number, 12, is produced by the preceding number, 8, and half 8; and that the third number, 18, is in like manner produced by the preceding number, 12, and half 12; and so on for the rest. They can also see how rapidly the sums increase as the ratio proceeds. The difference between the two first numbers is but four; but the difference between the two last is forty five: and from thence they may see with what immense rapidity the national debt has increased, and will continue to increase, till it exceeds the ordinary powers of calculation, and loses itself in cyphers.

I come now to apply the ratio as a rule to determine all the cases.

I began with the war that ended in 1697, which was the war in which the funding system began. The expense of that war was twenty-one millions and an half. In order to ascertain the expense of the next war, I add to twenty-one millions and an half, the half thereof (ten millions and three quarters) which makes thirty-two millions and a quarter for the expense of that war. This thirty-two millions and a quarter, added to the former debt of twenty-one millions and an half, carries the national debt to fifty-three millions and three quarters. Smith, (chapter on Public Debts) says, the national debt was at this time fifty-three millions.

I proceed to ascertain the expense of the next war, that of 1739, by adding, as in in the former case one half to the expense of the preceding war. The expense of the preceding war, was thirty-two millions and a quarter ; for the sake of even numbers, say thirty-two millions ; the half of which (16) makes forty-eight millions for the expense of that war.

I proceed to ascertain the expense of the war of 1756, by adding, according to the ratio, one half to the expense of the preceding war. The expense of the preceding war was taken at 48 millions, the half of which (24) makes 72 millions for the expense of that war. Smith (chapter on Public Debts) says, the expense of the war of 1756, was 72 millions and a quarter.

I proceed to ascertain the expense of the American war, of 1775, by adding, as in the former cases, one half to the expense of the preceding war. The expense of the preceding war was 72 millions, the half of which (36) makes 108 millions for the expense of that war. In the last edition of Smith, (chapter on Public Debts,) he says, the expense of the American war was *more than an hundred millions.*

I come now to ascertain the expense of the present war, supposing it to continue as long as former wars have done, and the funding system not to break up before that period. The expense of the preceding war was 108 millions, the half of which (54) makes 162 millions for the expense of the present war. It gives symptoms of going beyond this sum, supposing the funding system not to break up ; for the loans of the last year and of the present year, are twenty-two millions each, which exceeds the ratio compared with the loans of the preceding war. It will not be from the inability of procuring loans that the system will break up. On the contrary, it is the facility with which loans can be procured, that hastens that event. The loans are altogether paper transactions ; and it is the excess of them that brings on, with accelerating speed, that progressive depreciation of funded paper money that will dissolve the funding system.

I proceed to ascertain the expense of future wars, and I do this merely to show the impossibility of the continuance of the funding system, and the certainty of its dissolution.

The expense of the next war after the present war, according to the ratio which ascertained the preceding cases, will be   243 millions,

Expense of the second war	364
———————— third war	546
———————— fourth war	819
———————— fifth war	1228

3200 millions,

which, at only four per cent. will require taxes to the nominal amount of one hundred and twenty-eight millions to pay the annual interest, besides the interest of the present debt, and the expenses of government, which are not included in this account. Is there a man so mad, so stupid, as to suppose this system can continue?

When I first conceived the idea of seeking for some common ratio that should apply as a rule of measurement to all the cases of the funding system, so far as to ascertain the several stages of its approach to dissolution, I had no expectation that any ratio could be found that would apply with so much exactness as this does. I was led to the idea merely by observing that the funding system was a thing in continual progression, and that whatever was in a state of progression might be supposed to admit of, at least, some general ratio of measurement, that would apply without any very great variation. But who could have supposed that falling systems, or falling opinions, admitted of a ratio apparently as true as the descent of falling bodies? I have not *made* the ratio any more than Newton made the ratio of gravitation. I have only discovered it, and explained the mode of applying it.

To show at one view the rapid progression of the funding system to destruction, and to expose the folly of those who blindly believe in its continuance, and who artfully endeavor to impose that belief upon others, I exhibit in the annexed table, the expense of each of the six wars since the funding system began, as ascertained by the ratio, and the expense of the six wars yet to come, ascertained by the same ratio.

FIRST SIX WARS.				SECOND SIX WARS.			
1	-	-	21 millions	1	-	-	243 millions
2	-	-	33 millions	2	-	-	364 millions
3	-	-	48 millions	3	-	-	546 millions
4	-	-	72 millions*	4	-	-	819 millions
5	-	-	108 millions	5	-	-	1228 millions
6	-	-	162 millions	6	-	-	1842 millions

Total 444   Total 5042 millions

Those who are acquainted with the power with which even a small ratio, acting in progression, multiplies in a long series, will see nothing to wonder at in this table. Those who are not acquainted with that subject, and not knowing what else to say, may be inclined to deny it. But it is not their opinion one way, nor mine the other, that can influence the event. The table exhibits the natural march of the funding system to its irredeemable dissolution. Supposing the present government of England to continue, and to go on as it has gone on since the funding system began, I would not give twenty shillings for one hundred pounds in the funds to be paid twenty years hence. I do not speak this predictively; I produce the data upon which that belief is founded: and which data it is every body's interest to know, who have any thing to do with the funds, or who are going to bequeath property to their descendants to be paid at a future day.

Perhaps it may be asked, that as governments or ministers proceeded by no ratio in making loans or incurring debts, and as nobody intended any ratio, or thought of any how does it happen that there is one? I answer, that the ratio is founded in necessity; and I now go to explain what that necessity is.

* The actual expense of the war of 1739 did not come up to the sum ascertained by the ratio. But as that which is the natural disposition of a thing, as it is the natural disposition of a stream of water to descend, will, if impeded in its course overcome by a new effort what it had lost by that impediment, so it was with respect to this war and the next (1756,) taken collectively; for the expense of the war of 1756 restored the equilibrium of the ratio, as if it had not been impeded. A circumstance that serves to prove the truth of the ratio more fully than if the interruption had not taken place. The war of 1739 was languid; the efforts were below the value of money at that time: for the ratio is the measure of the depreciation of money in consequence of the funding system; or what comes to the same end, it is the measure of the increase of paper. Every additional quantity of it, whether in bank notes or otherwise, diminishes the *real*, though not the *nominal*, value of the former quantity.

It will always happen, that the price of labor, or of the
produce of labor, be that produce what it may, will be in
proportion to the quantity of money in a country, admitting
things to take their natural course. Before the invention of the funding system, there was no other money
than gold, and silver; and as nature gives out those metals
with a sparing hand, and in regular annual quantities from
the mines, the several prices of things were proportioned to
the quantity of money at that time, and so nearly stationary as to vary but little in any fifty or sixty years of that
period.

The funding system was a substitute for gold and silver. That substitute was paper; and the quantity increased as the interest increased upon accumulated loans. This
appearance of a new and additional species of money in
the nation soon began to break the relative value which
money and the things it will purchase bore to each other
before. Every thing rose in price; but the rise at first
was little and slow, like the difference in units between the
two first numbers, 8 and 12, compared with the two last
numbers 90 and 135, in the table. It was however sufficient
to make itself considerably felt in a large transaction.
When, therefore, government, by engaging in a new war,
required a new loan, it was obliged to make a higher loan
than the former loan, to balance the increased price to
which things had risen; and as that new loan increased
the quantity of paper in proportion to the new quantity of
interest, it carried the price of things still higher than before. The next loan was again higher, to balance that
further increased price; and all this in the same manner
though not in the same degree, that every new emission of
continental money in America, or of assignats in France,
were greater than the preceding emission, to make head
against the advance of prices, till the combat could be
maintained no longer. Herein is founded the necessity of
which I have just spoken. That necessity proceeds with
accelerating velocity, and the ratio I have laid down is the
measure of that acceleration; or, to speak the technical
language of the subject, it is the measure of the increasing
depreciation of funded paper money, which it is impossible
to prevent, while the quantity of that money and of bank
notes continues to multiply. What else but this can account
for the difference between one war costing 21 millions, and
another war costing 160 millions?

The difference cannot be accounted for on the score of extraordinary efforts or extraordinary achievements. The war that cost twenty-one millions was the war of the confederates, historically called the grand alliance, consisting of England, Austria, and Holland, in the time of William III. against Louis XIV. and in which the confederates were victorious. The present is a war of a much greater confederacy; a confederacy of England, Austria, Prussia, the German empire, Spain, Holland, Naples, and Sardinia, eight powers against the French republic singly, and the republic has beaten the whole confederacy. But to return to my subject.

It is said in England, that the value of paper keeps equal with the value of gold and silver. But the case is not rightly stated : for the fact is, that the paper has *pulled down* the value of gold and silver to a level with itself.— Gold and silver will not purchase so much of any purchasable article at this day as if no paper had appeared, nor so much as it will in any country in Europe where there is no paper. How long this hanging together of money and paper will continue, makes a new case ; because it daily exposes the system to sudden death, independent of the natural death it would otherwise suffer.

I consider the funding system as being now advanced into the last twenty years of its existence. The single circumstance, were there no other, that a war should now cost *nominally* one hundred and sixty millions, which when the system began cost but twenty-one millions, or that the loan for one year only (including the loan to the emperor) should now be *nominally* greater than the whole expense of that war, shows the state of depreciation to which the funding system has arrived. Its depreciation is in the proportion of eight for one, compared with the value of its money when the system began; which is the state the French assignats stood a year ago (March 1795) compared with gold and silver. It is, therefore, that I say, that the English funding system, has entered on the last twenty years of its existence, comparing each twenty years of the English system with every single year of the American and French systems as before stated.

Again, supposing the present war to close as former wars have done, and without producing either revolution or reform in England, another war, at least, must be looked for in the space of the twenty years I allude to ; for it

has never yet since happened that twenty years have
passed off without a war, and that more especially since
the English government has dabbled in German politics,
and shown a disposition to insult the world, and the world
of commerce, with her navy. The next war will carry the
national debt to very nearly seven hundred millions, the
interest of which, at four per cent. will be twenty-eight
millions besides the taxes for the (then) expenses of government, which will increase in the same proportion, and
which will carry the taxes to at least forty millions ; and
if another war only begins, it will quickly carry them to
above fifty ; for it is in the last twenty years of the funding system, as in the last year of the American and French
systems without funding, that all the great shocks begin to
operate.

I have just mentioned that paper, in England has *pulled
down* the value of gold and silver to a level with itself ; and
that this *pulling down* of gold and silver money has created
the appearance of paper money keeping up. The same
thing, and the same mistake, took place in America and in
France, and continued for a considerable time after the
commencement of their system of paper ; and the actual
depreciation of money was hidden under that mistake.

It was said in America, at that time, that every thing was
becoming *dear ;* but gold and silver could then buy those
dear articles no cheaper than paper could ; and therefore
it was not called depreciation. The idea of *dearness* established itself for the idea of depreciation. The same
was the case in France. Though every thing rose in price
soon after assignats appeared, yet those dear articles could
be purchased no cheaper with gold and silver than with
paper, and it was only said that things were *dear.* The
same is still the language in England. They called it
dearness. But they will soon find that it is an actual depreciation, and that this depreciation is the effect of the
funding system ; which, by crowding such a continually-
increasing mass of paper into circulation, carries down the
value of gold and silver with it. But gold and silver will,
in the long run, revolt against depreciation, and separate
from the value of paper ; for the progress of all such systems appears to be, that the paper will take the command
in the beginning, and gold and silver in the end.

But this succession in the command of gold and silver
over paper, makes a crisis far more eventful to the funding

system than to any other system upon which paper can be issued; for, strictly speaking, it is not a crisis of danger, but a symtom of death. It is a death stroke to the funding system. It is a revolution in the whole of its affairs.

If paper be issued without being funded upon interest, emissions of it can be continued after the value of it separates from gold and silver, as we have seen in the two cases of America and France. But the funding system rests altogether upon the value of paper being equal to gold and silver; which will be as long as the paper can continue carrying down the value of gold and silver to the same level to which itself descends, and no longer. But even in this state, that of descending equally together, the minister, whoever he may be, will find himself beset with accumulating difficulties; because the loans and taxes voted for the service of each ensuing year will wither in his hands before the year expires, or before they can be applied.— This will force him to have recourse to emissions of what are called exchequer and navy bills, which, by still increasing the mass of paper in circulation, will drive on the depreciation still more rapidly.

It ought to be known that taxes in England are not paid in gold and silver, but in paper (bank notes.) Every person who pays any considerable quantity of taxes, such as malsters, brewers, distillers. (I appeal for the truth of it to any of the collectors of excise in England, or to Mr. Whitebread) knows this to be the case. There is not gold and silver enough in the nation to pay the taxes in coin, as I shall show; and consequently there is not money enough in the bank to pay the notes. The interest of the national funded debt is paid at the bank in the same kind of paper in which the taxes are collected. When people find, as they will find, a reservedness among each other in giving gold and silver for bank notes, or the least preference for the former over the latter, they will go for payment to the bank, where they have a right to go. They will do this as a measure of prudence, each one for himself, and the truth or delusion of the funding system will then be proved.

I have said in the foregoing paragraph that there is not gold and silver enough in the nation to pay the taxes in coin, and consequently that there cannot be enough in the bank to pay the notes. As I do not choose to rest any thing upon assertion, I appeal for the truth of this to the publications of Mr. Eden (now called lord Auckland) and

George Chalmers, secretary to the board of trade and plantation, of which Jenkinson (now called lord Hawkesbury) is president. [These sort of folks change their names so often, that it is as difficult to know them as a thief.] Chalmers gives the quantity of gold and silver coin from the returns of coinage at the mint; and, after deducting for the light gold recoined, says, that the amount of gold and silver coin is *about twenty millions*. He had better not have proved this, especially if he had reflected, that *public credit is suspicion asleep*. The quantity is much too little.

Of this twenty millions (which is not a fourth part of the quantity of gold and silver there is in France, as is shown in M. Neckar's Treatise on the administration of the Finances) three millions, at least, must be supposed to be in Ireland, some in Scotland, and in the West-Indies, Newfoundland, &c. The quantity therefore in England cannot be more than sixteen millions, which is four millions less than the amount of the taxes. But admitting that there are sixteen millions, not more than a fourth part thereof can be in London, when it is considered that every city, town, village, and farm-house in the nation must have a part of it, and that all the great manufactories, which most require cash, are out of London. Of this four millions in London, every banker, merchant, tradesman, in short, every individual must have some. He must be a poor shopkeeper indeed, who has not a few guineas in his till. The quantity of cash therefore in the bank, never can, on the evidence of circumstances, be so much as two millions; most probably not more than one million; and on this slender twig, always liable to be broken, hangs the whole funding system of four hundred millions, besides many millions in bank notes. The sum in the bank is not sufficient to pay one-fourth of only one year's interest of the national debt, were the creditors to demand payment in cash, or demand cash for the bank notes in which the interest is paid. A circumstance always liable to happen.

One of the amusements that has kept up the farce of the funding system is, that the interest is regularly paid. But as the interest is always paid in bank notes, and as bank notes can always be coined for the purpose, this mode of payment proves nothing. The point of proof is, can the bank give cash for the bank notes with which the interest is paid? If it cannot, and it is evident that it cannot, some

millions of bank notes must go without payment, and those
holders of bank notes who apply last will be worst off.
Were the present quantity of cash in the bank paid away,
it is next to impossible to see how any new quantity is
to arrive. None will arrive from taxes, for the taxes will
all be paid in bank notes; and should the government refuse bank notes in payment of taxes, the credit of bank
notes will be gone at once, no cash will arise from the
business of discounting merchant's bills; for every merchant will pay off those bills in bank notes, and not in cash.
There is therefore no means left for the bank to obtain a
new supply of cash, after the present quantity be paid
away. But, besides the impossibility of paying the interest of the funded debt in cash, there are many thousand
persons in London and in the country, who are holders of
bank notes that came into their hands in the fair way of
trade, and who are not stockholders in the funds; and as
such persons have had no hand in increasing the demand
upon the bank, as those have had, who, for their own private interest, like Boyd and others, are contracting, or pre-
tending to contract, for new loans, they will conceive they
have a just right that their bank notes should be paid first.
Boyd has been very sly in France, in changing his paper
into cash. He will be just as sly in doing the same thing
in London; for he has learned to calculate: and then it is
probable he will set off for America.

A stoppage of payment at the bank is not a new thing.
Smith, in his Wealth of Nations, book ii. chap. 2. says,
"that in the year 1696, exchequer bills fell forty, fifty,
and sixty per cent.—bank notes twenty per cent. and the
bank stopped payment." That which happened in 1696,
may happen again in 1796. The period in which it happened was the last year of the war of king William. It
necessarily put a stop to the further emission of exchequer
and navy bills, and to the raising of new loans; and the
peace which took place the next year was probably hur-
ried on by this circumstance, and saved the bank from
bankruptcy. Smith, in speaking from the circumstances
of the bank, upon another occasion says, (book ii. chap. 2.)
" This great company had been reduced to the necessity
of paying in sixpences." When a bank adopts the expedient of paying in sixpences, it is a confession of insolvency.

It is worthy of observation, that every case of failure in
finances, since the system of paper began, has produced a

revolution in government, either total or partial.   A failure
in the finance of the assignats broke up the revolutionary
government, and produced the present French constitution.
A failure in the finances of the old congress of America
and the embarrassments it brought upon the commerce,
broke up the system of the old confederation, and produced the federal constitution.   If, then, we admit of reasoning by comparison of causes and events, the failure of the
English finances will produce some change in the government of that country.

As to Mr. Pitt's project of paying off the national debt
by applying a million a-year for that purpose, while he
continues adding more than twenty millions a-year to it, it
is like setting a man with a wooden leg to run after a hare.
The longer he runs the further he is off.

When I said that the funding system had entered the
last twenty years of its existence, I certainly did not mean
that it would continue twenty years, and then expire as a
lease would.   I meant to describe that age of decrepitude
in which death is every day to be expected, and life cannot continue long.   But the death of credit, or that state
that is called bankruptcy, is not always marked by those
progressive stages of visible decline, that mark the decline
of natural life.   In the progression of natural life, age cannot counterfeit youth, nor conceal the departure of juve-
nile abilities.   But it is otherwise with respect to the death
of credit; for though all the approaches to bankruptcy
may actually exist in circumstances, they admit of being
concealed by appearances.   Nothing is more common
than to see the bankrupt of to-day a man in credit but the
day before; yet no sooner is the real state of his affairs
known, than every body can see that he had been insolvent long before.   In London, the greatest theatre of bankruptcy in Europe, this part of the subject will be well and
feelingly understood.

Mr. Pitt continually talks of credit, and of the national
resources.   These are two of the feigned appearances by
which the approaches to bankruptcy are concealed.   That
which he calls credit may exist, as I have just shown, in a
state of insolvency, and is always what I have before described it to be, *suspicion asleep.*

As to national resources, Mr. Pitt, like all the English
financiers that preceded him since the funding system began, has uniformly mistaken the nature of a resource; that

is, they have mistaken it consistently with the delusion of
the funding system; but time is explaining the delusion.
That which he calls, and which they called, a resource, is
not a resource, but is the *anticipation* of a resource. They
have anticipated what *would have been* a resource in another
generation, had not the use of it been so anticipated. The
funding system is a system of anticipation. Those who
established it an hundred years ago, anticipated the resources of those who were to live an hundred years after;
for the people of the present day have to pay the interest
of the debts contracted at that time, and of all debts contracted since. But it is the last feather that breaks the
horse's back. Had the system began an hundred years
before, the amount of taxes at this time to pay the annual
interest at four per cent. (could we suppose such a system
of insanity to have thus continued) would be two hundred
and twenty millions annually; for the capital of the debt
would be 5486 millions, according to the ratio that ascer-
tains the expense of the wars for the hundred years that
are past. But long before it could have reached this period, the value of bank notes, from the immense quantity
of them, (for it is in paper only that such a nominal revenue could be collected) would have been as low or lower
than continental paper money has been in America or assignats in France; and as to the idea of exchanging them
for gold and silver, it is too absurd to be contradicted.

Do we not see that nature, in all her operations, disowns
the visionary basis upon which the funding system is built?
She acts always by renewed successions, and never by
accumulating additions, perpetually progressing. Animals
and vegetables, men and trees, have existed since the
world began; but that existence has been carried on
by succession of generations, and not by continuing the
same men and the same trees in existence that existed first;
and to make room for the new she removes the old. Every
natural ideot can see this. It is the stock-jobbing ideot
only that mistakes. He has conceived that art can do
what nature cannot. He is teaching her a new system:
that there is no occasion for man to die; that the scheme
of creation can be carried on upon the plan of the funding
system; that it can proceed by continual additions of new
beings like new loans, and all live together in eternal
youth. Go, count the graves, thou ideot, and learn the
folly of thy arithmetic.

But besides these things, there is something visibly farcical in the whole operation of loaning. It is scarcely more than four years ago that such a rot of bankruptcy spread itself over London, that the whole commercial fabric tottered; trade and credit were at a stand; and such was the state of things, that to prevent, or suspend a general bankruptcy, the government lent the merchants six millions in *government* paper, and now the merchants lend the government twenty-two millions in *their* paper; and two parties, Boyd and Morgan, men but little known, contend who shall be the lenders. What a farce is this! It reduces the operation of loaning to accommodation paper, in which the competitors contend, not who shall lend, but who shall sign, because there is something to be got for signing.

Every English stock-jobber and minister boasts of the credit of England. Its credit, say they, is greater than that of any country in Europe. There is a good reason for this ; for there is not another country in Europe that could be made the dupe of such a delusion. The English funding system will remain a monument of wonder, not so much on account of the extent to which it has been carried, as of the folly of believing in it.

Those who had formerly predicted that the funding system would break up when the debt should amount to one hundred or one hundred and fifty millions, erred only in not distinguishing between insolvency and actual bankruptcy ; for the insolvency commenced as soon as the government became unable to pay the interest in cash, or to give cash for the bank notes in which the interest was paid, whether that inability was known or not, or whether it was suspected or not. Insolvency always takes place before bankruptcy ; for bankruptcy is nothing more than the publication of that insolvency. In the affairs of an individual, it often happens that insolvency exists several years before bankruptcy, and that the insolvency is concealed and carried on till the individual is not able to pay one shilling in the pound. A government can ward off bankruptcy longer than an individual ; but insolvency will inevitably produce bankruptcy, whether in an individual or in a government. If then the quantity of bank notes payable on demand, which the bank has issued, are greater than the bank can pay off, the bank is insolvent; and when that insolvency is declared, it is bankruptcy.*

I come now to show the several ways by which bank notes get into circulation. I shall afterwards offer an estimate on the total quantity or amount of bank notes existing at this moment.

The bank acts in three capacities. As a bank of discount; as a bank of deposite; and as a bank for the government.

1st, As a bank of discount. The bank discounts merchants' bills of exchange for two months. When a merchant has a bill that will become due at the end of two months, and wants payment before that time, the bank advances that payment to him, deducting therefrom at the rate of five per cent. per annum. The bill of exchange remains at the bank as a pledge or pawn, and at the end of two months it must be redeemed. This transaction is done altogether in paper; for the profits of the bank, as a bank of discount, arise entirely from its making use of paper as money. The bank gives bank notes to the merchant in

* Among the delusions that have been imposed upon the nation by ministers, to give a false coloring to its affairs, and by none more than by Mr. Pitt, is a motley, amphibious-charactered thing called the *balance of trade.* This balance of trade, as it is called, is taken from the custom-house books, in which entries are made of all cargoes exported, and also of all cargoes imported, in each year—and when the value of the exports, according to the price set upon them by the exporter or by the custom-house, is greater than the value of the imports, estimated in the same manner, they say, the balance of trade is much in their favor.

The custom-house books prove regularly enough that so many cargoes have been exported, and so many imported—but this is all that they prove, or were intended to prove. They have nothing to do with the balance of profit or loss; and it is ignorance to appeal to them upon that account: for the case is, that the greater the loss is in any one year, the higher will this thing called the balance of trade appear to be according to the custom-house books. For example, nearly the whole of the Mediterranean convoy has been taken by the French this year—consequently those cargoes will not appear as imports on the custom-house books, and therefore the balance of trade, by which they mean the profits of it, will appear to be so much the greater, as the loss amounts to—and, on the other hand, had the loss not happened, the profits would have appeared to have been so much the less. All the losses happening at sea, to returning cargoes, by accidents, by the elements, or by capture, make the balance appear the higher on the side of the exports—and were they all lost at sea, it would appear to be all profit on the custom-house books. Also every cargo of exports that is lost and occasions another to be sent, adds in like manner to the side of the exports, and appears as profit. This year the balance of trade will appear high, because the losses have been great by capture and by storms. The ignorance of the British parliament in listening to this hackneyed imposition of ministers about the balance of trade, is astonishing. It shows how little they know of national affairs—and Mr. Grey may as well talk Greek to them, as to make motions about the state of the nation. They understand only fox-hunting and the game-laws.

discounting the bill of exchange, and the redeemer of the bill pays bank notes to the bank in redeeming it. It very seldom happens that any real money passes between them.

If the profits of a bank be, for example, two hundred thousand pounds a-year, (a great sum to be made merely by exchanging one sort of paper for another, and which shows also that the merchants of that place are pressed for money for payments, instead of having money to spare to lend to government) it proves that the bank discounts to the amount of four millions annually, or 666,666*l.* every two months; and as there never remain in the bank more than two month's pledges, of the value of 666,666*l.* at any one time, the amount of bank notes in circulation at any one time should not be more than to that amount. This is sufficient to show that the present immense quantity of bank notes, which are distributed through every city, town, village, and farm-house in England, cannot be accounted for on the score of discounting.

2d, As a bank of deposite. To deposite money at the bank means to lodge it there for the sake of convenience, and to be drawn out at any moment the depositor pleases, or to be paid away to his order. When the business of discounting is great, that of depositing is necessarily small. No man deposites and applies for discounts at the same time; for it would be like paying interest for lending money, instead of for borrowing it. The deposites that are now made at the bank are almost entirely in bank notes, and consequently they add nothing to the ability of the bank to pay off the bank notes that may be presented for payment; and besides this, the deposites are no more the property of the bank than the cash or bank notes in a merchant's counting house are the property of his book-keeper. No great increase therefore of bank notes, beyond what the discounting business admits can be accounted for on the score of deposites.

3d. The bank acts as banker for the government. This is the connexion that threatens to ruin every public bank. It is through this connexion that the credit of a bank is forced far beyond what it ought to be, and still further beyond its ability to pay. It is through this connexion that such an immense, redundant quantity of bank notes have gotten into circulation ; and which, instead of being issued because there was property in the bank, have been issued because there was none.

When the treasury is empty, which happens in almost every year of every war, its coffers at the bank are empty also. It is in this condition of emptiness that the minister has recourse to emissions of what are called exchequer and navy bills, which continually generates a new increase of bank notes, and which are sported upon the public without there being property in the bank to pay them.— These exchequer and navy bills (being, as I have said, emitted because the treasury and its coffers at the bank are empty, and cannot pay the demands that come in) are no other than an acknowledgment that the bearer is entitled to receive so much money. They may be compared to the settlement of an account, in which the debtor acknowledges the balance he owes, and for which he gives a note of hand ; or to a note of hand given to raise money upon it.

Sometimes the bank discounts those bills as it would discount merchants' bills of exchange ; sometimes it purchases them of the holders at the current price ; and sometimes it agrees with the ministers to pay an interest upon them to the holders, and keep them in circulation. In every one of these cases an additional quantity of bank notes get into circulation, and are sported, as I have said, upon the public, without there being property in the bank, as banker for the government, to pay them ; and besides this, the bank has now no money of its own ; for the money that was originally subscribed to begin the credit of the bank with at its first establishment, has been lent to government, and wasted long ago.

" The bank (says Smith, book ii. chap. 2.) acts not only as an ordinary bank, but as a great engine of state ; it receives and pays the greater part of the annuities which are due to the creditors of the *public*." (It is worth observing, that the *public*, or the *nation*, is always put for the government, in speaking of debts.) " It circulates" (says Smith) "exchequer bills, and it advances to government the annual amount of the land and malt taxes, which are frequently not paid till several years afterwards." (This advancement is also done in bank notes, for which there is not property in the bank.) " In those different operations (says Smith) *its duty to the public* may sometimes have obliged it, without any fault of its directors, *to overstock the circulation with paper money*,"—bank notes. How its *duty to the public* can induce it *to overstock that public* with prom-

issory bank notes which it *cannot pay*, and thereby expose
the individuals of that public to ruin, is too paradoxical to
be explained ; for it is on the credit which individuals *give
to the bank*, by receiving and circulating its notes, and not
upon its *own* credit or its *own* property, for it has none,
that the bank sports. If, however, it be the duty of the
bank to expose the public to this hazard, it is at least
equally the duty of the individuals of that public to get
their money and take care of themselves ; and leave it to
placemen, pensioners, government contractors, Reeves'
association, and the members of both houses of parliament,
who have voted away the money at the nod of the minister, to continue the credit if they can, and for which their
estates individually and collectively ought to answer, as
far as they will go.

There has always existed, and still exists, a mysterious,
suspicious connexion, between the minister and the directors of the bank, and which explains itself no otherwise
than by a continual increase of bank notes. Without,
therefore, entering into any further details of the various
contrivances by which bank notes are issued, and thrown
upon the public, I proceed, as I before mentioned, to offer
an estimate on the total quantity of bank notes in circulation.

However disposed governments may be to extort money
by taxes from the people, there is a limit to the practice
established in the nature of things. That limit is the proportion between the quantity of money in a nation, be that
quantity of money what it may, and the greatest quantity
of taxes that can be raised upon it. People have other
uses for money besides paying taxes ; and it is only a proportional part of that money they can spare for taxes, as it
is only a proportional part they can spare for house-
rent, for clothing, or for any other particular use. These
proportions find out and establish themselves ; and that
with such exactness, that if any one part exceeds its proportion, all the other parts feel it.

Before the invention of paper money (bank notes,) there
was no other money in the nation than gold and silver, and
the greatest quantity of money that ever was raised in
taxes during that period, never exceeded a fourth part of
the quantity of money in the nation. It was high taxing
when it came to this point. The taxes in the time of William III. never reached to four millions, before the inven-

tion of paper, and the quantity of money in the nation at that time was estimated to be about sixteen millions. The same proportions established themselves in France. There was no paper money in France before the present revolution, and the taxes were collected in gold and silver money. The highest quantity of taxes never exceeded twenty-two millions sterling; and the quantity of gold and silver money in the nation at the same time, as stated by M. Neckar, from returns of coinage at the mint, in his Treatise on the Administration of the Finances, was about ninety millions sterling. To go beyond this limit of a fourth part, in England, they were obliged to introduce paper money; and the attempt to go beyond it in France, where paper could not be introduced, broke up the government.

This proportion therefore of a fourth part, is the limit which the nature of the thing establishes for itself, be the quantity of money in a nation more or less.

The amount of taxes in England at this time is full twenty millions; and therefore the quantity of gold and silver, and of bank notes, taken together, amounts to eighty millions. The quantity of gold and silver, as stated by lord Hawkesbury's secretary (George Chalmers,) as I have before shown, is twenty millions; and therefore the total amount of bank notes in circulation, all made payable on demand, is sixty millions. This enormous sum will astonish the most stupid stock-jobber, and overpower the credulity of the most thoughtless Englishman: but were it only a third part of that sum, the bank cannot pay half a crown in the pound.

There is something curious in the movements of this modern complicated machine, the funding system; and it is only now that it is beginning to unfold the full extent of its movements. In the first part of its movements it gives great powers into the hands of government, and in the last part it takes them completely away.

The funding system set out with raising revenues under the name of loans, by means of which government became both prodigal and powerful. The loaners assumed the name of creditors, and though it was soon discovered that loaning was government-jobbing, those pretended loaners, or the persons who purchased into the funds afterwards, conceived themselves not only to be creditors, but to be the *only* creditors.

But such has been the operation of this complicated machine, the funding system, that it has produced, unperceived, a second generation of creditors, more numerous and far more formidable, and withal more real than the first generation; for every holder of a bank note is a creditor, and a real creditor, and the debt due to him is made payable on demand. The debt, therefore, which the government owes to individuals is composed of two parts; the one about four hundred millions bearing interest, the other about sixty millions payable on demand. The one is called the funded debt, the other is the debt due in bank notes.

The second debt (that contained in the bank notes) has, in a great measure, been incurred to pay the interest of the first debt; so that in fact little or no real interest has been paid by government. The whole has been delusion and fraud. Government first contracted a debt in the form of loans with one class of people, and then run clandestinely into debt with another class, by means of bank notes, to pay the interest. Government acted of itself in contracting the first debt, and made a machine of the bank to contract the second. It is this second debt that changes the seat of power and the order of things; for it puts it in the power of even a small part of the holders of bank notes (had they no other motive than disgust at Pitt and Grenville's sedition bills) to control any measure of government they found to be injurious to their interest; and that not by popular meetings, or popular societies, but by the simple and easy operation of with-holding their credit from that government; that is, by individually demanding payment at the bank for every bank note that comes into their hands. Why should Pitt and Grenville expect that the very men whom they insult and injure, should at the same time continue to support the measures of Pitt and Grenville, by giving credit to their promissory notes of payment? No new emissions of bank notes could go on while payment was demanding on the old, and the cash in the bank wasting daily away; nor any new advances be made to government or to the emperor to carry on the war; nor any new emission be made on exchequer bills.

"*The bank,*" says Smith, (book ii. chap. 2) is "*a great engine of state.*" And in the same paragraph he says, "*The stability of the bank is equal to that of the British government:*" which is the same as to say that the stability of the government is equal to that of the bank, and no more. If then the bank cannot pay, the *arch-treasurer of the holy Roman empire* (S. R. I. A.*) is a bankrupt. When folly invented titles, she did not attend to their application; for ever since the government of England has been in the hands of *arch-treasurers*, it has been running into bankruptcy; and as to the arch-treasurer *apparent*, he has been a bankrupt long ago. What a miserable prospect has England before its eyes!

Before the war of 1755, there were no bank notes lower than twenty pounds. During that war bank notes of fifteen pounds and of ten pounds were coined; and now, since the commencement of the present war, they are coined as low as five pounds. These five pound notes will circulate chiefly among little shopkeepers, butchers, bakers, market people, renters of small houses, lodgers, &c. All the high departments of commerce, and the affluent stations of life were already *overstocked*, as Smith expresses it, with the bank notes. No place remained open wherein to crowd an additional quantity of bank notes but among the class of people I have just mentioned, and the means of doing this could be best effected by coining five pound notes. This conduct has the appearance of that of an unprincipled insolvent, who, when on the verge of bankruptcy to the amount of many thousands, will borrow as low as five pounds of the servants in his house, and break the next day.

But whatever momentary relief or aid the minister and his bank might expect from this low contrivance of five pound notes, it will increase the inability of the bank to pay the higher notes, and hasten the destruction of all; for even the small taxes that used to be paid in money will now be paid in those notes, and the bank will soon find itself with scarcely any other money than what the hairpowder guinea tax brings in.

The bank notes make the most serious part of the business of finance; what is called the national funded debt is but a trifle when put in comparison with it; yet the case of the bank notes has never been touched upon. But it certainly ought to be known upon what authority, whether that of the minister or of the directors, and upon what foundation, such immense quantities are issued. I have

* Part of the inscription on an English guinea.

stated the amount of them at sixty millions; I have produced data for that estimation ; and besides this, the apparent quantity of them, far beyond that of gold and silver
in the nation, corroborates the statement. Were there
but a third part of sixty millions, the bank cannot pay
half a crown in the pound; for no new supply of money,
as before said, can arrive at the bank, as all the taxes will
be paid in paper.

When the funding system began, it was not doubted that
the loans that had been borrowed would be repaid. Government not only propagated that belief, but it began paying them off. In time this profession came to be abandoned : and it is not difficult to see that bank notes will march
the same way ; for the amount of them is only another
debt under another name ; and the probability is that Mr.
Pitt will at last propose funding them. In that case bank
notes will not be so valuable as French assignats. The
assignats have a solid property in reserve, in the national
domains ; bank notes have none; and besides this, the
English revenue must then sink down to what the amount
of it was before the funding system began—between three
and four millions: one of which the *arch-treasurer* would
require for himself, and the arch-treasurer *apparent* would
require three-quarters of a million more to pay his debts.
" *In France*," says Sterne, " *they order these things better.*"

I have now exposed the English system of finance to the
eyes of all nations; for this work will be published in all
languages. In doing this, I have done an act of justice to
those numerous citizens of neutral nations who have been
imposed upon by that fraudulent system, and who have
property at stake upon the event.

As an individual citizen of America, and as far as an individual can go, I have revenged (if I may use the expression without any immoral meaning) the piratical depreda-
tions committed on the American commerce by the English government. I have retaliated for France on the subject of finance : and I conclude with retorting on Mr. Pitt
the expression he used against France, and say, that the
English system of finance "IS ON THE VERGE, NAY EVEN IN
THE GULF OF BANKRUPTCY."

THOMAS PAINE.

Paris, April 8, 1796.

THE PEOPLE OF FRANCE.

Fellow citizens,

I receive with affectionate gratitude, the honor which the late national assembly has conferred upon me, by adopting me a citizen of France; and the additional honor of being elected by my fellow citizens a member of the national convention. Happily impressed, as I am, by those testimonies of respect shown towards me as an individual, I feel my felicity increased by seeing the barrier broken down that divided patriotism by spots of earth, and limited citizenship to the soil, like vegetation.

Had those honors been conferred in an hour of national tranquillity, they would have afforded no other means of showing my affection, than to have accepted and enjoyed them; but they come accompanied with circumstances that give me the honorable opportunity of commencing my citizenship in the stormy hour of difficulties. I come not to enjoy repose. Convinced that the cause of France is the cause of all mankind, and that liberty cannot be purchased by a wish, I gladly share with you the dangers and honors necessary to success.

I am well aware that the moment of any great change, such as that accomplished on the 10th of August, is unavoidably the moment of terror and confusion. The mind highly agitated by hope, suspicion, and apprehension, continues without rest till the change be accomplished. But

let us now look calmly and confidently forward, and success
is certain.   It is no longer the paltry cause of kings, or of
this or that individual, that calls France and her armies
into action.   It is the great cause of ALL.   It is the establishment of a new era, that shall blot despotism from the
earth, and fix, on the lasting principles of peace and citizenship, the great republic of man.

It has been my fate to have borne a share in the commencement and complete establishment of one revolution,
(I mean the revolution of America.)   The success and
events of that revolution are encouraging to us.   The
prosperity and happiness that have since flowed to that
country, have amply rewarded her for all the hardships
she endured, and for all the dangers she encountered.

The principles on which that revolution began, have
extended themselves to Europe ; and an over-ruling Providence is regenerating the old world by the principles of
the new.   The distance of America from all the other parts
of the globe, did not admit of her carrying those principles
beyond her own boundaries.   It is to the peculiar honor of
France, that she now raises the standard of liberty for all
nations ; and in fighting her own battles, contends for the
rights of all mankind.

The same spirit of fortitude that insured success to
America ; will insure it to France ; for it is impossible to
conquer a nation determined to be free !   The military circumstances that now unite themselves to France, are such
as the despots of the earth know nothing of, and can form
no calculation upon.   They know not what it is to fight
against a nation.   They have only been accustomed to
make war upon each other, and they know from system
and practice, how to calculate the probable success of despot against despot ; and here their knowledge and their
experience end.

But in a contest like the present, a new and boundless
variety of circumstances arises, that deranges all such customary calculations.   When a whole nation acts as an army, the despot knows not the extent of the power against
which he contends.   New armies rise against him with the
necessity of the moment.   It is then that the difficulties of
an invading enemy multiply, as in the former case they
diminished ; and he finds them at their height when he expected them to end.

The only war that has any similarity of circumstances with the present, is the late revolutionary war in America. On her part, as it now is in France, it was a war of the whole nation. There it was that the enemy, by beginning to conquer, put himself in a condition of being conquered. His first victories prepared him for defeat. He advanced till he could not retreat, and found himself among a nation of armies.

Were it now to be proposed to the Austrians and Prussians, to escort them into the middle of France, and there leave them to make the most of such a situation, they would see too much into the dangers of it to accept the offer, and the same dangers would attend them could they arrive there by any other means. Where then is the military policy of their attempting to obtain by force, that which they would refuse by choice. But to reason with despots is throwing reason away. The best of arguments is a vigorous preparation.

Man is ever a stranger to the ways by which Providence regulates the order of things. The interference of foreign despots may serve to introduce into their own enslaved countries the principles that they come to oppose. Liberty and equality are blessings too great to be the inheritance of France alone. It is an honor to her to be their first champion; and she may now say to her enemies, with a mighty voice, "O! Ye Austrians, ye Prussians! Ye who now turn your bayonets against us, it is for all Europe; it is for all mankind, and not for France alone, that she raises the standard of liberty and equality!"

The public cause has hitherto suffered from the contradictions contained in the constitution of the former constituent assembly. Those contradictions have served to divide the opinions of individuals at home, and to obscure the great principles of the revolution in other countries. But when those contradictions shall be removed, and the constitution made conformable to the declaration of rights; when the bagatelles of monarchy, royalty, regency; and hereditary succession, shall be exposed, with all their absurdities, a new ray of light will be thrown over the world, and the revolution will derive new strength by being universally understood.

The scene that now opens itself to France extends far beyond the boundaries of his own dominions. Every nation is becoming her colleague, and every court is become her enemy. It is now the cause of all nations against the cause of all courts. The terror that despotism felt, clandestinely begot a confederation of despots; and their attack upon France was produced by their fears at home.

In entering on this great scene, greater than any nation has been called to act in, let us say to the agitated mind, be calm. Let us punish by instructing, rather than by revenge. Let us begin the new era by a greatness of friendship, and hail the approach of union and success.

Your fellow citizen,

THOMAS PAINE.

REASONS

———————

CITIZEN PRESIDENT,

My hatred and abhorrence of monarchy are sufficiently known; they originate in principles of reason and conviction, nor except with life, can they ever be extirpated; but my compassion for the unfortunate, whether friend or enemy, is equally lively and sincere.

I voted that Louis should be tried, because it was necessary to afford proofs to the world of the perfidy, corruption, and abomination of the monarchical system. The infinity of evidence that has been produced, exposes them in the most glaring and hideous colors; thence it results, that monarchy, whatever form it may assume, arbitrary or otherwise, becomes necessarily a centre, round which are united every species of corruption, and the kingly trade is no less destructive of all morality in the human breast, than the trade of an executioner is destructive of its sensibility.

I remember during my residence in another country, that I was exceedingly struck with a sentence of M. Autheine, at the Jacobins, which corresponds exactly with my own idea,—" Make me a king to-day," said he, " and I shall be a robber to-morrow."

Nevertheless, I am inclined to believe that if Louis Capet had been born in an amiable and respectable neighborhood, at liberty to practice the duties of domestic life, had he been thus situated, I cannot believe that he would have shown himself destitute of social virtues: we are, in a moment of fermentation like this, naturally little indulgent to his vices, or rather to those of monarchical governments; we regard them with additional horror and indignation; not that they are more heinous than those of his predecessors, but because our eyes are now open and the veil of delusion is at length withdrawn ; yet the lamentable, degraded state to which he is actually reduced, is surely far less imputable to him, than to the constituent assembly, which of its own authority, without consent or advice of the people, restored him to the throne.

I was in Paris at the time of the flight or abdication of Louis XVI. and when he was taken and brought back. The proposal of restoring him to supreme power struck me with amazement ; and although at that time I was not a French citizen, yet as a citizen of the world, I employed all the efforts that depended on me to prevent it.

A small society, composed only of five persons, two of whom are now members of the convention, took at that time the name of the Republican club, (societe republicaine.) This society opposed the restoration of Louis, not so much on account of his personal offences, as in order to overthrow the monarchy, and to erect on its ruins the republican system, and an equal representation.

With this design, I traced out in the English language certain propositions, which were translated with some trifling alterations, and signed by Achilles Duchatlet, actually lieutenant-general in the army of the French republic, and at that time, one of the five members which composed our little party : the law requiring the signature of a citizen at the bottom of each printed paper.

The paper was indignantly torn by Malouet ; and brought forth in this very room as an article of accusation against the person who had signed it, the author and their adherents, but such is the revolution of events, that this paper is now received and brought forth for a very opposite purpose : to remind the nation of the error of that unfortunate day, that fatal error of not having then banished Louis XVI. from its bosom, and not to plead this day in favor of his exile, preferably to his death.

The paper in question, was conceived in the following terms :

" Brethren and fellow citizens,

" The serene tranquillity, the mutual confidence which prevailed amongst us, during the time of the late king's escape, the indifference with which we beheld him return, are unequivocal proofs that the absence of a king is more desirable than his presence, and that he is not only a politi-eal superfluity, but a grievous burden, pressing hard on the whole nation.

" Let us not be imposed upon by sophisms ; all that concerns this, is reduced to four points.

" He has abdicated the throne in having fled from his post.   Abdication and desertion are not characterized by the length of absence ; but by the single act of flight.   In the present instance, the act is every thing, and the time nothing.

" The nation can never give back its confidence to a man who, false to his trust, perjured to his oath, conspires a clandestine flight, obtains a fraudulent passport, conceals a king of France under the disguise of a valet, directs his course towards a frontier covered with traitors and deserters, and evidently meditates a return into our country. with a force capable of imposing his own despotic laws.

" Whether ought his flight to be considered as his own act, or the act of those who fled with him ?   Was it a spontaneous resolution of his own, or was it inspired into him by others? The alternative is immaterial: whether fool or hypocrite, idiot or traitor, he has proved himself equally unworthy of the important functions that had been delegated to him.

" In every sense that the question can be considered, the reciprocal obligation which subsisted between us is dissolved.   He holds no longer any authority.   We owe him no longer obedience.   We see in him no more than an indifferent person; we can regard him only as Louis Capet.

" The history of France presents little else than a long series of public calamity, which takes its source from the vices of the kings : we have been the wretched victims that have never ceased to suffer either for them or by them. The catalogue of their oppressions was complete, but to complete the sum of their crimes, treason yet was wanting. Now the only vacancy is filled up, the dreadful list is full ; the system is exhausted: there are no remaining errors for them to commit, their reign is consequently at an end.

" What kind of office must that be in a government which requires neither experience nor ability to execute?   That may be abandoned to the desperate chance of birth, that may be filled with an idiot, a madman, a tyrant, with equal effect, as by the good, the virtuous and the wise?   An office of this nature is a mere nonentity : it is a place of show not of use.   Let France then, arrived at the age of reason, no longer be deluded by the sound of words, and let her deliberately examine, if a king, however insignificant and contemptible in himself, may not at the same time be extremely dangerous.

"The thirty millions which it costs to support a king in the eclat of stupid brutal luxury, presents us with an easy method of reducing taxes, which reduction would at once release the people, and stop the progress of political corruption. The grandeur of nations consists, not, as kings pretend, in the splendor of thrones, but in a conspicuous sense of their own dignity, and in a just disdain of those barbarous follies and crimes, which, under the sanction of royalty, have hitherto desolated Europe.

"As to the personal safety of Louis Capet, it is so much the more confirmed, as France will not stoop to degrade herself by a spirit of revenge against a wretch, who has dishonored himself. In defending a just and glorious cause it is not possible to degrade it, and the universal tranquillity which prevails, is an undeniable proof, that a free people know how to respect themselves."

Having thus explained the principles and the exertions of the republicans at that fatal period, when Louis was reinstated in full possession of the executive power, which by his flight had been suspended, I return to the subject, and to the deplorable situation in which the man is now actually involved.

What was neglected at the time of which I have been speaking, has been since brought about by the force of necessity; the wilful, treacherous defects in the former constitution have been brought to light; the continual alarm of treason and conspiracy roused the nation, and produced eventually a second revolution. The people have beat down royalty, never, never to rise again; they have brought Louis Capet to the bar, and demonstrated in the face of the whole world, the intrigues, the cabals, the falsehood, corruption and rooted depravity, the inevitable effects of monarchical governments. There remains then only one question to be considered, what is to be done with this man?

For myself, I seriously confess, that when I reflect on the unaccountable folly that restored the executive power to his hands, all covered as he was with perjury and treason, I am far more ready to condemn the constituent assembly than the unfortunate prisoner Louis Capet.

But abstracted from every other consideration, there is one circumstance in his life which ought to cover, or at least to palliate a great number of his transgressions, and this very circumstance affords to the French nation a blessed occasion of extricating itself from the yoke of kings, without defiling itself in the impurities of their blood.

It is to France alone, I know, that the United States of America owe that support which enabled them to shake off the unjust and tyrannical yoke of Britain. The ardor and zeal which she displayed to provide both men and money, were the natural consequences of a thirst for liberty. But as the nation at that time, restrained by the shackles of her own government, could only act by the means of a monarchical organ, this organ—whatever in other respects the object might be, certainly performed a good, a great action. Let then these United States be the safeguard and asylum of Louis Capet. There, hereafter, far removed from the miseries and crimes of royalty, he may learn, from the constant aspect of public prosperity, that the true system of government consists not in kings, but in fair, equal, and honorable representation.

In relating this circumstance, and in submitting this proposition I consider myself as a citizen of both countries. I submit it as a citizen of America, who feels the debt of gratitude which he owes to every Frenchman. I submit it also as a man, who, although the enemy of kings, cannot forget that they are subject to human frailties.

I support my proposition as a citizen of the French republic, because it appears to me the best, and most politic measure that can be adopted.

As far as my experience in public life extends, I have ever observed, that the great mass of the people are invariably just, both in their intentions and in their object; but the true method of accomplishing that effect, does not always show itself in the first instance.

For example; the English nation had groaned under the despotism of the Stuarts. Hence Charles I. lost his life; yet Charles II. was restored to all the plenitude of power, which his father had lost.

Forty years afterwards, the same family strove to reestablish their ancient oppressions; so the nation then banished from its territories the whole race. The remedy was effectual. The Stuart family sunk into obscurity, crowded itself with the multitude, and is at length extinct.

Two brothers of Louis Capet have banished themselves from the country; but they are obliged to bear with the spirit and etiquette of the courts where they reside. They can advance no pretensions on their own account, so long as Louis Capet shall live.

Monarchy, in France, was a system pregnant with crimes and murders; cancelling all natural ties, even those by which brothers are united. We know how often they have assassinated each other to pave a way to power. As those hopes which the emigrants had reposed in Louis XVI. are fled, the last which remains rests upon his death, and their situation inclines them to desire this catastrophe, that they may once again rally round an active chief, and try one further effort under the fortune of the ci-devant monsieur and d'Artois.

That such an enterprise would precipitate them into a new abyss of calamity and disgrace, it is not difficult to foresee; but yet it might be attended with mutual loss, and it is our duty, as legislators, not to spill a drop of blood, when our purpose may be effectually accomplished without it.

It has already been proposed to abolish the punishment of death. This cause must find its advocates in every corner, where enlightened politicians, and lovers of humanity exist; and it ought above all to find them in this assembly.

Monarchical governments have trained the human race, and inured it to the sanguinary arts and refinements of punishment; and it is exactly the same punishment which has so long shocked the sight and tormented the patience of the people, that now, in their turn, they practise in revenge on their oppressors. But it becomes us to be strictly on our guard against the abomination and perversity of monarchical examples: as France has been the first of European nations to abolish royalty, let her also be the first to abolish the punishment of death, and to find out a milder and more effectual substitute.

In the particular case now under consideration, I submit the following propositions: 1st, that the national convention shall pronounce sentence of banishment on Louis and his family. 2d, That Louis Capet shall be detained in prison till the end of the war; and at that epoch the sentence of banishment to be executed.

AGRARIAN JUSTICE,

OPPOSED TO

AGRARIAN LAW,
AND TO AGRARIAN MONOPOLY.

AGRARIAN JUSTICE.

To preserve the benefits of what is called civilized life, and to remedy, at the same time, the evil which it has produced, ought to be considered as one of the first objects of reformed legislation.

Whether that state that is proudly, perhaps erroneously, called civilization, has most promoted or most injured the general happiness of man, is a question that may be strongly contested. On one side, the spectator is dazzled by splendid appearances; on the other, he is shocked by extremes of wretchedness; both of which he has erected. The most affluent and the most miserable of the human race are to be found in the countries that are called civilized.

To understand what the state of society ought to be, it is necessary to have some idea of the natural and primitive state of man; such as it is at this day among the Indians of North-America. There is not, in that state, any of those spectacles of human misery which poverty and want present to our eyes, in all the towns and streets of Europe.

* The occasion of the publication of the following piece, was a Sermon preached by Watson, bishop of Landaff, entitled "The wisdom and goodness of God, in having made both *rich* and *poor* : with an appendix, containing reflections on the present state of England and France."

The error contained in the title of this Sermon, determined me to publish my Agrarian Justice. It is wrong to say that God made *rich* and *poor* ; he made only *male* and *female*, and he gave them the earth for their inheritance.

Poverty, therefore, is a thing created by that which is called civilized life. It exists not in the natural state. On the other hand, the natural state is without those advantages which flow from agriculture, arts, science, and manufactures.

The life of an Indian is a continual holiday, compared with the poor of Europe; and, on the other hand, it appears to be abject when compared to the rich. Civilization, therefore, or that which is so called, has operated two ways; to make one part of society more affluent, and the other more wretched, than would have been the lot of either in a natural state.

It is always possible to go from the natural to the civilized state, but it is never possible to go from the civilized to the natural state. The reason is, that man, in a natural state, subsisting by hunting, requires ten times the quantity of land to range over, to procure himself sustenance, than would support him in a civilized state, where the earth is cultivated. When, therefore, a country becomes populous by the additional aids of cultivation, arts and science, there is a necessity of preserving things in that state; because without it, there cannot be sustenance for more, perhaps, than a tenth part of its inhabitants. The thing, therefore, now to be done, is, to remedy the evils, and preserve the benefits that have arisen to society, by passing from the natural to that which is called the civilized state.

In taking the matter up on this ground, the first principle of civilization ought to have been, and ought still to be, that the condition of every person born into the world, after a state of civilization commences, ought not to be worse than if he had been born before that period. But the fact is, that the condition of millions, in every country in Europe, is far worse than if they had been born before civilization began, or had been born among the Indians of North-America at the present day. I will show how this fact has happened.

It is a position not to be controverted, that the earth, in its natural, uncultivated state, was, and ever would have continued to be, *the common property of the human race.* In that state every man would have been born to property. He would have been a joint life-proprietor with the rest in the property of the soil, and in all its natural productions, vegetable and animal.

But the earth, in its natural state, as before said, is capable of supporting but a small number of inhabitants compared with what it is capable of doing in a cultivated state. And as it is impossible to separate the improvement made by cultivation, from the earth itself, upon which that improvement is made, the idea of landed property arose from that inseparable connexion; but it is nevertheless true, that it is the value of the improvement only, and not the earth itself, that is individual property. Every proprietor therefore, of cultivated land, owes to the community, a *ground-rent;* for I know of no better term to express the idea by, for the land which he holds: and it is from this ground-rent that the fund proposed in this plan is to issue.

It is deducible, as well from the nature of the thing, as from all the histories transmitted to us, that the idea of landed property commenced with cultivation, and that there was no such thing as landed property before that time. It could not exist in the first state of man, that of hunters. It did not exist in the second state, that of shepherds: neither Abraham, Isaac, Jacob, nor Job, so far as the history of the Bible may be credited in probable things, were owners of land. Their property consisted, as is always enumerated, in flocks and herds, and they travelled with them from place to place. The frequent contentions, at that time, about the use of a well in the dry country of Arabia, where those people lived, show also that there was no landed property. It was not admitted that land could be claimed as property.

There could be no such thing as landed property originally. Man did not make the earth, and, though he had a natural right to *occupy* it, he had no right to *locate as his property* in perpetuity any part of it: neither did the Creator of the earth open a land-office, from whence the first title-deeds should issue. Whence, then, arose the idea of landed property? I answer as before, that when cultivation began, the idea of landed property began with it, from the impossibility of separating the improvement made by cultivation from the earth itself, upon which that improvement was made. The value of the improvement so far exceeded the value of the natural earth, at that time, as to absorb it; till, in the end, the common right of all became confounded into the cultivated right of the individual.

But they are, nevertheless, distinct species of rights, and will continue to be so long as the earth endures.

It is only by tracing things to their origin that we can gain rightful ideas of them, and it is by gaining such ideas that we discover the boundary that divides right from wrong, and which teaches every man to know his own. I have entitled this tract Agrarian Justice, to distinguish it from Agrarian Law. Nothing could be more unjust than Agrarian Law in a country improved by cultivation ; for though every man, as an inhabitant of the earth, is a joint proprietor of it in its natural state, it does not follow that he is a joint proprietor of cultivated earth. The additional value made by cultivation, after the system was admitted, became the property of those who did it, or who inherited it from them, or who purchased it. It had originally no owner. Whilst, therefore, I advocate the right, and interest myself in the hard case of all those who have been thrown out of their natural inheritance by the introduction of the system of landed property, I equally defend the right of the possessor to the part which is his.

Cultivation is, at least, one of the greatest natural improvements ever made by human invention. It has given to created earth a tenfold value. But the landed monopoly that began with it, has produced the greatest evil. It has dispossessed more than half the inhabitants of every nation of their natural inheritance, without providing for them, as ought to have been done, an indemnification for that loss, and has thereby created a species of poverty and wretchedness that did not exist before.

In advocating the case of the persons thus dispossessed, it is a right and not a charity that I am pleading for. But it is that kind of right, which, being neglected at first, could not be brought forward afterwards, till heaven had opened the way by a revolution in the system of government. Let us then do honor to revolutions by justice, and give currency to their principles by blessings.

Having thus, in a few words, opened the merits of the case, I shall now proceed to the plan I have to propose, which is,

To create a national fund, out of which there shall be paid to every person, when arrived at the age of twenty-one years, the sum of fifteen pounds sterling, as a compensation in part, for the loss of his or her natural inheritance, by the introduction of the system of landed property.

And also, the sum of ten pounds per annum, during life, to every person now living, of the age of fifty years, and to all others as they shall arrive at that age.

MEANS BY WHICH THE FUND IS TO BE CREATED.

I have already established the principle, namely, that the earth, in its natural, uncultivated state, was, and ever would have continued to be, the *common property of the human race* ; that in that state, every person would have been born to property; and that the system of landed property, by its inseparable connexion with cultivation, and with what is called civilized life, has absorbed the property of all those whom it dispossessed, without providing, as ought to have been done, an indemnification for that loss.

The fault, however, is not in the present possessors.— No complaint is intended, or ought to be alleged against them, unless they adopt the crime by opposing justice. The fault is in the system, and it has stolen imperceptibly upon the world, aided afterwards by the Agrarian law of the sword. But the fault can be made to reform itself by successive generations, without diminishing or deranging the property of any of the present possessors, and yet the operation of the fund can commence, and be in full activity, the first year of its establishment, or soon after, as I shall show.

It is proposed that the payments, as already stated, be made to every person, rich or poor. It is best to make it so, to prevent invidious distinctions. It is also right it should be so, because it is in lieu of the natural inheritance, which, as a right, belongs to every man, over and above the property he may have created or inherited from those who did. Such persons as do not choose to receive it, can throw it into the common fund.

Taking it then for granted, that no person ought to be in a worse condition when born under what is called a state of civilization, than he would have been, had he been born in a state of nature, and that civilization ought to have made, and ought still to make, provision for that purpose, it can only be done by subtracting from property, a

portion equal in value to the natural inheritance it has absorbed.

Various methods may be proposed for this purpose, but
that which appears to be the best, not only because it will
operate without deranging any present possessors, or without interfering with the collection of taxes, or *emprunts*
necessary for the purposes of government and the revolution, but because it will be the least troublesome and the
most effectual, and also because the subtraction will be
made at a time that best admits it, which is, at the moment
that property is passing by the death of one person to the
possession of another. In this case, the bequeather gives
nothing; the receiver pays nothing. The only matter to
him is, that the monopoly of natural inheritance, to which
there never was a right, begins to cease in his person. A
generous man would not wish it to continue, and a just man
will rejoice to see it abolished.

My state of health prevents my making sufficient inquiries with respect to the doctrine of probabilities, whereon
to found calculations with such degrees of certainty as
they are capable of. What, therefore, I offer on this head
is more the result of observation and reflection, than of received information ; but I believe it will be found to agree
sufficiently enough with fact.

In the first place, taking twenty-one years as the epoch
of maturity, all the property of a nation, real and personal, is always in the possession of persons above that
age. It is then necessary to know as a datum of calculation, the average of years which persons above that age
will live. I take this average to be about thirty years, for
though many persons will live forty, fifty, or sixty years
after the age of twenty-one years, others will die much
sooner, and some in every year of that time.

Taking, then, thirty years as the average of time, it will
give, without any material variation, one way or other, the
average of time in which the whole property or capital of
a nation, or a sum equal thereto, will have passed through
one entire revolution in descent, that is, will have gone by
deaths to new possessors; for though, in many instances,
some parts of this capital will remain forty, fifty, or sixty
years in the possession of one person, other parts will have
revolved two or three times before those thirty years expire, which will bring it to that average ; for were one

half the capital of a nation to revolve twice in thirty years, it would produce the same fund as if the whole revolved once.

Taking, then, thirty years as the average of time in which the whole capital of a nation, or a sum equal thereto, will revolve once, the thirtieth part thereof will be the sum that will revolve every year, that is, will go by deaths to new possessors; and this last sum being thus known, and the ratio per cent. to be subtracted from it being determined, will give the annual amount or income of the proposed fund, to be applied as already mentioned.

In looking over the discourse of the English minister, Pitt, in his opening of what is called in England, the budget, (the scheme of finance for the year 1796,) I find an estimate of the national capital of that country. As this estimate of a national capital is prepared ready to my hand, I take it as a datum to act upon. When a calculation is made upon the known capital of any nation, combined with its population, it will serve as a scale for any other nation, in proportion as its capital and population be more or less. I am the more disposed to take this estimate of Mr. Pitt, for the purpose of showing to that minister, upon his own calculation, how much better money may be employed, than in wasting it, as he has done, on the wild project of setting up Bourbon kings. What, in the name of heaven, are Bourbon kings to the people of England? It is better that the people have bread.

Mr. Pitt states the national capital of England, real and personal, to be one thousand three hundred millions sterling, which is about one-fourth part of the national capital of France, including Belgia. The event of the last harvest in each country proves that the soil of France is more productive than that of England, and that it can better support twenty-four or twenty-five millions of inhabitants than that of England can seven, or seven and an half.

The thirtieth part of this capital of 1,300,000,000l. is 43,333,333l. which is the part that will revolve every year by deaths in that country to new possessors; and the sum that will annually revolve in France in the proportion of four to one, will be about one hundred and seventy-three millions sterling. From this sum of 43,333,333l. annually revolving, is to be subtracted the value of the natural inheritance absorbed in it, which perhaps, in fair justice, cannot be taken at less, and ought not to be taken for more, than a tenth part.

It will always happen, that of the property thus revolving by deaths every year, part will descend in a direct line to sons and daughters, and the other part collaterally, and the proportion will be found to be about three to one ; that is, about thirty millions of the above sum will descend to direct heirs, and the remaining sum of 13,333,333*l.* to more distant relations, and part to strangers.

Considering, then, that man is always related to society, that relationship will become comparatively greater in proportion as the next of kin is more distant, it is therefore consistent with civilization to say, that where there are no direct heirs, society shall be heir to a part over and above the tenth part *due* to society. If this additional part be from five to ten or twelve per cent. in proportion as the next of kin be nearer or more remote, so as to average with the escheats that may fall, which ought always to go to society and not to the government, an addition of ten per cent. more ; the produce from the annual sum of 43,333,333*l.* will be,

From 30,000,000*l.* at ten per cent.	3,000,000*l.*
From 13,333,333*l.* at ten per cent. with the addition of ten per cent. more	2,666,666
43,333,333*l.*	5,666,666*l.*

Having thus arrived at the annual amount of the proposed fund, I come, in the next place, to speak of the population proportioned to this fund, and to compare it with the uses to which the fund is to be applied.

The population (I mean that of England) does not exceed seven millions and an half, and the number of persons above the age of fifty will in that case be about four hundred thousand. There would not, however, be more than that number that would accept the proposed ten pounds sterling per annum, though they would be entitled to it. I have no idea it would be accepted by many persons who had a yearly income of two or three hundred pounds sterling. But as we often see instances of rich people falling into sudden poverty, even at the age of sixty, they would always have the right of drawing all the arrears due to them. Four millions, therefore, of the above annual sum of 5,666,666*l.* will be required for four hundred thousand aged persons, at ten pounds sterling each.

I come now to speak of the persons annually arriving at twenty-one years of age. If all the persons who died were above the age of twenty-one years, the number of persons annually arriving at that age, must be equal to the annual number of deaths, to keep the population stationary. But the greater part die under the age of twenty-one, and therefore the number of persons annually arriving at twenty-one, will be less than half the number of deaths. The whole number of deaths upon a population of seven millions and an half, will be about 220,000 annually. The number arriving at twenty-one years of age will be about 100,000. The whole number of these will not receive the proposed fifteen pounds, for the reasons already mentioned, though, as in the former case, they would be entitled to it. Admitting then that a tenth part declined receiving it, the amount would stand thus :

Fund annually   5,666,666*l.*

To 400,000 aged per-
    sons at 10*l.* each   4,000,000*l.*

To 90,000 persons of
21 years, 15*l.* ster. ea. 1,350,000

                         5,350.000

                  remains   316,666*l.*

There are in every country a number of blind and lame persons, totally incapable of earning a livelihood. But as it will always happen that the greater number of blind persons will be among those who are above the age of fifty years, they will be provided for in that class. The remaining sum of 316,666*l.* will provide for the lame and blind under that age, at the same rate of 10*l.* annually for each person.

Having now gone through all the necessary calculations, and stated the particulars of the plan, I shall conclude with some observations.

It is not charity but a right; not bounty but justice, that I am pleading for. The contrast of affluence and wretchedness continually meeting and offending the eye, is like dead and living bodies chained together. Though I care as little about riches as any man, I am a friend to riches

because they are capable of good. I care not how affluent some may be, provided that none be miserable in consequence of it. But it is impossible to enjoy affluence
with the felicity it is capable of being enjoyed, whilst so
much misery is mingled in the scene. The sight of the
misery, and the unpleasant sensations it suggests, which,
though they may be suffocated, cannot be extinguished,
are a greater drawback upon the felicity of affluence than
the proposed 10 per cent. upon property is worth. He
that would not give the one to get rid of the other, has no
charity, even for himself.

There are, in every country, some magnificent chari-
ties established by individuals. It is, however, but little
that any individual can do, when the whole extent of the
misery to be relieved is considered. He may satisfy his
conscience, but not his heart. He may give all that he
has, and that all will relieve but little. It is only by or-
ganizing civilization upon such principles as to act like a
system of pullies, that the whole weight of misery can be
removed.

The plan here proposed will reach the whole. It will
immediately relieve and take out of view three classes of
wretchedness. The blind, the lame, and the aged poor ;
and it will furnish the rising generation with means to prevent their becoming poor; and it will do this, without deranging or interfering with any national measures. To
show that this will be the case, it is sufficient to observe,
that the operation and effect of the plan will, in all cases,
be the same, as if every individual were *voluntarily* to
make his will, and dispose of his property, in the manner
here proposed.

But it is justice and not charity, that is the principle of
the plan. In all great cases it is necessary to have a principle more universally active than charity ; and with respect to justice, it ought not to be left to the choice of detached individuals, whether they will do justice or not.—
Considering, then, the plan on the ground of justice, it ought
to be the act of the whole, growing spontaneously out of
the principles of the revolution, and the reputation of it
ought to be national and not individual.

A plan upon this principle would benefit the revolution,
by the energy that springs from the consciousness of justice. It would multiply also the national resources ; for

property, like vegetation, increases by offsets. When a young couple begin the world, the difference is exceedingly great, whether they begin with nothing or with fifteen pounds apiece. With this aid they could buy a cow, and implements to cultivate a few acres of land; and instead of becoming burdens upon society, which is always the case, where children are produced faster than they can be fed, would be put in the way of becoming useful and profitable citizens. The national domains also would sell the better if pecuniary aids were provided to cultivate them in small lots.

It is the practice of what has unjustly obtained the name of civilization (and the practice merits not to be called either charity or policy) to make some provision for persons becoming poor and wretched, only at the time they become so. Would it not, even as a matter of economy, be far better, to devise means to prevent their becoming poor. This can best be done, by making every person, when arrived at the age of twenty-one years, an inheritor of something to begin with. The rugged face of society, chequered with the extremes of affluence and of want, proves that some extraordinary violence has been committed upon it, and calls on justice for redress. The great mass of the poor, in all countries, are become an hereditary race, and it is next to impossible for them to get out of that state of themselves. It ought also to be observed, that this mass increases in all countries that are called civilized. More persons fall annually into it, than get out of it.

Though in a plan, in which justice and humanity are the foundation-principles, interest ought not to be admitted into the calculation, yet it is always of advantage to the establishment of any plan, to show that it is beneficial as a matter of interest. The success of any proposed plan submitted to public consideration, must finally depend on the numbers interested in supporting it, united with the justice of its principles.

The plan here proposed will benefit all, without injuring any. It will consolidate the interest of the republic with that of the individual. To the numerous class dispossessed of their natural inheritance by the system of landed property, it will be an act of national justice. To persons dying possessed of moderate fortunes, it will operate as a tontine to their children, more beneficial than the sum of

money paid into the fund : and it will give to the accumulation of riches a degree of security, that none of the old
governments of Europe, now tottering on their foundations,
can give.

I do not suppose that more than one family in ten, in any
of the countries of Europe, has, when the head of the family dies, a clear property left of five hundred pounds sterling. To all such, the plan is advantageous. That property would pay fifty pounds into the fund, and if there were
only two children under age, they would receive fifteen
pounds each, (thirty pounds) on coming of age, and be entitled to ten pounds a-year after fifty. It is from the overgrown acquisition of property that the fund will support itself ; and I know that the possessors of such property in
England, though they would eventually be benefited by
the protection of nine-tenths of it, will exclaim against the
plan. But, without entering into any inquiry how they
came by that property, let them recollect that they have
been the advocates of this war, and that Mr. Pitt has already laid on more new taxes to be raised annually upon
the people of England, and that for supporting the despotism of Austria and the Bourbons, against the liberties of
France, than would pay annually all the sums proposed in
this plan.

I have made the calculations, stated in this plan, upon
what is called personal, as well as upon landed property.
The reason for making it upon land is already explained ;
and the reason for taking personal property into the calculation, is equally well founded, though on a different principle. Land, as before said, is the free gift of the Creator
in common to the human race. Personal property is the
effect of society ; and it is as impossible for an individual to
acquire personal property without the aid of society, as it
is for him to make land originally. Separate an individual from society, and give him an island or a continent to
possess, and he cannot acquire personal property. He
cannot become rich. So inseparably are the means connected with the end, in all cases, that where the former
do not exist, the latter cannot be obtained. All accumulation, therefore, of personal property, beyond what a man's
own hands produce, is derived to him by living in society ;
and he owes, on every principle of justice, of gratitude,
and of civilization, a part of that accumulation back again

to society from whence the whole came. This is putting the
matter on a general principle, and perhaps it is best to do
so ; for if we examine the case minutely, it will be found,
that the accumulation of personal property is, in many instances, the effect of paying too little for the labor that produced it; the consequence of which is, that the working
hand perishes in old age, and the employer abounds in affluence. It is, perhaps, impossible to proportion exactly
the price of labor to the profits it produces ; and it will
also be said, as an apology for the injustice, that were a
workman to receive an increase of wages daily, he would
not save it against old age, nor be much better for it in
the interim. Make, then, society the treasurer, to guard
it for him in a common fund ; for it is no reason, that because he might not make a good use of it for himself, that
another should take it.

The state of civilization that has prevailed throughout
Europe, is as unjust in its principle, as it is horrid in its
effects; and it is the consciousness of this, and the apprehension that such a state cannot continue. when once investigation begins in any country, that makes the possessors
of property dread every idea of a revolution. It is the hazard and not the principles of a revolution that retards their
progress. This being the case. it is necessary as well for
the protection of property, as for the sake of justice and
humanity, to form a system, that whilst it preserves one part
of society from wretchedness, shall secure the other from
depredation.

The superstitious awe, the enslaving reverence, that
formerly surrounded affluence, is passing away in all countries, and leaving the possessor of property to the convulsion of accidents. When wealth and splendor, instead of
fascinating the multitude, excite emotions of disgust ; when.
instead of drawing forth admiration, it is beheld as an insult upon wretchedness ; when the ostentatious appearance
it makes, serves to call the right of it in question, the case
of property becomes critical, and it is only in a system of
justice that the possessor can contemplate security.

To remove the danger, it is necessary to remove the antipathies, and this can only be done by making property
productive of a national blessing, extending to every individual. When the riches of one man above another shall
increase the national fund in the same proportion : when

it shall be seen that the prosperity of that fund depends on the prosperity of individuals; when the more riches a man acquires, the better it shall be for the general mass; it is then that antipathies will cease, and property be placed on the permanent basis of national interest and protection.

I have no property in France to become subject to the plan I propose. What I have, which is not much, is in the United States of America. But I will pay one hundred pounds sterling towards this fund in France, the instant it shall be established; and I will pay the same sum in England, whenever a similar establishment shall take place in that country.

A revolution in the state of civilization, is the necessary companion of revolutions in the system of government. If a revolution in any country be from bad to good, or from good to bad, the state of what is called civilization in that country, must be made conformable thereto, to give that revolution effect. Despotic government supports itself by abject civilization, in which debasement of the human mind, and wretchedness in the mass of the people, are the chief criterions. Such governments consider man merely as an animal; that the exercise of intellectual faculty is not his privilege; *that he has nothing to do with the laws, but to obey them;** and they politically depend more upon breaking the spirit of the people by poverty, than they fear enraging it by desperation.

It is a revolution in the state of civilization, that will give perfection to the revolution of France. Already the conviction that government, by representation, is the true system of government, is spreading itself fast in the world. The reasonableness of it can be seen by all. The justness of it makes itself felt even by its opposers. But when a system of civilization, growing out of that system of government, shall be so organized, that not a man or woman born in the republic, but shall inherit some means of beginning the world, and see before them the certainty of escaping the miseries that under other governments accompany old age, the revolution of France will have an advocate and an ally in the hearts of all nations.

An army of principles will penetrate where an army of soldiers cannot; it will succeed where diplomatic manage-

---

* Expression of Horsley, an English bishop, in the English parliament.

ment would fail; it is neither the Rhine, the Channel, nor the Ocean, that can arrest its progress; it will march on the horizon of the world, and it will conquer.

MEANS FOR CARRYING THE PROPOSED PLAN INTO EXECUTION, AND TO RENDER IT AT THE SAME TIME CONDUCIVE TO THE PUBLIC INTEREST.

I. Each canton shall elect in its primary assemblies, three persons, as commissioners for that canton, who shall take cognizance, and keep a register of all matters happening in that canton, conformable to the charter that shall be established by law, for carrying this plan into execution.

II. The law shall fix the manner in which the property of deceased persons shall be ascertained.

III. When the amount of the property of any deceased person shall be ascertained, the principal heir to that property, or the eldest of the co-heirs, if of lawful age, or if under age, the person authorized by the will of the deceased to represent him or them, shall give bond to the commissioners of the canton, to pay the said tenth part thereof within the space of one year, in four equal quarterly payments, or sooner, at the choice of the payers. One half of the whole property shall remain as security until the bond be paid off.

IV. The bond shall be registered in the office of the commissioners of the canton, and the original bonds shall be deposited in the national bank at Paris. The bank shall publish every quarter of a year the amount of the bonds in its possession, and also the bonds that shall have been paid off, or what parts thereof, since the last quarterly publication.

V. The national bank shall issue bank notes upon the security of the bonds in its possession. The notes so issued, shall be applied to pay the pensions of aged persons, and the compensations to persons arriving at twenty-one years of age. It is both reasonable and generous to suppose, that persons not under immediate necessity, will suspend their right of drawing on the fund, until it acquire, as it will do, a greater degree of ability. In this case, it is proposed, than an honorary register be kept in each canton, of the names of the persons thus suspending that right, at least during the present war.

VI. As the inheritors of property must always take up their bonds in four quarterly payments, or sooner if they choose, there will always be *numeraire* arriving at the bank after the expiration of the first quarter, to exchange for the bank notes that shall be brought in.

VII. The bank notes being thus put in circulation, upon the best of all possible security, that of actual property, to more than four times the amount of the bonds upon which the notes are issued, and with *numeraire* continually arriving at the bank to exchange or pay them off whenever they shall be presented for that purpose, they will acquire a permanent value in all parts of the republic. They can therefore be received in payment of taxes or *emprunts* equal to *numeraire*, because the government can always receive *numeraire* for them at the bank.

VIII. It will be necessary that the payments of the ten per cent. be made in *numeraire*, for the first year, from the establishment of the plan. But after the expiration of the first year, the inheritors of property may pay ten per cent. either in bank notes issued upon the fund, or in *numeraire*. If the payments be in *numeraire*, it will lie as a deposite at the bank, to be exchanged for a quantity of notes equal to that amount ; and if in notes issued upon the fund, it will cause a demand upon the fund equal thereto ; and thus the operation of the plan will create means to carry itself into execution.

THOMAS PAINE.

THE END.

ABOUT THE AUTHOR

Thomas "Tom" Paine (February 9, 1737 – June 8, 1809) was an author, pamphleteer, radical, inventor, intellectual, revolutionary, and one of the Founding Fathers of the United States. He has been called "a corsetmaker by trade, a journalist by profession, and a propagandist by inclination."

Born in Thetford, in the English county of Norfolk, Paine emigrated to the British American colonies in 1774 in time to participate in the American Revolution. His principal contributions were the powerful, widely read pamphlet *Common Sense* (1776), the all-time best-selling American book that advocated colonial America's independence from the Kingdom of Great Britain, and *The American Crisis* (1776–1783), a prorevolutionary pamphlet series. His writing of *"Common Sense"* was so influential that John Adams reportedly said, "Without the pen of the author of *'Common Sense,'* the sword of Washington would have been raised in vain."

In 1789 Paine visited France, and lived there for much of the following decade. He was deeply involved in the early stages of the French Revolution. He wrote the *Rights of Man* (1791), in part-defence of the French Revolution against its critics, in particular the British statesman Edmund Burke. In Great Britain, for this publication he was later tried and convicted *in absentia* for the crime of seditious libel. Despite not speaking French, he was elected to the French National Convention in 1792. The Girondists regarded him as an ally, so, the Montagnards, especially Robespierre, regarded him as an enemy. In December of 1793, he was arrested and imprisoned in Paris, then released in 1794. He became notorious because of *The Age of Reason*, his book that advocates deism, promotes reason and freethinking, argues against institutionalised religion and Christian doctrines. He also wrote the pamphlet *Agrarian Justice* (1795), discussing the origins of property, and introduced the concept of a guaranteed minimum income.

Paine remained in France during the early Napoleonic era, but condemned Napoleon's dictatorship, calling him *"the completest charlatan that ever existed"*. In 1802, at President Jefferson's invitation, he returned to America where he died on June 8, 1809.

www.ingramcontent.com/pod-product-compliance
Lightning Source LLC
Chambersburg PA
CBHW020653270326
41928CB00005B/91